THE FARMER'S COOKBOOK

THE FARMER'S COOKBOOK

A Back to Basics Guide to
Making Cheese • Curing Meat • Preserving Produce • Baking Bread • Fermenting • and More

Marie W. Lawrence

Skyhorse Publishing

THE FARMER'S COOKBOOK

Skyhorse Publishing books may be purchased in bulk at special discounts for sales promotion, corporate gifts, fund-raising, or educational purposes. Special editions can also be created to specifications. For details, contact the Special Sales Department, Skyhorse Publishing, 307 West 36th Street, 11th Floor, New York, NY 10018 or info@skyhorsepublishing.com.

Skyhorse® and Skyhorse Publishing® are registered trademarks of Skyhorse Publishing, Inc.®, a Delaware corporation.

www.skyhorsepublishing.com

10 9 8 7 6 5 4 3 2 1

Library of Congress Cataloging-in-Publication Data

Lawrence, Marie W.
  The farmer's cookbook : a back to basics guide to making cheese, curing meat, preserving produce, baking bread, fermenting, and more / Marie W. Lawrence.
      p. cm.
  Includes bibliographical references and index.
  ISBN 978-1-61608-380-9 (alk. paper)
  1. Cooking, American—New England style. 2. Cooking, American. 3. Cookbooks. 4. Farm life—New England. I. Title.
  TX715.2.N48L39 2011
  641.5974—dc23

                          2011014984

Printed in China

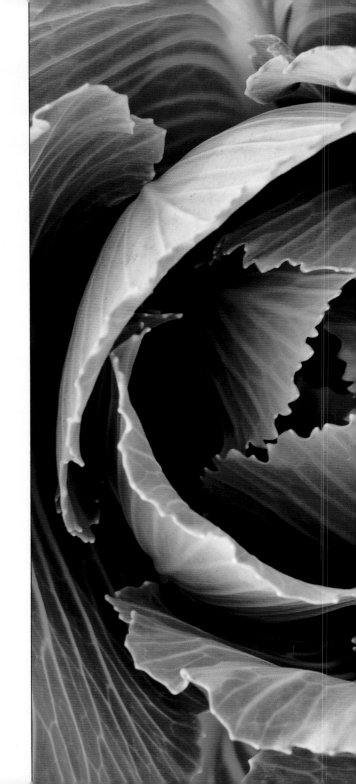

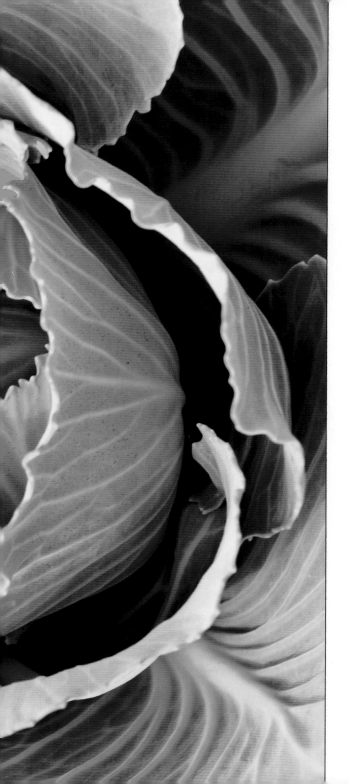

To my family, past, present, and future, with love . . .
and for the farmer in each of us.

Contents

The Farmer's Cookbook
Growing Up in Farm Country

My parents, Evelyn and William Wheelock, circa 1935.

WHEN MY PARENTS decided to buy a piece of land out in the country, they did my brothers and me the biggest favor we could have imagined. We grew up in Vermont during the 1950s and 1960s, living a rural lifestyle that in many aspects has since disappeared. Folks in our neighborhood were, for the most part, either full-time farming families or those such as my parents who kept gardens; raised a few animals for meat, milk, or pets; and generally felt the benefits of living in the country far outweighed the drawbacks.

A country upbringing gives you an appreciation of fresh air, fresh water, and good, fresh food. You also learn to appreciate the long hours farm folk put in every day of the week to care for their animals, crops, and the land that sustains them (and us) all. Self-reliance and pride of a job well done go hand in hand in this profession.

Farming has been around this good green planet for a number of centuries now, and it is probably one of the most universal occupations in the world. It may take many forms, from tiny subsistence holdings in remote areas to immense factory farms that bear little resemblance to the family farmsteads of not so long ago. And a whole lot of it takes place outside of Vermont!

Although I have incorporated a few recipes with an international flavor, much of my perspective is from rural New England, land of my paternal grandfather. You'll also notice the influence of my immigrant grandparents, from Scotland, Sweden, and Finland. No matter what the origins of any recipe may be, this cookbook is about getting back to the basics in order to produce delicious food. I really like to know just what it is I'm putting in my mouth before I eat it, and preparing food from scratch is a great way to figure that out. You don't have to spend a fortune at the grocery store in order to do this, although you do need to be willing to take a little bit of time. Understanding how to create your own homemade products can be pleasantly empowering and a lot of fun as well.

If you're able to grow a fair amount of your own food as I do, that's a wonderful thing. However, modern society being what it is, many folks no longer have this option. Fortunately for us all, even as some kinds of farming have slid by the wayside, other types are becoming more prevalent. Farmer's markets are flourishing, and in many areas, there are local farm stands dotting the roadsides. If you happen to live in an urban area, don't despair. Community gardens and inner-city farmer's markets are becoming more viable by the day. Even if all you have is a sunny window, you might just be able to grow a few herbs or some radishes. For when you get right down to it, there's a little bit of the farmer in us all.

General Cooking, Baking, and Preserving Guidelines
Safety First!

Safe Cooking Techniques for Eggs

THE ISSUE OF possible salmonella contamination from eggs is a tricky one. Ingesting an undercooked salmonella-infected egg may cause unpleasant symptoms like nausea, vomiting, and intestinal cramping. The very young, very old, pregnant women and those with compromised immune systems carry the potential for more serious complications. Approximately one in every twenty thousand eggs may contain salmonella. Although at one time the shells were considered the sole purveyor of this pathogen, there is now the slim chance a contaminated hen may carry it in her intestines or ovaries, in which case you could become ill from eating any part of the egg. Cooking your eggs to at least 160°F is the safest solution. I've read a number of articles on home-pasteurization techniques for eggs, several of which recommend coddling the whole eggs in the shell in water at a temperature of 150°F for four minutes and then chilling them quickly. I'm not sure what the safest technique is, although I strongly recommend not cutting corners when you purchase eggs. Commercially pasteurized eggs are available in some areas of the country, or if you raise your own chickens, you'll be able to control such variables as growing conditions and freshness. Your chickens and the quality of the eggs they produce will depend on your good husbandry for their good health, and ultimately yours. If you purchase eggs, buy the freshest, best quality you can find and check that the shells are clean and solid. Refrigerate them promptly at 40°F or cooler and maintain cooked eggs at 140°F or higher for brief periods only.

Pasteurization of Milk

Commercially sold milk in this country is pasteurized, and with very good reason. Heating the milk to a minimum temperature for a given length of time effectively kills off disease-producing organisms and prolongs the shelf life of the milk. Milk used to be sold either pasteurized (with the cream still floating on the top) or homogenized (pasteurized milk, which had undergone a separate procedure to emulsify the milk and cream together). Over the years, dairy manufacturers have discovered a process called ultrapasteurization. Whereas regular pasteurization would require holding the milk at a steady temperature for about half an hour before chilling it down, ultrapasteurization heats the milk to a much higher initial temperature for a much shorter amount of time. While this saves time and may prolong the milk's shelf life even longer, ultrapasteurization is a very mixed blessing. The higher temperatures used during this process alter the protein makeup of the milk, rendering it useless for making certain types of cheese, especially hard cheeses. Unfortunately for the home cheese maker, it is increasingly difficult to find milk that has not been ultrapasteurized. While I was constructing the cheese recipes in this book, I was able to purchase raw organic milk, which then I home-pasteurized. I placed the milk in a large double boiler, bringing the temperature to 150°F, and held it there for a full half hour, making sure the temperature of the milk never

dropped below that point the entire time. I then quick chilled it by placing the bowl of warm milk in an ice water–filled kitchen sink. Once chilled, the milk was poured into clean bottles and refrigerated (never use same bottles the raw milk was collected in before washing and sterilizing them). I based my pasteurization time and temperature on information from various cheese-making books and extension service websites; if you choose to home-pasteurize milk, I would encourage you to do similar research *and* to be very sure of your milk source. Unfortunately, there is still so much concern about contamination of raw milk that it can be extremely difficult to obtain if you don't own your own dairy cows, goats, or sheep. If you don't have a milk source and really want to try the recipes for cheeses such as mozzarella or cheddar, do a little sleuthing and try to find milk that is pasteurized but *not* ultrapasteurized; smaller, more local microdairies would probably be your best bet. The milk will be more expensive, but in the end, the results will be worth it.

Jam and Jelly Preserving Guidelines

The first and foremost rule when attempting any kind of preservation method is *absolute attention to cleanliness!* All utensils need to be thoroughly washed at the very least; I generally sterilize all of mine by submerging them in boiling water. If you're using a cloth to wipe rims, for goodness' sake, don't use a ratty old dishrag, but rather the cleanest, freshest cloth you can find. All work surfaces must be clean; and if you place implements on the stove, table, or shelf, make sure they have their own little spotless tray to rest upon. It doesn't do much good to wash or ster-

ilize them if you then lay them on a contaminated surface. Make sure the fruit you're preserving is clean as well—freshly washed and free of any insect residue. It goes without saying that it should also be in pristine condition, with no sign of mold or rot.

For many years, boiling hot jellies and jams were poured directly into sterilized jars. The lids would be applied, and the preserves would be left to seal. I discovered recently the hot jars of jam should also be submerged in a boiling water bath for ten minutes, a procedure I previously utilized for pickles but not sweet preserves. Properly confused, I conducted research, looking for answers. It turns out unpleasant little organisms called mycotoxins have been discovered living in the mold, which grows on underprocessed jams and jellies. Mycotoxins have been shown to cause cancer in animals. Apparently you might be exposed to them even if you scrape off the mold before eating the jam. Now, in all honesty, why would you want to eat a moldy jam in the first place? That being said, I'm not about to scoff at new and improved food safety standards. If the extra processing time ensures a higher probability that mold won't grow on my preserves, it's the right thing to do. I guess I can kiss all those cute little jars of Christmas jelly with the cloud of whipped white paraffin wax on top good-bye; you certainly can't use paraffin in a boiling water bath.

Therefore, utilizing a canning kettle or other large pan deep enough to submerge your jelly jars with a couple inches of water over the tops would be the final step in making cooked jam or jelly. I can't fit the little quarter pint jelly jars I use in my canning kettle because they slip right through the canning jar rack, so instead, I use my largest roasting pan with a metal cooling rack set in the bottom and a large baking sheet for a cover. Don't place jars directly on the bottom of the pan or they may crack open—a sorry state of affairs. Begin heating the water in the pan while you're making your jam or jelly. Place the filled hot-lidded jars into the very hot (not boiling) water, making sure they are completely immersed. Add extra water if need be for adequate coverage; boiling water is OK for this step. Bring the water in the pan or canner to a boil and continue to boil, covered, for ten minutes. Turn off the heat and remove the jars with tongs to cool on a level surface padded by a dishtowel, again to guard against the hot jars of jelly cracking or breaking apart from the temperature variation. Allow them to cool entirely, checking to make sure they've all sealed (the tops will have become concave and will not pop back when pressed with your fingertip). Don't worry if the rings seem a little loose; what's important is the seal of the lids.

Do not store any jars without a proper seal; refrigerate them to use first or reapply fresh lids and process them again in the boiling water bath for the full ten minutes. Poor overcooked jam? Let's hope it processes correctly the first time around! Jams and jellies prepared in this manner should last on your shelves (cool and dry is best) for a year. Be sure to label them with variety and date; what you think you'll remember in July may be quite different from what you actually remember in January.

Pickling Guidelines

You will need a large, deep kettle in order to safely can pickles. Canning kettles, including a metal or wire jar holder/lifter, are generally available in hardware stores or the housewares departments of larger department stores, especially around harvesttime. You must be able to entirely cover each jar with two inches or more of water over the top of the lids to ensure your product reaches safe canning temperatures. This canning method is referred to as a boiling water bath, and it is only effective for fruits and high-acid foods such as pickles. Any home-canning of most vegetables would *require a pressure canner*, which is a different story altogether! Quality canning jars with screw-type seals and lids, a large-mouthed funnel for pouring liquids, a jar lifter, and a noncorroding large kettle for the initial brining/cooking of ingredients are also important. If this sounds like a lot, just keep in mind that once you've made the initial investment, you may reuse everything except for the sealing lids, which can usually be purchased separately from the jars. Follow the initial procedures as outlined for preserving jams and jellies; cleanliness and proper sterilization techniques are very important. And as per jellies, once the pickles have processed for the proper amount of time, remove the jars to a clean, dry, level surface while they cool and seal. Any jars that don't seal must be used at once or processed again using new seals. Store your jars of pickles in a cool, dry place to use within a year, if they hang around for that long!

Baking Tips

Measure Accurately

Although measuring by weight is arguably the most accurate method for producing fine-baked goods, most folks simply measure by the cup or spoonful.

Use *liquid measuring cups* for all liquids—including milk, water, oil, and raw eggs or egg whites—if necessary. The majority of liquid measuring cups are of glass, with a pouring spout and with units of measurement clearly marked on the outside. Hold the cup at eye level when measuring out liquids; if it's below eye level, you can't accurately tell if the liquid is level with the indicated line.

Use *dry measuring cups* for all dry or solid measures, such as flour, sugar, mayonnaise, or shortening. Dry measuring cups are generally made from metal or plastic and come in sets of graduated sizes: ¼, ⅓, ½, and 1 cup sizes. Combine two for amounts called for such as ⅔ cup or ¾ cup. *Spoon white sugar or flour* into the desired size and gently level off with a frosting spatula or straight knife blade. Be sure to use a light touch with the flour so as not to compact it down. *Brown sugar*, on the other hand, *should be packed* down firmly enough so that it holds its shape when emptied from the cup; all recipes in this book calling for brown sugar should be packed in this manner. Solids such as shortening should be pushed in firmly to avoid air pockets and leveled off. Butter, unless you buy it in bulk, can easily be measured using the handy markings on the side of each stick wrapper.

Measuring spoons are used for both liquid and dry measures of smaller proportions; again, follow the guidelines above in order to measure each component accurately.

Temperature Counts

It's important to chill dough that relies on butter or shortening for leavening and texture, such as puff pastry, piecrust, and cookie. This enables the butter to remain in solid form, creating air pockets in pastry dough or making the cookie dough sturdy enough to successfully roll out with a minimum of breakage.

Warming egg whites to room temperature helps to increase their volume when whipping them. Making sure butter and cream cheese are at room temperature before integrating them into cakes, cookies, and frostings will give smoother and better results.

Bake breads, pies, and cakes on middle shelves of the oven while cookies, cupcakes, and muffins on upper shelves. These smaller pastries are more prone to burning on the bottom, whereas the larger baked goods need the more even heat a middle rack provides. Pies generally bake at an initial higher temperature, which is reduced after ten to fifteen minutes; this will produce a less soggy golden brown piecrust. Evenly gauged oven temperatures are a must for light cakes such as sponge, chiffon, and angel food. If these cakes consistently fall for no apparent reason, you may wish to invest in an oven thermometer to monitor what might be going on in there.

In general, cookies should be removed from baking sheets as soon as possible after removing from the oven; otherwise, they may stick to the pan or become brittle and break. Butter-based cakes should cool in the pans for about ten minutes and then loosened and turned out of the pans to finish cooling on wire racks. Try to remove them too soon and they will fall apart; leave them in too long and they'll stick to the pan. If you are using a large rectangular pan, it's often easier just to leave the cake in the pan, cooling it on a rack, frosting if desired, and serving in pieces right from the pan. Tube cakes such as angel food should be cooled in the tin upside down. Do not remove them until they are thoroughly cooled or the cake may collapse.

The Right Stuff

Use the correct ingredients for the recipe. This is especially true when baking, and particularly when it comes to flour. Use all-purpose flour for muffins, quick breads, pancakes, waffles, and cookies. Some cake recipes call for all-purpose flour, but the majority of them utilize cake flour, which is finer and lighter and will therefore give you a finer, lighter cake. If you don't have any cake flour, you may try spooning two level tablespoons of all-purpose flour from each cup called for and replacing it with two level tablespoons of cornstarch. It's not a perfect fix, but worth a try. Bread flour is higher in gluten content, the stuff that gives yeast breads their elasticity and spring. Use it for breads and pizza dough. In general, use no more than half whole wheat or rye flour, with equal or greater amounts of the specified white flour in your recipes; otherwise, your bread will come out heavy and rather unpalatable.

Butter and shortening are not interchangeable, nor are butter and oil. Butter contains a fair amount of air and also traces of milk and salt; hydrogenated shortening is denser and less flavorful. I prefer not to use solid shortening or margarine, as the hydrogenation process has come under increasing scrutiny in recent years. Although there are now nonhydrogenated shortenings out there, I prefer to stick to butter and oil; the more pure the product, the better the end result. Oil is a more concentrated form of fat than any of the solids, which is why recipes frequently call for less of it in proportion to other ingredients than if it were butter or the like.

Most baked goods require a leavening agent—something that helps the batter or dough to form little bubbles before and/or during the baking process. In general, these agents fall into two main categories. One of them encompasses cakes, cookies, and quick breads, which utilize baking powder, baking soda, cream of tartar, or some combination of the aforementioned. Batters should be baked as soon as they are mixed in order to best utilize the leavening power of these products, although some dough (as for cookies) may be refrigerated or even frozen before use. It's also important to recognize that cakes and quick breads are very temperature sensitive in the first few minutes of baking time; do not open the oven door or otherwise disturb them for at least ten to fifteen minutes or the baked good may cave in on itself ("fall") and never recover. The other category includes yeast and sour dough raised products, most often breads. Yeast must be kept within a fairly narrow temperature range in order to activate properly. When bought in bulk, it should be stored in a cool, dry place; I leave mine right in the refrigerator. Yeast must then be warmed to lukewarm to begin the growth process by placing it in liquid to dissolve (some yeast now is formulated to mix directly into the dough). However, if yeast is overheated, it will kill the tiny organisms that cause the bread dough to rise. The liquid should feel warm on the inside of your wrist but not hot; check by placing your wrist on the outside of the bowl or by placing a drop or two directly on the skin. One packet of yeast is the equivalent to about 2½ teaspoons. Because I use bulk yeast, I simply add 1 tablespoon to most recipes. Chances are you could use one packet in place of each tablespoon if you prefer.

Unless specified otherwise, I use extra large eggs in all my recipes. I also use 1 percent milk, although I suspect in the majority of recipes, the butterfat content of the milk won't make or break the finished product. Over the years, I've frequently utilized instant dry milk while baking, adding an appropriate amount of water; it's easy and economical. One other important tip: use only pure flavorings; why go to all the trouble of baking from scratch if you're going to compromise on flavor?

THE FARMER'S COOKBOOK

"When the Days Begin to Lengthen, the Cold Begins to Strengthen"

ANOTHER JANUARY HAS rolled around, with the requisite New Year's resolutions and two and a half feet of snow blanketing my garden, berry bushes, and fruit trees. Following so closely on the heels of December's winter equinox, I think at first we might wonder if January isn't just toying with us. Any slight increase in daylight is more than offset by bitter cold, and just when we've suffered through entirely too many snowstorms, a deluge of freezing sleet comes along to remind us things really could be worse.

Hmm . . . when you get right down to it, maybe snow isn't such a bad companion to have hanging around after all! It buffers the roots of perennial plants, keeping them safe from extremes of cold. It's great for snowshoeing, skiing, sliding, and snowboarding, and for bragging to our Southern friends and relatives about how many feet of the white stuff we're suffering through this time around! Judging from the multiple trucks stacked with logs that come roaring down the road in front of my house daily, it isn't so bad for the loggers, either.

January is a slow month as far as gardening is concerned hereabouts; the only green things growing at this point are my houseplants and that little tub of mint I dug from my herb garden last fall. Fortunately, the freezer and pantry shelves are still well stocked with pickles, jams, and produce from last year's gardening ventures. And because by the end of the month the days really are becoming noticeably longer, I can once again look forward to starting seedlings for next summer's garden sometime

soon. What a good thing January's here after all; when else would I have a chance to look at all those seed catalogs?

Because January begins in celebration, some of the recipes in this first chapter are of a festive nature. However, festive doesn't necessarily mean expensive; with a little bit of know-how, you can produce a wide variety of delicious dishes for very little cost and effort. As we journey through the year together, you're going to learn lots of tricks about producing delicious home-cooked food, whether utilizing what you've raised yourself or purchased from others who've worked hard to provide it for you.

January is a month of rest, renewal, and planning. As I plot out next summer's garden, which of course will be bigger and better than ever, let's begin our journey together through a country year. With a culinary treat or two getting us off to an optimistic start, even better things are sure to follow.

Squirrel trails from the orchard lead to our bird feeders as the apple trees wait for summer.

January

Breakfast Delight

January mornings begin with sunlight filtering golden though the trees overlooking my back meadow. The birds are busy eating at the feeders, hoping to get their fill before the squirrels join in the fun. We all know eating a proper breakfast is the best way to start your day. Oatmeal is a great source of fiber and nutrients; adding some fruit and nuts while we're at it can only improve things. Make an individual serving for one, or multiply the ingredients for the whole family.

For One

½ c. (cup) rolled oats, old-fashioned or quick cooking
1 c. water
dash salt
1 T. (tablespoon) chopped walnuts/almonds
1 T. raisins or other dried fruit
½ c. diced fresh apple
1 T. maple syrup or honey
A few drops of vanilla
A pinch of cinnamon
A pinch of nutmeg
Milk or light cream for pouring

For Four

2 c. rolled oats of choice
1 c. water
¼ t. (teaspoon) salt
¼ c. raisins
2 c. diced fresh apple
¼ c. chopped walnuts/almonds
2 T. honey
2 T. maple syrup
¼ t. cinnamon
¼ t. nutmeg
½ t. vanilla
Milk or light cream for pouring

Combine the oats, salt, and water in a small saucepan. Bring to a boil and cook from 1–3 minutes, depending on whether you're using quick cooking or old-fashioned oats. Remove from heat and stir in everything else except the milk or cream. Allow it to stand for about a minute to blend the flavors and then enjoy with milk or cream.

Orange Date Bran Muffins

Bran muffins are a great way to add fiber and nutrients to your diet, but only if they're properly moist and sweet. As with so many foods, the manner in which they're prepared is as important as the ingredients they contain. There's nothing like a little zing of orange to help get rid of those winter blahs. These muffins are particularly good with a dab of cream cheese, although you can't go wrong with butter, either.

1¾ c. bran cereal
¼ c. corn oil
¾ c. milk
1 t. grated orange zest
¾ c. orange juice
1 egg
1 t. baking powder
1 t. baking soda
½ c. sugar
1¼ c. flour
½ t. salt
½ c. chopped dates

Soak the cereal in the milk and orange juice for 5 minutes. Whisk in the egg and oil. Combine the sugar, flour, baking powder, baking soda, and salt. Stir into the wet ingredients along with the chopped dates and orange zest. Divide evenly among 12 lined or well-greased muffin cups. Bake on an upper rack of the oven at 400°F for 15–20 minutes. Cool in the muffin tin for about 5 minutes before turning out. These are at their best served while still warm, although they're easier to remove from the wrappers when a bit cooler.

Cream Cheese Coffee Cake

If you want something a little rich and indulgent for your winter breakfast or brunch, this recipe is the one for you. It's based on a recipe given me by Christine Jefferson, a friend of Finnish heritage who understands the value of a stick or two of butter. Try eating some fresh and freezing some for a rainy (or snowy) day. Wrap your extra coffee cake in two layers of foil or plastic wrap, label with the date, and freeze to enjoy within a month. If you cut into serving portions before freezing, you can remove a slice or two at a time.

Dough

½ c. milk
6 T. butter
1 egg
⅓ c. sugar
½ t. salt
½ t. vanilla
1 T. dry yeast
¼ c. warm water
2 c. flour, plus more rolling out

Cheese Filling

1 lb. cream cheese, softened
1 c. sugar
3 eggs
2 t. vanilla

1 t. grated orange or lemon zest

2 c. preferred fruit; berries, cut-up peaches or pears, etc.

Crumb Topping

½ c. sugar

1 c. flour

½ c. butter

1 t. vanilla

½ c. rolled oats

Glaze

1 c. confectioner's sugar

½ t. vanilla

1 T. orange juice, lemon juice, or milk

Prepare the dough right in the saucepan. Heat the butter and milk in; it saves on dishes and time. Heat the milk and butter together until the butter is melted and the milk is hot but not boiling. Allow this to cool slightly before stirring in the sugar and slightly-beaten egg. Meanwhile, dissolve the yeast in the ¼ c. of warm water; make sure the water isn't too hot or it will kill the yeast. It should be about 130°F, or feel pleasantly warm when you put a drop on the inside of your wrist. When the milk mixture has reached a comparable temperature, stir in the yeast and a cup of the flour. This forms what we refer to as a sponge—a soft yeast batter. Allow the yeast to "work" for about 5 minutes; you will see bubbles form on the top of the batter. Now stir in the second cup of flour to make a fairly soft dough. Cover and allow the dough to rise for about an hour. Meanwhile, prepare the cheese filling and crumb topping. For the filling, beat the cream cheese until it is soft and smooth. Add the other ingredients except the fruit and beat again until it is smooth and creamy. Melt the butter in a small saucepan; stir in the rest of the topping ingredi-

ents until the mixture is crumbly. To assemble the coffee cake, butter a 9 × 13" cake pan. Punch down the yeast dough and roll it somewhat larger in size than the pan; you want it up over the edges to help contain the filling once it's poured in. Fit the dough in pan and pour in the filling, smoothing it out toward the edges. Top the filling with your

fruit of choice and fold the dough over the edges of the filling (it won't fully cover it). Sprinkle evenly with the crumb topping. Bake at 350°F for about 40 minutes, until the edges and crumb topping are golden brown. Allow it to cool before cutting; the filling will firm up as it cools. Drizzle with glaze, if desired, and enjoy.

Farmhouse White Bread (Two Loaves)

There's nothing like a nice, warm loaf of fresh-baked bread to whet your appetite. Whey is a by-product of the cheese-making process and has the added benefit of making absolutely wonderful yeast-raised bread. If you want to try making cheese, there are several recipes included in the "June" chapter of the cookbook; then you'll have your own whey, as well! However, whey is not readily available commercially, so if you don't have a source, simply substitute milk and water in the proportions given; the bread comes out just fine either way. Be sure to use bread flour when making yeast-raised breads and rolls; the higher gluten content is what gives these breads their characteristic light, springy texture.

1½ c. whey or 1 c. water and ½ c. milk
2 T. butter
2 T. honey
1½ t. salt
1 scant T. (1 pkg.) dry yeast
Approximately 5 c. bread flour

In a large heatproof bowl or saucepan, warm the whey or the milk and water until the liquid is just lukewarm; a drop or two dribbled on the inside of your wrist should feel pleasantly warm but not hot. Stir in the honey, salt, and butter until the butter melts. Stir in the yeast until it is dissolved. Next stir in two cups of the flour; set the resulting batter aside in a warm (not hot) place for about 5 minutes, until it begins to form bubbles and becomes springy when stirred. This is referred to as allowing the yeast to "work," and it helps produce a finished product of a finer quality. Next, stir in two more cups of flour. Now comes the fun part; remove any rings that you don't wish to become mired in bread dough and knead in approximately one more cup

Farmhouse white bread, plain or swirled with cinnamon sugar, is a treat in both winter and summer.

of flour. Kneading is accomplished by using the heel of your hand and the knuckles to push the dough under and over until it is springy and resilient but still fairly soft. Adding too much flour will result in tough bread that doesn't rise particularly well; adding too little will result in too soft dough that sticks to your fingers and generally makes a mess. If in doubt, go for the softer product. Some folks prefer to turn their dough out onto a floured surface to knead it; over the years, I've simply begun using an oversized mixing bowl in which I mix, knead, and allow the dough to raise without having to go through the rigmarole of providing a clean, greased bowl for the rising process. Do whichever feels more comfortable to you. Once the dough is smooth and elastic feeling, place it in a warm (not hot) space, free from drafts, covered with a damp dishtowel, and allow it to hang out for up to an hour. If you find the dough adheres to the dishtowel, you could either place a bit of waxed paper in between the towel and dough, or place a bowl of hot water in the oven along with the dough and not use the dishtowel. Once it has doubled in bulk (when you stick your finger into the dough, it should leave a nice indent), give it a good punch with your fist and turn it out of the bowl onto a lightly floured surface for the shaping process. Divide it in half, kneading and shaping each into a rectangle approximately 9" × 12". Tightly roll the longer side of the dough up to form a cylinder 9" long and fit each cylinder into a buttered 9" bread pan. Again, leave it in a warm place (an unlit oven or the back of the stove works well for me), until the dough reaches to top of the pan, approximately another hour. Bake in a preheated 375°F oven for about 35–40 minutes, until the tops of the loaves are golden brown and the bread sounds hollow when tapped with your knuckle. Brush the top of each loaf with soft or melted butter and turn out of the pans sideways to cool on wire racks. Although it's delicious still warm from the oven, it will slice better once it's entirely cooled. Store your cooled loaves wrapped in plastic; I find the 1-gallon-sized plastic bags available in bulk work well, although I prefer the ones with twist ties to the zipper types, as they contour better to the size of the loaf. This will yield two loaves of bread.

Cinnamon Raisin Bread

Use the farmhouse white bread recipe as the base for your cinnamon raisin bread. You may make both loaves into raisin bread, or just one, leaving the other as is for white bread. The proportions given here are for one loaf of bread, so adjust according to how much you wish to make.

Per Loaf

> 1 T. softened butter
> 2 T. sugar
> 1 t. cinnamon
> ¼ c. raisins

Icing (optional)

> ½ c. confectioner's sugar
> 2 t. milk

When you have kneaded and shaped the bread dough prior to rolling it up, lightly spread the softened butter over the dough. Sprinkle it with the combined sugar and cinnamon and then with the raisins. Roll up and place in the pan, seam-side down. Allow it to rise until doubled and bake in a 375°F oven for approximately 35–40 minutes, as per farmhouse white bread. Once it has been removed from the oven, you may either brush it with butter, or if you prefer, allow it to cool and drizzle it with the confectioner's sugar and milk, which have been combined to make the icing. Be sure to let the icing firm up before packaging the bread. A looser wrapping is preferable so that the icing doesn't soften and stick to the plastic; you may wish to use waxed paper or foil, or place the bread in a small air-proof container.

Snacks and Such

Somewhere in between eating breakfast and bedtime come those moments in the day when you'd really like a little something savory to snack on. You can enjoy the following tidbits as part of a New Year's celebration, or just keep them handy for any old time. They're easy to make and store well. They even mail well, if you've some faraway friends or relatives you'd like to surprise with a tasty homemade treat.

Tangy-Herbed Oyster Crackers

Little munchies are always fun to have around the holidays. These herbed oyster crackers are also great as toppers for tomato soup, or crumbled as a cracker topping on casseroles. Powdered buttermilk is available in the baking section of most supermarkets and provides an easy shortcut to many dishes. Store it in the refrigerator once opened for a longer shelf life.

14–16 oz. oyster crackers
2 T. powdered buttermilk
1 t. salt
1 t. sugar
½ t. onion powder
½ t. garlic powder
1 t. parsley flakes
1 t. dill weed
¼ t. pepper
1 c. corn oil
1 t. lemon juice

Combine all the dry ingredients, including herbs, whisking well to combine. Using a 2-quart measuring cup or mixing bowl, whisk together the dry mixture with the corn oil and lemon juice. Stir in the oyster crackers, mixing well to coat all. Bake on the upper shelf in a 350°F oven for about 5–7 minutes, until heated through but not browned. Store the crackers in an airtight canister or plastic bag.

A Bit about Beef

I suspect the majority of people in this country, if asked to define the all-American meat, would think of beef first. Beef cattle, large animals that require plenty of room and plenty of food, have roamed the Western states for a few hundred years. They first made the trip from Spain to the New World during Christopher Columbus's second voyage, in 1493. After running wild for the next century or so, they eventually were semitamed into range animals. With the increasing interest in locally produced foods, it's now not uncommon to see a field of grazing beef cattle even in Vermont.

Here are a few beef recipes for you to try. Since January is a time of celebration and the start of a new year, it seemed a special offering might be in order. If you're not in the market for such things, there are also some economical and delicious variations on beef included, as well as a few for "ridge beef," if there are any hunters in our midst.

A neighbor's beef cow grazes near the Ames Hill Brook.

Nutty Cereal Snack Mix

Just about everybody loves a crunchy, flavorful snack mix. It not only costs less to make your own; it's also fresher and tastier because you decide on the flavorings. This is a favorite around our house from Thanksgiving through New Year's.

8 c. crispy corn/rice cereal
2 c. salted cashews
2 T. Worcestershire sauce
½ c. butter
1½ t. seasoned salt
1 t. onion powder
½ t. garlic powder
½ t. Tabasco sauce, or to taste

Melt the butter in a large saucepan. Stir in the seasonings until well blended. Stir in the cereal, coating it well with the butter mixture. Spread on a large baking sheet and bake at 350°F for about 5–7 minutes, stirring once. The mix should be nicely heated through but not browned. Remove from the oven and immediately toss with the cashews. Store airtight once cooled. You may alternatively toasted the mix in your microwave for about 3–6 minutes, again stirring once and mixing in the cashews once it's heated through. This makes about 10 cups of snack mix.

Creamy Clam Dip

How about ringing in the New Year with a nice dish of creamy clam dip? Add some crackers or chips and a few fresh veggies, and you're good to go! Although the dip should store, covered, in your refrigerator for up to a week, it goes without saying you won't be mailing this particular snack to anyone!

8 oz. cream cheese
¼ c. sour cream
2 cans minced clams, drained
1 T. chopped fresh parsley or 1 t. dried
1 T. lemon juice
¼ t. salt
1 t. Worcestershire sauce
¼ t. garlic powder
¼ t. Tabasco sauce

Beat the softened cream cheese until smooth and creamy. Beat in the sour cream, clams, and lemon juice. Stir in all the remaining ingredients until everything is well blended. Chill the dip for an hour or two before serving for best flavor. Serve with chips and veggies for dipping. This makes about 2 cups of dip.

Roast Beef Tenderloin

I do love beef tenderloin, although admittedly I only splurge about once a year. If you've been industrious enough to raise your own beef, this is a great time to remove that special roast from the freezer and enjoy the fruits of your labors. If you're buying one instead and can afford the initial cost, a larger tenderloin cut will generally cost you less per pound, providing you with more than one gourmet meal. It's probably the easiest cut to butcher; simply gauge by the total purchase weight how you'd like to divide it, slicing off into either roasts or steaks. Double wrap what you won't use right away, separating steaks with waxed paper or freezer paper for easier thawing, label with contents, amount, and date, and then freeze. Plan to use within 2–3 months for best results.

2 lb. (pounds) beef tenderloin
3 T. olive oil
1 t. freshly ground sea salt
¼ t. freshly ground black pepper
¼ c. minced fresh shallots
1 t. crumbled rosemary
1 T. Dijon mustard

Preheat oven to 475°F. Place tenderloin in an oiled roasting pan. You may use a rack in the pan or not, as you wish. Lightly brush the roast with 1 T. of the olive oil. Combine the salt, pepper, mustard, shallots, rosemary, and 2 T. of the olive oil. Rub half of this mixture over the surface of the beef, coating it evenly. Set aside the rest for the mushroom gravy. Roasting the tenderloin for 25 minutes to ½ hour should give you a medium-rare roast. It's really helpful if you have an instant-read roasting thermometer; with many cuts you can guess at doneness, but tenderloin is too much a treat to risk under- or overcooking. Insert the thermometer at one end of the roast and also in the middle. A 140°F indicates rare and 160°F, medium. You definitely don't want to go higher than that with a roast this tender. Remove the meat to a serving platter and allow it to rest for about 10 minutes while making gravy and bringing your other dishes to the table.

Mushroom Gravy

2 T. butter
2 T. flour
2 c. sliced mushrooms
½ c. red wine
½ c. water or veggie cooking water
Reserved mustard and shallot mixture
Salt to taste
Pepper to taste

Deglaze the roasting pan with the water. In a small saucepan, melt the butter and add the mushrooms, sautéing them until tender. Stir in the flour to make a roux. Whisk in the mustard shallot mixture, deglazing liquid from the roasted pan and the wine and bring to a full boil. Season the gravy to taste with salt and pepper, pour into your gravy boat, and serve alongside the roast.

Beef Paprikash (Goulash)

Goulash is a central European specialty that has broad-based appeal. Use tomatoes from your freezer or fresh ones for the best flavor, although canned may be substituted if necessary. Serve this with noodles or mashed potatoes; add a green vegetable and some crusty bread for a satisfying winter meal.

1 lb. steak tips or stew beef
1 lg. onion, sliced
2 T. olive oil
1 t. salt
1½ t. paprika
½ t. thyme
¼ t. pepper
1 clove garlic, minced, or ¼ t. garlic powder
2 tomatoes, cut in chunks (1½ c.)
1½ c. water
1 c. sour cream

In a Dutch oven or large, heavy kettle, heat the olive oil over medium high. Brown the meat on one side, turning it over. Add the onions and seasonings while the meat continues browning, stirring occasionally. Add the tomatoes and water, bring to a boil, lower the heat and simmer, covered, for about an hour, until the meat is tender and the liquid reduced to a thick sauce. Stir in the sour cream and serve to four hungry people.

Festive tenderloin of beef surrounded by roasted potatoes—ready for a New Year's feast.

Pot Roast

Use tougher cuts of meat for pot roasting: bottom-round, eye-of-round, or tip roasts from the hindquarters or a brisket from just-behind-the-front-leg quarters. Although chuck roasts are also considered pot roast material, I find them too fatty and full of gristle to make a particularly good pot roast; there really is a reason why ground beef has become so popular over the years. I always cook my pot roasts on top of the stove in a heavy pan such as a Dutch oven. After an initial browning, the meat braises slowly for a few hours to tenderize and bring out the delicious flavors only a pot roast can achieve. Another added bonus to pot roasting your meat is that you'll be assured of plenty of gravy to go around!

Old-Fashioned Pot Roast

3 lb. beef for pot roasting
2 T. corn oil
1–2 bay leaves
Black pepper
Rosemary
2 lg. onions, sliced
2 t. salt
2 garlic cloves
2 stalks celery, chopped, optional
1 c. red wine *or* 2 T. cider vinegar
1 lb. of carrots, scrubbed and sliced lengthwise
Mashed potatoes or buttered noodles

Heat the corn oil in a 4-qt. pan or Dutch oven. Season the beef on all sides with the pepper and rosemary; I sprinkle enough on to lightly coat but not overwhelm. Brown it evenly over medium heat. When the browning process is about half completed, add the onions and garlic, allowing them to brown alongside the beef. Once everything is nicely browned, add about 2 t. of salt, the bay leaves, and water just to cover. This is also when you may wish to add a stalk or two of sliced celery and also the red wine or vinegar. It's your pot roast, so season it as you like! Bring everything to a boil, reduce the heat to medium low, and simmer at a low boil for approximately 2 hours, until the meat is very tender when poked with a fork. During the last half hour, add in the carrots. Remove the meat and carrots to a serving platter. If you have extra vegetable cooking water, as from the potatoes, and you would like extra gravy, add that into the liquid in the pan. To thicken the gravy, use about 1 T. of flour per cup of cooking liquid. Mix the flour with a little cold water until it is a smooth liquid and whisk into the gravy until it's thickened as you'd like it. Don't ever add plain flour to a hot liquid, as it will immediately turn into lumps! Some folks may prefer to cook potatoes in with the roast, although I prefer mashed on the side to enjoy with all that good gravy. This will serve 6–8 easily; leftovers are fine too.

Ridge Beef

Now that we're celebrating beef roasts of all sorts, it's time to mention the "other red meat." Out in the country, chances are that will be venison, a.k.a. ridge beef. My husband, Bruce, like so many other country boys, got his hunting license while he was still in high school. The mounted head of the eight-point buck he shot back when he was sixteen has graced our living room wall throughout the entire course of our wedded bliss. Supplementing the family meat larder with wild game is a time-honored tradition here in Vermont, and in many other parts of the country too, I'm sure. Venison is a lean red meat with a rich flavor. It's important to trim away what fat there may be, as it imparts a rather tallowlike taste. Instead, lard your roasts with thin strips of bacon or salt pork, and don't overcook the tender cuts.

A trio of young white-tail bucks, their antlers still in velvet, wander through our field.

Roast Saddle of Venison with Cumberland Sauce

As with all such meats, the tenderloin or saddle of venison is the prime cut, so you'll want to treat it with due respect. It should be roasted in a similar manner to beef tenderloin, although the accompanying sauce reflects the venison's unique flavor. I haven't prepared a saddle of venison in a while, but when I did, I larded it with bacon and roasted it quickly in a hot oven. Although the entire saddle can be in the vicinity of 5–8 pounds, I'm utilizing a smaller roast, which is more manageable and more affordable. Some folks like to sprinkle on a few crushed juniper berries when roasting venison, but I prefer it without; use sparingly if you decide to.

2 lb. boneless venison tenderloin, trimmed of all fat
4 slices bacon, halved
Salt to taste
Pepper to taste

Season the venison with salt and pepper to taste and drape the half slices of bacon over the roast at intervals along the length of it. Roast the venison in a 475°F oven for about 30 minutes. This should produce a medium-rare roast. If you're one of those people who prefer your venison still roaming around the woods blatting when you cut into it, start checking your roast after 20 minutes. Again, an instant-read thermometer is an excellent investment; try 140°F for a rare roast, 160°F for medium. Remove to a serving platter to rest for 5–10 minutes. This allows the juices to remain in the meat rather than running all over the platter when it is sliced.

Cumberland Sauce

Cumberland sauce is a traditional English recipe containing currant jelly, port wine, and citrus. Homemade crab apple jelly may be substituted for the currant, if you prefer, and/or a sweet wine such as blackberry merlot for the port. Cumberland sauce is also a good accompaniment to turkey, duck, or pork.

1 c. red currant or crab apple jelly
2 t. grated orange rind
¼ c. orange juice
1 t. grated lemon rind
2 T. lemon juice
½ c. port wine
1 t. Dijon mustard
1 t. fresh grated ginger, or ½ t. powdered ginger
Salt to taste
Pepper to taste

Combine all ingredients in a small saucepan and bring to a boil, stirring until the sauce is smooth. Serve at room temperature; cover and refrigerate leftovers. This will make about 1½ c. sauce.

Venison Stew

I freely admit to not being as much a fan of venison as is Bruce. Therefore, when he'd proudly drag his harvest of the year home from the woods surrounding Brattleboro, I'd spend much of my time trying to convince myself it was beef. With this recipe for venison stew, I was almost able to succeed.

1 lb. venison, trimmed of all fat and cut in stew-sized pieces
2 T. corn oil
2 T. flour
2 c. 1" potato chunks
1 c. carrot slices
1 c. ½" cubes rutabaga
1 T. Worcestershire sauce
1 lg. onion, chopped (1 c.)
2 stalks celery, sliced
1 t. salt
¼ t. pepper
2 c. beef broth
2 bay leaves
½ c. dry red wine (optional, or add more broth)
6 juniper berries, tied in cheesecloth, optional; they add a slightly bitter, "wild" taste

Combine the flour, salt, and pepper in a medium bowl. Dredge the venison in this mixture, coating it well. In a heavy kettle or Dutch oven, brown the venison in the hot oil. Add the onions and celery and continue to cook a few minutes longer. Add the bay leaves, juniper berries, broth and wine. Bring to a boil, reduce the heat, and simmer, covered, for half an hour. Add the vegetables and cook for another half hour, until everything is tender and the stew has thickened somewhat. Remove the bay leaves and juniper berries before serving the stew. This easily serves 4–6.

Venison Mincemeat

My father hunted when he was a younger man, at one time bagging a semilegendary 10-point buck. Sadly, as the story went, he sold his trophy head to some collector from down country, so I never was able to view the magnificent beast. By the time I came along, our main supply of venison was courtesy of the local game warden, a man who just happened to have the same last name as we did. Perhaps it was his way of thanking my dad for taking all those wildlife nuisance calls directed to the wrong person. Because this venison was from deer that had been hit and killed by cars, some of it was quite young and tender—good enough to cook as steaks. However, the odd, tough portions were plopped into my mother's trusty pressure cooker therein to process until the meat literally fell off the bones. Then she would be ready to make one of her specialties— venison mincemeat. Mother used to can hers in glass jars—dark, foreboding little vessels of spiced meat and fruit waiting to cover vanilla ice cream or to be plopped into pie shells. If the thought of it all is too overwhelming, I've also included a smaller recipe for those of a more timid persuasion.

3 lb. venison or beef shoulder meat, boiled tender and chopped fine (not ground)
6 lb. tart apples—pared, cored, and chopped
1 lb. suet (beef fat) chopped fine
1 lb. diced citron*
1½ c. candied diced lemon peel
1 ½ c. candied diced orange peel
¾ c. cider vinegar
2 lb. dark seedless raisins
2 lb. dried currants
6 c. apple cider or apple juice
2 lb. brown sugar
2 T. cinnamon
1 T. allspice
1 T. nutmeg
1 T. salt
1 T. cloves
2 c. brandy, optional

Combine all ingredients except the brandy and portion them into one or two large, heavy pans. Cook over low heat for about an hour, until the liquid is mostly absorbed and everything is quite tender. This will burn easily, so be vigilant! Stir in the brandy at the end of the cooking process. Although old recipes for mincemeat call for keeping it in a crock in a cool cellar, pressure canning is a safer mode of preservation. Follow the directions for canning meat found in your pressure canner guidelines, checking seals to make sure everything is properly canned. Pressure canning is necessary because of the meat in the mincemeat; the pressure canner reaches a higher temperature (240°F) than a boiling water bath is capable of. Alternatively, place your mincemeat in pint or quart freezer containers, seal, and freeze. The texture of the mincemeat may be slightly altered from the freezing process. This recipe will produce about 6 quarts or 12 pints of mincemeat.

Mini Mincemeat

Here's the promised minirecipe for mincemeat. For this version, simply cook the meat right along with the fruits and spices, another time saver. Although it's possible to substitute ground beef or venison for the diced meat, the texture and taste may suffer somewhat; make sure to invest in top-quality low-fat ground meat if you do and break it up really well during the cooking process.

½ lb. venison or beef, chopped fine
1 lb. tart apples—peeled, cored, and chopped (3 c.)
3 T. unsalted butter or 6 T. diced suet
½ c. citron*
¼ c. candied diced lemon peel
¼ c. candied diced orange peel
1 c. raisins
1 c. dried currants
1 c. cider or apple juice
2 T. cider vinegar
1 c. packed brown sugar
1 t. cinnamon
½ t. nutmeg
½ t. allspice
½ t. salt
½ t. cloves
1/3 c. brandy, optional

Stew beef works well for this amount of mincemeat. Mincing the meat while raw is easy to do when working with such a small amount and will cut down on cooking time; partially freezing it first makes the process even easier. (Although it's possible to substitute ground beef, the texture and taste may suffer somewhat; make sure to invest in top-quality low-fat beef if you do and break it up really well during the cooking process.) Combine all ingredients in a large, heavy pan. Bring to a boil, reduce the heat, and cook slowly until the liquid is mostly absorbed, stirring frequently to prevent burning, about ½ hour. Add the brandy, cool, and use as desired. This amount should produce about 4 cups of mincemeat—enough for one solid-citizen pie, a couple of more modest ones, or several tarts. You could also serve it warm over ice cream. Keep unused portion refrigerated, covered up to two weeks.

*A note about citron: Citron is the candied peel of an ancient citrus fruit indigenous to India and later the Mediterranean regions. It's perhaps best known as an ingredient in fruitcake or certain sweet Christmas breads. Although it's now also grown in the Southern United States, citron is not as popular or widely available as many ingredients; around here we're most apt to find it during the months of November and December. Although another dried or candied fruit such as apricots or pineapple may be substituted in a pinch, the flavor of your mince will be somewhat altered.

13

Meatless Mince Fruit

If you prefer a meatless version for your mince pies or cookies, here is a nice alternative. An added advantage to meatless mince fruit is that it's easier to use for filling cookies and the like, as it doesn't require the refrigeration of mincemeat. The slightly different combination of ingredients used to make mince fruit gives it a characteristic mince flavor with a fresh twist.

1½ c. diced peeled apple
1½ c. diced peeled pear
½ c. whole cranberry sauce
2 T. diced candied orange peel
2 T. diced candied lemon peel
¾ c. packed brown sugar
½ c. dark raisins
½ c. chopped walnuts
¼ c. orange juice
1 T. lemon juice
½ t. cinnamon
½ t. salt
½ t. ginger
1 T. butter
¼ t. nutmeg
¼ t. cloves
¼ t. allspice

Combine all ingredients in a large, heavy saucepan. Bring to a boil over medium heat, stirring frequently. Lower heat somewhat and continue to cook and stir for about 10–15 minutes, until the fruits are cooked through and the mixture has thickened somewhat. Allow it to cool before using. This will yield about 3 cups, enough for 1 nice pie or for some tarts and filled cookies. It's also good warm over ice cream or cold over cheesecake.

Mince fruit (top), while having many of mincemeat's characteristics, is lighter and brighter in color and taste.

Napoleon of Butternut Squash

Speaking of meatless dishes, are you looking for a vegetarian entrée fancy enough for company? Try these little stacks of roasted butternut squash rounds and savory rice patties, enhanced with cranberries, nuts, and maple liquor. It'll brighten your winter night, for sure.

12½" thick butternut squash slices (from the neck of the squash)
2 T. olive oil
2 T. corn oil
½ t. salt
½ t. pepper
2 T. maple liquor
Or 1 T. each rum and maple syrup
1 egg
1 c. cooked rice
¼ c. cashews
¼ c. walnuts
¼ c. dried cranberries
1 t. soy sauce
1 t. dried minced onion
1 t. dried parsley flakes
6 T. maple syrup
1 T. cider vinegar
1 T. butter
1 T. maple liquor or rum
Cooked greens such as spinach, kale, or chard

Combine the olive oil, ½ t. salt, ¼ t. of the pepper, and 2 T. maple liquor in a foil-lined 9" × 13" pan. Add the squash slices, turning to coat well. Distribute the slices so they are all flat and evenly spaced in the pan. Roast in a 375°F oven for twenty minutes, carefully turn with a spatula, and roast for 15 more minutes, until they are golden and tender. Remove from the oven, leaving the slices on the pan until assembling. While the squash is roasting, prepare the maple vinegar sauce and the rice patties. Chop half of the cashews and half of the walnuts, setting aside the remainder. Stir the chopped nuts and half of the dried cranberries into the cooked rice, along with the soy sauce, onion, parsley, and the egg, which has been beaten first. Place the 2 T. corn oil in a heavy cast-iron skillet or fry pan over medium-high heat. Drop 8 equal portions of the rice mixture onto the hot oil, flattening each with a spatula into a thin patty approximately the same diameter as your squash slices. Fry until golden on one side, turn, and brown on the other. Place the 6 T. maple syrup plus the butter, vinegar, and additional 1 T. maple liquor or rum in a small saucepan and bring to a full boil. Remove from the heat and set aside. Assemble the Napoleons by placing the hot cooked greens on a serving platter. Arrange 4 squash slices evenly on the greens. Top each with a rice patty and then another squash slice. Continue this with remaining squash and rice patties to form 4 stacks with 3 squash slices and 2 rice patties in each. Sprinkle the stacks and greens with the remaining nuts and cranberries, pour the hot maple vinegar sauce over all, and serve. As an entrée complete with soup or salad, crusty bread, and dessert, this will serve 4. By itself, with hearty appetites, it may better serve 2.

Napoleon of butternut squash makes a tasty vegetarian alternative to your January fare. Its bright colors and flavors make the winter's night seem a little more enjoyable.

Orange Anise–Glazed Carrots

Carrots are an inexpensive and nutritious addition to your winter table. They will last for months in a refrigerator vegetable keeper or, if you've enough of them and are industrious enough to construct one, in a root cellar. This side dish is a nice variation on an old favorite. Add a little zip, and plain carrots go from blah to "ah"!

2 c. sliced carrot rounds
½ c. water
2 T. butter
¼ t. salt
½ t. anise seed
1 t. grated orange rind
3 T. dark brown sugar
2 T. orange juice

Cook the carrots in the water for 5–7 minutes, until crisp tender. Drain off any remaining water. Stir all other ingredients into the carrots in the cooking pan. Continue to cook over medium heat, stirring occasionally, until the liquid is almost all absorbed and the carrots are nicely glazed. Be careful not to let them burn. This makes 4 generous servings.

Brussels Sprouts with Blue Cheese Dressing

Brussels sprouts respond beautifully to the creamy tang of good blue cheese dressing. Brussels sprouts are one of those hearty cold vegetables that may be harvested directly off the stalk

long after most vegetables in the garden have been destroyed by freezing temperatures. By January here in Vermont, I've already harvested them, so my choices are fresh from the store, or frozen; either will work well. A pound of brussels sprouts equals approximately three cups.

3 c. fresh or frozen brussels sprouts
½ c. sour cream
½ c. mayonnaise
2 T. milk
1 T. snipped chives
¼ t. cracked black pepper
¼ t. salt
¼ t. Tabasco sauce
½ c. crumbled blue cheese
4 slices bacon, crisp cooked and crumbled (optional)

Combine all dressing ingredients except blue cheese and milk (and bacon if using) in a small mixing bowl, blending until smooth. Stir in milk to thin slightly and then add in the blue cheese, mixing lightly. Allowing the dressing to rest an hour or two in the fridge will help develop its flavor more fully. Cook the brussels sprouts in water about ⅔ the depth of the sprouts until tender but still bright green—approximately 10–12 minutes. Drain the sprouts well and place in serving dish. Crumble the bacon over the dressing and serve on the side. Generously serves 6. You may well have leftover dressing, which can be refrigerated up to a week. It's also great on cooked cauliflower, steak, as a dip for crudités or french fries, or as a salad dressing for green and/or winter fruit salads.

Warm Winter Salad

Kale, a true winter vegetable, is packed with vitamins and minerals. It's readily available fresh during those months when other fresh produce may be in short supply. I feel the flavor of the kale is enhanced by brief steaming, as in this hearty salad, just right for a cold winter's day.

8 c. lightly packed bite-sized pieces of kale, torn from the stem
¼ c. dried cranberries
¼ c. crumbled gorgonzola cheese
1 firm green pear, such as Anjou, cored and sliced

Dressing
¼ c. balsamic vinegar
¼ c. olive oil
2 T. maple syrup
1 T. and 1 t. soy sauce
¼ t. ground ginger or 1 t. grated fresh

It's probably easier to make your dressing in advance, as once the kale is steamed you'll want to assemble your salad and serve. Whisk together the balsamic vinegar, soy sauce, maple syrup, and ginger. Whisk in the olive oil until well blended. Allow it to sit at room temperature for up to a day; for longer storage, place in the refrigerator, but be sure to take it out at least an hour in advance so that the olive oil will again liquefy. Place the kale in a metal strainer or steaming dish. Steam it over boiling water for 5 minutes, until it's warm and slightly soft but still bright dark green. Divide it evenly between 4 individual salad bowls or place it all in 1 large bowl. Top with the sliced pear and sprinkle with the dried cranberries and the gorgonzola. Drizzle with the dressing and serve at once. This makes 4 generous servings.

Warm winter salad is colorful, flavorful, and nutritious.

Mashed Potatoes

Because we always had a garden, we always had plenty of homegrown potatoes. We'd carefully dry and then store them, away from light, in a cool closet room on the north side of the house. There are a number of potato varieties, each suited to one or more uses. In order to get the best results from your recipe, it's important to know your potato types well enough to choose the right one. At least we've only a few main varieties to choose from in the United States, unlike Peru, land of the potato's origin. At last count, I believe that country boasted over a thousand different kinds. Imagine trying to sort that collection for your mashers; it would take until the next New Year's just to get through them all! My favorite potato for mashing is a variety called purple Viking; it's a beautiful round potato with purple skin and snowy-white flesh. However, chances are you won't be finding any of those little guys unless you grow your own. Some folks may prefer one of the mild-flavored "gold" potatoes now increasingly available, although because their moisture content is somewhat higher than many varieties, it's easy to make that type of potato too mushy when mashed with this ratio of ingredients. Therefore for this recipe, I recommend a russet-type potato, both for flavor and texture. They're widely available and won't disappoint.

1 lb. potatoes—washed, peeled, and quartered
½ t. salt

1½ c. water
½ c. milk *or* half and half
2 T. butter
¼ t. seasoned salt *or* ¼ t. pepper

Place the potatoes in a medium saucepan. Add the salt and enough of the water to almost cover the potatoes; you don't want to drown them. To me, there's nothing more pathetic than a pan full of waterlogged, anemic potatoes staring sadly at you. Bring the potatoes to a boil, reduce the heat, and boil gently, covered, for 20–30 minutes, until the potatoes are very tender and the liquid has partially cooked away. Just don't let the liquid totally cook down; a pan of dried-out, burned potatoes staring at you is almost as depressing as their waterlogged cousins. Here is where my years of 4-H cooking lessons come into play; when you drain your potatoes, save the cooking water for use in gravy, soup, or even making bread. Don't throw all those valuable nutrients down the drain! With the potatoes still in the pan over low heat, add in the milk, butter, and seasonings; cover; and let the mixture heat through for a minute or so. Now it's time to mash or whip your potatoes until they're as smooth or lumpy as you wish. Add another pat of butter to the top, if you wish, and serve them while they're hot! If you must make these a little in advance, place the covered pan into a larger pan of simmering water. Once the potatoes start to cool down, they become hard and not nearly as appetizing. This recipe is very easy to halve or double, as you wish.

Scalloped Corn

Scalloped corn is a tasty side dish on a cold winter night. Extra corn from last summer's garden is easy enough to freeze. Blanch your ears in boiling water for 5 minutes, chill in icy water for another 5, drain, and cut from the cob. I freeze my kernels spread out on cookie sheets, ready to pop into sealed freezer bags once they've frozen. This method is referred to as "loose pack." You may use either loose-pack frozen corn or canned, drained whole kernel corn for this recipe. If using frozen, there's no need to thaw in advance; you can thaw it stove-top during preparation.

2 c. corn
¼ c. butter
½ sleeve saltine crackers, crushed
¼ t. celery seed
¼ t. Tabasco sauce *or* black pepper
1 t. dried minced onion
½ c. milk

Melt the butter in a medium-sized saucepan over moderate heat. Stir in the crackers and seasonings, coating the cracker crumbs well. Add the corn and milk. If the kernels are still frozen, you may heat them a few minutes, stirring occasionally. Turn into a well-buttered casserole dish. Bake in a 375°F oven for about ½ hour, until heated through. This serves 4 generously or 6 moderately.

The Tale of the Rabbit

Rabbit is a rather ignored meat in this country. Perhaps this is a bit of a shame; rabbit meat is very lean, with a delicate flavor. Rabbits are also much more economical to care for than some of the larger meat-producing animals. The flavor is somewhere between dark meat chicken and light meat pork, although the texture is more dense. Rabbit should either be brined before frying or braised in a stew, as it has a tendency toward dryness. You should also beware of the rabbit's fragile bones; they splinter easily when you're busy cutting the meat. An increasing number of specialty meat shops and even some supermarkets now offer rabbits, whole or cut up. If you choose to raise your own, as we did for one incredibly brief period of time, you'll need to learn to skin and gut the little critters. However, that is another kettle of rabbit entirely. In general, if you need to cut up your rabbit, remove the large hind legs and much smaller front legs at the joints where they connect into the main body. These portions of meat are especially good for frying. The rest of the rabbit can be braised or stewed to make a flavorful pot pie.

Rabbit Casserole Provencal

The white wine adds a bit of an exotic flavor, although you can as easily substitute water or chicken stock. Serve the rabbit as is with an accompaniment of crusty bread, or top it with herbed drop biscuits.

1½–2 lb. rabbit parts (white meat, backbone, and ribcage, or add some leg meat)
  ½ c. dry white wine
  1½ c. water
  2 bay leaves
  3 small sprigs fresh thyme
  3 slices bacon
  1 small onion, chopped: ½ c.
  1 medium carrot, sliced in rounds: ½ c.
  ½ t. salt
  ¼ t. white pepper
  1 c. sliced mushrooms

Dice the bacon and place in a large skillet or saucepan. Fry it gently along with the rabbit, onions, celery, and carrot. After the vegetables have softened and browned somewhat, add in the water, broth or wine, seasonings, and mushrooms. Bring to a boil, reduce heat, and simmer for 30–40 minutes, until the rabbit meat is very tender. Remove the rabbit from the broth and allow it to cool enough so that you can pick it with the meat off the bones. Add the rabbit back into the pan. You may now either reheat the rabbit in the pan and serve with crusty bread or turn the hot mixture into a casserole dish, top with the herbed biscuits, and bake at 375°F until the biscuits are browned and cooked through—about 20 minutes. This serves around 4.

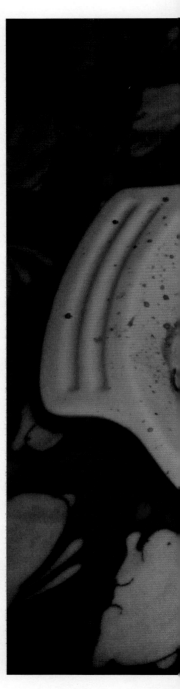

A nice casserole of rabbit Provencal is waiting to warm you up.

Herbed Biscuits

These biscuits are also nice accompaniments to a chicken stew or served as is for breakfast or brunch. You could even drop teaspoons of the dough onto simmering soup, cover tightly, and cook for 7–9 minutes, until your little herbed dumplings are cooked through.

¾ c. flour
1 t. baking powder
¼ t. salt
¼ t. dried thyme
1 t. chives
1 t. parsley
2 T. butter, melted
½ c. milk

Stir together the dry ingredients and seasonings. Combine the milk and melted butter and stir into the flour mixture. Drop spoonfuls onto the hot rabbit in the casserole and immediately place it in the oven to bake. You could also gently pat out the dough to about ½" thickness on a floured surface and cut it into circles or squares. Bake the biscuits separately for about 10 minutes, until they are puffed and golden brown.

Country-Fried Rabbit

A good presoak in salted water is the trick to producing moist fried rabbit. Set your rabbit to soaking early on the day you plan to serve it.

1½ lb. rabbit legs
1 qt. water
2 t. salt
¼ c. corn oil
½ c. flour
½ t. paprika
½ t. salt
¼ t. poultry seasoning

You may wish to cut the much-larger hind legs of the rabbit in half, using a good, sharp knife. Place the rabbit legs, water, and salt in a plastic or stainless steel container, preferably with a tight cover, and refrigerate for 8 hours. Drain the legs well, patting them lightly to somewhat dry them. Combine the flour and seasonings in a bowl or plastic bag and dredge the rabbit legs, coating them well. Heat the oil in a heavy skillet over medium, adding the rabbit pieces when it is hot. Fry the rabbit, covered, until it is deep golden brown on one side. Turn the rabbit and brown the other side. Keeping the pan covered during the frying process will help the meat to cook more evenly and to retain moisture. Remove the rabbit to a serving plate. If you wish gravy, add a tablespoon or two of flour to the cooking pan. Cook and stir a minute or two and then deglaze the frying pan with a cup or so of chicken stock or water. Serves 3–4.

Piecrust . . . or Piecrust

Once upon a time, I thought the only way to make a good piecrust was with solid shortening. As time went by, I began to appreciate more the effect of butter on a pastry shell. Eventually, as news of the ills associated with hydrogenated foods swirled about, I decided to eliminate solid shortening from my cooking entirely. The only two foods this proved difficult for were whoopie pies and piecrust. I've now settled on satisfactory recipes for both, ironically just as nonhydrogenated solid shortenings such as those made from palm oil have made their way to the grocery store shelves. I'm sharing two of my piecrust recipes here. There's still plenty of room for others, if you prefer. For years lard was the standard utilized in turning out a flaky crust, and some folks swear by a crust made with just oil. However, for now we'll take a middle-of-the-road approach with one shortening and one shortening-less crust recipe.

My Favorite Piecrust

This crust takes a little extra effort to prepare properly. If the butter and water aren't cold enough, or if your proportions are off by just a little, you may end up with piecrust that tastes good but is somewhat tough. However, when properly prepared, this is a golden, slightly crispy crust with a wonderful flavor. Always chill it before rolling for best results.

½ c. cold, unsalted butter
¼ c. corn oil
2 T. milk
2 c. flour

1 t. salt
2 t. sugar
4 T. ice-cold water

Combine the flour, sugar, and salt in a large mixing bowl. This will give you adequate space to cut in the butter and to mix the crust without it spilling over the edges of the bowl. Using a pastry cutter or two sharp knives, cut the butter into the flour mixture until it forms tiny lumps the size of baby peas. In a small bowl, stir together the oil and milk with a fork; it will become a creamy white. Mix this quickly into the flour/butter mixture. Add the ice water and stir again with the fork; the dough should form a nice stiff, slightly crumbly consistency. Divide the dough in two and quickly roll each half into a ball. Cover with waxed paper or plastic wrap and refrigerate at least half an hour before rolling it out. This recipe is easy to double or triple, which I frequently do. Wrap each single crust-sized ball of dough separately and freeze them for up to two months. When you need some piecrust dough, allow it to thaw in the fridge overnight or at room temperature for a couple of hours. In a pinch, carefully microwave it, a few seconds at a time, until the dough is soft enough to roll out but still cold. Be wary of this method! It's awfully easy to let the piecrust overheat, which spoils the whole purpose of having chilled it in the first place.

Basic Piecrust

This is a standard piecrust, enough for one or two crust pies or for two pastry shells. Save any scraps to make piecrust cookies!

2 c. flour
½ c. solid shortening
¼ c. cold butter

1 t. salt
1 t. sugar
Approximately 4 T. ice-cold water

Combine the flour, salt, and sugar in a large mixing bowl; this will give you plenty of room to work without spilling your flour. Use a pastry cutter or two knives to cut the shortening and cold butter into the flour mixture until they resemble the size of baby peas throughout. Sprinkle on the ice water and toss together with a fork until everything is just blended; you don't want to overmix. Gather up the piecrust dough with your hands and form it into two balls; wrap in plastic or waxed paper and refrigerate until firm, at least ½ hour. If you wish, you can make your piecrust in advance. Store it 3–4 days in the refrigerator, or wrap it airtight and freeze it for up to a couple of months.

Piecrust Cookies

Whenever I make piecrust, any scraps of dough are saved to be made into these delectable little pastries. They're especially popular with the under-twelve set, although "adults" enjoy them too.

Leftover scraps of piecrust
Milk
Sugar *or* cinnamon sugar

Roll out the scraps of dough into as large a circle as necessary to make a thin crust. Brush the top of the circle with milk and sprinkle it generously with sugar or cinnamon sugar. Cut the circle pizza style into thin wedges. Carefully transfer to a cookie sheet and bake on the upper shelf of your oven at 375°F for about 8–10 minutes, until they are golden brown and slightly crispy. Cool just slightly before removing them to enjoy.

Pineapple Pie

My mother-in-law, Lucretia "Kitty" Lawrence, generally made three pies for special occasions: pumpkin, pecan, and pineapple. Pineapple pie provides a welcome spot of bright color and flavor in the midst of a cold New England winter. I use crushed canned pineapple in mine, as I believe Kitty did too. Although she also added egg to hers, I prefer to simply use cornstarch for thickening, along with just a hint of lemon and spice for added flavor. This makes a nice big pie with lots of tasty fruit filling.

2 crust pie pastry
2 20-oz. cans crushed pineapple in juice
1 c. sugar
5 T. cornstarch
1 T. butter
1 T. lemon juice
½ t. pure lemon extract *or* 1 t. grated lemon zest
¼ t. mace
¼ t. ginger

Combine everything but the piecrust in a large, heavy saucepan. Bring to a full boil over medium-high heat, stirring frequently to prevent burning. Once it has thickened slightly, remove from the heat and allow it to cool to room temperature. Roll out the crust half at a time, fitting one loosely into a 9" pie plate. Pour in the filling and cover with the top crust. If you wish, cut a decorative shape from the upper crust before fitting it on top, or simply cut a few slits in it afterward. Brush the top lightly with milk and sprinkle with sugar.

Bake at 375°F until the top is nicely browned, about 45 minutes. It's best to allow the pie to cool before cutting, as the filling is quite soft when hot.

This will serve 8–12, depending on slice size and appetites involved. It's quite tasty with a scoop of vanilla ice cream, if you feel like splurging.

How about ringing in the New Year with a slice of golden pineapple pie?

Puff Pastry

Classic puff pastry contains very simple ingredients: flour, salt, butter, and water. It is the way in which these are combined that will produce heavenly results. Do not try to hurry puff pastry; it can't be done. However, by allotting small spaces of time over a day or two, you'll produce fine puff pastry with relatively little effort. As this freezes easily, it can be prepared well in advance, wrapped and frozen to be used at your leisure. For years I followed a "single-batch" recipe, having read somewhere or another that my pastry would be ruined if I tried doubling it. Now older and wiser, especially since having produced 300 of the little delicacies for son Timothy and daughter-in-law Abigail's wedding, a larger batch has become my standard. For all this commitment, you deserve a plentiful finished product.

2 sticks cold salted butter (no substitutes!)
1½ c. all-purpose flour
½ c. and 1 T. ice-cold water

You will note I don't add salt to this recipe, choosing instead salted butter to add that component. The flavor to me is just fine when made in this manner. Begin by placing the flour in a large mixing bowl. Stir in the water to form dough that is stiff but malleable. Cover this mixture and allow it to "rest" at room temperature for at least 5 minutes or up to ½ hour. This allows the gluten in the flour to develop and will result in a more elastic product for the next step. Next, knead the dough a few times and roll it out on a lightly floured surface to a 12" square. To me, this is the most difficult part of the whole procedure: don't be afraid to pull at the dough's edges with your fingers to get it large enough. It will take quite a bit of tension—just don't pull it too hard; you don't want to rip any of the edges if you can help it. Slice each of the sticks of cold butter lengthwise into three equal parts. Place them side by side on one-half of the dough's surface, leaving about ½" around the outer edges. Fold the dough up and over the butter, pinching the edges all around to seal it entirely. Roll the dough out to twice its height again (you'll discover it spreads out in the direction of the butter sticks). Fold the dough over on itself into thirds starting with the pinched edge and then turn it one-quarter turn on your work surface. The turning is done so that the next time you roll out the dough, you'll fold it over on the opposite edges from the previous turn. Lightly flour your work surface as needed and roll the dough out one more time. Fold the previously unfolded edges over in thirds to make a neat flat package of dough about 6" on each side. You have officially completed two "turns" of your pastry. Now comes your first break: wrap the dough airtight in plastic wrap, waxed paper, or foil and then place it flat in the refrigerator for at least a couple of hours to firm up the butter again. Trying to roll out puff pastry dough filled with soft butter is a recipe for buttery disaster; it will leak out the edges, and you never will attain the exquisite layers, which make this pastry so unique. Once it has sufficiently chilled, again roll the dough out to double or triple its original size, folding it over in thirds. Give the dough a quarter turn and repeat one more time before again chilling. You will repeat this chilling, rolling, and folding procedure one more rotation (two more turns), which in the end will yield you 729 gloriously buttery layers within your pastry, if I've done my math correctly! The puff paste is now ready to be used; refrigerate it again until ready to roll it out if using within a couple of days. For longer storage, securely wrap it and lay it flat on the freezer shelf to use within a month or two.

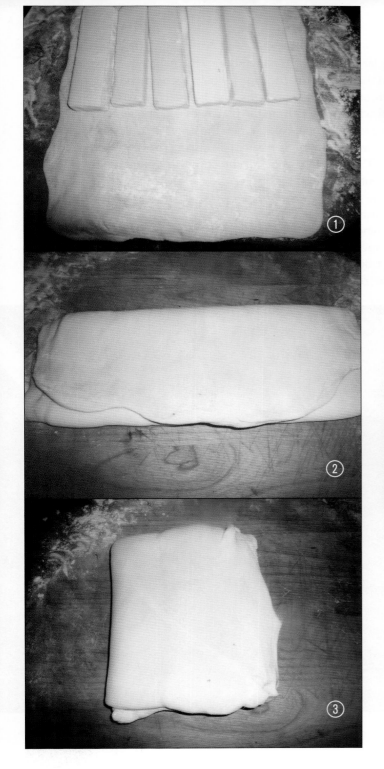

①

②

③

The initial stages of puff pastry: After placing cold butter in the rolled-out dough base, the edges are sealed. Once it has been rolled thin, the pastry dough is folded in thirds, rolled thin, turned, and folded in thirds again. It is then chilled prior to the next series of rolling and folding.

29

Chocolate Layer Cake with Fudge Frosting

When our son Gregory married a lady from Minnesota, I was suddenly confronted with a new and, at times, unfamiliar cuisine: upper Midwestern cooking. Wild rice and walleye pike notwithstanding, I was relieved to note one of Elizabeth's favorite desserts was actually quite familiar to me: chocolate cake with fudge frosting. This cake bakes up moist and flavorful, for you to frost as plain or fancy as you wish. It's equally delicious to top off a festive meal, or simply to savor with a glass of cold milk or a cup of coffee. Although I almost always use cake flour when baking cakes, this is one recipe where you may substitute all-purpose; the cake will still be moist and light, but a little denser. If you don't wish to buy a box of cake flour, you may also try substituting a ratio 2 T. of cornstarch in place of 2 T. of all-purpose flour per cup of flour used.

2 c. all-purpose or cake flour
1¾ c. sugar
⅔ c. dark cocoa powder
½ c. corn oil
1½ t. baking powder
1½ t. baking soda
1 t. salt
1 t. vanilla
1 c. milk
3 eggs
¾ c. water

Combine everything but the water in a large mixing bowl. Beat at low speed to blend and then at medium speed until everything is smooth and well blended. You can also do this by hand with a wire whisk. Stir in the water; you will have a thin, smooth batter. Pour it into two greased and floured 9" round cake pans or a prepared 9" × 13" cake pan. Bake at 350°F for 30–35 minutes for the round pans or 35–40 minutes for the 9" × 13" pan. The top will be shiny, slightly raised, and will spring back when lightly touched when the cake is done. Cool in the pans on wire racks for 10 minutes. If you plan to remove the cakes from the pans, run a knife gently around the rim of each pan and turn the cake out on the rack to finish cooling. I would recommend this only for the round tins; the larger cake will be easier to serve from the pan unless you're decorating it as a sheet cake. When the cakes are fully cooled, frost them as desired. The fudge frosting here is especially good for the chocoholics among us.

Fudge Frosting

This rich dark frosting is also delicious on yellow, white, or angel food cakes. The recipe is easy to halve or double as need be. This frosts two layers or a 9" × 13" rectangle. To decorate

a layer cake as well as generously frost it, I suggest adding ½ again the ingredients listed here. Adding the optional coffee or coffee liquor creates an extra element of flavor.

2 c. best-quality semisweet chocolate chips
1 c. cream
2 T. light corn syrup
2 T. dark cocoa powder
¼ c. butter
1½ c. confectioner's sugar
2 T. coffee liquor *or* cold coffee *or* cream

Heat the cream in a medium saucepan until it just comes to boiling. Remove from the heat and stir in the chocolate chips until they are completely melted. Add in order the corn syrup, butter, and confectioner's sugar, stirring well after each addition. Stir in the coffee liquor, coffee, or cream. Place the pan in a larger pan or bowl of cold water (ice water for faster chilling) and allow it to cool somewhat, stirring occasionally, until it becomes slightly cooler than room temperature. Beware—if it chills too much, your frosting will be too stiff to spread easily. Beat it with an electric mixer to a creamy spreading consistency, being careful not to overbeat, and frost your cake at once.

Winter Mornings . . .

THE EARLY HOURS of the day during a New England winter are also when temperatures drop to their lowest point. If you're able to overlook small inconveniences such as defrosting windshields on cars and trucks, and making sure your water pipes don't freeze and burst, you may even be able to enjoy their beauty. Temperatures well below freezing cause crystalline formations on every tree branch and bush. When the early sun rises, you're treated to thousands of sparkling diamonds reflecting its light. Hungry birds are out and about, feathers fluffed for insulation, making them look larger than they really are. Blue jays flashing brilliant blue and cardinals' intense crimson play counterpoint to earth-toned sparrows and slate gray juncos. Soon the squirrels appear as well, bounding over the snow from the cover of the apple trees, their conduit from the relative safety of the woods to the heady allure of fresh bird seed.

The amount of snow in any given winter usually predicates whether I'll be seeing deer in the dim light of predawn. Years with a thick blanket of snow, they seldom venture my way, instead forming deer yards on south-facing slopes, where there's safety in numbers and lots of browse to eat. However, when only a few inches of the white stuff covers the ground, I may be awakened to the crunching sound of hooves on the hard-packed surface and the sight of the graceful critters only a few feet from my back door, feasting on last autumn's fallen apples.

When I was growing up, intensely cold mornings also meant I'd be heading out to the barn with pails of warm water sweetened with molasses, a restorative treat for the goats waiting there. The sweet steam from the water coupled with the fresh scent of a newly opened bail of hay always made the goat barn seem a little more hospitable by the time morning chores were done. I'd trudge back to the house, leaving the goats contentedly munching, occasionally wishing I could just stay there with them rather than ready myself to board the large yellow school bus, barely warmer than the outdoors itself, which would soon arrive, bearing me away on the long journey to school.

No matter what your occupation may be on a winter morning, be sure to start it right, with a nourishing breakfast to sustain you along the way. It's sure to make your winter day a little brighter.

Multiflora rose hips, encased in sparkling ice, hang suspended above the Ames Hill Brook.

February

Scandinavian Sunrise

Although the blending of ingredients for this cereal breakfast dish is influenced by Nordic lands, it lends itself just as well to New England. You don't need to spend hours slaving over pastry to produce a delicious and spectacular breakfast treat. Prepare your custard and fruit sauce the night before. In the morning, simply whip up a batch of cooked cereal, and you're ready to go! I use frozen berries picked from my garden the previous summer—easy and economical! (Try freezing berries you get on special or "in season" if you don't have your own supply. Simply spread the clean dry berries on a cookie sheet until frozen and then pop them in labeled ziplock freezer bags for future use.)

Vanilla Custard Cream

¾ c. milk
¾ c. cream
⅓ c. sugar
2 egg yolks
1 t. vanilla

Red Fruit Sauce

1½ c. red raspberries *or* strawberries
½ c. red currants *or* cranberries *or* tart cherries
½ c. water
1 t. cornstarch
⅓ c. sugar
To Assemble
4 servings of farina (cream of rice or cream of wheat cereal)
2 T. sugar
½ t. cinnamon
½ t. ground cardamom

1 recipe custard cream
1 recipe red fruit sauce

For the custard, place the milk and cream in a medium, heavy saucepan and heat them to just under boiling. Meanwhile, beat the egg yolks and sugar together. Add a little of the hot liquid to this mixture to "temper" it and then return everything to the pan, whisking constantly. Stir and cook over medium heat to just under boiling; the custard will have thickened slightly but not have curdled. Immediately remove from the heat and stir in the vanilla. Chill quickly by placing the pan into a large bowl of cold water. Once it has cooled to room temperature, pour into a small bowl and refrigerate until you're ready to use it. Next combine the berries and water in a small saucepan and heat them to just under boiling, crushing them with the back of a spoon to help release their juices. Pour into a blender and puree until smooth. Pour the juice back into the pan through a wire mesh strainer to remove most of the seeds. Stir in the combined sugar and cornstarch. Bring the mixture to a full boil. Remove from the heat, cool the sauce to room temperature, and then chill it until serving time. When you're ready to enjoy your treat, place a serving of cereal in each of four large soup bowls. Sprinkle the combined sugar, cinnamon, and cardamom in a thin rim around the edges. Make a depression in the center of each to hold the custard cream. Finally, place the fruit sauce in a pastry bag or a plastic sandwich bag with the tip of one corner snipped off. Pour it carefully in a circle around each center. Using a sharp knife tip, pull the sauce at intervals out toward the edge of the bowl to form your "sunrise." As with the real thing, once you begin eating, it won't last long!

Start your day with a Scandinavian sunrise! Who needs Danish when your cereal looks like this?

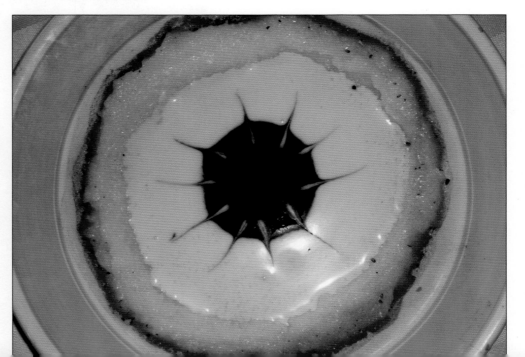

Bagels

An easy and satisfying on-the-go breakfast, bagels may be served plain or fancy. The trickiest part of making bagels at home is having them rise to the optimal height for submerging in boiling water. Under- or over-risen dough will produce perfectly respectable bagels, but they may be somewhat wrinkly. If you're able to use two large pans of boiling water (each seasoned with the requisite amount of salt and sugar), you'll be able to boil all your bagels at once for optimal results. You'll then pop them into the oven to brown and complete the cooking process. Warm bagels and cream cheese are a classic. Add some homemade jam or a bit of gravlax or smoked salmon to top, and you've transformed your bagel into a gourmet treat.

2½ c. bread flour, approximately
1 T. dry yeast
2 T. sugar, divided
2 t. salt, divided
1 t. oil
1 c. warm water
Optional: poppy seeds, sesame seeds, minced garlic or onion, coarse salt, etc.

Combine the warm water, 1 T. sugar, 1 t. salt, and oil. Stir in the yeast until dissolved. Stir in 2 c. of the flour and allow the mixture to rest for about 15 minutes. Divide the dough into 6 larger or 12 smaller equal balls. Form each into a hollow circle, using your finger to poke out the center and then thinning the ring until it's about 4" in circumference (2" for smaller bagels). Allow them to rest for another 15–20 minutes, while you bring to a boil about 4 quarts of water. Add in the remaining 1 T. of sugar and 1 t. of salt. Reduce to a gentle boil. Cook half the bagels at a time, 3 minutes on each side for large or 1½ minutes per side for small. Remove them to a pan lined with a damp dishtowel while the boiling process is completed. Meanwhile, have your oven preheating to 425°F. Place the parboiled bagels on an oiled baking sheet, which has been dusted with cornmeal, if you wish. Bake on an upper rack for about 20–25 minutes (less time for smaller bagels) until they are golden brown.

Homemade bagels topped with homemade cream cheese ("June") and homemade crab apple jelly and peach preserves ("August"). What could be better?

Soft Pretzels

Pretzels are another example of yeast-raised minibread that is treated with brief immersion in warm water before baking. In this case, the water is combined with baking soda, which adds both flavor and color to the finished product. Pretzels are often featured during the pre-Easter period of Lent, perhaps because the unique pretzel shape depicts arms crossed in prayer. Don't feel you must wait for Lent to enjoy soft pretzels; they're an easy to eat treat any time of the year.

1 T. yeast
2 T. brown sugar
1 t. salt
1 c. very warm water
1 c. bread flour
1¾ c. all-purpose flour
¼ c. unsalted butter
4 c. water
2 T. baking soda
Coarse salt for sprinkling
Cinnamon sugar for sprinkling, optional

Dissolve the sugar and salt in the warm water in a large bowl. Stir in the yeast and the cup of bread flour. Set it aside and allow it to work for about 5 minutes. Stir in enough all-purpose flour to form a stiff dough. Knead the dough until it is smooth and elastic. Cover the bowl and allow the dough to rise in a warm place for about 1 hour, until it has doubled in bulk. Near the end of the raising time, place the 4 cups of water and the baking soda in a large frying pan or kettle and bring it to just under simmering. Divide the dough into 8 equal portions and roll each piece in between your hands until it forms a long thin strip about 16" long. Twist and loop each dough strand into a pretzel shape and place on a greased baking sheet, leaving room for expansion. Once you have formed all eight pretzels, dip them one at a time into the warm baking soda water, submerging each side for about 10 seconds; replace on the baking sheet. Allow them to rise again for about half an hour. Bake the pretzels on the upper racks in a preheated 425°F oven for 12–15 minutes, until they are golden brown. Keep a close watch on them; the difference between browning and burning at such a high oven temperature is a very small window of time. Once they've baked, brush each pretzel generously with melted butter and sprinkle with coarse sea salt. If you prefer a sweeter pretzel, you may sprinkle them with cinnamon sugar instead. The salty pretzels are tasty with a bit of mustard, or try them as a dip with your favorite cheese sauce or fondue.

Pretzels after their baking soda bath, waiting to be baked . . . and the finished product—salty, buttery, and ready to be enjoyed for breakfast, lunch, or snack.

Ice Fishing in Little Shanty Towns . . .

One winter phenomenon up here in the north, for those who live near lakes, ponds, or setbacks in rivers (and that amounts to quite a few of us), is the sport of ice fishing. There are ice fishers who spend much of the warm-weather months crafting ice shanties to be pulled and parked out on the frozen surface, once the ice is thick enough. Woe to those who don't exercise proper caution in this respect; fishers who venture on too-thin ice may submerge their shanties, and occasionally their cars or trucks, in icy water. Fortunately, the majority of folks who enjoy ice fishing also understand such things, whether they hole up in a sturdy little shack complete with heating system and furnishings or simply hike out on the ice with auger for drilling and fish pole in hand.

The largest body of water for ice fishing around Vermont would be Lake Champlain, which forms a boundary between us and upper New York State. Ice fishers there may be lucky enough to snag a landlocked salmon for their efforts. And Lake Willoughby, in the northeast corner of the state, has lake trout of world-record proportions. However, down in this end of Vermont, folks are more apt to be found on smaller local bodies of water, perhaps Harriman Reservoir over in Wilmington or the Retreat setback on the West River right here in Brattleboro. According to Bruce, the fish likely to be caught hereabouts are perch, small white fleshed little critters best suited to frying.

A little village of fishing shanties springs up each winter on the West River setback.

Oven-Fried Perch

Freshwater perch may be caught in summer or winter. If you don't enjoy fishing, it's easy enough to pick up a pound of fillets at the local supermarket or fish store. The key to buying any fish is making sure it's scrupulously fresh; in this instance, firm white flesh and no fishy smell! You may substitute another white fleshed fish for the perch, if you prefer.

1 lb. perch fillets
4 T. butter
½ c. fine bread crumbs
½ t. salt
1 t. paprika
1 T. Parmesan cheese

Combine the bread crumbs (finely grated cheese), salt, and paprika in a small bowl. Melt the butter in a medium baking dish; coat each fillet with the melted butter and dip both sides in the seasoned crumbs, coating well. Place the breaded fillets back in the buttery baking dish and bake in a 425°F oven for 10 minutes or until the fish flakes lightly when a fork is inserted. Serve your oven-fried perch with lemon wedges, if desired, to 4 people.

Gravlax

Gravlax is raw salmon that has been cured in a mixture of salt, sugar, pepper, and fresh dill. It may then be sliced thin and eaten as you wish, accompanied by sweet mustard sauce. Gravlax, roughly translated, means "ground salmon." The meaning is literal, in all actuality, because in the days before refrigeration, the salmon was kept cool during the curing process by being buried underground. Fortunately, refrigeration has made the curing of gravlax both simpler and safer.

Per Pound of Best-Quality Salmon (fillet)
¼ c. each sugar and sea salt, a bunch of fresh dill, about 1 c. of the fronds
1 t. fresh-cracked pepper: white is traditional, but black works as well

Place the whole fillet, skin and all, on a piece of extra-strength foil large enough to totally encompass and fold around the fish. Rub the combined sugar and salt generously over both sides of the salmon, patting it on well. Grind on the pepper and cover both sides with fresh dill sprigs. Wrap in the foil and allow it to cure in the fridge for 48 hours, turning over about every 12 hours or so. Slice thin and serve as above or turn it onto a casserole with potatoes and cream.

Rubbed with sugar, pepper, and salt, topped with dill; the gravlax is ready to cure.

Sweet Mustard Sauce

Try marinating boiled shrimp in this mustard sauce for an interesting variation on shrimp cocktail.

¼ c. prepared mustard
¼ c. sugar
½ t. salt
1 T. cider vinegar *or* lemon juice
½ c. oil
A few grinds of pepper
½ c. chopped fresh dill

Whisk together the mustard, sugar, salt, and pepper. Slowly drizzle in the oil, whisking constantly, until the mixture is smooth and thick. Stir in the chopped dill and you're good to go. This amount will take care of about a pound of gravlax, boiled shrimp, or other protein of your choice.

Scalloped Salmon and Potatoes

Here's a nifty way to use up that extra little bit of gravlax you may have hanging around. Smoked salmon will substitute in just fine if you're not in the mood for curing your own. The leek adds an especially nice flavor, so try to use it if you can. You'll note there's no added salt in this recipe; the saltiness of the fish should suffice in this regard.

1 lb. potatoes (3 c. thinly sliced)
6 oz. gravlax or smoked salmon
1 medium onion *or* leek, white part only, thinly sliced
2 eggs
2 T. butter
1 c. milk
¼ c. cream
1 t. Dijon mustard
1 T. fresh chopped dill

Lightly sauté the sliced onion or leek in the butter until tender but not brown. Place ½ of the potatoes in a buttered 1-qt. casserole dish. Top with the sautéed onion and then with the thinly sliced salmon. Top with the rest of the potatoes. Whisk together the eggs, milk, cream, and mustard until smooth; pour over all. Bake covered at 350°F for ½ an hour. Uncover and continue baking another 15–20 minutes, until the top is golden and the potatoes feel tender when poked with a fork. This makes 4 hearty servings.

Soup's on . . . Mother's Chicken Rice Soup

Back in the 1960s, the A&P store on Main Street would occasionally have sales on chicken necks. This was cause for great . . . well, at least moderate celebration at our house. My mom would buy several pounds of the scrawny little guys and bring them home to make soup. They'd simmer in a couple of large kettles, accompanied by onions, celery, and carrots. The most exciting part of the venture would be pulling whatever usable meat there was off the cooked necks while avoiding the countless tiny bones. Talk about your family bonding projects. Once this was accomplished, the meat went back into the kettles along with the veggies and some rice. You don't have to rely on chicken necks to make this, although if you're up for the challenge, you'll have a very tasty soup for very little expense.

2–3 lb. chicken necks and wings *or* 1–2 lb. chicken thighs
2 lg. onions
4 stalks celery
½ lb. of carrots
1 c. uncooked rice
2 bay leaves
1 T. parsley flakes
Salt to taste
Pepper to taste
8 c. of water

Place the chicken, onions, 1 T. of salt, and 1 t. of pepper in a Dutch oven or soup kettle. Bring to a boil, lower the heat, and cook gently until the meat is tender, about an hour. Remove the chicken from the broth and allow it to cool enough to pull it from the bones in small pieces, discarding the skin. You may wish to skim excess fat from the top of the broth at this time as well. Add the sliced celery, sliced carrots, parsley, and rice to the soup kettle and bring to a boil, augmenting the soup with a bit more water if it seems too thick. Reduce the heat to simmering, add the chicken, and season further, if you wish. Remove the bay leaves and serve once the vegetables and rice are tender.

Chicken Vegetable Rice Soup

This version is zestier than Mother's original and has a more complex blend of ingredients. Either can be tasty, depending on your mood and personal taste.

1 small broiler/fryer chicken, whole or cut up
2–3 q. water
3 garlic cloves, peeled and chopped
1 lg. onion, peeled and chopped
2–3 stalks celery with leaves, chopped
1 lg. carrot, chopped
3 bay leaves
1 t. paprika
1 t. thyme
1 t. rosemary
2 T. corn oil
1 T. parsley flakes
¼ t. Tabasco sauce
1 T. salt
1 c. uncooked brown rice
1½ c. diced rutabaga

1½ c. canned, diced tomatoes in juice *or* 3 c. diced fresh
½ red bell pepper, diced
1 box frozen mixed vegetables (unseasoned)

Sprinkle the chicken with half the combined paprika and herbs and brown it slowly in a large soup kettle or Dutch oven. Near the end of the browning time, add the onion, garlic, celery, and carrot. Add the bay leaves, Tabasco, salt, and water to cover. Bring it to a boil and then reduce the heat and cook, covered, until the chicken is tender, about ¾ hour. Remove the chicken, place it in a large strainer over another pot or large bowl, and pour the cooking broth through the strainer. Return the broth to the cooking pot, adding the rest of the herbs, the brown rice, and the rutabaga. Cook for about ½ an hour. In the meanwhile, skin the lightly cooled chicken and pull all the meat from the bones. Discard the skin and bones and save the white meat for sandwiches. Place the shredded dark meat back in the kettle, along with the tomatoes and red bell pepper. Check for adequate liquid and seasonings. Lastly, add in the mixed vegetables and allow the soup to cook for 10 minutes more. This makes a large amount of soup; cool and freeze some for later, if you wish.

Creamy Potato Soup with Crispy Kale

As a hot dish for a cold winter's day, this soup is creamy and comforting. Add the crispy kale as a healthy and delicious alternative to croutons. When chilled, it becomes velvety smooth vichyssoise, equally appropriate for balmier weather. Use a russet-type potato for best results.

½ c. sliced leeks, white and light green parts only
2 c. peeled cubed potatoes
1 t. salt
⅛ t. white pepper
2 T. butter
2 c. water
¼ c. sour cream
Chopped chives

Melt the butter in a medium saucepan over moderate heat. Add the leeks and sauté for about 5 minutes, stirring occasionally, to soften but not brown them. Add the potatoes, salt, pepper, and water. Bring to a boil, reduce heat slightly, and simmer for 15–20 minutes, until the vegetables are tender. Puree in a blender until smooth, being careful the hot liquid doesn't try to escape during the process. Return to the pan and stir in the sour cream. Serve warm or chilled, garnished with chopped chives if you desire. This serves 2–3.

Creamy potato soup with crispy kale—a midwinter treat waiting to be enjoyed.

Crispy Kale

Kale, a versatile and nutritious vegetable, tolerates and even benefits from cold weather. Folks around this area frequently are still harvesting kale from their gardens at Thanksgiving or even later, as long as the snowfall cooperates and doesn't bury it. Oh, and providing the deer don't decide to harvest it first! There are different varieties of kale; this recipe utilizes curly leaved for best results.

1 bunch curly kale
¼ c. corn oil
Salt to taste

Rinse the kale under cold water, shaking as much water from it as possible; strip the leaves from the tough stems, discarding the stems. Tear each leave into two or three sections, which should yield between 6–8 cups of lightly packed leaves. Preheat oven to 350°F. Toss the torn kale leaves in a large mixing bowl with the oil, coating each evenly. Divide them between two large metal cooling racks, each situated on a cookie sheet or baking pan. Bake them for about 15–20 minutes, rotating and shaking the racks occasionally. When done, the leaves should be crispy and dry, still retaining their deep green color. Remove from the oven and sprinkle with salt to taste. Serve with soup, or just enjoy them on their own!

Broccoli Cheddar Soup

I have fallen prey to the siren song of prepared vegetable broth for this recipe. I suppose if you wish to be a purist, you could make your own, but sometimes a little less preparation time can be a good thing. Whether you choose to or not, you'll have the classic flavor combination of broccoli and cheddar cheese to enjoy in this soup.

1 medium-head broccoli, finely chopped
14–16 oz. can of vegetarian broth (2 c.)
4 T. flour
4 T. butter
2 c. milk
½ t. salt
A few sprinkles of pepper
A few sprinkles of nutmeg
1½ c. shredded cheddar cheese, mild or sharp to suit your preference

Cook the broccoli in the broth until just tender. Meanwhile, make a roux of butter and flour by melting the butter and stirring in the flour, cooking for a couple of minutes. Stir in the seasonings and add the milk, cooking and stirring until thick and bubbly. Stir in the broccoli and broth, simmering a few minutes to blend the flavors. Just before serving, stir in the cheddar cheese, allowing it to melt without boiling the soup. Add the nutmeg and pepper, adjust for seasoning, and serve.

New England Clam Chowder

New England clam chowder consists of clams and potatoes cooked in a creamy broth. Rich and comforting, it makes a fine Saturday lunch or Sunday supper. Since many of us don't have regular access to clams in the shell, this recipe relies on canned instead. If you prefer your chowder meat-free, substitute 2 more table-spoons of butter for the bacon or salt pork.

2–6.5 oz. can chopped clams in broth
2 slices bacon *or* salt pork, diced
¼ c. diced onion
1½ c. diced raw potatoes
½ t. salt
¼ t. pepper
2 T. butter
2 T. flour
1½ c. milk
1 t. dried parsley flakes

Drain the clams, reserving the broth. In a heavy pan over low heat, cook the onions with the bacon or salt pork until they are tender and translucent. Add the diced potatoes, salt, pepper, and the clam broth combined with enough water to equal 1 cup. Cook covered, until the potatoes are just tender, about 7–8 minutes. Meanwhile, melt the butter in a small saucepan. Add the flour and stir until smooth, cooking the mixture for just a minute. Pour in the milk all at once and whisk the mixture until it comes to a boil. Combine the hot milk with the potatoes, clams, and parsley, stirring well. Heat the chowder just to combine the flavors, adjusting salt and pepper to taste. Serve with your favorite crackers. This serves 3–4 and is easy to double or triple for more.

Beef Barley Soup

Beef shins are an inexpensive conduit to a kettle of delicious and hearty soup. The secret to making your homemade beef soup rich and flavorful is in the slow browning of the beef and aromatic vegetables before adding water. Once the browning process is complete, the rest of the soup simply simmers on a back burner until you're ready to enjoy it.

1 lb. beef shin
8 c. water
2 T. olive oil
1 lg. onion, sliced
2 stalks celery, chopped
1 carrot, chopped
2–3 bay leaves
1 T. salt
2 cloves garlic
¾ t. oregano
¾ t. rosemary
½ t. thyme
½ t. pepper
¾ c. uncooked barley
2 carrots, thinly sliced: 1 c.
1 med. tomato, diced: 1 c.
2 c. sliced mushrooms

In a large, heavy soup pan or Dutch oven, heat the oil over medium-low heat. Add the beef shin and cover, browning the beef well on one side. Turn the beef over and add the onion, peeled halved garlic, chopped carrot, and celery. Cover the pan again and continue to brown both the meat and vegetables, stirring occasionally, until the meat is deep brown and the vegetables are golden brown. Please note that there is a difference between browning and burning; you want to caramelize the surface of the vegetables for a rich, but not burned, flavor. Once the meat and vegetables are nicely browned, add the salt, barley, seasonings, and the water. Bring to a boil, reduce heat to a simmer, and cook, covered, for about 1½ hours, until the barley and beef are both tender. Remove the beef to a bowl and allow it to cool enough to tear bite-sized pieces from it. Meanwhile, add the tomato and sliced carrots to the pan, again bringing to a boil. Cook for about 15 minutes and then add the beef and mushrooms and cook for another 10–15 minutes, until everything is nicely cooked. This makes about 2 quarts of soup.

③

④

Cheese Biscuits

While these soups go well with crusty bread or crackers, cheese biscuits make a nice change. These require no patting or cutting, being a drop-type biscuit. Flavor them as you wish with garlic or onion and serve them hot with butter. Leftovers warm up nicely for breakfast.

2 c. flour
4 t. baking powder
½ t. salt
1 T. sugar
1½ c. shredded Colby *or* cheddar cheese
6 T. cold butter
½ t. onion powder *or* garlic powder
1 c. milk

Combine the flour, baking powder, salt, sugar, and onion or garlic powder in a large mixing bowl. Add the cheese and butter and work them in with your fingers until the butter is in small (pea-sized) lumps. Stir in the milk and allow the dough to firm up for just a minute. Scoop out 12 even portions onto a buttered 9" × 13" pan. Bake on the upper rack of a 375°F oven for 20–25 minutes, until golden brown. This makes 12 good-sized biscuits.

Beef barley soup step-by-step . . .
The beginning . . . Browning the base
components . . . More to add . . . The
finished product . . .

Fondue Memories

Thoughts of fondue take me back to high school, college, and newlywed days, when a significant fondue craze was making its way across the land. Little pots of bubbling cheese put in an appearance everywhere from book study groups to neighborhood potlucks. After dying down somewhat in the interim, fondue appears to have made a comeback of sorts, good news for the cheese lovers among us. Indeed, it's perhaps good news for lovers in general. What better way to spend a snowy February evening than feeding your one and only morsels of crusty bread and mellow fruits sensuously coated in a velvety cheese sauce? The best-known fondue is arguably cheese, slowly melted in white wine and served with crusty bread and crudités. A variation on fondue, almost resembling a hot pot, requires heated oil in which to individually fry tender pieces of steak or shrimp, which are then enhanced with a variety of savory sauces. Last but not least are the dessert fondues, generally a rich chocolate sauce just right for immersing fruits and little pieces of cake. Fondue is relatively inexpensive and relaxed way to eat while entertaining. Whether your fondue party is for two or twenty, fondue makes eating more fun.

February Fondue

This is the classic variation on fondue, mellow and rich. Chunks of good crusty bread are a given accompaniment. Other go-withs are limited only by your personal taste and imagination.

12 oz. Gruyère cheese
8 oz. Emmentaler Cheese
4 oz. cheddar cheese
1¼ c. dry white wine
1 clove garlic, peeled and halved
2 T. kirsch, optional
¼ t. pepper
¼ t. nutmeg
2 T. flour

For dipping. Raw or blanched vegetables such as carrot sticks, broccoli florets, mushrooms, bell peppers; crusty breads; fruits such as pear and apple wedges and seedless grapes; bite-sized pieces of cooked sausages such as kielbasa.

Heat the wine and garlic in a large, heavy saucepan over low heat. Shred or dice the cheeses into tiny cubes. Toss the cheese with the flour. Once the wine mixture just starts to emit tiny bubbles (much lower heat than boiling), stir in the cheese. This is the tricky part of making fondue; it must warm gently over low heat so that the cheeses melt together without overheating. If the mixture becomes too hot, the cheese will clump together, leaving a watery wine mixture and a hard, stringy ball. Stir constantly during the melting stage, which might take about 5 minutes altogether. Although some recipes call for a wooden spoon, I've found a heavy-duty whisk works well also. Once the cheese has melted into the wine, stir in the pepper and salt, and the kirsch if using. Pour the fondue into a fondue pot, which has a little flame to keep the mixture warm, and serve immediately. If you don't have a fondue pot, you can improvise by balancing a flame-proof bowl on three empty soup cans with a tea light candle centered underneath or use an electric hotplate on the very lowest setting.

Kid-Friendly Fondue

This fondue is especially nice for the younger set or those not wishing to use wine in their cooking. It's similar to a rich cheese sauce and, as with all cheese sauces, should not be overcooked lest the cheese and liquid go their separate ways, an unfortunate state of affairs for all concerned. This fondue is especially tasty with crisp apple slices or lightly cooked, chilled broccoli.

2 T. flour
2 T. butter
1½ c. milk
¼ t. salt
¼ t. nutmeg
¼ t. dry mustard
⅛ t. pepper
⅛ t. garlic powder (optional)
2 c. shredded cheese of choice—Swiss, cheddar, Gruyère
(A combo of flavors is nice)

Melt the butter in a heavy saucepan over medium-low heat. Stir in the flour and seasonings, cooking and stirring for a minute. Add the milk all at once, whisking until smooth and thickened and the entire mixture is bubbling briskly. Remove from the heat; whisk in the cheese until it is just melted. Pour into a fondue pot as above. Serve with your choice of accompaniments.

Classic Chocolate Fondue

This is my favorite New Year's Eve dessert, although it could also be a special Valentine's treat. It's easy to make and lends itself well to a variety of dippers. Try fresh fruits such as strawberries, cherries, banana slices, orange sections, and pineapple wedges. Cubes of angel food, sponge, and pound cake are good choices, as are marshmallows and crisp cookies.

12 oz. (2 c.) quality semisweet chocolate chips *or* chopped chocolate

4 oz. (1 c.) quality milk chocolate chips *or* chopped chocolate

1 c. cream

2 T. orange-flavored liqueur *or* 2 T. orange juice and 1 t. orange zest

Bring the cream to just a boil in a medium saucepan. Remove from the heat and stir in the chocolate until it is all melted. Stir in the orange liqueur or juice and zest and pour into a fondue pot or heated bowl as above. Surround with the fruits and cakes of choice and enjoy!

Welsh Rarebit . . . a Rare Rabbit

Contrary to its sometimes title, this dish contains no rabbit whatsoever. Welsh rarebit, also referred to as Welsh rabbit, is a hearty melted cheese dish originally from the British Isles. A sharp cheese such as cheddar or Stilton is melted in beer to make this robust cousin of a fondue. Hot-buttered toast is the accompaniment of choice here.

3 T. butter
2 T. flour
½ t. dry mustard
½ t. salt
¼ t. pepper
2–3 drops Tabasco
1 t. Worcestershire
1 c. beer
12 oz. sharp cheddar, grated
1 egg, beaten

Melt the butter in a heavy saucepan over medium-low heat. Stir in the beer, mustard, salt, pepper, Tabasco, and Worcestershire sauces; raise heat slightly; and bring just to a simmer. Toss together the cheese and flour. Add handfuls of the shredded cheese to the simmering beer mixture, stirring constantly with a wooden spoon or whisk. Once it is just melted, quickly stir in the beaten egg. Remove from heat and spoon over crisp white or rye toast.

Cherries . . . Sweet and Tart

Although I suppose the legend of George Washington cutting down the cherry tree with his little hatchet has been thoroughly debunked by now, I still think of February as the month to enjoy cherries. Perhaps Valentine's Day, with its perpetual red theme, has something to do with this. Perhaps it's also because these highly perishable little fruits are frequently easier to find canned or frozen than fresh. One of my goals for the new decade is to have producing cherry trees on our property by the end of it. Finally varieties are being developed that tolerate the cold of a Vermont winter, which is exciting news indeed for a person whose favorite fruit in the whole world is a sweet golden cherry, with that gorgeous blush of red on its little cheek. Such delicacies notwithstanding, here are some recipes using their red (sometimes even artificially red) cousins.

Cherry Cobbler

My mom was fond of relating to me how my brother John had once assured her that he thought he'd do extra well in school if only they could start out the day with cherry cobbler for breakfast. Cherries not only contain vitamins C, K, and A but also the antioxidant anthocyanin, increasingly recognized as a potent weapon in fighting gout and arthritis, and melatonin, helpful in regulating sleep and circadian rhythms. Considering how much nutrition is packed in these little fruits, cherry cobbler for breakfast doesn't sound like such a bad idea at all.

1 can (14–16 oz.) sour pitted cherries
¾ c. sugar, divided
1 T cornstarch
½ t. cinnamon
¼ t. almond extract
1 c. flour
1 t. baking powder
¼ c. butter
½ c. milk
¼ c. slivered almonds, optional but good

Combine ½ c. sugar, cinnamon, and the cornstarch in a medium saucepan. Add the cherries and their juice, stirring gently to combine. Cherries are fragile, so try not to jostle them around too much. Bring just to a boil, stirring gently to prevent sticking. Pour them into a buttered 8" × 8" pan or a small casserole dish and place in the oven while it preheats to 375°F. Combine the ¼ c. sugar, the flour, and baking powder in a small bowl. Melt the butter and combine with the milk and almond extract. Stir quickly into the dry ingredients. Spoon the batter evenly over the hot cherries in the pan. Sprinkle with the almonds. Bake for 20–25 minutes, until the cobbler is lightly browned and cooked through. Serve warm or cool to 4 or more. Add some vanilla yogurt for a tasty and nutritious accompaniment.

Chocolate-Cherry Granola

Chocolate and cherries are a natural go-together. If you'd like something a little less rich than cheesecake or torte that's even good for breakfast, how about trying some granola? The cherry juice in this recipe is reduced by half before combining with the other coating ingredients, stirred into the oats, and then slow baked to remove the additional moisture. It adds nice overtones of cherry along with the chocolate right into the oats themselves. Store your granola in an airtight canister or ziplock-type plastic bags.

½ c. pure black cherry juice
½ c. lt. brown sugar
¼ c. corn oil
¼ c. dark cocoa powder
3 c. rolled oats
½ c. dried cherries
½ c. slivered almonds
¼ c. mini chocolate chips

Place the cherry juice in a small, heavy saucepan. Bring to boiling, reduce heat, and boil gently for about 7–10 minutes, until the juice has been reduced by half. Be careful it doesn't cook down too much or too quickly in order to avoid a burned flavor. Stir together the warm juice with the sugar, cocoa powder, and oil in large mixing bowl. Stir in the rolled oats to coat well. Place on a waxed paper–lined baking sheet, spreading it out evenly. Bake in a 325°F oven for 30–35 minutes, stirring every 5–10 minutes for even heating and to prevent it from clumping together. Stir in the almonds during the last 10–15 minutes of baking time. Be cautious during the last few minutes; you want it properly dried and crunchy, but not burned. Remove from the oven and cool completely before stirring in the cherries and mini chocolate chips. This makes about 6 cups of granola.

Cherry Berry Pie

When I was a vendor at the Brattleboro Farmers' Market, one of my specialties was little triangles of homemade puff pastry filled with either savory veggie or sweet fruit fillings. The cherry-berry combination was one of my favorites, here revised to make a standard pie.

2 c. tart cherries (frozen are fine) *or* 1 can of tart cherries, not drained
2 c. fresh or unsweetened frozen red raspberries
1¼ c. water (measure the canned cherry juice first, adding extra water to equal this amount)
3 T. cornstarch
1 t. grated lemon rind *or* ¼ t. pure lemon extract
½ t. almond extract
1 T. kirsch *or* other cherry liquor
Unbaked 2 crust pie pastry

Combine everything except the extracts, liquor, and crust in a heavy saucepan. Cook over medium heat, stirring gently, until thickened and bubbly. Remove from heat and add the flavorings. Allow the filling to cool for about 15 minutes. Meanwhile, roll out half the chilled piecrust and fit into a 9" pie plate. Add the filling and moisten the out rim of the bottom piecrust with water or milk. Roll out and fit the top crust, fit it over the pie, and trim excess overhang from both crusts, leaving about an inch extra. Fold the top crust down over and under the bottom crust to seal. Press the edges and flute decoratively. Cut slits in the top crust or prick with a fork to allow steam to escape during baking. Brush the top crust with milk or cream and sprinkle lightly with sugar. Bake at 425°F for

10 minutes. Reduce heat to 350°F and continue baking until the crust is nicely browned and the filling is bubbly, about 30 minutes longer. Cool before cutting.

Classic Cherry Pie

Although George Washington may not have chopped down that cherry tree, the legend still enables us to celebrate his birth with a piece of classic cherry pie. Or . . . maybe we'll simply enjoy it because we like cherry pie!

Unbaked pastry for 2 crust pie
Milk or cream for glazing
2 cans pitted tart cherries in juice *or* 4 c. fresh or frozen
1 c. sugar
¼ c. granulated ("minute") tapioca
¼ t. salt
½ t. almond extract
2 T. cherry liquor, optional

Combine the cherries and juice, sugar, salt, and tapioca in a medium, heavy saucepan. Allow about 15 minutes for the tapioca to absorb some of the juice and soften. If you are using frozen or fresh cherries, heat them so the juices just start to flow before adding the other ingredients. In either case, once the mixture has set for 15 minutes, cook over medium heat until it comes to a boil. Remove from heat and stir in the almond extract and the cherry liquor, if using. Allow the filling to cool for best results. Roll out the chilled pie pastry for the bottom crust, fitting it loosely into a 9" pie plate. Pour in the filling. Roll the upper crust, fitting it over the top. Crimp the edges and cut slits for steam to escape. Brush the top lightly with

milk or cream and sprinkle with sugar. Bake in a preheated 375°F oven for about 45 minutes, until the crust is golden brown and nicely glazed. Cool the pie before cutting into 8 servings. It's especially tasty topped with vanilla ice cream.

Classic cherry pie: a treat any time of the year.

Cherry Walnut Sandwich Filling

Mom made this special treat sandwich filling when I was growing up. I think it tastes especially good on soft whole wheat bread. Try cutting it in little heart shapes for a slightly less sweet Valentine's treat.

8 oz. cream cheese
½ c. chopped, drained maraschino cherries
½ c. chopped walnuts
Cherry juice to moisten

Beat the cream cheese and cherries together. Add a bit of cherry juice, if necessary, for a good spreading consistency. Fold in the walnuts. Refrigerate any leftover filling, covered.

Maraschino Party Cake

Maraschinos are a bird of a different feather in the cherry world. They probably contain too much sugar and artificial coloring to be particularly healthy, but I must admit they've always held a special place in my heart. This cake—light, pink, and delectable—is perfect party fare.

¾ c. unsalted butter, softened
1½ c. sugar
1 t. vanilla
½ t. almond extract
¼ c. maraschino cherry juice
20 maraschino cherries, well drained, cut in eighths
2½ c. cake flour

3 t. baking powder
1 t. salt
½ c. milk
5 egg whites
½ c. chopped toasted almonds, optional

Place all ingredients except the egg whites and almonds in a large mixer bowl. Beat on low speed to blend and then beat on medium speed until the mixture is smooth and creamy. Add the egg whites and again beat until smooth. Fold in the almonds, if using. Pour into 2 greased and floured 9" round cake pans. Bake at 350°F approximately 30–35 minutes, until the tops are lightly browned and spring back when touched. Cool in the pans for 10 minutes and then turn out on wire racks to complete cooling. Fill and frost as desired. The filling and frosting below go nicely with this cake although a boiled (fluffy white) icing or butter cream frosting would also be good. This serves 12–16 easily.

Cherry-Chocolate Filling

8 oz. cream cheese
1 c. confectioner's sugar
1–2 T. cherry juice
½ c. chopped maraschino cherries, well drained
½ c. mini chocolate chips

Beat the cream cheese and confectioner's sugar until they are smooth and creamy, adding a little cherry juice if necessary; just don't add too much or the mixture will become too runny. Fold in the cherries and chocolate chips. Use this to fill in between the two layers.

Creamy Chocolate Frosting

1 c. semisweet chocolate chips

1 c. milk chocolate chips
½ t. almond extract
½ c. cream
½ c. butter
1 c. confectioner's sugar

Heat the cream to just under boiling. Remove from heat and stir in the chocolate chips until they are melted. Cool slightly. Beat the butter, almond extract, and confectioner's sugar until light and fluffy. Beat in the chocolate mixture until well blended. Frost the top and sides of the cherry cake. Garnish with maraschino cherries, if you wish.

Sweet Chocolate Cake

Rich and delicate, sweet chocolate cake has a milder flavor than most chocolate desserts. Perhaps the gold standard for sweet chocolate cakes comes from the Baker's German's Sweet Chocolate bar. My version uses semisweet chocolate chips for a slightly more defined flavor and offers a pair of toppings to mix or match. You may also wish to freeze one layer to thaw and enjoy another day.

1 c. semisweet chocolate chips
¼ c. water
1½ c. sugar
¾ c. butter
1 t. vanilla
1½ c. flour
1 t. baking soda
¼ t. salt
3 eggs, separated
¾ c. buttermilk or sour milk*

Melt together the chocolate chips and water, either in a small saucepan over low heat or microwave on high for about 1½ minutes (don't overheat; stir smooth while the chocolate is still partially melted). Meanwhile, combine the butter, sugar, and vanilla in a large mixing bowl. Beat on low to combine and then on high speed until the mixture is light and fluffy. Reduced speed and beat in the melted chocolate and then the egg yolks, one at a time. Beat in the combined dry ingredients alternately with the buttermilk. In a separate smaller bowl with clean beaters, whip the egg whites to stiff peaks. Fold them lightly but thoroughly into the batter. Divide the batter evenly between two generously greased and floured 9" round cake pans. Bake at 350°F for about ½ hour, until the tops spring bake when lightly touched. Gently run a spatula around the edge of each cake. Allow the cakes to cool in the pans for about 15 minutes, as they are quite delicate when hot. Then carefully loosen them and turn out onto racks to complete cooling. Once it has cooled, frost the cake as desired. If you wish to freeze a layer, line a clean 9" cake pan with foil or waxed paper and place the cooled cake layer back in the pan. Once frozen, wrap the top of the cake airtight as well. Plan to use within a month.

*Use buttermilk from the dairy case or reconstituted powdered buttermilk. In a pinch, simply add 1 t. of lemon juice or vinegar to ¾ c. of fresh milk to sour it.

Sweet Cherry Cream Cake

This topping and cake combination reminds me a little of a Black Forest torte. It's easy to prepare and makes a dessert with lots of eye appeal.

14–15 oz. can of dark sweet cherries in juice
1 T. cornstarch
2 T. cherry liquor
1 c. heavy cream
¼ c. sugar
1 t. vanilla
⅓ c. semisweet chocolate chips
1 T. butter
1 T. light corn syrup
1 layer sweet chocolate cake

Combine the cherries and cornstarch in a medium saucepan. Cook, stirring occasionally, over medium heat until the mixture bubbles and thickens. Remove from the heat, stir in the cherry liquor, and cool completely. Whip the cream with the sugar and vanilla until the mixture is fairly stiff. Frost the cake with the whipped cream and refrigerate. Before serving (this can be done in advance), top the cake with the cooled sweet cherries. Melt together the chocolate chips, butter, and corn syrup, stirring until smooth. Drizzle the melted chocolate decoratively over the cherries and cream. Chill until serving; refrigerate leftovers as well. This serves 8.

Maple Butternut Topping

The combination of nuts, maple, and butter is a natural; here's a Northern variation on a Southern classic. If you don't have access to granulated maple sugar, an equal amount of lightly packed brown sugar may be substituted. This recipe frosts one 9" cake layer, enough to serve 8.

½ c. granulated maple sugar
½ c. cream
1 T. butter
¼ t. salt
1 t. cornstarch
½ t. vanilla*
1 egg, beaten
½ c. flaked coconut
½ c. chopped pecans

Combine the sugar, cream, salt, cornstarch, and butter in a small, heavy saucepan. Bring to a full boil over medium-low heat, stirring constantly. Stir a little of the hot liquid into the beaten egg and then add the tempered egg mix back into the pan, stirring constantly. Immediately remove from the pan and from the heat. Stir in the vanilla, coconut, and pecans. Allow the hot topping to cool for about 5 minutes before spreading evenly over one layer of sweet chocolate cake.

*If you use brown sugar, add ½ t. natural maple flavoring along with the vanilla.

Pudding Cakes

If you've grown tired of cherries by now, it's time to move on to other flavors. Pudding cakes are old-fashioned comfort food. For most pudding cakes, batter is spread in a pan, sprinkled with dry ingredients, and topped off with hot water before popping into the oven to bake, forming a layer each of pudding and cake in the process. Lemon pudding cake, more spongy and delicate than the others, is the exception to this rule. Here is a trio of flavors for you to try, and nary a cherry among them.

Fudge Pudding Cake

If you'd like something fudgy but not too terribly fancy, try this dark-chocolate pudding cake. Served warm with vanilla ice cream, it's a winter treat that's sure to please.

Batter

1 c. flour
½ c. sugar
3 T. cocoa powder
¼ c. corn oil
1 t. baking powder
¼ t. salt
½ t. vanilla
¾ c. milk
½ c. chopped pecans or walnuts (optional)

Sauce

¾ c. sugar
2 T. cocoa
2 t. cornstarch
1 ½ c. hot water

Whisk together the dry ingredients for the batter. Add in the milk and vanilla, stirring until smooth. Stir in the walnuts or pecans. Spread the batter in a buttered 8" or 9" square cake pan. Combine the sugar, cocoa, and cornstarch and sprinkle evenly over the top. Place the pan on the middle rack of a preheated 350°F oven. Carefully pour the hot water evenly over the top. Bake approximately 30–35 minutes, until the cake portion is set and the sauce is bubbly. Serve warm or cool.

Farmhouse Pudding

Farmhouse pudding is a butterscotch version of pudding cake, accentuated with raisins and walnuts. It's tasty served with whipped cream or light cream. Try combining sweetened whipped cream and sour cream for a special topping treat.

Batter

¼ c. butter
¾ c. packed brown sugar
1 t. vanilla
1 t. baking powder
½ t. salt
1 c. flour
¾ c. milk
½ c. chopped walnuts
½ c. raisins

Sauce

1 c. packed brown sugar
1 T. cornstarch
1½ c. water
2 T. butter

Cream together the butter, brown sugar, and vanilla. Beat in the combined dry ingredients alternately with the milk. Stir in the walnuts and raisins. Spread in a buttered 8" or 9" square cake pan. Combine the brown sugar and cornstarch in a medium saucepan. Stir in the water and butter and bring to a boil, stirring constantly. Place the pan of batter on a cookie sheet for stability. Carefully pour the boiling sauce over the batter. Bake in a 350°F oven until the cake is light and golden and the sauce is bubbly, about 30–35 minutes. Serve warm or cool.

Lemon Pudding Cake

If you're in the mood for lemon, try this old-fashioned recipe for lemon pudding cake. It's a recipe I've revised over the years from one in a Fannie Farmer Cookbook. The top bakes into a spongy cake while the bottom cooks into a lemony pudding. This is especially tasty served with fresh whipped cream.

1 c. sugar
½ c. flour
¾ t. baking powder
¼ t. salt
3 eggs, separated
½ c. sugar
¼ c. lemon juice
2 t. grated lemon rind *or* ½ t. pure lemon extract
2 T. melted butter
1½ c. milk or water

Preheat oven to 350°F. Place a 9" × 13" cake pan in the oven with about ½" of hot water covering the bottom. Combine the flour, 1 c. sugar, baking powder, and salt in a medium mixing bowl. Beat the egg whites with ½ c. of sugar until stiff and glossy. Beat the egg yolks with the butter, lemon juice, lemon rind or extract, and milk, or water. Pour this mixture over the combined dry ingredients, mixing well. Fold in the egg whites. Pour into a buttered 2 qt. casserole or 8" × 8"–deep cake pan. Place this in the larger pan of hot water. Bake for 45 minutes; the top will appear puffy and lightly browned, but the bottom will be semiliquid. Remove from the larger pan and cool at least an hour before serving for best results. This serves 6–8.

Sweetheart Cookies

We couldn't let February slip away without including at least one Valentine recipe, could we? When our now-adult children first headed off to college, I wanted to still be able to share a little taste of home baking with them. I devised my recipe for sweetheart cookies about the time our older son Greg departed for the halls of higher academia. The nice thing about these crispy little sugar cookies is that the frosting is sandwiched inside, making them easy for transporting and even for mailing to someone special who's far away.

Sweetheart Valentine cookies—sure to win anyone's heart.

1 c. unsalted butter
1 t. vanilla
½ t. almond extract
1 c. granulated sugar
½ t. salt
1 egg
1 t. baking powder
2 c. flour
Colored sugar and/or sprinkles
Milk for brushing tops

Pink Buttercream Filling/Frosting

½ c. butter
3 c. confectioner's sugar
1 T. water
1 t. flavoring of choice (vanilla, cherry, raspberry)
2–3 drops of red food coloring (optional)

Beat the butter and sugar together until smooth and creamy. Add the egg and extracts, beating again until light and fluffy. On low speed with a heavy mixer blade or by hand with a wooden spoon, stir in the flour, baking powder, and salt until thoroughly combined. Cover the dough or place in a plastic bag and refrigerate for about 1 hour (or more) before rolling and baking. The chilling time is important for a couple of reasons; it makes the fragile dough more manageable, and it decreases the amount of flour necessary for rolling and therefore the amount absorbed when rerolling scraps. When you're ready to bake your cookies, roll portions of the dough at a time thin (⅛"). Cut out with heart-shaped cookie cutters. Lightly brush the tops with milk and sprinkle generously with colored sugar. Bake on ungreased cookie sheets on upper shelf of a 350°F for about 10–12 minutes, until light golden brown around the edges. Cool for a minute or two on the sheets before carefully removing to cooling racks. For the filling, beat the softened butter with the extract of choice at medium speed until it's nice and fluffy. Gradually add the confectioner's sugar, beating well. Mix in the water and a few drops of red coloring, if you wish. The frosting will be creamy, yet stiff enough to sandwich between cookies without running out or turning the cookies soggy. If you prefer to ice your cookies, you may wish to beat in another tablespoon or so of water. Use 1–2 teaspoons of filling per cookie; this batch should yield enough for approximately 2½–3 dozen heart sandwich cookies, depending on the size of the cookie.

Season of Change . . .

MARCH IS A season of change here in the Northeast. There's still plenty of winter's snow and cold, but signs abound that spring is on the way. Buds on trees and bushes are beginning to swell, while streams and rivers break free of ice and begin to flow (and occasionally flood) freely once again. The vernal equinox, one of two times during the year when daylight and darkness are most nearly equal, takes place during the third week in March. From then on, daylight wins out, lengthening steadily all through spring, until the longest day of the year is reached in June. The sun's angle changes as well, slanting in with warmer light, conducive to greening all those plants on the windowsill and melting away snow on the south sides of houses and barns. If spring comes early, a few hardy crocuses might even poke their heads up through, making way for daffodils in April.

Even with such promise of warmer days to come, sunlight alone is seldom strong enough to produce sturdy seedlings, so this is also the time of year when my grow lights come out. I have a portable stack of four shelves, each with its own fluorescent light hanging above, which I situate next to a south-facing window. The bottom shelf also has room for a warming pad, essential for urging those tender little pepper seeds to actually sprout, rather than just sitting there in the growing mix acting coy. Soon flats of seeds, the underside of their covers moist with condensation, morph into open flats of tiny green seedlings straining toward the light. Two of my neighbors who sell plants and vegetables for a living rather than just for the home garden as I do have greenhouses that are in full swing at this time. Wandering through a warm greenhouse while snow is still blanketing the countryside is a great way to shake off those late winter blues and to think expectantly of things to come . . .

Even with two feet of snow still outside, the amaryllis in my window gives a hopeful glimpse of things to come.

March

Sugaring Off

In the northeastern United States and south-eastern Canada, vast forests of mixed conifers and hardwood trees cover much of the landscape. One tree almost unique to the area is the sugar maple. These deciduous beauties, which turn the mountains crimson and gold each autumn, reward us in early spring with a sweet sap that boils down into the liquid ambrosia known as maple syrup. Vermont is famous for its maple syrup, and rightly so. It produces more than almost any other place on earth, second only to our neighbor Quebec just to the north. Almost every Vermont kid has either been to or worked in a sugarhouse or sugar shack, depending on what part of the state you happen to be from. Pure maple syrup is a rare commodity because it can only be produced for a certain window of time each year, when temperatures rise to above freezing during the day and dip back down below freezing at night. It is then that the sap in the sugar maples begins to run and that the trees are tapped. Once collected, the sap boils down to a fraction of its former self in order to produce maple syrup and maple sugar. Maple syrup's unique qualities are best enjoyed in their purest form; please don't try to dilute it. Once you've enjoyed it, you'll see why.

A vintage sugaring picture Mother took of our neighbors at Lilac Ridge Farm collecting sap back in the 1960s. The horses are long since gone, and plastic tubing has largely replaced individual buckets, but the sugaring continues.

Sugar on Snow

The most elemental way to enjoy pure maple syrup is by boiling it down and pouring it over bowls of snow—hence, the name sugar on snow. Traditional accompaniments for sugar on snow are sour pickles, usually dill, and homemade doughnuts. Countless church, grange, and volunteer fire department suppers throughout the North country are held during sugaring season. They generally feature baked beans, although chicken pot pie is not unheard-of. However, the surefire ending for each is sugar on snow.

½ c. maple syrup per serving (more than one serving at a time works better)

Clean snow (or shaved ice in a pinch), packed into soup bowls

1–2 doughnuts per serving

2–3 pickles, depending on size, per serving

Place the syrup in a heavy saucepan; even with a small pan, you'll probably need at least a cup in order to immerse the thermometer adequately. However, you also need to leave a few inches at the top of the pan, as the syrup has a tendency to bubble up while cooking. Heat it to boiling and cook over moderate heat until it reaches 230–232°F on a candy thermometer. This is known as soft ball stage; if you place a drop of the hot syrup in a cup of cold water, it will form a lightly flattened ball. Remove from the heat and immediately pour into a heatproof pitcher, or serve directly from the pan. Lightly swirl it over the bowls of packed snow, using a fork to pick up the chewy syrup and bits of snow. Enjoy your sugar on snow with pickles and doughnuts!

Sugar on snow with homemade doughnut and pickles is a quintessential Vermont treat.

Maple Cream

Did you ever enjoy those little molded maple candies available in some specialty shops? Would you like something sweet and creamy to slather on hot biscuits or a piece of toast? The answer to both is right here: homemade maple cream. Prepare your syrup as above, heating it just slightly more, to about 235°F, for candies. Rather than swirling it on snow, allow it to cool slightly and then stir it with a heavy spoon until it turns thick and creamy. Smooth it into flexible candy molds; once it has cooled thoroughly, you can unmold it for candy. If you prefer spread, heat the syrup to about 230°F, beating as above. Place in a jar or dish and cover it tightly, scooping out what you want for topping hot toast or biscuits. Even if it seems hard on the outside, the texture will be velvety smooth and creamy within. As with sugar on snow, don't even think about trying to make this with anything other than pure maple syrup; aside from the unique flavor of real maple, the makeup of blended or fake syrups will ensure a burned, sticky disaster if you try heating them in this manner.

Maple Yogurt Cream

Quick, easy, and delicious, maple yogurt cream has the benefit of being healthy enough to enjoy as a snack, for breakfast, or even for dessert. Alternatively, use it as a dip with fresh fruits and crackers. The amount given will make 1 serving.

½ c. plain Greek-style yogurt
or 6 T. plain yogurt and 2 T. sour cream
1 T. maple syrup
1 T. chopped walnuts

Combine the yogurt, syrup, and walnuts in a small bowl. Serve at once or refrigerate to enjoy within a day or two; with this dish, the fresher it is, the better it is.

Hot Spiced Maple Milk

With the increasing popularity of hot drinks such as chai, I though it might be nice to experiment with a hot maple drink. It's a nice way to warm up after a long day in the great outdoors and has the added advantage of being kid as well as adult-friendly. The hint of vanilla adds a mellow note.

1 c. milk, *or* for adults, ½ c. each milk and hot tea
1 T. maple syrup
½ t. chai spice mix
¼ t. vanilla
Chai spice mix: uses ground spices
1 T. cardamom
1 T. ginger
1½ t. cinnamon
1 t. cloves
1 t. allspice
1 t. mace *or* nutmeg
¼ t. fresh ground black pepper (optional)

Combine all the spices together, mixing well. Measure ½ t. into a mug or small saucepan. Mix in the maple syrup and vanilla, stirring to combine well. Add the milk or milk and tea and heat to just under boiling. Serve at once; if you'd like a nice frothy beverage, whirl it in the blender for a few seconds before serving. It's easy to double, triple, or quadruple the amounts as you desire. Store any extra spice mix, tightly covered, in the refrigerator to maintain flavor.

Old-Fashioned Doughnuts

Bruce's mom, Lucretia "Kitty" Lawrence, made excellent baking powder doughnuts, as does my coworker, Dot Class. Dot originally got her recipe from my sister-in-law, Veronica's mother, Vivian Thomas; I guess a love of fine doughnuts runs strong in these parts. The following is a composite of their recipes along with a few touches of my own. Although old-timers might swear by lard for frying, and Kitty always used solid shortening, I prefer corn oil.

¼ c. butter
⅞ c. sugar
4 c. flour
½ t. salt
¼ t. ginger
½ t. baking soda
2 t. baking powder
½ t. nutmeg
½ t. mace*
¼ t. pure lemon extract
or 1 t. grated lemon zest
1 c. buttermilk *or* sour milk**
2 eggs
Oil for frying; enough for 2" in a large, heavy skillet

Heat the oil to 375°F, using a candy thermometer clipped to the side of the pan to monitor the temperature. I never was able to produce decent doughnuts until I stopped trying to use a deep fat fryer and instead started frying them stove top in a cast-iron skillet; I find the temperature can be controlled much more accurately in this manner. Melt the butter. Mix together the melted butter, sugar, and eggs in a large bowl until they are well blended. Combine the flour, baking powder, baking soda, salt, nutmeg, mace, and ginger. Add to the sugar mixture alternately with the combined buttermilk and lemon extract. Roll or pat the dough out, half at a time, on a lightly floured board to ½" thickness. If the dough seems too soft, refrigerate it, covered, for about an hour. Cut out the dough with a floured doughnut cutter, or with a well-floured jar top, drinking glass, or can. If using the latter, cut out the holes with a well-floured bottle neck or spice jar lid. Fry in the hot oil until they are deep golden brown on each side. Drain on paper towels. If desired, shake the doughnuts with confectioner's sugar or sugar and cinnamon. This makes about 1½ dozen doughnuts.

*Mace and nutmeg are different parts of the same plant, although mace isn't as widely available. You may substitute an additional ½ t. of nutmeg for the mace if you prefer.

** To sour milk, stir 1 t. of vinegar or lemon juice into a cup of fresh milk.

No matter what the icing, homemade raised doughnuts are delicious.

Raised Doughnuts

The secret to a great raised doughnut, as with many yeast breads, rests not only in the ingredients but also the method of preparation. These doughnuts require a little extra time for rising, but the results are well worth the effort. Try to disturb them as little as possible when transferring to the hot oil; commercial doughnut shops often have raising racks that fit right in the deep fryer, although with a gentle touch you should be able to successfully move them from one to the other. I find placing my cut doughnuts on a fine mesh rack in a warm oven with a bowl of hot water for moisture works well and cuts down on the required raising time.

1 c. milk
¼ c. warm water
1 T. dry yeast
1 t. salt
½ c. sugar
¼ c. butter
1 egg
¼ t. mace, optional
½ t. vanilla
3½ c. flour, plus more for dusting
Glazes or fillings as desired

Heat the milk to lukewarm in a medium saucepan; dissolve the yeast in the warm water. Stir the dissolved yeast and 1 T. of the sugar into the lukewarm milk. Stir in 1½ c. of the flour, mixing well; this forms a sponge, a kind of soft yeast batter that enables the yeast to feed and interact with the starch and sugar. Cover the pan and allow the sponge to work for about ¾ hour. Cream together the remaining sugar with the butter and salt in a large mixing bowl. Mix in the yeast sponge and the beaten egg until everything is well blended. On low speed, beat in the remaining flour until the mixture forms into cohesive dough. Cover the bowl and allow the mixture to rise in a warm spot for another hour. (At this point you may refrigerate all or part of the dough, covered with foil or plastic wrap, overnight.) Roll or pat out the dough, ½ at a time, to ½" thickness and cut with a well-floured doughnut cutter. You can substitute a well-floured can, drinking glass, or jar if you don't have the doughnut cutter, making the holes with the well-floured top of a soda or wine bottle or a spice jar lid. For jelly doughnuts, cut them without the center hole. Allow the doughnuts to rise for about ½ hour, while the oil heats to 375°F. Fry 3–4 at a time, depending on the size of the pan. They will float to the surface once cooked enough on one side; flip them with a fork and continue frying, turning once or twice more as needed, until the doughnuts are uniformly golden brown. Drain them on paper towels, filling or frosting as desired once they have cooled. This recipe will make approximately 16 doughnuts and doughnut holes, depending on their size. The chocolate, vanilla, or orange glazes below should frost about 8 doughnuts each; strawberry and maple may vary.

Glazes

Vanilla

2 c. confectioner's sugar
½ t. vanilla
2 T. warm water
Stir all together until smooth.

Fresh Strawberry

2 T. diced fresh strawberries
1½ –2 c. confectioner's sugar
Stir together the strawberries and confectioner's sugar. Important: this will initially seem dry, but will liquefy considerably as the strawberries and sugar form strawberry juice.

Maple

Maple cream (above)
Hot water
Combine the maple cream with a very small amount of hot water, until it's of a good glazing consistency.

Chocolate

2 c. confectioner's sugar
2 T. unsweetened cocoa powder
2 T. warm water
Stir all together until smooth, adding a drop or two more of water if necessary.

Fresh Orange

2 T. orange juice
1 t. grated orange zest
2 c. confectioner's sugar
Combine the juice, zest, and confectioner's sugar, stirring until smooth.

Fried Cinnamon Buns

Use half of the raised doughnut recipe to make this amount of buns. Leaving the dough refrigerated overnight makes it easier to roll out and fill the following morning. Of course, if you're hungry for fried cinnamon buns, you may use all the dough and double the other ingredients.

½ recipe raised doughnut dough
1 T. sugar
1 t. cinnamon oil for frying

Glaze

1 c. confectioner's sugar
1–2 T. cream
⅛ t. cinnamon
½ t. vanilla

On a lightly floured surface, roll the dough out into about a 12" square. Brush it lightly with water and then sprinkle evenly with the combined sugar and cinnamon. Roll the dough up tightly and cut into 8–10 equal pieces. Flatten the cinnamon buns to as thin as possible for each and allow them to rest on a lightly floured surface in a warm location while the oil is heating. Fry them at 365°F until golden brown on both sides, turning with a fork as necessary. The middle of the buns should have some spring when they are lightly touched. Combine the confectioner's sugar and cream until they are smooth. Stir in the vanilla and cinnamon. Frost each bun with a swirl of icing. Serve warm or at room temperature. Loosely cover leftovers; if they're covered too tightly, the frosting will liquefy and run off the doughnuts.

From the raising to the frying to the warm cinnamon bun—fried, frosted, and ready to eat.

73

Corn Bread

Corn bread is equally tasty served for breakfast or to accompany a later meal of the day. Sadly, the corn bread of my youth tended to be somewhat hard and crumbly, not allowing it to reach its full potential. I prefer a softer, sweeter product, which is what this recipe produces. The batter may also be baked in muffin tins, producing about a dozen. A variation on the base recipe follows.

1⅓ c. flour
⅔ c. yellow cornmeal
½ c. sugar
1 t. salt
2 t. baking powder
⅓ c. melted butter
2 eggs
1 c. milk

Stir together all the dry ingredients and set aside. Melt the butter and combine in a large mixing bowl with the milk and eggs, whisking together until well blended. Stir in the dry ingredients all at once until just well blended. Pour into an 8" or 9" square baking pan, which has been well buttered to prevent sticking. Bake at 350–360°F for approximately 30 minutes, until lightly browned and the top surface feels firm to touch. Serve warm or cold; makes about 9 good-sized squares. If you prefer to make muffins, use either paper liners or butter the individual cups before adding batter. Increase the oven temperature to 375°F and bake for about 20 minutes, until puffed and golden.

Cranberry-Orange Corn Bread

Prepare corn bread (above) with the following alterations:

Substitute orange juice for the milk in the base recipe.

Stir in when combining wet and dry ingredients:

1 c. dried cranberries
2 t. grated orange rind

Orange Icing

2 T. orange juice
2 c. confectioner's sugar

After the corn bread is baked, pierce the top with a fork or wooden skewer. Stir together the orange juice and confectioner's sugar until smooth. Evenly pour the icing over the entire surface, spreading so that it will absorb.

Irish Soda Bread

Here's a nice go-with for your St. Patrick's Day boiled dinner. Traditional Irish soda bread is an unembellished loaf made simply with wheat and white flours, baking soda, salt, and buttermilk. It reflects what was available to country folk in Ireland back in the nineteenth century, when baking soda was first utilized. The Irish soda bread I'm more familiar with is richer and sweeter, with added raisins and also caraway seeds, if you wish. Some folks refer to this type of soda bread as spotted dog, so I shall too.

Traditional Irish Soda Bread

Although it contains only a few simple ingredients, this quick bread bakes up surprisingly light and springy. It's best fresh, especially straight out of the oven slathered with butter. A bit of jam or marmalade wouldn't hurt matters any, either.

⅔ c. whole wheat flour
1⅓ c. all-purpose flour
½ t. salt
1 t. baking soda
1¼ c. buttermilk

Combine the flour, salt, and baking soda in a mixing bowl. By hand, stir in the buttermilk; this will form a stiff dough. Pat it into an 8" or 9" round buttered cake or baking pan, adding a little flour to the top. Cut a deep cross in the dough. Bake at 350°F for approximately 40–45 minutes, until the top is golden and firm to touch. Serve hot with lots of butter.

Spotted Dog

Spotted dog is softer, sweeter bread than the traditional loaf above, although the buttermilk still works its magic to give it a special kind of "spring." It's tasty with butter, but also rich enough to enjoy just as it is.

2 c. all-purpose flour
¼ c. sugar
½ t. salt
½ t. baking soda
1 t. baking powder
2 T. butter, melted
1 egg, beaten
¾ c. buttermilk
1 c. raisins, soaked in 1 c. warm water
1 T. caraway seeds, optional

Melt the butter and combine in a large mixing bowl with the buttermilk and beaten egg. Combine all the dry ingredients and stir them into the liquid along with the well-drained raisins and the caraway seeds. Pour into a buttered 8" or 9" round cake pan and bake at 350°F for 40–45 minutes, until the top is golden brown and springs back slightly when touched. Serve warm or at room temperature.

Fish Every Friday

When I was growing up, everyone in school ate fish on Friday whether they were Catholic or not. This was especially true during Lent, a part of the church year frequently observed in the month of March. So, in perhaps not-so-fond memory of all those soggy fish sticks, here are a few fish recipes that are both simple and tasty.

Fish-and-chips with homemade tartar sauce.

Beer Batter Fish-and-Chips with Homemade Tartar Sauce

I suppose you could go British with this and serve with malt vinegar. I personally like french fries with vinegar, although everyone else in the family seems to be a ketchup fan. It must be that folks in Canada prefer vinegar, also, as I was happily surprised to discover little packets of it in a fast-food restaurant we stopped at while traveling through Ontario on our way to visit Greg and Biz in Minnesota. This recipe is easy to halve, if there are only 2–3 of you to eat it. In that case, lucky you! You'll only have one batch of each to fry, making your meal that much faster to serve.

1 lb. white fish fillets, such as cod or haddock
¾ c. milk
½ c. cornstarch
Corn oil for frying
1 c. flour
1 t. salt
½ t. paprika
¼ t. pepper
1 c. beer
2–3 large russet potatoes
Lemon wedges

Tartar sauce

Buy the freshest fish you can find. Rinse it and cut into thick finger-sized portions. (Hint: partially frozen fish cuts a bit easier, if you have time for this step.) Place it in a small bowl along with the milk and allow it to soak while preparing the batter and cooking the chips—a.k.a. french fries—about 20 minutes. Combine the flour, salt, paprika, and pepper in a medium-sized bowl. Whisk in the beer (it will probably foam some) until smooth and set aside. Preheat about 2" of corn oil in a heavy cast-iron skillet. Attach a cooking or candy thermometer if you have one to the side of the pan and allow the oil to become quite hot, 375–400°F. Meanwhile, scrub the potatoes and trim any irregularities, but don't bother to peel them. Cut lengthwise in one direction and then the other to form long matchstick-shaped pieces. Rinse in cold water and quickly pat dry. Add the potatoes to the hot oil in 2 batches so that the bottom is covered with potatoes and they are covered with the hot oil. The temperature will drop down abruptly but will head back up again as the fries cook. Stir one or twice during the frying process. Once they are golden brown, remove to a baking sheet and place in a 200°F oven to keep warm while you cook the others. Once the fries have cooked, reduce the heat slightly so that your thermometer gets down to around 350°F. Drain the milk off the fish and discard. Quickly roll each piece in the cornstarch and dip into the batter, coating on all sides. Add the fish to the hot oil in the pan; again, this will probably take 2 batches. The frying temperature should stay between 325 and 350°F throughout the cooking process. Once the fish is golden brown on one side, flip over with a slotted spoon and cook until golden on the other. Again, remove to the baking sheet once done. Serve hot, garnished with lemon wedges and lots of tartar sauce. Serves 4–5.

Tartar Sauce

Variations on commercially produced tartar sauce seem to run the gamut from sublime to ridiculous. Since I'm a devoted fan of sublime, I decided years ago the only way to ensure the tartar sauce we ate fit that category was to concoct it myself. It doesn't take much time and is so very worth the effort.

½ c. mayonnaise or more to taste
1 t. snipped dill weed
2 T. diced dill pickle
2 T. diced stuffed green olives
2 T. chopped capers
1 T. parsley flakes
1 T. snipped chives
1 t. lemon juice (optional)

Combine all ingredients in a small bowl. Serve immediately, cover, and refrigerate leftovers. If you need to substitute dry herbs for some of the fresh, use about ⅓ as much by volume. This makes a thick tartar sauce; if you prefer it to be less dense, simply add a little more mayonnaise.

Homemade Ketchup (Catsup)

Did you ever wonder what went in to all those plastic squeeze bottles of ketchup, a.k.a. catsup, lining the shelves of your grocery store? In too many cases, a lot of unnecessary fillers and sweeteners we perhaps wouldn't otherwise be ingesting. Even if such things aren't of concern to you, it's still a bit empowering to know how to make your own, whenever you wish. And of course, you may customize it: a little sweeter, a little tarter—whatever direction your culinary preference moves you in, just follow your taste buds! Although there are large and cumbersome recipes for making ketchup from fresh tomatoes, I'd rather spend my end-of-summer time as unencumbered as possible. To me it makes more sense to stir up a batch or two of tomato paste, which can then be parceled out and preserved for use in a myriad of recipes sometime later—like, for instance, a snowy day in March! Tomato ketchup is just such a recipe; and if you don't happen to have any homemade tomato paste hanging around, a small can of it from the store will serve your purpose very nicely.

12 T. (¾ c. or 1 sm. can) tomato paste
¾ c. water
1–2 T. honey
1–2 T. brown sugar
¼ t. salt
¼ t. cinnamon
¼ t. dry mustard
¼ t. onion powder
⅛ t. allspice
⅛ t. cloves
⅛ t. celery salt
1 T. cider vinegar

Combine all ingredients in a small nonreactive saucepan, stirring until smooth. Vary the amounts of sugar and honey to taste. Bring to just barely boiling, reduce heat, and simmer for about 5 minutes to blend the flavors. Store in a covered container in the fridge for about a month; the sugars and vinegar provide some preservative value, but it is still more perishable than many commercial brands. This makes just under a pint of ketchup.

Tasty Tuna Mousse

I have a nifty little fish mold that is just right for shaping this mousse. You may use any mold you happen to have on hand, or just place the mousse in a 9" × 5" loaf pan that has had plastic wrap draped down one side, across the bottom, and up the other. The wrap will help it slide right out once you dip the pan in hot water and invert it. This is my favorite Lenten appetizer or snack, good with pretzels, breadsticks, crackers, or crudités, which is just a fancy way of saying veggies for dipping.

8 oz. pkg. cream cheese
1 pkg. unflavored gelatin
6 or 7½ oz. can water pack light tuna, drained and flaked
¾ c. milk
1 T. parsley flakes
1 T. lemon juice
½ t. dried dill weed
¼ t. Tabasco sauce
½ c. sour cream
Salt to taste
⅓ c. snipped scallions or chives
⅓ c. minced celery
⅓ c. sliced stuffed olives

Combine the tuna, scallions, celery, olives, parsley, dill, lemon juice, and Tabasco sauce. Soften the gelatin in ¼ c. of the milk. Meanwhile, heat the remaining milk to just below boiling. Stir in the gelatin mixture until dissolved and then chill it until lukewarm; don't let it chill too much or it will set before you want it to! Once it has cooled, beat the cream cheese with an electric mixer, adding in the gelatin milk mixture and the sour cream, until smooth. Fold in the tuna mixture. Pour into a lightly greased 2-cup mold and chill until well set, at least 2 hours. Dip the mold or pan quickly in hot water to unmold, inverting onto your serving platter. If you've used a fish mold, decorate with an olive slice for an eye and garnish with any combination of scallions, dill weed, and/or parsley. Refrigerate promptly and plan to use within a day or two.

Creamed Tuna and Peas

This must surely be the official fish dish comfort food. It's a little bit bland and a little bit savory, with a hint of richness thrown in on the side—a winning combination in the comfort foods category. In some cases, it's even morphed into something referred to as "tuna wiggle"—although not in this case!

3 T. butter
3 T. flour
¼ t. Tabasco sauce
1 t. lemon juice
¼ t. dried dill weed
½ t. salt

½ t. dried onion flakes
2 c. milk
1 6–7-oz. can tuna, drained and flaked
1 c. green peas (I use frozen, either thawed or "as is")

Melt the butter in a medium-sized saucepan over low heat. Stir in the Tabasco sauce, onion flakes, dill weed, and salt. Stir in the flour until smooth. Whisk in the milk and cook over medium heat, whisking frequently, until mixture thickens and bubbles. Stir in the lemon juice, tuna, and peas. In using thawed peas, this will be ready to eat as soon as it bubbles again. If the peas are frozen, cook a minute or two longer, until they are just warmed through. Serve over toast, baked potatoes, or in a real fix, saltine crackers. This serves 2 generously.

Seafood Artichoke Casserole

If you'd like something just a bit fancier in the canned seafood category, try branching out with a bit of crabmeat and shrimp. This simple casserole still fits the comfort food category, just perhaps slightly more sophisticated comfort food.

1 c. pasta, cooked and drained
1 13-oz. can quartered artichoke hearts, drained
6 oz. crabmeat, drained and flaked
1 c. tiny shrimp, cooked
2 T. butter
2 T. flour
1 t. dill
1 t. chives
½ t. salt
¼ t. Tabasco sauce
½ t. nutmeg
½ t. dry mustard
1½ c. milk
1 c. cheddar cheese, shredded
4 oz. cream cheese
Paprika for topping

Make sauce by melting the butter in a medium saucepan over low heat. Stir in the flour and all the seasonings. Increase heat to medium and stir in the milk all at once. Cook and stir until the mixture bubbles. Remove from hat and stir in the cheddar cheese until it just melts. Stir in the cream cheese, hot cooked pasta, drained artichoke, crabmeat, and shrimp. Turn into a buttered casserole dish and sprinkle with paprika. Bake at 350–375°F for about ½ hour, until the casserole is heated through and just bubbly. Serves 4–6.

Citrus Poached Salmon

Cold water salmon has turned out to be one of those omega-3 "healthy" fish, especially good for your heart. If you're able to purchase salmon that has been designated "wild caught," so much the better. Salmon is one instance where the term "farmed" doesn't necessarily denote a superior product. The rich flavor of these colorful fish lends itself well to the mustard and citrus overtones in this recipe.

4 salmon fillets, about 1 lb. total
2 T. coarse grainy mustard
1 t. dried dill
1 t. dried tarragon
1 t. dried chives
2 T. butter
2 T. lime juice
½ c. orange juice

Combine the mixed herbs and the mustard. Spread thinly on each fillet, cover loosely with plastic wrap, and refrigerate to blend flavors at least 1 hour. When ready to prepare, heat the butter in a heavy skillet just large enough to hold the 4 fillets. Add the salmon, mustard-side down, and cook over medium heat until just slightly browned. Turn the fillets over and cook a minute longer. Pour in the orange and lime juice and allow the salmon to cook gently (poach) until it just flakes when pulled at with a fork. Serve with the juices poured over each piece. This dish is good with a rice pilaf and/or mashed sweet potatoes.

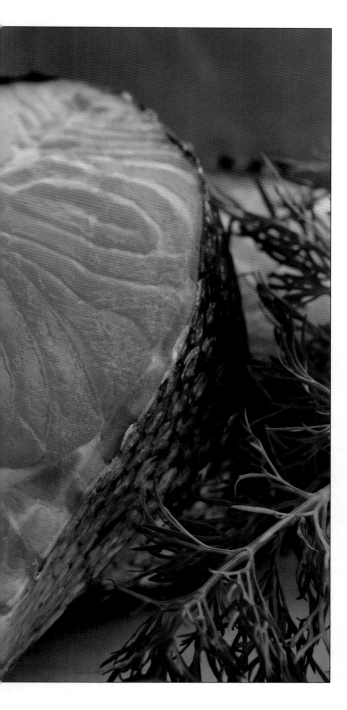

Mashed Sweet Potatoes

Sweet potatoes, sometimes called yams in the South, are a member of the morning glory family. They should not be confused with the other large tuber referred to as a yam, which is often associated with African cuisine. Sweet potatoes have thin skins, flesh ranging from pale yellow to deep golden, and a sweet, mellow flavor. They're also a great source of vitamin A and potassium.

1 lb. sweet potatoes, peeled and cut in chunks
1 T. butter
1 T. packed brown sugar
2 T. cream
2 T. orange juice
¼ t. salt
¼ t. cinnamon
⅛ t. nutmeg
⅛ t. ginger

Place the sweet potatoes in a medium saucepan with 1½ c. of water. Bring to a boil, reduce heat to medium low, and boil gently, covered, until they are tender, about 20 minutes. Drain any excess liquid from them. Add in the butter, brown sugar, orange juice, cream, salt, and spices. Mash or beat the sweet potatoes smooth. This makes 4 servings, although the amounts are easy to double.

Colcannon

This hearty cabbage and potato dish is tasty with everything from pork chops to frankfurters. It's not bad as a vegetarian entrée, either—perhaps with a dish of farmer cheese or cottage cheese on the side.

1 lb. russet-type potatoes, peeled and cut in chunks
½ lb. cabbage, shredded or chopped fine
¼ c. milk
1 small yellow onion, diced;
or 2 scallions, sliced
3 T. butter, divided
Salt to taste
Pepper to taste

Cook the potatoes with ½ t. salt and water just to cover until they are tender. Melt 1 T. of the butter in a large, heavy skillet. Add the onion and cook just until tender. Add the cabbage and pour some of the potato cooking water over the top. Cover, bring to a boil, and cook until the cabbage is tender, stirring occasionally. The water should have mostly evaporated. Mash the potatoes with the remaining 2 T. butter, the milk, and salt and pepper to taste. Stir in the cabbage and onions and serve. This makes 4 servings.

New England Boiled Dinner

When I was growing up, New England boiled dinners were an important part of our winter menu. The most noticeable difference between these and a corned beef dinner was the meat. We always used a smoked ham for the New England version; frequently a cut of meat so large we had a hard time fitting it in the cooking kettle. In essence, the smoked ham, its skin (a.k.a. rind) still on, was precooked in a large pot of gently boiling water until the skin loosened up enough to trim it off with a butcher knife. Depending on the saltiness of the ham, it was either returned to the same water, or if need be, placed in a fresh pan full. The cooking process could take the better part of an afternoon, as the ham was not only large but also raw. Once it was nearly cooked, easy to establish when a fork was inserted near the bone, vegetables would be added. As with the corned beef, carrots would be added first, although if rutabagas or parsnips were included, bits of them would be added at the same time. Cabbage always brought up the end of the process, with potatoes and beets again cooked in separate pans. Plan on about 4 hours cooking time for a large (7 lb.) smoked ham, although the added vegetables will only require about one of them.

Of Corned Beef and Other Such Things...

How could we get through March without mentioning Saint Patrick's Day? And how could we remember Saint Patrick's Day without mentioning corned beef?

Corned Beef Brine

By corning your own beef, you get to control what goes into it as well as the cut of meat you use. I prefer not to use sodium nitrate, also known as saltpeter. The only difference you'll notice is that the meat will cook to a natural brown rather than the typical reddish pink. You must cool your brine completely before immersing the beef in it; otherwise, you'll risk spoilage of your meat. You'll also need a noncorrosive container, such as glass, stainless steel, or plastic, preferably with a tight-fitting lid. You may also weight your meat down with a clean plate or use a large-sized plastic food-grade bag (not a generic plastic bag, please!) to encase the meat and brine. This amount will brine a 2–3 pounds cut of beef; double for a larger cut. You should plan on 5–7 days of brining time for your beef, in your refrigerator.

1 qt. water
½ c. canning salt
¼ c. packed brown sugar
2" stick cinnamon
1 t. mustard seeds
2–3 bay leaves
½ t. whole allspice
½ t. peppercorns
½ t. whole cloves
2 T. cider vinegar
2 lg. or 4 small cloves of garlic

Place all ingredients in a large stainless steel kettle and bring to a boil. Remove from heat and allow it to cool to room temperature. Place in refrigerator to complete the chilling process. Prick the beef all over with a metal or wooden skewer, which will better enable the corning solution to permeate it. Once it is *cold*, add your piece of beef, making sure it is covered entirely. Weight down if necessary, cover and refrigerate for 5–7 days, turning occasionally. I like using a flat cut for this purpose.

Corned Beef and Cabbage

What a symphony of flavors is produced from such humble beginnings! Corned beef and cabbage doesn't only please the palate, but it's also a treat for the eye: juicy slices of meat surrounded by garnet red, deep orange, creamy white, and green vegetables—all nestled together on the serving platter just waiting to be devoured. It's even tasty if you've chosen to purchase your corned beef from a store.

2–3 lb. corned beef
1 lg. onion, halved
1 small head of cabbage cut in 6 wedges
6 carrots, scrubbed and cut in sticks
Potatoes cooked separately
Beets cooked separately (optional)

Remove the beef from the brining solution. Place in a large kettle of water just to cover. Add the onion and bring to a boil. (I also like to add in the garlic and bay leaves from the brine.) Reduce heat and simmer the beef for 2–2½ hours, until it becomes quite tender. During the last ½ hour, add the carrots. Add the cabbage 15 minutes later and simmer until they are both tender but still colorful. Remove the beef to a serving platter and surround by the cabbage and carrots. Add red-skinned potatoes that have been boiled in lightly salted water in their jackets (unpeeled). Note: beets generally take longer to cook than most vegetables; it wouldn't be amiss to plan on up to an hour of cooking time in boiling water if you'd like to include them. Serve with melted butter to which chives and parsley have been added and a variety of mustards. Some Irish soda bread is a nice touch for St. Patrick's Day. This serves 6, with leftovers.

Corned beef and cabbage—traditional Irish fare.

Red Flannel Hash

Baking is an exacting skill; precise measurements are important for the end result. Cooking, on the other hand, is more a two-pronged avocation consisting of proportion and personal taste. The creation of a red flannel hash, an old New England dish that is commonly the by-product of a boiled dinner, is a classic example. In general, I use approximately 1 part either corned beef or ham to 3 parts vegetables, which will always include potatoes, beets, and onions, with others added as fit the occasion. I personally don't consider it a good hash unless it also contains carrots and cabbage, both cooked during an earlier meal. The ingredients here are approximate; quantity is dictated by the amount of leftovers available, the number to be fed, and the heartiness of their appetites.

1 med. onion, diced
2 T. corn oil

2 c. diced cooked or raw potatoes
2 c. chopped or shredded cooked ham *or* corned beef
2 c. diced cooked beets
1 c. cooked chopped carrots
1 c. cooked chopped cabbage
Salt to taste
Pepper to taste

Sauté the onions in the oil in a large cast-iron skillet until they soften slightly but are not brown. If using raw potatoes, add a couple minutes into this process and allow them to cook together until crisp tender. Add the chopped meat and remaining vegetables and continue to cook over medium heat, scraping the pan and lifting the hash with a spatula occasionally, for about 15 minutes. Season it to taste and serve the hash as is or with hard-cooked eggs as an accompaniment. Dill pickles and corn bread also lend themselves well to the occasion.

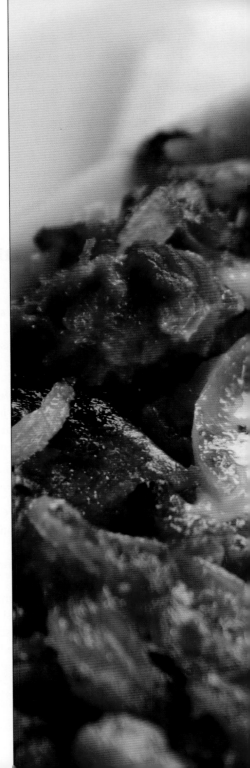

Red flannel hash, with a side of spotted dog and homemade pickles.

Corned Beef Hash

Corned beef hash is a simple-enough dish to make. I usually combine equal parts cooked corned beef and cubed potatoes, along with some onion for flavor. It's another one of those recipes that can make as much or as little as you wish quite easily. Anadama bread and corn bread are both good go-withs, as are dill pickles or pickled beets. Some folks swear by ketchup as an accompaniment, although I prefer mine unembellished. Try topping some with your favorite eggs for a hearty breakfast or brunch.

3 c. ground or finely diced cooked corned beef
3 c. diced potatoes, either cooked or raw
1 medium onion, diced
2 T. oil
2 T. butter
Chopped parsley
Diced green pepper, optional
Salt to taste
Pepper to taste

Heat the oil and butter in a large, heavy skillet. Add the onions and the potatoes if you're using raw ones. Cook for just a minute or two, to partially soften them, if cooking only the onions. If you're cooking potatoes as well, it will probably take closer to 5 minutes. Add the corned beef, cooked potatoes if using them, and about ¼ c. minced green pepper if you wish. Season the hash with salt and pepper to taste. Mix everything together well and allow it to fry on one side for about 5 minutes to form a crust on the underside. Using a spatula, lift up and turn over the underside and allow it to cook about 5 minutes longer. At this point, your hash should be heated through

with some nice crusty browned areas. Sprinkle with parsley and serve hot with your choice of accompaniments. This serves 4–6, depending on appetites.

Hot Dog Hash

While we're on the subject of hash, here's an old favorite that's thrifty, easy to make, and really tasty. Unfortunately it probably wouldn't be considered the healthiest fare in the world, but with the advent of reduced this-and-that frankfurters, it can be made a little more so than once upon a time. Add on some healthy sides such as steamed broccoli, stewed toma-toes, or even pickled beets to help redeem it even more. As with its companion hashes, this one also lends itself well to an accompaniment of corn bread. When I was young, we used to make this from leftovers; my mom would cook a large number of boiled potatoes at one meal and occasionally hot dogs as well, leaving plenty for pursuits such as this later.

    4 medium-cooked potatoes (about 2–3" each) or fewer larger ones
    1 small onion, diced
    2 T. corn oil
    4–6 hot dogs
    ½ t. salt
    ½ t. paprika
    ¼ t. pepper
    ⅛ t. celery seed, optional

Cut the potatoes in small cubes. If they've been cooked in the jackets with their skins on, I don't bother to peel them. If you're dealing with baked potatoes, you may wish to remove the skins. Slice the hot dogs thinly. Heat the corn oil in a large cast-iron skillet over medium-high heat. Add the onions and sauté, turning them occasionally until they begin to soften. Add the sliced hot dogs and continue to cook, turning occasionally, until they start to brown. Add the potatoes and seasonings and cook until the potatoes are nicely browned. Some folks will enjoy ketchup with this, others just as is. This serves 4.

Heavenly Hash

Here's a hash of a different inclination entirely. Don't try serving this one with pickles or hard-cooked eggs! It's for dessert only.

    ¾ c. jasmine rice
    1 lg. can crushed pineapple in juice
    ¼ c. sugar
    1½ c. heavy cream
    2 c. mini-marshmallows (white or colored)
    ½ c. chopped maraschino cherries
    ½ c. chopped walnuts (optional)

Drain the pineapple juice into a small bowl or large measuring cup. Add water to equal 1½ cups. Combine the pineapple juice/water and rice in a small saucepan. Bring just to a boil, stirring to blend. Cover the pan, reduce heat to a simmer, and let the rice cook until it is quite soft and all the cooking liquid has been absorbed. Combine the pineapple, rice, and marshmallows in a medium bowl. Refrigerate until the mixture is thoroughly chilled. Whip the cream and sugar to soft peaks. Fold the cherries, walnuts, and whipped cream into the rice and pineapple mixture. Serve garnished with additional cherries or marshmal-lows, if you wish. This make about 8–10 servings.

Chocolate Pudding

What better comfort food on a chilly March evening than a smooth dish of chocolate pudding topped with a dollop of sweet whipped cream? This is a dish that can easily be made with powdered milk, which is how I usually make it. When my kids were little, it was a more economical choice, and it's still fully as easy as using fresh milk. You can even mix up batches of the dry ingredients in advance, bagging them airtight, and have your own pudding mix to cook up quickly any time you want some. If you decide to use powdered milk in this recipe, use 1 cup of the dry powder, which you'll combine with the dry ingredients. When it's time to add the fresh milk, simply substitute 3 cups of water.

3 c. milk
2 T. butter
4–6 T. cornstarch*
3 T. unsweetened cocoa powder
¾ c. sugar
1 t. vanilla

Stir together the sugar, cocoa, and cornstarch. Melt the butter in a large saucepan over low heat. Whisk in the dry ingredients and milk until all is smooth. Increase the heat to medium and cook, stirring occasionally to prevent sticking, until the pudding comes to a full boil. Remove from the heat and stir in the vanilla. Allow the pudding to cool before serving. A piece of waxed paper placed over the top will prevent a "skin" from forming on the surface, although to me that's the best part! *The lesser amount of cornstarch will produce a softer pudding, the larger amount a slightly firmer one, which could also be used as filling for a chocolate cream pie. Serve plain or topped with fresh whipped cream. It's extra festive with a maraschino cherry for garnish. This serves 6–8.

Maple Cream Pie

There's a truck-stop diner in Wells River, Vermont, that makes some of the best maple cream pie around. The folks up there know not to skimp on either the real maple syrup or the real whipped cream—worthy advice for us all. A sprinkling of chopped walnuts atop the cream provides the crowning touch on my version of this quintessential Vermont treat.

1 baked 9" piecrust
2½ c. milk
1 c. maple syrup
6 T. cornstarch
2 T. butter
1 egg, beaten
Pinch of salt
1 c. heavy cream
¼ c. sugar
½ t. vanilla
Chopped walnuts for topping, optional

Combine the cornstarch and maple syrup in a heavy saucepan, whisking until smooth. Stir in the milk, salt, and butter and cook over medium heat, stirring frequently, until the mixture comes to a full boil. Remove from the heat and immediately whisk in the beaten egg, stirring to combine thoroughly. Allow the filling to cool in the pan for about 10 minutes, stirring once or twice, before pouring into the prepared pie shell. Refrigerate the pie for at least 2 hours, until it is chilled completely. Whip the cream, sugar, and vanilla together until it is just stiff. Spread the cream evenly over the chilled pie filling. Sprinkle with chopped walnuts, if desired. An extra little swirl of maple syrup on top of each piece makes it taste even better. This serves 8; make sure to refrigerate leftovers.

Maple cream pie topped with walnuts—it's hard to top this.

Maple Nut Pie

This New England variation on a pecan pie features maple syrup and your choice of just pecans or a combination of pecans and walnuts. (In the good old days, butternuts would have been the nut of choice; sadly, there aren't that many of them around anymore.) Maple nut pie is a Thanksgiving classic around our house, but can easily be enjoyed any time of the year.

1 unbaked 9" pastry shell
⅔ c. pure maple syrup*
⅔ c. packed brown sugar
⅔ c. light corn syrup
3 eggs, beaten
¼ c. melted butter
1 t. vanilla extract
½ t. natural maple flavoring; if you can only find artificial, please omit it
1½ c. nuts of choice; I use halves, although you could use some chopped also

Combine everything but the pastry shell and nuts, mixing well. Stir in the nuts and pour the mixture into the prepared crust, which has been fluted up around the edges of the pan. Bake at 425°F for 10 minutes. Reduce the heat to 350°F and bake 25–30 minutes longer, until the filling is slightly puffed in the center. Cool completely before slicing and serving topped with whipped cream. As my father used to say, this is "rich and delicious," so what might normally serve 8 could presumably be stretched into 10–12 servings.

*Although you can be a purist and use only maple syrup in this pie, I prefer the more classic texture the addition of brown sugar and corn syrup give; this can only be achieved by the blending of different sugar types. If you prefer just maple, increase the syrup to 2 cups and omit the brown sugar and corn syrup.

Boston Cream Pie

Boston cream pie is a New England favorite; it's even the official state dessert of Massachusetts. They're clever folk, those Bostonians. It's not a pie in the traditional sense, but rather a custard cream pudding sandwiched between layers of vanilla cake, the top covered in chocolate glaze. It makes a delicious ending to a hearty New England supper on a cold March evening.

½ c. butter
1 c. sugar
1 t. vanilla
1½ c. cake flour
1½ t. baking powder
½ t. salt
½ c. milk
2 eggs

Combine the softened butter, sugar, and vanilla in a large mixing bowl. Beat on high speed until light and fluffy, pausing occasionally to scrape bowl. Combine the flour, baking powder, and salt. Add these to the butter and sugar mixture, along with the milk. Beat on medium speed until smooth and creamy. Last, add the eggs, beating until just smooth and creamy, again scraping the bowl as needed. Pour batter into a greased and 9" round floured cake pan. Bake at 350°F until golden brown and firm to touch, approximately 30 minutes. Cool in pan for 10 minutes. Run a knife around the edges to loosen and turn it out on a cooling rack. While the cake finishes cooling, prepare the custard pudding filling.

2 T. butter
3 T. cornstarch

½ c. sugar
1 c. milk
½ c. cream
1 t. vanilla extract
1 egg, well beaten

In a medium-sized saucepan (preferably heavy-grade stainless steel for more even cooking), melt the butter over low heat. Remove from heat and whisk in the sugar and cornstarch until all are integrated and the mixture looks grainy. Whisk in the milk and cream. Return the pan to medium and cook, whisking almost constantly to prevent sticking, until the mixture thickens and comes to a full boil. Turn off the heat and immediately whisk in the beaten egg. Stir in the vanilla extract. Cool, whisking occasionally, to room temperature. Place the entire pan in a larger pan or bowl filled with cold water to hasten this process. Using a long serrated knife, carefully cut the cake in half horizontally, making two even layers. Place one layer, cut-side up, on a serving platter. Spoon the filling evenly over the cake, smoothing to ½" of the edge. Carefully place the second layer, cut-side down, over the filling, pressing lightly. Refrigerate the filed layers while preparing the glaze.

1 T. butter
2 T. cream
2 T. light corn syrup
¼ c. semisweet chocolate chips
1 T. unsweetened cocoa powder
½ c. confectioner's sugar

Melt the butter in a small saucepan over low heat. Add the cream, corn syrup, and chocolate chips, stirring and heating until the chips melt. Remove from heat and stir in the cocoa powder and confectioner's sugar. Immediately pour the

How about a nice helping of Boston cream pie to finish?

glaze over the cooled cake layers, smoothing evenly and allowing a little to run over the edges. Serve Boston cream pie thoroughly chilled, cover any leftovers with foil and refrigerate, and plan to eat within two days. Serves 8–12.

Oatmeal Shortbread Cookies

Although my maternal grandparents were Scandinavian emigrants, my paternal grand-mother, Matilda Jane Calhoun, was born in Scotland. Here's a tasty recipe utilizing that grand Scottish staple rolled oats. These cookies are quite tasty with a mug of cocoa, hot spiced maple milk, or a nice cup of tea.

1½ c. butter
1 c. sugar
1 c. flour
2 t. vanilla
3 c. rolled oats and extra for rolling

Cream together the softened butter, vanilla, and the sugar in a large mixing bowl. Once they are light and fluffy, stir in the flour and rolled oats. Form the mixture into 1" balls, rolling in extra oats for manageability and place about 2" apart on ungreased baking sheets. Use the bottom of a drinking glass to flatten the balls out. Bake on the upper rack of a 375°F oven for 15 minutes, until they are lightly browned around the edges. Allow to cool for a minute or two on the baking sheets before carefully removing with a spatula to cooling racks. This makes 30 cookies.

Maple Leaf Cookies

Here is our last maple recipe of the month. Crispy maple-flavored butter cookies are topped with a smooth maple icing, which dries to a rich glaze. Use maple leaf–shaped cookie cutters to shape these if you have any; yield will depend on the size of the cutters involved. If you're feeling adventuresome, try adding a sprinkle of colored sugar or finely chopped walnuts as a finishing touch.

1 c. unsalted butter
1 t. pure maple flavoring
1 c. granulated sugar *or* ½ c. each granulated and maple sugar
½ t. salt
1 egg
1 t. baking powder
2 c. flour

Maple Icing

½ c. pure maple syrup
¼ c. butter
¼ c. cream
4 c. confectioner's sugar

Beat the butter and sugar together until smooth and creamy. Add the egg and the maple extract, beating again until light and fluffy. On low speed with a heavy mixer blade or by hand with a wooden spoon, stir in the flour, baking powder, and salt until thoroughly combined. Either cover the dough or place in a plastic bag and refrigerate for about 1 hour (or more) before rolling and baking. The chilling time is important for a couple of reasons; it makes the fragile dough more manageable, and

Maple leaf cookies: a tasty maple snack.

it decreases the amount of flour necessary for rolling and therefore the amount absorbed when rerolling scraps. When you're ready to bake your cookies, roll portions of the dough at a time thin (⅛"). Bake on ungreased cookie sheets on upper shelf of a 350°F for about 10–12 minutes, until light golden brown around the edges. Cool for a minute or two on the sheets before carefully removing to cooling racks. The number of cookies you get will depend on the size and shape of your cutters; I have a large maple leaf cutter that makes about 1½ dozen per batch, although smaller cutters will obviously yield more. Once the cookies are completely cooled,

frost them with maple icing. For the icing, bring the butter, cream, and maple syrup to a boil in a medium saucepan. Turn off the heat and beat in the confectioner's sugar until smooth; the icing will be thin. Quickly dip the top of each cookie in the hot icing, lightly smoothing off extra with a flat spatula or knife blade. Lay the cookies flat to dry and cool completely before attempting to move them. The heat of the icing will temporarily soften the cookies, making breakage a possibility if they're moved too soon. When you're ready to transfer them, slide a spatula carefully underneath to loosen any hardened icing.

Spring Is on Its Way . . .

APRIL IS WHEN spring first begins to look like spring here in southern Vermont. Sugaring is done by now, and the trees and shrubs are just beginning to bud. Even though fall is Vermont's prime foliage season, and with good reason, spring brings more subtle colors to the hills. Each woodland tree sports its own unique blossom before leafing out in pale green. Maples, reflecting their brilliant fall foliage, sport delicate miniature crimson blooms. Elms offer tiny hanging clusters of pink and mauve, while shad trees, another early bloomer, are covered with little white flowers. Shad trees even feature in traditional rural planting guidelines. Planting of peas should be done when their leaves are the size of a mouse's ears, although I must admit I've never tried a comparison of the two to see just what that size might be. And who can resist those soft little buds of silver appearing on the twigs of marsh-loving pussy willows? The first crocus and daffodils are poking their heads up on lawns, bringing a spot of bright color soon to be mirrored by flowering forsythias.

Flocks of migratory birds are making their way back north as well, pausing to feed in last year's corn stubble and hayfields. Soon the whistles of red-winged male blackbirds echo from willow bushes where they perch, alert and territorial, preparing for the nesting season ahead. By now seedlings are beginning to look like the plants they will become, and early perennial herbs are again making their outdoor advent.

It's no wonder April is frequently also the month of Easter, the holiday of rebirth. It fits nicely that so many favorite Easter dishes include eggs, historically in more plentiful supply during spring, thanks to the lengthening of the days and the chickens' industry.

April

Egg-xactly What the Doctor Ordered . . .

When I was five or six years old, I managed to catch just about every contagious childhood disease in the book, in the course of only a few short months. At that point our family physician, a pioneering lady doctor by the name of Grace Burnett, instructed my mother that I was to eat an egg a day to build up my resistance to such things. There followed a series of egg-oriented breakfast dishes, some of which probably don't bear repeating here, but many of which were very tasty indeed. Frequently a well-cooked egg or two can be fully as satisfying as any number of sandwiches or burgers. Thank goodness much of the furor about avoiding eggs at all costs has gone away by now. The average egg has only 75 calories and contains a complex mix of nutrients, including B vitamins and antioxidants, even omega-3 fatty acids. There is one other issue you must be aware of when cooking with eggs. Possible food-borne illness from such nasty pathogens as salmonella may develop from eating undercooked eggs. Please refer to the "General Guidelines" section for more in-depth information regarding safe cooking temperatures for eggs. Although some of the recipes I've used over the years do call for uncooked eggs and I've made them many times with no ill effects, I must reiterate that you should serve undercooked eggs only if you fully understand the risk involved. Fortunately for us all, most of my recipes call for thoroughly cooking them, alleviating our fears! Here are a few recipes that are tasty for breakfast, brunch, or even a light supper. I hope you'll enjoy them too.

The Basics . . .
Poached Eggs

A soft poached egg or two, sprinkled with salt and pepper and placed on hot-buttered whole-grain toast, can be a kind of breakfast ambrosia. I still leave the yolks runny, as long as I know my egg source. Leaving them a minute or two longer will firm up the yolks and ensure their safety for all. Don't poach more than 2 at a time, or they may not cook properly.

Bring about 3" of water to a boil in a medium saucepan. Break your eggs, one at a time, into a saucer or small dish and slide them into the water. This should keep the yolks unbroken and eggshells out of the water. Once the egg has slid in, make sure the white is firm around the egg yolk. While some spreading of the white

is normal, one that loosens away from the yolk indicates the egg is not as fresh as it should be and should either be discarded or thoroughly cooked. The cooking water generally will froth up some during the initial poaching process. Turn off the heat and cover the pan. Allow it to sit 3 minutes for liquid yolks, up to 5 for firmer ones. Carefully remove the eggs with a slotted spoon and place on your hot-buttered toast. Season to taste and enjoy!

Hard-Cooked Eggs

You'll note I've designated these to be "hard cooked" rather than hard boiled. Boiling an egg, especially overboiling it, results in a tough product with an unattractive grayish ring around the yolk. With the method used here, the only boiling takes place at the beginning of the process. Depending on how many eggs you'll be cooking at once, place 3–4" of water in a saucepan with a cover. Carefully add in the number of raw eggs in the shell you wish; each should be fully immersed in the water. Oh, and fresh eggs will lie sideways in the water. If any of your eggs float end up, it means they're past the first blush of youth. It's a good thing you'll be thoroughly cooking those little guys! Bring the water with the eggs in it to a full boil, then turn off the heat, and allow the eggs to sit, covered, for 10 minutes. Pour off the hot water and place the eggs in a pan of cold water. If

you're using your eggs for sandwiches, simply cut the cooled eggs in half and scoop out the insides for mashing or chopping. If you need to retain the eggs' shape, tap the shells all over to crack them and allow the eggs to sit in the cool water a few minutes. You should then be able to carefully pull the shell and outer membrane away from the cooked egg.

Creamy Scrambled Eggs

Slow cooking is essential to creamy scrambled eggs. Cooking too long or over high heat can result in watery, tough, or even burned eggs, none of which are very appealing. Serve your eggs with hot-buttered toast or an English muffin for a tasty breakfast or a light supper.

Per Serving

2 eggs
Salt to taste
Pepper to taste
(I prefer 5 sprinkles of salt and 2 of pepper per egg)
2 T. milk
2 t. butter
2 T. shredded cheese, optional

Beat the eggs until the whites and yolks are well incorporated. Add the milk, salt, and pepper—stir-

ring to combine. Melt the butter in a small, heavy pan over low heat. Pour in the eggs and cook slowly, occasionally scraping the cooked egg up from the bottom of the pan, until set as you wish. They will continue to cook slightly after removing from the heat. Fold in the cheese, if desired, just before serving.

Pan-Scrambled Eggs

If you prefer your scrambled eggs firmer, as does Bruce, try this variation. There's no milk included because the higher cooking temperature would make the eggs watery if it was used. They're especially tasty if you scramble them in a little bacon fat.

2 eggs
Salt to taste
Pepper to taste
2 t. butter or bacon fat

Beat together the eggs and seasonings; I use about 10 shakes or grinds of salt and half as much pepper for 2 eggs. Heat the butter or bacon fat in a moderately hot pan, or just drain your excess grease from cooking bacon and pour the eggs directly in. Push them back and forth with a spatula until they are firm scrambled. Serve at once.

Fried Eggs

The amount of heat you use when frying eggs will determine whether they have tender whites or crispy ones; either is fine in my book. Slow and low will make for more tender eggs; I would recommend using butter for this method. Higher heat will give your white a nice brown crust; I here prefer corn oil. Once your eggs are broken in the pan, season them to taste with salt and pepper. Use about 1 t. fat per egg.

Sunny-side up. Eggs are not flipped, although some of the cooking fat may be splashed over the top to help them cook slightly. Sunny-side up eggs are not considered a "safe" way to guard against salmonella because the yolks don't reach a high-enough temperature.

Over easy. The eggs are fried on one side and turned just briefly without breaking the yolks, cooking the whites but leaving the yolks soft. The food safety rules are the same as for sunny-side up eggs.

Over hard. The eggs are cooked on both sides. The yolks are broken when the eggs are flipped, causing them to cook through. This is considered a "safe" way to fry eggs.

Mixed up. Beat the eggs lightly with the salt and pepper before frying. They are flipped over while frying and result in a "safe" cooked egg.

Either over-hard or mixed-up eggs make good egg sandwiches; add a slice of cheese once the eggs have been flipped over, allowing it to melt on slightly. Sandwich the eggs in between toasted English muffins or bagels, adding bacon, sausage, or ham if you wish.

Westerns

You don't need to be perched in front of a black-and-white television watching guys in Stetsons racing their trusty steeds through rugged terrain to enjoy one of these. Sandwich each in between toast or English muffins and add a splash of ketchup for good measure. If you prefer a "Denver" instead, add a little diced green pepper along with the onion.

2 eggs, beaten
2 T. diced cooked ham
1 T. diced onion
Salt (a pinch or 5 shakes)
Pepper (a small pinch or 2 shakes)
1 t. corn, canola, or olive oil
1 slice cheese, optional

Heat the oil in a small frying pan. Add the onion and sauté for just a minute. Combine the ham, eggs, and seasonings and pour over the onions. Cook over medium heat until the bottom is set and browned; flip over and fry on the other side until the middle of your Western is cooked through. If you've used an individual-sized frying pan, you'll now have a perfect little circle of goodness to plunk upon your buttered toast. If it's spread a bit, just fold it over as needed; it'll still taste every bit as good.

Eggs Goldenrod

A variation of this whimsically titled egg dish was printed in one of my 4-H cookbooks. The cookbook and the original recipe have long since disappeared. Hopefully this version will help preserve "eggs goldenrod" for posterity. You will note the cream sauce base is fairly thin; although you may add just a bit more flour if you'd prefer it thicker, I like being able to mush everything on my tastefully presented plate together before eating. It almost gives the veneer of again consuming those nice runny egg yolks some of us may now prefer to avoid. This recipe yields 1 hearty serving.

2 peeled hard-cooked eggs
1 T. butter
1 T. flour
1 c. milk
¼ t. salt
⅛ t. pepper
⅛ t. dry mustard
2 T. shredded cheese of choice, optional
Snipped chives *or* chopped parsley, optional
1 toasted, buttered English muffin *or* 2 slices buttered toast

Cut each egg in half and separate the whites from the yolks. Chop the whites and set aside. Mash the yolks lightly with a fork to produce a fine, almost-pollenlike mixture. Make a white sauce by melting the butter in a small saucepan over medium heat. Stir in the flour and seasonings and allow the mixture to cook, stirring, for about a minute. Whisk in the milk all at once and allow it to come to a boil and thicken. Add the cheese, if desired. Stir in the chopped egg whites. Pour this mixture over the buttered English muffin and sprinkle with the mashed egg yolks to produce the "goldenrod" effect, adding chives or parsley for color if desired. Serve at once. This is surely a dish fit for the garden fairies.

Eggs goldenrod is an egg dish that offers something a little out of the ordinary.

Easter Sunday Crepes

Here's a slightly sweeter use for eggs—easy and elegant at the same time. We shared these crepes with Tim and Abbey the Easter we visited them in New Jersey. They made a lovely après church Easter brunch. We chose strawberries and bananas to go with, although crepes are delectable with savory fillings as well. The accompaniments are limited only by your imagination.

1 c. flour
2 eggs
½ c. milk
½ c. water
¼ t. salt
2 T. butter, melted

Accompaniments

Confectioner's sugar
Fresh strawberries
Sliced bananas
Chocolate-hazelnut spread or chocolate ganache*
Orange butter sauce
Orange slices
Whipped cream

Combine the flour and salt in a small, deep bowl. Add the eggs, melted butter, and milk and whisk until the mixture is smooth. Add the water and whisk again; the batter should now be approximately the consistency of heavy cream. Set it aside for about 5 minutes, while you prepare your fruit and other accompaniments. Preheat a small skillet or crepe pan over medium-high heat. Swirl a little butter over the bottom to coat and add about ¼ cup of the crepe batter, swirling the pan to coat it evenly with a thin layer. Allow it to cook until the top appears somewhat dry, flip the crepe, and continue cooking about a minute longer. Immediately remove the crepe from the pan, fold it in half and then in fourths, and set aside on a serving platter while you prepare the others. Half the fun of eating crepes is customizing them to your individual preference. Use toppings of choice; spread each with a thin layer of chocolate, if desired, and top with fruit, whipped cream, and a sprinkle of confectioner's sugar. A nice alternative is a drizzle of orange butter sauce accompanied by slices of peeled oranges, with or without whipped cream for added luxury. This recipe makes about a dozen crepes.

*Ganache is a blend of melted chocolate and heavy cream; try 6 oz. good-quality chopped chocolate or chocolate chips stirred into ½ c. of hot cream until it's melted; use warm or at room temperature.

Orange Butter Sauce

This is a variation on a recipe that originally utilized orange juice concentrate. That's not as commonly available anymore, thanks to all the fresh and bottled juices we can now choose from. Enjoy this on pancakes, waffles, or French toasts as well as crepes.

1 c. orange juice
¼ c. honey *or* light corn syrup
¼ c. butter
2 t. cornstarch

Heat the honey or corn syrup and butter together until the butter just melts. Meanwhile, whisk the cornstarch into the cold juice until smooth. Add to the honey butter mixture and heat just to boiling. Serve the sauce warm or at room temperature. If you have leftover sauce, refrigerate it, covered. This makes about 1½ c. sauce.

Waffles

If you're one of those folks who thinks there's nothing finer on a lazy morning than a mass-produced frozen waffle popped into the toaster, this recipe may not be for you. However, if you long for a light, fluffy waffle with a crispy exterior just waiting for butter and syrup or berries and cream to top things off, then by all means give it a whirl! The single most important step you can take for waffle success is to oil or spray the waffle grids prior to cooking and probably a few times in between waffles as well. Many waffle grids are touted as stick resistant, but in practice, very few are. Nothing spoils the fun of waffle making more thoroughly than having the sides of your waffle stick to the grid, making removal a pain and the finished product looking not at all as a good waffle should. Either brush oil on with a pastry brush or a paper towel, or invest in a good can of cooking spray. The batter for these waffles is fairly fluffy and may take a bit longer to cook than a thinner one. You'll need to gauge cooking time dependent on your individual iron; in general, wait until most of the steaming has stopped, which is a good indicator that the batter is cooked through.

2 eggs, separated
1 c. milk
¼ c. corn oil
1 T. sugar
½ t. salt
1 c. flour
2 t. baking powder

Preheat your waffle iron; it must be really hot for the waffles to cook properly. Most irons feature a temperature-control indicator that will let you know when it's time to start cooking. Whip the egg whites at high speed until soft peaks form; set aside. Combine the egg yolks, milk, and oil in a medium bowl and whisk until smooth. Whisk in the combined flour, sugar, and salt. Once the batter is smooth, fold into it the egg whites until they are just well incorporated. The less mixing you do from now on, the better. Measure out enough batter to cover the inner part of the iron while leaving an uncovered edge perhaps ½" wide around it; the batter will expand while cooking. Lower the top and cook as above; remove the waffles by their edges with a fork. Serve your waffles nice and hot with butter and maple syrup. For a special treat, serve them with sweetened berries or other juicy fruit such as peaches and top with whipped cream, ice cream, or sour cream. This recipe should produce 4 large waffles. If you have a crowd, double it and consider getting a second iron so you don't end up cooking waffles all morning!

A golden waffle with butter and maple syrup tastes even better with a bit of bacon.

Pancakes

My mom's pancakes were generally thinner and smaller than the traditional American flapjack, more resembling the little Swedish pancakes called plattar. She'd make sure the pan was sufficiently heated for proper frying by sprinkling a few drops of water directly onto its surface. If the droplets balled up and skittered across the pan, it was deemed hot enough. She'd dollop three or four spoons of the thin batter onto the greased pan at once, turning them over when the tops were covered with bubbles and browning the other side. My dad evidently preferred his own method for frying pancakes. Once Mother had stopped pancake production for the day, he'd take over the frying pan, pouring great quantities of batter dead center of the zealously heated skillet. Such oversized griddle cakes required a longer cooking period than their diminutive counterparts, although Daddy never did get the knack of lowering the heat commensurately. The end result wasn't always pretty, but he seemed to enjoy them regardless. I suppose enough butter and maple syrup applied to almost anything will make it more palatable. These pancakes resemble those I remember Mother making; a stack of three is a considerably lighter prospect than anything you'll encounter in your average restaurant.

1 c. milk
1 egg
1 T. corn oil
2 t. sugar
1 c. flour
3 t. baking powder
½ t. salt
Corn oil for frying
Toppings as desired

Combine the milk, oil, and egg in a medium mixing bowl. Whisk in the combined dry ingredients until the batter is nice and smooth, and allow it to sit for a minute while heating the frying pan. I prefer a heavy cast-iron skillet or griddle, as this surface conducts the heat more evenly, giving you golden pancakes without burning. Once the water drop skitters across, pour in just a bit of corn oil to cover the bottom evenly. Pour in 3 large spoonfuls to form 3 small pancakes and cook until the tops are speckled with bubbles. Flip with a spatula and continue cooking until they've risen slightly and stopped steaming. This recipe makes 12 little pancakes, or 4 servings.

Variations. Add mini chocolate chips or wild blueberries to the batter or, better yet, quickly sprinkle a few over each pancake before flipping. Although butter and maple syrup are always grand toppings, I especially like confectioner's sugar with the blueberry or chocolate-chip pancakes.

French Toast

The nice thing about French toast is that it's easy to prepare as much or as little as you'd like. This is a lightly pan-fried version that's moist and fluffy inside, crispy on the outside, and not too greasy. I recommend a heavy cast-iron frying pan for best results. You can vary this recipe to your heart's desire, by using whatever type of bread you'd like or experimenting with different types of spice, extracts, or even citrus rind for flavor. This base recipe serves one.

1 egg, well beaten
¼ c. milk
1 t. sugar
⅛ t. vanilla
2–3 slices bread, depending on size and thickness

Combine the egg, milk, sugar, and vanilla in a small, shallow bowl. Dip each slice of bread on both sides so that the egg mix is absorbed throughout. Fry in a small amount of oil in a preheated pan over medium-high heat, flipping once. The toast will puff up while frying on the second side, letting you know the filling is cooking. Serve with butter and syrup.

Suggested variations. Add a pinch of cinnamon and/or nutmeg. Use brown sugar and add a pinch of ginger.

Add a couple drops of almond extract and coat the battered bread in finely chopped almonds before frying. Add a grating or two of orange or lemon peel.

Popovers

Daughter Amanda and I share a predilection for golden hot popovers. This recipe makes 6 small popovers; just double the ingredients for a dozen. Although I understand there are actual popover pans, which are larger and deeper than muffin tins, I've never used such things. Muffin tins are convenient and make a nice-sized popover for children. These are best eaten hot, and although you can store leftovers briefly in the fridge, popovers are really intended to be eaten straight out of the oven. As with cream puffs and Yorkshire pudding, popovers rise due to the buoyancy of the eggs as they heat. Having ingredients at room temperature will help with this. Place the egg in its shell in a dish of very hot tap water for about a minute, as a quick way to warm it up. Try your popovers dabbed with strawberry or raspberry jam for a real treat.

1–2 T. butter
½ c. milk
2 eggs
½ c. flour
¼ t. salt

Preheat oven to 400°F. Beat together the flour, eggs, milk, and salt until very smooth. Utilizing a large liquid measuring cup for this will make pouring the batter into the muffin cups easier for you. Place ½–1 teaspoon of butter in each of 6 muffin cups and place in the oven for about a minute, until the butter melts and starts to bubble. Don't heat it or too long or it will burn. Pour even amounts of batter into each muffin cup and immediately place in your preheated oven. Bake for 35 minutes, resisting the urge to peek at them as this may cause them to fall. When done, they will be puffed and golden brown. Serve at once with butter and jam.

Asparagus Omelet

Asparagus is a welcome friend returning to the spring garden, just when you want something fresh and green the most. A few asparagus roots, planted in deep rich soil and adequately mulched, will reward you annually within a couple of years. Make sure you put it in a spot where it won't be disturbed, as asparagus doesn't transplant particularly well. As the season draws to a close, around the end of June here, leave some of the little spears to turn into asparagus fern, ensuring the plants' health for another year.

Per Serving

2 eggs
⅛ t. salt
3 drops Tabasco sauce
1 T. water
2 t. butter or olive oil
3–4 stalks cooked, drained asparagus
3 shakes of lemon pepper seasoning
¼ c. (1 oz.) shredded Havarti, dilled Havarti, or cheddar cheese

Whisk together the eggs and water with salt and Tabasco sauce to taste. I use about 5 sprinkles or twists of salt per egg, so a fair-sized pinch should do for this recipe. Swirl the butter or oil in a heavy skillet over medium-high heat. Pour in the egg mixture and cook, lifting up the edges to let uncooked portion run underneath until the egg is mostly cooked. This is where omelet purists might simply add the fillings and fold over. I prefer to fully cook mine, so I flip the whole thing quickly and then place the asparagus, seasoned with a little lemon pepper, slightly to one side of the middle. Top with the shredded cheese and tip the uncovered half of the egg up over the filling. You can allow it to heat just for a minute in the pan or remove immediately, allowing the cheese to melt on retained heat. Serve with crusty bread or hot-buttered toast.

Farmer's Frittata

I like frittatas especially well because they're relatively easy to cook—not as finicky as some omelet recipes seem to insist on being. If you happen to have a set of cast-iron skillets, you can vary your frittata size considerably, serving from 1 to 10 in the process. This frittata is a hearty one, utilizing many good homegrown foods you can produce with just a little land and effort. Leafy green vegetables, root cellared potatoes, and fresh pork sausage all combine happily herein. Add some crusty bread and perhaps a bit of fruit, and you'll have a hearty enough meal for any self-respecting farmer.

8 slices bacon, diced
or ½ lb. pork sausage, crumbled
2 c. diced raw potatoes
1 med. onion, diced
1 clove minced garlic

2 T. butter
2 T. olive oil
8–12 oz. chopped, cooked greens, such as chard or spinach
4 extralarge eggs
2 T. water
¼ t. Tabasco sauce
¼ t. salt, or to taste
⅛ t. pepper, or to taste
A pinch of parsley *and/or* oregano
4 oz. shredded cheddar, Colby or Jack cheese (1 cup)

Brown the bacon or sausage (or use half of each) in a large cast-iron skillet until cooked. Remove with a slotted spoon and drain on paper toweling. Pour the excess fat from the pan and add the butter and olive oil. Sauté the onions and potatoes until lightly browned, adding the garlic near the end of the cooking process. Stir in the bacon or sausage and the cooked greens, seasoning to taste with salt, pepper, parsley, and oregano. Beat the eggs, ½ t. salt, Tabasco sauce, and water in a bowl until well blended. Pour over the hot ingredients in the pan and cook, lifting the edges as needed for the raw egg to slide under and cook. I now lower the heat and cover the pan for about 5 minutes to facilitate the eggs cooking through. Although this step could also be accomplished in a 375°F oven, it would probably take a little longer. Whichever method you choose, the final step is to top your frittata with the shredded cheese, either returning briefly to the oven or again covering for a minute to melt the cheese. This makes 4 servings.

Deviled Eggs

Deviled eggs are one of those universal dishes to be found at countless potluck dinners and holiday tables running the gamut from Easter to the Fourth of July. They're certainly kid-friendly food but can be gussied up just as easily for adult tastes. Whether enjoyed as an appetizer or as a side dish staple, deviled eggs are an economical and delicious addition to a variety of meals.

8 hard-cooked eggs
½ t. salt
¼ c. mayonnaise
1 T. prepared mustard
¼ t. onion powder
¼ t. pepper
⅛ t. celery seed
Paprika for sprinkling
16 pimento stuffed green olives (optional)

Carefully slice each peeled egg in half lengthwise. Remove the yolks to a small bowl and arrange the cooked white halves on a serving plate. Mash the yolks with a fork until they are quite smooth. Stir in the remaining ingredients to form a creamy filling; spoon or pipe evenly into each of the halves. Sprinkle with paprika and press a stuffed olive into the center of each, if desired. Cover loosely and refrigerate until serving time. Refrigerate any leftovers to eat within two days.

Easter Egg Buns

Starting Easter morning with a bit of egg and bread will leave room for the festivities later in the day. Use your choice of colored or natural eggs to fill each bread "nest." There's no need to boil the eggs in advance; the oven will cook them as the buns bake. If it's safer for little fingers to color hard-cooked eggs, they may also be used, although the twice-cooked approach may render them a bit tough.

Festive and frosted, Easter egg buns are set for your Easter breakfast or brunch.

6 T. butter
⅔ c. milk
6 T. sugar
½ t. salt
1 egg
1 t. grated lemon zest
1 t. grated orange zest
1 t. vanilla extract
1 T. dry yeast
⅓ c. warm water
3½–4 c. bread flour
6 plain or colored uncooked eggs in the shell

Glaze

2 T. butter
1 t. lemon juice
1 T. orange juice
½ t. vanilla extract
2 c. confectioner's sugar
Colored sprinkles, if desired

Heat together the butter and milk until the butter is just melted. Stir in the sugar, salt, and beaten egg and cool to lukewarm. Meanwhile, dissolve the yeast in the ⅓ c. warm water. Combine the two liquids and stir in 2 c. of the flour. Allow the batter to rest and work for about 15 minutes. Blend in 1½ c. more of the flour. Allow the dough to rise for about 1 hour. Punch down and knead in a bit of extra flour, if needed, for manageability. Divide the dough into 6 equal sections. Divide each section into two and roll the individual pieces of dough into long, thin strips about 15" long. Twist the two sections together to form a cord and loop each cord into a hollow circle, pinching the ends together well. Place each on a buttered baking sheet and center an egg in the middle of each. At this point you may cover and refrigerate overnight, or allow the buns to rise in a moist, warm place for another hour, until they are mostly doubled in bulk. Placing them in an oven on the lowest setting with a pan of hot water for moisture will speed the process. Bake the buns on an upper-middle rack of a 375°F oven for about 15–20 minutes, until they are uniformly golden and sound hollow when tapped. Allow to cool slightly while preparing the glaze. (If you've refrigerated the unbaked buns overnight, place them in the warm oven as mentioned above, for about ¾ to 1 hour and bake as above.) For the glaze, melt the butter in a medium saucepan over low heat, remove from heat, and stir in the lemon and orange juices and the vanilla. Mix in the confectioner's sugar until it's nice and smooth, adding a few drops of water if needed. Frost the warm buns and decorate as desired. Serve immediately; refrigerate any leftovers to eat within 2–3 days. This makes 6 large buns, which will feed at least 6 or possibly more.

113

Easter Ham

If you're looking for a little epicurean adventure to liven up your spring dining pleasure, why not cure your own ham? It takes a bit of advance planning and a smoke source, which could be a small commercial smoker or even a gas grill with cover. Talk about impressing your guests. However, if you don't feel quite that adventuresome, simply forego the curing process, buy a ready-cured and precooked ham, and glaze it as below, using the 20-minute-per-pound reheating guidelines.

5 lb. fresh pork shoulder, rind off or on
1 c. salt, not iodized
2 c. apple chips for smoking

Brine

½ c. salt, not iodized
½ c. packed dark brown sugar
½ t. black peppercorns
½ t. whole cloves
2 c. apple juice
6 c. water

Glaze

¾ c. crab apple or apple jelly
2 T. cider vinegar
¼ t. ground cloves
¼ t. ginger
1 T. Dijon mustard
Whole cloves

A week before you plan to serve your ham, rub the pork shoulder evenly with the 1 cup of salt. Place it in a noncorrosive bowl or container and place it in the refrigerator for about 24 hours, turning it 2–3 times. A fair amount of liquid should

be drawn out of the pork during this time. The next day, drain any liquid from the ham, rinse off the salt, and pierce the ham all over with a skewer. You should also prepare your brine the same day you salt your ham, as it needs to cool thoroughly before using. Combine 4 c. of the water, the ½ c. of salt, brown sugar, peppercorns, and cloves in a

Easter ham and bacon just finished smoking.

large pan and bring just to boiling. Remove from the heat and add the apple juice and remaining 2 cups of water. Allow it to cool to room temperature and then chill the brine down to at least 40°F; a cool porch may work in the fall or winter. Your refrigerator should do the trick any time of year if you have room. Just make sure the temperature stays cool enough; you don't want to risk spoilage! Use stainless steel, food-grade plastic, or a 2½-gallon-sized ziplock bag for the next step in the brining process. If using the bag, set it in a bowl or other container, as a safeguard against leaking liquid. Place the drained and perforated ham in the ziplock bag or noncorrosive container and add the brining solution, making sure the liquid covers as much of the ham as possible. If necessary, weight the ham down with a clean plate. Place it back in the refrigerator and allow it to brine for the next 5 days, turning it once a day. On the sixth day, remove the ham from the brine, rinse it and pat dry with paper towels. Allow it to sit overnight in the refrigerator, uncovered. This allows the surface area of the ham to dry, which ensures it will properly smoke, the next step. You may now smoke the ham at 250°F (hot smoke) until the internal temperature registers 165°F on an instant-read meat thermometer. If you have a home smoker, follow the manufacturer's directions. I use my covered gas grill; combine 2 c. of apple chips with an equivalent amount of water in doubled disposable pie plates. Set the chips aside for ½ hour so that they absorb the water. Place the pan on one side of the grill, over a lighted burner on a low setting. Place the ham on the opposite side, over an unlit burner. Try to maintain the 250°F temperature as consistently as you can during the smoking process. Turn the ham every hour or so; it may take up to an hour per pound to reach the necessary temperature. If you don't wish to attempt smoking it, you may bake the ham in a 300°F oven until it reaches the same temperature. The flavor will be somewhat different if you choose to bake rather than smoke your ham. Serve as is or reheat the ham in a 350°F oven for about 20 minutes per pound. Combine all the glaze ingredients in a small saucepan, heating until everything has melted together. Brush the ham with this mixture during the last hour of baking time.

Apple-glazed Easter ham soon to be enjoyed.

A Little Bit of Lamb

Although cattle may play a dominant role in modern American agriculture, never underestimate the power of the sheep! Sheep have played an integral part in our history as a nation, even including a role in the steps leading to the American Revolution. (By the turn of the eighteenth century, the burgeoning wool trade in what later became the United States so alarmed folks back in England that it was outlawed. Scofflaws risked having their right hands cut off if they were caught trading in wool, which didn't set well at all with the colonists.) Vermont's hilly topography is well suited to raising sheep, and during the mid-nineteenth century, annual sheep drives occurred, with large flocks of them herded en masse to market areas such as Boston.

Sheep may be divided into three categories: meat, milk, and wool producers. Although each is important in its own right, when thoughts of Easter dinner roll around, it's time to contemplate the meat-producing varieties. Because meat of mature sheep, referred to as mutton, tends to have a strong and tallowlike flavor, the sheep meat of choice comes from lambs. For many folks, lamb is the centerpiece of the Passover or Easter table. Whether a leg of lamb sumptuously roasted or more humble ground meat or stew recipes, lamb can claim an important place on your spring table.

Citrus-Marinated Leg of Lamb

This is a little different approach to lamb than many. The meat takes on almost-Oriental overtones, as opposed to the more common rosemary and garlic approach. Allow at least 24 hours for marinating time; 48 will be even better.

4–5 lb. boneless leg of lamb, trimmed of fat
3 T. Dijon mustard
¼ c. soy sauce
¼ t. red pepper flakes
⅓ c. packed brown sugar
¼ c. lemon juice
¼ c. olive oil
½ c. orange juice
1 T. chopped cilantro
2 lg. cloves garlic, peeled and minced
½ c. scallions, white and green parts, minced

Whisk or shake together all the marinade ingredients, which would include everything in this recipe except the lamb itself. Once they are blended smooth, place the lamb in a large plastic ziplock bag or in a nonreactive covered bowl or container just large enough to contain the meat and marinade. Pour the marinade over the lamb, making sure it's covered as evenly as possible. Seal or cover and refrigerate for one or two days, turning the lamb over every 12 hours or so for even marinating. About an hour before you're ready to roast the lamb, remove it from the marinating container, discarding the marinade (it's contaminated with the raw meat juices). Pat the lamb dry with paper towels

Spring lambs enjoying a bite to eat; it doesn't take them long to grow.

and place it on a metal rack in a roasting pan. Allow it to warm almost to room temperature before roasting. Begin the roasting process in a 450°F oven for 20 minutes. Reduce the heat to 325°F and continue roasting the lamb for approximately 25 minutes per pound for medium rare, 30 for medium. A meat thermometer will register between 140–160°F depending on the degree of rareness desired. Remove the lamb from the oven and allow it to rest for about 15 minutes before serving. This amount of lamb should easily serve 8–12 with leftovers.

Lamb Curry

This curry doesn't need to limit itself to lamb; chicken, shrimp, beef, or pork may be utilized, dependent on personal taste and what's in the freezer or refrigerator. Even firm tofu could step in for those of vegetarian persuasion. If using shrimp or tofu, sauté briefly in a little oil and add for the last 5 minutes of cooking time only.

1 lb. good-quality lamb cut in ¾" cubes
1 T. oil
1 lg. onion, chopped: 1 c.
2 lg. cloves garlic, diced
2–3 t. curry powder, or to taste
1 t. salt
1 lg. tomato—peeled, seeded, and chopped
½ c. raisins
½ c. cashew pieces
Hot cooked rice

Heat the oil in a large, heavy skillet. Brown the lamb over medium heat, adding the onions and garlic once it is mostly browned. Continue cooking until the vegetables are tender. Add the curry powder, salt, and 1 cup of water. Bring to a boil, reduce heat, and cook for about 20–25 minutes, until the lamb has become somewhat tender. Add in the tomato, raisins, and cashews and continue cooking until the sauce reaches a good serving consistency, about 10 minutes more. Serve with hot cooked rice to about 4 people.

Bobotie

I believe this dish is South African, although its origins apparently stretch back to Malaysia and Indonesia. It's a kind of a southern hemisphere take on moussaka. Try substituting ground turkey or beef if you wish. Serve it with hot yellow rice (geel rys) and a side of peach or mango chutney for an authentic touch.

1 lb. ground lamb
1 lg. onion, sliced
1 T. butter
2 eggs
1 T. sugar
2 t. curry powder
1 c. milk
1 t. salt
¼ t. pepper
¼ t. turmeric
2 slices bread, torn in pieces (½ c. packed)
1 T. lemon juice
3 bay leaves
¼ c. sliced almonds
¼ c. raisins
½ c. diced apple

In a large skillet, sauté together the butter, thinly sliced onion, and meat until the onion is tender and the meat has lost its pinkness. Mix together 1 egg, ¼ c. of the milk, and the bread crumbs. Add in the fruits, almonds, lemon juice, sugar, curry powder, and salt and pepper. Combine with the meat mixture and turn into an ungreased 8" × 8" baking pan. Cut each bay leaf in half length- wise and press them evenly over the surface of the meat mixture. Bake at 350°F for ½ hour. Meanwhile, beat together the remaining egg, the ¾ c. milk, and the turmeric. Take the meat from the oven, remove the bay leaves, and pour the custard mixture over the top. Bake 15 minutes longer to set custard. Serve hot or slightly cooled; refrigerate leftovers promptly. This makes 4–6 servings.

Geel Rys

Many cultures have variations on rice colored and flavored with turmeric. This South African version includes raisins, cinnamon, and a touch of brown sugar for sweetness. Try it as an accompaniment to chicken as well as with bobotie.

2½ c. chicken broth or water
1 c. uncooked white rice
½ t. turmeric
½ t. cinnamon
1 T. brown sugar
¼ c. raisins
2 T. butter
1 t. salt (only if using water rather than broth)

Melt the butter in a medium saucepan over medium-low heat. Add the rice and cook, stir- ring occasionally, for 2–3 minutes. Add the rest of the ingredients, bring to a boil, and reduce the heat. Simmer the *geel rys*, covered, for about 20 minutes, until the rice is tender and the liquid is absorbed. Fluff the rice before serving.

Shish Kebab

Mention shish kebab and many folks think of lamb. This recipe combines influences from several countries to produce a kebab that's moist and flavorful. Although these flavors meld particularly well with lamb, beef or venison would make nice substitutes. Lean stewing meat works fine in this recipe, as the long marinating period helps tenderize it.

1 to 1½ lb. lamb cut in 1" chunks
⅓ c. plain yogurt
⅓ c. diced onion (1 small)
2 T. lemon juice
¼ c. olive oil, divided
1 t. dried oregano
1 t. salt
1 t. cumin
2 small zucchini, cut into 1" slices
¼ t. each salt and black pepper

Make sure the meat pieces are of a fairly uniform size; I prefer about 1" square. Combine the yogurt, onion, lemon juice, and 2 T. of the olive oil in a nonreactive container. Add the 1 t. salt, oregano, and cumin. Stir in the lamb, coating the pieces thoroughly. Cover and refrigerate at least 24 hours or up to 48. When you're ready to grill, remove the meat from the marinade, wiping off any extra. Thread the chunks on skewers. Broil or grill over medium-hot coals or heat about 5 minutes per side. I find using a wire mesh rack over the regular grill works well for this purpose; be sure to oil it lightly before use. Meanwhile, pare ribbon-thin strips of the zucchini using a vegetable peeler. Combine with the remaining 2 T. olive oil, salt, and pepper in a medium saucepan with a cover. Heat it quickly, stirring, for about 1–2 minutes; turn off the heat, cover tightly, and allow it to cook on retained heat for 2–3 minutes longer. Serve alongside the shish kebabs with pistachio apricot rice for a mellow counterpoint. This serves 4.

Pistachio Apricot Rice

Brown is rice sautéed in butter, parboiled, and finished with orange juice, spice, and condiments. It's a nice accompaniment to chicken or spicy meatballs as well as shish kebabs.

1 c. brown rice
2 c. water
2 T. butter
¼ t. salt
½ c. orange juice
½ t. cinnamon
⅓ c. diced dried apricots
⅓ c. chopped salted pistachios

Melt the butter over medium heat and add the rice, stirring and cooking until it lightens somewhat and just slightly begins to brown. Add the salt and water, cover, bring to a boil, and reduce heat to lowest setting. Simmer the rice until it is tender but still slightly chewy and the water is all absorbed, about 30 minutes. Stir in the orange juice, cinnamon, apricots, and pistachios. Set aside for about 5 minutes for the flavors to blend and orange juice to absorb. This makes about 3½ cups of cooked rice.

Mint Apple Jelly

Mint jelly is a traditional accompaniment to lamb dishes. This is a back-to-basics recipe— easy to make and inexpensive as well. I move a little of my garden mint to an indoor container in late autumn, making a handy source of fresh mint during the winter and early spring.

However, fresh mint is also increasingly available in grocery stores. Because the pectin content is higher in fresh apples, you may have already stored a little premade jelly juice in your freezer for just such an occasion. If starting from scratch, look for the crispest apples you can find. As the pectin is most concentrated in the skin, I strongly recommend using organically grown apples for this. Also avoid wax-coated ones; you don't want those unwanted "extras" in your jelly.

2 c. chopped apples, peel left on
1 c. water
⅔ c. sugar
1 T. lemon juice
¼ c. loosely packed fresh mint leaves

Place the chopped apples and water in a small saucepan. Cover and bring to a boil. Reduce heat and simmer gently about 20 minutes. Remove from heat and strain the mixture through a double layer of cheesecloth. Many jelly recipes recommend not squeezing the cheesecloth in order to keep your jelly clear. I'm not above squeezing a little to get enough juice for my batch of jell; the choice is up to you. You should end up with about ¾ cup of juice. Combine the apple juice, lemon juice, and sugar in a small saucepan. Bring to a boil, skimming off any foam. Add the mint leaves and continue to boil, stirring frequently, for about 5 minutes, until the mixture sheets from a spoon. This simply means that when you slowly pour a little sideways off a metal spoon, it will start to congeal and form a sheet of jelly rather than just dripping. Remove from the heat and pour through a small metal sieve to remove the mint leaves.

This makes just under a cup of mint jelly. If you've used red-skinned apples, the color will be a lovely pale pink. If you prefer green jelly, use yellow- or green-skinned apples and add a drop or two of green food coloring along with the mint leaves.

Mint apple jelly makes a sparkling accompaniment to many lamb dishes.

Parsnips

Although some folks think of parsnips as a fall vegetable, New Englanders in the know leave theirs to winter over in the garden. The cold temperatures bring out sweetness in the parsnips you don't otherwise get to experience. April is a good time to enjoy parsnips; the ground has thawed enough to dig them but not warmed enough for them to try and produce new tops, at which point they won't be palatable anymore.

Browned Parsnips

This dish is similar to glazed carrots but uses less sugar. The natural sweetness of the parsnips combined with the heat of browning results in an almost–caramel-like flavor. Browned parsnips make a nice accompaniment to most meat dishes but are especially nice with pork, ham, rabbit, or poultry.

2 c. peeled, sliced parsnips
2 T. butter
¼ t. salt
¼ t. sugar
⅛ t. pepper

Cook the parsnips in water, covered, for about 5 minutes, until they are barely tender. Drain them well. Melt the butter in a medium, heavy skillet. Add the parsnips, salt, pepper, and sugar and sauté them for an additional 5 minutes, until they turn golden brown. Makes 4 servings.

Parsnip Puree

Sweet springtime parsnips bring out the flavor of this dish. Properly sweet parsnips have nutty overtones almost reminiscent of coconut. Try this puree in place of mashed potatoes for an intriguing alternative.

1 lb. parsnips peeled and chopped (8 small or 4–6 larger)
2 T. cream
2 T. butter
¼ t. salt
⅛ t. pepper
⅛ t. nutmeg

Place the parsnips in a medium-sized saucepan, adding water just to cover them. Bring to a boil and cook, covered, until they are very tender and the water has mostly evaporated, about 15 minutes. Please resist the urge to drown your parsnips in water; as with so many other vegetables, the little extra effort of watching to make sure they don't burn will reward you with a product superior in both taste and nutritive value. Drain any residual water and mash the parsnips very smooth, adding the butter, cream, and seasonings to taste.

Kid-Friendly Shepherd's Pie

If you're all ham and lambed out and just want some simple comfort food, how about a bit of shepherd's pie? Presumably the original did include lamb; otherwise, wouldn't it be rancher's pie? However, most folks think of the version made with good old ground beef. I don't recall my mother making shepherd's pie when I was a kid, so my introduction was the lunchroom version from grade school. As an adult, I preferred to use leftover pot roast for such things. Tender little pieces of flavorful beef and abundant gravy happily welcomed diced-up leftover carrots and the requisite whole kernel corn. Mashed potatoes piled on top browned nicely in the oven, topped with a bit of butter and paprika. It's the only kind of shepherd's pie my kids ever had, at least at home. However, over the years I've become privy to another kind of shepherd's pie, this one made with cream-style corn. It's much tastier than the old-school lunchroom version, flavorful without being overspiced and easy to eat. The trick is dicing your onions and carrots very fine and adding a little extra milk to the potatoes.

¾ lb. lean ground beef
¼ c. diced onion *or* 1 T. instant minced

½ t. salt
¼ t. paprika
¼ t. black pepper
1 can cream style corn
1 lg. or 2 small carrots, diced fine
2 c. diced red-skinned potatoes
2 T. butter
¼ t. salt
¼ c. milk
Parsley flakes (optional)

Place the potatoes, ¼ t. salt, and water just to cover in a small saucepan and bring to a boil. Cook them, covered, until they are tender, about 10 minutes. In a large, heavy skillet, over medium-low heat, cook the ground beef, carrots, and onions, stirring to break the beef up thoroughly, until it looses its color and the vegetables are crisp tender; don't brown them. Add the cream-style corn and about ½ c. of the potato-cooking water and allow it to simmer while mashing the potatoes. Drain any extra water from them and add the butter and milk. Mash or whip until they are smooth, adding a little extra milk if needed, and additional salt and pepper to taste. Pour the beef mixture into a medium-small casserole dish or glass pie plate. Top with the mashed potatoes and sprinkle with parsley, if desired. Bake in a 400°F oven until everything is piping hot, which won't take long at all. This serves 4 nicely.

Angel Food Cake

If you've never had homemade angel cake, you don't know what you're missing; it truly is a heavenly treat when properly prepared. Much as I love it, over the years it's also proved rather finicky to perfect, my numerous attempts somewhat resembling the triumphs and tragedies of an ancient Greek drama. As with so many from-scratch baked goods, it's not that difficult to make but does require strict attention to technique in order to produce the desired results. In this instance, the volume of the egg whites is what will make or break your finished product. Making sure they are totally free from any trace of the yolks or any other source of fat, even a smidge of it in the mixing bowl, is essential, as is a prolonged and vigorous whipping period; plan on at least 10–15 minutes using a powerful large mixer. Being careful to bake until the cake is entirely cooked through will ensure a light, high product rather than a sorrowfully crumpled one. Angel food is one of the best-keeping cakes; it actually improves if left overnight before slicing. If not used within the week (or perhaps a bit sooner if the weather is very hot and humid), you may wish to double-wrap individual slices, label, and freeze to eat within a month.

1 ⅔ c. egg whites: about 11–12 extra large
½ t. salt
1½ t. cream of tartar
½ t. almond extract
2 t. vanilla
1¼ c. granulated sugar
1¼ c. confectioner's sugar
1 c. sifted cake flour

Combine the egg whites, salt, cream of tartar, and flavorings in a large mixing bowl. Beat with the whisk attachment until soft peaks begin to form. Very gradually add the granulated sugar to the still-beating egg whites; this will probably take about 2–3 minutes. Continue beating; the egg whites should be very stiff and glossy by the time you are done. Depending on the mixer size and strength, the total whipping process will probably take around 10–15 minutes. You don't need to hover near the mixer the entire time; just make sure this step is completed adequately before moving on! Sift together the flour and confectioner's sugar, either using a sifter or a wire mesh strainer. Unless you have an extra-large mixer bowl, carefully pour the egg whites into the largest mixing or salad bowl you have and sprinkle the flour mixture over them. Working quickly, lightly, but thoroughly, use a large wooden spoon or scraper to fold the egg white mixture over and under until it is all incorporated—about 20–25 strokes. Lightly spoon the batter into an ungreased tube pan, gently smoothing out the top if need be. Bake in a preheated 375°F oven for about 30–35 minutes, until the top is puffy, golden, and cracked, and feels dry to touch. It occasionally may not develop cracks but hopefully will not appear concave. If it does, that's simply an indication that the egg white deflated a bit too much. Don't despair, the cake will still be tasty, and imperfections can always be covered with judicious applications of whipped cream or other such toppings. Be sure not to underbake, or the cake may fall. Invert the pan over a bottle neck or other such thing to cool *completely* before removing the cake; a too-warm angel cake may also collapse. This easily serves 12–16.

Angel food cake is a heavenly treat whether served plain or fancy.

Daffodil Cake

As the title suggests, this light and airy two-toned cake is reminiscent of the yellow and white colors of a daffodil. It's somewhat of a hybrid—part angel food cake and part sponge cake. The fresh lemon flavor meshes well with Easter meals and other such pursuits of spring.

1¾ c. sugar, divided
1¼ c. cake flour
1¾ c. egg whites (12–13)
1½ t. cream of tartar
¼ t. salt
1½ t. vanilla
5 egg yolks
1 T. lemon juice
2 T. flour
2 T. sugar
2 t. grated lemon rind

Sift together or stir well the cake flour and ¾ c. of the sugar with a wire whisk. In a large mixing bowl, combine the egg whites, salt, cream of tartar, and vanilla. Beat until frothy. At high speed, gradually beat in the remaining 1 c. of sugar, beating at high speed until the mixture is stiff and glossy. This may take awhile; don't underbeat! Gently fold in the flour/sugar mixture. In a medium bowl, combine the 2 T. each of flour and sugar, the lemon juice, lemon rind, and egg yolks. Beat at high speed until thick and lemon colored, about 2–3 minutes. Note that you can use the same beaters for the yolks as for the whites without rinsing, but never try beating egg whites with beaters that already have yolks on them; they won't whip properly. Carefully fold ⅓

of the egg white mixture into the beaten yolks. Alternately drop spoonfuls of the two batters in an ungreased 10" tube pan. Swirl lightly with a long, thin knife. Bake on the lower rack in a preheated 350°F oven for 30–35 minutes, until the top is cracked and dry appearing and the color golden. Cool thoroughly in the pan upside down. A glass wine or soda bottle with a thin neck works well to center the funnel on while cooling. Run a thin knife around the inner and outer edges of the cake pan to help in removal. This is good with a lemon or vanilla glaze, a fluffy white frosting, or whipped cream.

Lemon Meringue Pie

Lemon meringue is a classic beauty of a pie. The curd filling for this version is lighter than some, with a nice, fresh lemon flavor. Be sure to bake the meringue sufficiently to cook the whites; it will give you a safer and, in my opinion, superior product—nice golden brown swirls disclosing creamy white meringue within. Promptly refrigerate leftovers, if you have any. Lemon meringue pie is best eaten within a day or two of when it's been made.

1¼ c. sugar
1¾ c. water
2 T. flour
3 T. cornstarch
2 egg yolks
2 T. butter
¼ c. lemon juice
2 t. grated lemon rind *or* ½ t. pure lemon extract
9" baked pastry shell
4 egg whites

½ c. sugar
2 t. lemon juice
¼ t. salt

Combine sugar, flour, and cornstarch in a medium saucepan. Whisk in the water and cook over medium-low heat, stirring frequently, until it bubbles and becomes very thick. Whisk a little of the hot mixture into the combined egg yolks and lemon juice. Return all to the pan along with the lemon rind or extract, coking for just a minute. Remove from the heat and stir in the butter until melted. Pour into the baked pastry shell and immediately prepare the meringue topping. Beat together the egg whites, lemon juice, and salt, gradually adding the ½ c. of sugar. Beat until glossy peaks form. Pile over the warm filling, covering the surface entirely and swirling it into peaks. Bake in a preheated 350°F oven for about 15 minutes, until it is nicely browned. I prefer a moderate oven temperature for the browning process so that the meringue cooks all the way through. Allow the pie to cool in the oven with the door slightly ajar until the oven is cool. This helps prevent the meringue from "weeping," or forming droplets of moisture on the surface. Finish chilling in the refrigerator; serve when thoroughly cold. Refrigerate leftovers and eat within 2–3 days. This serves around 8, depending on how hungry for pie they might be.

Banana Cream Pie

I consider banana cream to be the "companion" pie to lemon meringue because it lets you use up those two extra egg yolks. This is my husband Bruce's birthday treat; he prefers it to cake, and I've made him one for his birthday every year since we've been married. At this point, that amounts to quite a few banana cream pies!

3 c. milk
¾ c. sugar
6 T. cornstarch
3 T. butter
2 egg yolks
1 t. vanilla
¼ t. almond extract
2 large bananas
9" baked pie shell
1 T. rum *and/or* banana liquor (optional)
1¼ c. heavy cream
½ c. confectioner's sugar
1 t. vanilla

Melt the butter in a large, heavy saucepan. Whisk in the cornstarch and sugar and then whisk in the milk. Cook over medium heat, stirring frequently to prevent sticking or burning, until the mixture bubbles and thickens. Beat the egg yolks in a small bowl, whisk a little of the hot mixture into them and quickly return all to the hot filling, whisking constantly to blend and cook evenly. Once the mixture has just returned to a boil, remove from the heat and stir in the flavorings. Allow to cool at room temperature for about ½ hour, until warm but still able to pour. If you wish to place a piece of waxed paper over the surface while it cools, it will prevent a skin from forming, although you'll also lose a bit of your pie filling on the waxed paper. Place ½ the filling into the baked pie shell, slice the bananas evenly over the surface and top with the remaining filling, covering the bananas completely so they don't discolor. Chill in the refrigerator at least 2 hours, until completely cool. Whip the cream with the confectioner's sugar and vanilla until it forms fairly stiff peaks; just remember not to beat too much or you'll end up with sweetened butter! Swirl the whipped cream over the pie, garnish as desired, and serve. This serves 8 generously.

For It Is the Month of May—Oh, It Is the Month of May!

THE WORDS OF this old English folk song couldn't have put it better—what a wonderful month May is. Last winter's snow has finally lost its battle with the green grass springing up in every direction, and the air carries a sweet scent of apple blossoms and sun-warmed earth. May sunshine is pleasant but not too hot, just right for doing some spring yard work, and chances are, the garden has finally dried out enough for tilling and early plantings. May is also when perennial crops such as rhubarb and asparagus again begin to sprout and grow. In the countryside, it's a time to start foraging for delicacies such as fiddlehead ferns and wild violets. I can't get enough of May—brooks flowing cold and clear, emerald green grass playing counterpoint to the chartreuse of newly leaved trees.

My farmer neighbors are out plowing and planting the moist brown earth. They're also busy enriching it by spreading multiple batches of what my 4-H gardening record sheet referred to as "loads barnyard" (as opposed to "pounds commercial" . . . far tamer stuff). Good for the barnyard, good for the ground . . .

May is a time of rebirth as well. Spring lambs, calves, piglets, and kids have arrived; chicks are hatched; and in the spring twilight, an occasional early fawn makes an appearance. Birdsong is with us morning, noon, and night, as our small winged friends go about producing families as well. It's time to get organized about what will be planted when in this year's garden and to set out seedlings to toughen up a bit before transplanting them. There may not be a lot of fruits and vegetables to harvest yet, but the ones there are taste all the better for the effort. By the time the lilacs are in fragrant lavender bloom around Memorial Day, chances are there will be peas, lettuce, and spinach punctuating the garden with green. Perhaps a few fat brook trout will even have found their way to the dining room table.

May

Baking Powder Biscuits

My mother occasionally used to serve biscuits with maple syrup for breakfast. She made "drop" biscuits, mounding spoonfuls of soft dough onto the baking sheet rather than kneading and cutting out first. I prefer that approach for scones; when I'm making biscuits, the extra step of patting and cutting makes flaky little squares or rounds, just right for pulling apart to slather with butter, jam, or honey. These biscuits also taste fine with fresh rhubarb sauce or with some of the chicken recipes to follow.

2 c. flour
6 T. cold butter
1 t. salt
2 t. sugar
4 t. baking powder
¾–1 c. milk

Combine the flour, sugar, salt, and baking powder in a medium mixing bowl. Cut in the butter using a pastry cutter or two knives until the mix resembles coarse crumbs about the size of peas. Stir in the milk; the greater amount will produce a more tender biscuit, but also softer dough. Turn out onto a lightly floured clean surface and knead gently, turning the dough over and under, about a dozen times, sprinkling on flour as necessary.

Pat the dough about ½" thick and either cut out with a round floured cutter, the floured top of a thin-rimmed glass, or simply cut into squares. You can gently combine and pat out scraps to make more biscuits. If you cut the dough into squares, you'll waste no dough, but be aware that the uncut sides won't rise in the same manner as the cut ones do. Place the biscuits a couple inches apart on ungreased baking sheets. Alternately, simply drop spoonfuls of the soft dough directly onto the baking sheets, although in this case you'll probably want to grease the sheet lightly first. Bake on an upper rack in a 375°F oven for about 10–15 minutes, depending on biscuit size. When they are done, they will be puffed and golden brown. This makes approximately 6 large biscuits or 8–10 smaller ones.

Naan (Indian Flat Bread)

The proportions of this recipe will make 4 good-sized pieces of flat bread or 6 smaller. Once the dough has risen, preheat two cookie sheets for about 5 minutes at 425°F before dividing the dough evenly between them. Naan makes nice breakfast bread, or you could enjoy it with the coconut cashew chicken you'll find later in this chapter.

½ t. salt
½ t. sugar
2 t. yeast (or use 1 individual packet)
½ c. hot water
2 T. oil
2 T. melted butter*
1 c. flour, plus more for shaping

Combine the water, sugar, and salt in a medium mixing bowl. Once it is lukewarm, dissolve the yeast in the water. Add the oil and then stir in the flour. Allow the dough to rise in a warm place, covered, for about ½ hour. I leave it right in the mixing bowl for this. Once the oven and pans have preheated to 425°F, divide the dough into four or six pieces. Dip the dough lightly in flour only so it won't stick to your fingers and gently shape and pull it as thin as possible. Traditional naan shape is an elongated oval, almost like a teardrop. Spray the pans lightly with nonstick spray or use a paper towel to quickly apply a thin coating of oil (I don't recommend doing this in advance, as the heat will make the oil smoke). Quickly place the breads on the hot sheets, pulling their edges out a little more if needed. Bake on an upper rack for about 10 minutes, until puffed and browned on the bottom. Brush generously with the melted butter and serve at once.

*Ghee, or clarified butter, is the traditional accompaniment for naan. If you prefer to use ghee, melt about double the amount of butter to just under browning, allow it to cool slightly, and skim or pour the clarified liquid from the top, leaving the solids in the pan.

Pie Plant

Spring gardens in Vermont eagerly await the reappearance of that old-fashioned favorite, rhubarb. Sprouting up from the ground, slender red stalks unfurl large, spreading triangular leaves of dark green. Pie plant has returned! Rhubarb is technically not a fruit; it is a member of the Asian buckwheat family. Although the leaves are inedible, the tart, fibrous stems with a texture resembling a softer version of celery and with a flavor all their own are ready and waiting to be incorporated into sauce, pies, and puddings. As soon as strawberries come into season, even greater delights await, as the pair combine to produce flavorful desserts. Once your rhubarb has sprouted, you know spring is here to stay.

Rhubarb Sauce

My mother used to like a bowl of this topped with "pour" cream along with toast or biscuits for her spring breakfast. Rhubarb sauce also makes a very tasty parfait; just layer the cooled sauce with vanilla yogurt. Make some extra while you're at it to use in spring surprise pudding.

    4 c. rhubarb, in 1" pieces
    1–1½ c. water
    1–1½ c. sugar, or to taste

Combine the rhubarb and water in a medium saucepan. Bring to a boil over high heat, lower to medium, and continue cooking until the rhubarb is tender. Stir in the sugar, cooking a bit longer, until the sauce is the consistency you'd like it. Remove from the heat and serve either warm or chilled. It will thicken just slightly on standing, although not to anywhere near the degree some other fruit sauces will.

Spring Surprise Pudding

Surprise! Just when you think you're cutting into an orange cake, a layer of rosy rhubarb sauce peeks out to greet you. This pudding cake–type dessert is tasty as is, even better with a bit of whipped cream or vanilla ice cream. Some folks might even have a bit for breakfast—there's just no accounting.

2 c. (hot) rhubarb sauce

Cake Batter

1 c. flour
1 t. baking powder
¼ c. butter
¾ c. sugar
1 t. grated orange rind
½ t. vanilla
1 egg
¾ c. milk

Preheat oven to 350°F. Cream together the sugar, butter vanilla, and orange rind. Beat in the flour and baking powder alternately with the milk. Lastly, beat in the egg. Pour the batter into a buttered 8" or 9" pan. Evenly pour the bubbling hot rhubarb sauce over the batter and immediately place in the preheated oven. Bake for about 35–40 minutes, until the cake top is baked through. Serve warm or cold. This will make about 6 servings.

Rhubarb Custard Pie

Because rhubarb is so tart, it requires more sugar than many fruits. The custard filling in this pie helps to mellow out some of that tartness. Be sure to refrigerate leftovers. Rhubarb custard pie is a perfect example of what my late father would have called a "rich and delicious" dessert.

2 c. diced rhubarb
1 c. sugar
2 T. flour
1 c. light cream
2 eggs, beaten
1 t. vanilla
½ t. nutmeg
9" unbaked pie shell

Beat together the eggs, sugar, flour, cream, vanilla, and nutmeg. Stir in the rhubarb and pour into your unbaked pie shell. Bake at 425°F for 10 minutes, reduce heat to 350°F, and continue baking until the filling is slightly puffed and mostly firm, jiggling slightly when the pan is wiggled, about 45–50 minutes longer. Cool before slicing.

Sweet custard gives rhubarb custard pie a velvety texture and luxurious taste.

Strawberry Rhubarb Pie

As the first strawberries appear, this pie follows close behind. It's a particularly good way to utilize some berries that might not be quite as sweet and juicy as you'd prefer for shortcakes or for topping ice cream. Speaking of which, this pie tastes mighty fine with a scoop or two of vanilla to keep it company.

2 c. sliced strawberries
2 c. diced rhubarb
4 T. cornstarch
1½ c. sugar
¼ t. salt
1 t. grated orange rind
Unbaked pastry for 2 crust pie

Combine all the filling ingredients in a large bowl, mixing to coat well. Roll and fit the lower crust into a 9" pie plate. Pour in the filling. Smooth a little water or milk around the rim of the lower crust to help it adhere to the top crust. Cover with the rolled top crust, trimming excess and folding the edge of the upper crust over the lower crust to seal. Crimp the edges, prick or cut slits into the top crust, and brush the surface with milk or cream. Sprinkle lightly with sugar. Bake in a 425°F oven for 10 minutes, reduce heat to 350°F, and continue baking for another 35–40 minutes, until the crust is nicely browned and the filling just starts bubbling in the center. Cool before cutting for best results, although it is yummy warm also.

Fiddlehead Ferns

Fiddlehead ferns are a springtime treat from the northern woods. Their flavor resembles asparagus with a hint of spinach thrown in on the side. Although ferns, in general, resemble small fiddleheads when they're first unfurling, only the ostrich fern produces the delectable edible variety. Thanks to an excellent website from the University of Maine, I finally became confident enough in my foraging abilities to head into the small stretch of woods and stream at the end of our garden and gather my own. Look for smooth green stems, flat or curved in on the inner side, with tightly rolled fronds of bright green and no spores apparent. Ostrich ferns do not have any white fuzz on them, although there is a thin brown tissue paper–like covering partially over each fiddle head. Please do some research and make absolutely sure you're gathering the real thing if you choose to forage for your own fiddlehead ferns; other varieties can make you ill. In our area, fiddleheads are occasionally available for purchase through local stores and restaurants. You may even be able to order them in a canned form. If growing conditions are right in your area, you can also order your own ostrich ferns to plant and enjoy both for their spring fiddleheads and for their large decorative fronds when mature.

Fiddlehead ferns exhibit unique characteristics. Be sure to identify them correctly before harvesting; many ferns are inedible. Always leave some ferns in each clump to mature.

Fresh-Cooked Fiddleheads

Many sources recommend cooking your fiddleheads thoroughly, as there have been some documented cases of illness following ingestion of undercooked fiddleheads. Some even suggest changing the water once during the cooking process; I'll leave that to your individual judgment. To prepare for cooking, rub the brown tissuelike husks from each coiled fern head. If the heads appear at all dirty, wash them well. Place them in a pan with water to cover and boil them for 10 minutes, drain,* and serve with butter and a splash of vinegar or lemon juice. If you plan to integrate the fiddleheads into another dish, such as a stir-fry, boil for only 7–8 minutes, drain,* and add them in about 5 minutes before serving.

*You need to discard the cooking liquid, rather than using as a soup or gravy base. There may be toxins in it which you won't wish to ingest.

Cream of Spring Soup

The best soup I have ever had the pleasure to enjoy was served one Mother's Day at the New England House restaurant in West Brattleboro. Although I don't know what was used in that recipe, I do know it was concocted from wild ramps, which are members of the allium family (onions, garlic, and such), and fiddlehead ferns. If you don't have access to either, a very respectable version can be made by substituting asparagus for the fiddleheads and scallions plus a bit of garlic for the ramp.

2 c. fiddlehead ferns or chopped asparagus
1 bunch scallions
1 clove garlic, minced
2 T. butter
½ t. salt
1½ c. milk
½ c. cream
Pinch of white pepper
Pinch of nutmeg

Place the cleaned fiddleheads in a small sauce pan, adding about 1 cup of water. Bring them to a boil and cook for 8 minutes; drain well. If using asparagus, cook as above, reducing the time to 5 minutes. Meanwhile, melt the butter in a medium saucepan. Add the scallions and garlic and cook over low heat for about 5 minutes, until they are wilted but not brown. Add in the fiddleheads or asparagus, the salt, pepper, nutmeg, and the milk and cream. Although the cream adds a lovely richness, feel free to substitute milk for any or all of it if you're watching your intake of such things. Simmer the soup over medium-low heat for another 5–10 minutes, until the flavors are well blended and the vegetables thoroughly cooked. This will serve 3–4.

Cream of spring soup adds a mellow touch to May.

Roasted Asparagus

The fiddlehead's domestic counterpart asparagus will be making its appearance now as well, although its season generally extends longer than the elusive ferns. With a little judicious harvesting, you should be able to enjoy stalks from a well-established asparagus bed through early to midsummer. Fresh asparagus takes on a whole new flavor when it's roasted rather than steamed. A little olive and some salt and pepper are all it takes to produce a delicious side dish. It may be served hot as is or can also be chilled and marinated in vinaigrette, a great take-along dish for a fancy spring picnic.

Fresh asparagus stalks
2–3 T. olive oil per pound of asparagus
Fresh ground salt
Fresh ground pepper

Snap and discard the tough ends from the asparagus by bending lightly at the lower end of each stem; the stalk will snap where the more tender part begins. Place the asparagus on a foil-lined baking sheet (for easier cleanup) and drizzle with the olive oil, shaking the pan to coat the stalks evenly. Sprinkle with salt and pepper and place on the upper rack in a preheated 350–400°F oven for about 25 minutes, stirring once or twice. When done, the asparagus should be bright green and slightly limp. If you prefer a light browning of your roasted asparagus, use the higher temperature, leaving it until it's as golden as you wish. A pound of asparagus should serve 4 people.

Wild Spring Greens

My late mother-in-law, Lucretia Lawrence, took full advantage of the first wild greens of spring. With nine hungry children to feed, it's no wonder she relied on Mother Nature to help out with such things. You don't want to wander on some pesticide-enhanced lawn looking for dandelion or milkweed greens; make sure what you gather has grown in a healthy environment. The trick is to pick while the plants are still very young; older dandelions especially turn bitter very quickly. Pluck the young leaves before any flower buds have formed and wash them well. Milkweeds have a milder flavor, but please-oh-please make sure you know what you're picking before you pick it! The last thing you need is an upset stomach from uninformed choices. Violets serve two purposes: the leaves may be cooked and eaten like spinach, and the blossoms may be candied or even used to make a delicately flavored jelly. If you're not able to find wild greens, simply substitute an equal amount of spinach.

10–12 oz. spring greens, about 6–8 loosely packed c.
    1½ T. butter
    or 1 T. olive oil
    or 2 slices bacon, diced
    1 T. cider vinegar
    ¼ t. salt
    Pinch of pepper

Wash the greens extremely well to remove any residual dirt, trim any tough ends, and chop into manageable pieces. Cook the greens in just-enough water to cover the bottom of your cooking pan; they should be tender enough within about 5 minutes from when the water begins to boil. The advantage to cooking greens in small amounts of water is more flavorful and nutritious food; the disadvantage is the possibility of your greens burning if the water cooks down too soon, so be vigilant. If there is any extra cooking liquid, drain it off lightly. While the greens are cooking, brown the diced bacon in a heavy skillet over medium-low heat; set aside. Add the butter, oil, or cooked bacon and the bacon fat. Next, stir in the vinegar, salt, and pepper and allow the greens to continue cooking, uncovered, for a minute or two longer to evaporate any excess liquid. This serves 4 or so.

Spinach Salad

Spring garden greens are now ripening as well. Spinach is one of the earliest, and you'll do well to plant it as early as you can. Even though more resilient varieties are produced every year, spinach is still a plant that loves cool temperatures and tends to bolt (go to seed) when the days become too warm. Although it's delicious steamed or sautéed, spinach also tastes great raw in salads.

10 oz. spinach—washed, drained, and torn into bite-sized pieces (about 6 c.)
    4 slices bacon, cooked crisp
    1 sm. red onion, sliced thin
    2 T. honey
    1 T. cider vinegar
    ¼ c. mayonnaise

Fry the bacon, reserving 2 T. of the bacon fat. Lightly sauté the onion in the fat until it's just wilted but not browned. Mix together the mayonnaise, honey, vinegar, and the onions. Pour over the spinach and toss lightly. Crumble the bacon over the top and serve immediately. This serves 6 as a side dish, or for smaller appetites. To serve 4 as a main course, add 4 sliced hard-cooked eggs and any combination of red bell pepper strips, croutons, Swiss cheese cubes, seedless grapes, or mandarin orange sections.

Creamed Spinach

Spinach prepared in this manner can be served as a side dish or as an accompaniment to fried polenta. If you don't have your own spinach, you may purchase a 10 oz. package of fresh spinach. Off-season, substitute 1 10-oz. box of frozen chopped spinach if you wish; just thaw it first.

10 oz. spinach, washed and coarsely chopped (6 c.)
    1 sm. clove garlic, crushed or minced
    ½ t. salt
    ⅛ t. pepper
    ¼ t. nutmeg
    2 T. olive oil
    ⅔ c. cream
    4 oz. cream cheese
    2 T. Parmesan cheese

Warm the olive oil in a large, heavy skillet over medium heat. Add the spinach and garlic and sauté until the spinach is wilted and dark green in appearance. Add the cream, pepper, and nutmeg and cook, stirring occasionally, until the mixture becomes slightly thickened. Stir in the cream cheese and Parmesan cheese and remove from the heat. Serve as is or use as below.

Fried Polenta with Creamed Spinach

Prepare the polenta well in advance, browning it in the butter as you cook the creamed spinach. If you prefer, use the butter-browned pieces as a side dish for breakfast or supper topped with maple syrup, accompanied with bacon, sausage, and/or eggs; or enjoy it as an accompaniment to fried brook trout.

1 c. yellow cornmeal
3½ c. water
1 t. salt
2 T. butter, divided

Bring the water and salt to boiling in a large saucepan. Whisking constantly, add the cornmeal and bring back to a boil. Lower the heat so that the mixture maintains a gentle boil and continue to cook, whisking frequently, until the mixture has cooked for 15 minutes. Remove from the heat, whisk in 1 T. of the butter, and pour into a buttered 9" square pan. Cool to room temperature and then chill thoroughly, at least 2 hours or overnight. Cut into 8 pieces for easier handling. Melt the remaining 1 T. of butter in a large, heavy frying pan or skillet over medium-high heat. Fit the polenta slices in, and sauté on both sides until light golden brown. Serve topped with the creamed spinach. This amount of polenta will serve 4.

Mediterranean Spinach Turnovers

These savory pastries were one of my specialties when I vended at the Brattleboro Farmers' Market back in the 1980s. At the time I only made about 2 or 3 dozen per market, although years later I turned out 300 miniturnovers for hors d'oeuvres at Tim and Abbey's wedding. Lucky thing for me (and you too!) that the unbaked pastries freeze beautifully, saving on time and trouble. Although premade puff pastry is available commercially, I always use homemade for these and any other turnovers I make; once you get used to the "real thing," you just don't want to settle for anything else.

1 lb. spinach—cooked, drained, and chopped
1 cup ricotta cheese
8 oz. mozzarella cheese cut in small cubes
2 cloves garlic, chopped
¼ c. chopped onion
2 T. olive oil
¼ t. white pepper
¼ t. fresh grated nutmeg
½ t. dill weed
½ t. oregano
1 T. flour
½ t. salt, or to taste
Puff pastry dough, homemade or purchased frozen, thawed

Combine the spinach, olive oil, flour, and seasonings in medium saucepan and cook them over medium heat for a minute or two. Remove from the heat, add the cheeses, and cool to room temperature or chill for future use. Roll out the puff pastry thin and cut it in 3" × 3" squares. Place a spoonful of spinach mixture in center of each. Fold into a triangle or rectangle using milk and pinching with fingers to seal edges. Bake on upper rack in 425°F oven until puffed and brown, about 15–25 minutes. Cool them on paper towels and serve warm or cold. Be sure to refrigerate any leftovers. This amount of filling will yield quite a few turnovers, although the quantity may vary somewhat depending on the size you make them.

Stromboli

Stromboli, which is essentially a variation on a pizza roll, is another great way to use a bit of spinach. Fillings may vary according to preference, although I like to integrate vegetables, cheese, and meat altogether in mine. If you don't wish to take the time to prepare your own bread dough, a loaf-sized refrigerated ready-to-bake French bread dough may be substituted; simply unroll and flatten it evenly.

1 recipe rustic bread dough
1 recipe pizza sauce (both in "August")
4 oz. thinly sliced mozzarella cheese
4 oz. thinly sliced provolone cheese
7–8 oz. fresh spinach
1 clove garlic, minced
1 T. minced onion
4 oz. thinly sliced ham
4 oz thinly sliced salami
2 T. olive oil
Coarsely ground black pepper
Coarsely ground salt
¼ c. grated Parmesan
Sesame and/or poppy seeds, optional

Prepare the rustic bread dough as instructed, omitting the salt glaze. Allow it to rise for 1 hour. Heat the olive oil in a large, heavy skillet, adding the garlic/onion and sautéing them for just a minute or two. Stir in the spinach, a sprinkle each of salt and pepper, and 2 T. water; heat and stir the spinach until it's just wilted. Set it aside to cool slightly; the water should have evaporated during the cooking process. Place the bread dough on a large oiled baking sheet and pat it out into a thin rectangle as close to the dimensions of the baking sheet as you can. Layer one cheese, one meat, the spinach, the other meat, and other cheese lengthways along one edge, leaving about an inch at each end and along the outer edge. Starting with the filled end, roll the Stromboli up as tightly as you can without causing the filling to leak out. Seal the edges and place seam-side down. Cut 4–5 short diagonal slashes across the top of the loaf. If desired, sprinkle the top with any combination of the Parmesan cheese, seeds, and/or salt and pepper. Bake on the upper shelf in a 375°F oven for about 35–40 minutes, until the loaf is nicely browned and sounds hollow when tapped. Serve the Stromboli warm with the pizza sauce. Refrigerate any leftovers.

Stromboli, hot from the oven, tastes even better with a bit of homemade marinara sauce ("August").

Fried Brook Trout

These shiny little fish are elusive lovers of cold water and quiet pools. Any quick movement will send them racing under sheltering brook banks and tree roots. If you're lucky enough to catch some, try them the way sons Tim and Greg used to enjoy them—dipped in seasoned flour and fried in butter. Tim especially became quite an epicurean over the years, savoring his annual catch with all due respect. The following amounts are open to adjustment, depending on the size of your trout.

Per Trout

    2 T. flour
    ¼ t. salt
    Pinch of paprika
    Pinch of pepper
    1–2 t. butter
    Lemon wedges, if desired

Clean and gut the trout, removing the head and intestines and rinsing it well to remove any residual blood. Combine the flour and seasonings in a small dish. Dip the trout, covering it evenly on all sides. Heat the butter in a small, heavy frying pan or skillet until it begins to bubble. Add the trout, cooking over medium heat for 2–3 minutes. Flip it over and cook on the other side for another 2–3 minutes. The tail will probably curl up during this process—just a normal reaction, as the thinner portion of the trout always cooks faster. You'll know your trout is done when it's a delicate brown and the flesh flakes easily when poked with a fork. Serve immediately with lemon wedges, if you wish. If cooking more than one trout, simply adjust the ingredient amounts up accordingly.

Everyone has his or her favorite fishing hole. If you look closely in the near left of the pool, you'll see a little ring in the water—a good indication a hungry fish is after an insect on the surface.

Spring Chickens

The chicken we love to eat roasted or fried traces its origins to the jungles of Southeast Asia. Domesticated there for centuries, the great-grandparents of our modern-day hens and roosters eventually found their way both east and west, becoming a delicacy in Europe by the Middle Ages. Early in the seventeenth century, chickens journeyed to the New World, where their Native American counterpart, the turkey, awaited them. Having wended our way through April's eggs, it seems only fair to now give equal attention to the proverbial spring chicken and to explore some of the many ways it delights our palates.

Country-Fried Chicken

Fried chicken must be one of America's top ten favorite dishes. There are probably as many ways to fry it as there are people willing to do so. Over the years, I've discovered the key to crispy brown fried chicken is low and slow cooking. I swear by my cast-iron cookware for frying chicken, just as I do for so many other purposes. The cast-iron conducts the heat more evenly, and once it's reached optimal frying temperature, it holds it longer than a lighter material might. I actually prefer dark-meat chicken for frying; it retains moistness better and is more flavorful than white. Cook up some pan gravy while you're at it to spoon over homemade mashed potatoes and maybe a biscuit or two.

½ c. flour
1 t. salt

1 t. paprika
2 t. parsley flakes, crumbled
¼ t. pepper
¼ t. garlic powder
4 chicken thighs
4 chicken drumsticks
Approximately ½ c. corn oil

Preheat the corn oil in a large cast-iron skillet over medium to medium-low heat. Rinse the chicken parts in cool water, leaving the skins damp. Combine the flour, salt, paprika, pepper, and garlic powder in a bowl or plastic bag. Dredge each chicken piece to coat thoroughly, starting with the thighs. Place the chicken pieces, skin-side down, into the hot fat, leaving a little space around each. Cover the pan and allow the chicken to cook for about 15 minutes, until it's nicely browned on one side. Turn each piece, cover, and continue cooking another 10 minutes, or until the other side is browned as well. Leave the pan uncovered and continue to cook the chicken for another 5–10 minutes, turning once, to crisp the skin. Remove to a hot serving plate. Drain all but about 2 T. of fat from the pan, leaving in the crispy bits from frying. Sprinkle on 2 T. of the remaining flour mixture, supplementing if necessary with plain flour. Discard any leftover dredging flour, as contact with the raw chicken may have contaminated it for further use. Allow the flour to brown slightly, stirring up the brown bits of goodness from the bottom of the pan. Now add 2 cups of chicken broth or vegetable cooking water, or a combination. You may use plain water in a pinch, although your gravy won't be quite as tasty. Season to taste with salt and pepper, but taste first; you may find the flavor's fine just the way it is.

Bread Stuffing

This is essentially the same stuffing as I use for turkey, just in a smaller quantity. I would divide the ingredients for the turkey in half or even thirds, depending on the size of your chicken. Although I find the poultry seasoning in the little yellow box to be tasty and handy, I've included a poultry seasoning blend recipe in case you'd prefer to make your own.

3–4 T. butter
⅓ c. diced onion
1 stalk celery, diced
6–8 slices toasted bread, torn in small pieces
2–3 t. poultry seasoning*
½–¾ c. water, more or less

Melt the butter in a medium saucepan. Sauté the onion and celery in the butter over medium-low heat until the mixture becomes somewhat tender but not browned. Stir in the bread and the poultry seasoning. Add enough water to moisten the dry ingredients to taste; some folks prefer a very moist stuffing, while others like it slightly dry. It will take a minute or two for the water to fully incorporate, so you may wish to add any extra cautiously. Stuff the chicken lightly; I've found I can push the stuffing in fairly firmly, but don't try to pack it too hard or it may "explode" during cooking time. Roast your chicken per instructions above.

*Commercial and homemade poultry stuffing may vary somewhat in pungency; I recommend using a lesser amount initially, tasting and adding more to your preference.

Poultry Seasoning Blend

I grew up with the poultry seasoning from the little yellow box and am still quite contented to use that much of the time. However, especially if you grow your own herbs, you may prefer to blend your own to order. This recipe does use dried herbs, as fresh dry at different rates and might end up spoiling if stored while there's still some water content in any of the individual components. (Hang your bunches of herbs by their stems, leafy parts down, until dry and crisp and then crumble the leaves and store for individual use.) Store extra seasoning in a small glass jar with a tight cork or in a ziplock bag in the fridge (the plastic may allow the essential flavor of the herbs to leach out somewhat).

1 T. oregano
1 T. marjoram
1 T. thyme
1 T. sage
1 T. parsley
2 t. rosemary
1 t. black pepper
1 t. ginger
½ t. celery seed

Combine all the seasonings together in a small bowl, crumbling them together well and stirring up lightly. Add 1–2 T. to chicken stuffing, 2–4 to turkey. Start with the lesser amounts, adding more to taste as you go along. This makes about ⅓ cup of poultry seasoning, although the amounts are easily increased proportionately.

Roast Chicken

Whole chickens for sale were much more plentiful when I was growing up. They could be divided into three main categories: roasters, broiler/fryers, and stewing chickens. There was also the occasional capon, essentially a castrated rooster, which along with the stewing hens is a rare find anymore. The two you're most apt to come in contact with now would be broiler/fryers and roasting chickens. Both are very young birds, although the broiler/fryers, coming in at around 1½–3½ lb., are lighter birds than the 3–5 lb. roasters. If you cut up your own frying chickens, hang on to any extra pieces, such as the bony back sections and wing tips. Bag, freeze, and label them; once enough have accumulated, you can cook up a delicious pot of homemade chicken soup or stock to flavor your other chicken dishes.

3–5 lb. roasting chicken (if frozen, allow about 2 days in the refrigerator for thawing time)
¼ c. butter
or 4 slices bacon
Salt
Pepper
Paprika

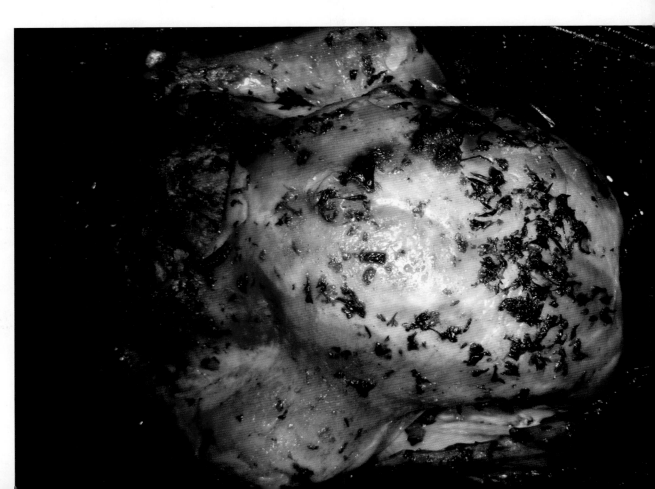

A duo of tasty oven-baked chicken dishes—herbed roasted chicken and easy oven chicken, featuring pieces of chicken roasted with buttery vegetables.

Additional Herbs
Parsley
Chervil
Thyme
Rosemary
1 small onion *and* 1 stalk celery *or* 2–3 c. stuffing

Rinse the chicken under cold running water, shaking out the excess. Place in an oiled roasting pan, breast-side up. Lightly stuff with your preferred stuffing or place the cut-up onion and celery inside, along with a knob of butter and some salt and pepper. Brush the skin with the melted butter combined with about ½ t. each salt and paprika, ¼ t. pepper, and a pinch or two of whatever herbs you might wish. If you're using bacon instead, sprinkle the surface with the seasonings first and then lay strips of the bacon evenly spaced over the top. Cover your pan and roast in a 375°F oven for approximately 1 hour. Smaller birds will take proportionately longer to cook per pound than large ones. Remove the cover and continue roasting for another 45–60 minutes, until the skin is deep golden and the chicken tender. When the bird is done, it should have an overall crisp brown appearance, and the drumstick should move up and down easily. The internal temperature of cooked poultry should be greater than that of red meats; 180°F for safety. Although overcooking can dry out the breast meat, chicken roasted in this manner should retain its moistness nicely. Allow it to stand for about 10 minutes for the juices to reabsorb into the meat.

Chicken Provincial

Even tender broiler fryers adapt well to braising over gentle heat. In this instance, it allows the bird to infuse with the flavors of the other ingredients. It's another good way to utilize the dark meat; you can decide whether to use a whole chicken or to just use thighs and drumsticks, saving the breast meat for another day. Serve this chicken with cooked rice and crusty bread for sopping up the juices.

1 frying chicken, cut in quarters, *or* 4 thighs and 4 drumsticks
¼ c. olive oil
1 lg. onion, sliced
2 cloves minced garlic
1 t. salt
¼ t. pepper
½ t. thyme
2 T. capers
1 med. tomato, diced (1 c. fresh or ½ c. canned)
½ c. dry white wine
Hot cooked rice

Brown the chicken well in the hot olive oil in a heavy skillet or Dutch oven. Sprinkle with the salt, pepper, and thyme and scatter the onions and garlic over all. Cover the pan and cook on medium-low heat for about 20 minutes. Add the tomato, capers, and wine; stir a bit; and continue to cook, covered, another 20–25 minutes. The chicken should be quite tender and the tomato and wine should have produced a nice sauce. This is good with a green vegetable such as peas or string beans. Serves 4.

Easy Oven Chicken Supper

I've been making this easy casserole dish since my children were little. It's economical enough for every day, yet fancy enough for company. And because it's essentially a meal in itself, it makes for a no-fuss presentation.

4 small chicken leg quarters, halved, *or* 4 large thighs
4 medium red-skinned potatoes, scrubbed and halved or quartered
4 large carrots, scrubbed and cut into 3" pieces
2 T. olive oil
2 T. butter
1 t. instant minced onion
1 t. parsley flakes
½ t. salt
½ t. paprika
½ t. thyme
¼ t. crumbled rosemary

Preheat the oven to 375°F. Melt the butter and olive oil together in a 9" × 13" baking pan. Stir in all the seasonings. Arrange the chicken pieces, skin-side down, and bake for 10 minutes. Add the carrots and potatoes, stirring to coat. Cover with foil and bake in a 375°F oven for 30 minutes. Uncover, stir the vegetables, and continue baking, uncovered, another 10–15 minutes, until everything is tender and the chicken is nicely browned. This serves 4, more if smaller appetites are involved.

Cashew-Coconut Chicken

This variation on Indian cuisine imparts a little flavor of Southeast Asia. It's best made with dark-meat chicken pieces, as they'll become moister with the slightly prolonged cooking period during which the sauce reduces. Serve with rice, chutney, steamed spinach, and naan (Indian flat bread) for an especially tasty meal.

4 medium chicken thighs and 4 drumsticks, skin on
2 T. oil
2 lg. cloves garlic, peeled and sliced
6 green onions (scallions), sliced in 1" pieces
¾ t. salt
1 t. curry powder, or to taste
1 14-oz. can coconut milk (not cream)
½ c. cashews

Slowly brown the chicken pieces, covered, in the oil over medium-low heat. This should take about 10 minutes. Add the garlic and scallions during the last couple of minutes. Sprinkle evenly with the curry powder and salt. Pour the coconut milk over all, increase the heat, and bring the mixture to a boil. Reduce the heat again and cook gently, covered, until the chicken is tender, about ½ hour. Remove the cover and cook a few more minutes to reduce the sauce to a good consistency. Sprinkle with the cashews and serve. This will feed 4–6; I frequently find a single thigh to be plenty for one.

Chicken and Broccoli with Pasta

Here comes the white meat! If you've been wondering what would become of all the chicken breast you haven't been using in the previous recipes, the next few should set your curiosity to rest. As for the wings, cut in half, bag, and freeze for later on to make all those tasty little appetizers we love to munch. Now on to the recipe at hand! Aside from cooking the pasta separately, chicken with broccoli is a one-cooking-pan wonder.

2 c. macaroni or ziti, cooked al dente (just tender) and drained

1 lb. skinless boneless chicken, cut in bite-sized pieces

1 bunch broccoli trimmed and cut into florets (3–4 c.)

2–3 scallions, sliced;
or ¼ c. minced onion

2 cloves garlic, minced

1 c. chicken broth

¼ c. butter

¼ c. grated Parmesan cheese

1 c. milk

Combine the chicken, onions, garlic, and broth in a large, heavy skillet and cook 3–4 minutes over high heat. Add the broccoli, pasta, milk, butter, and Parmesan cheese. Bring to a boil and then reduce heat to medium and cook, stirring occasionally, about 5 minutes longer. The broccoli should be crisp tender and the sauce somewhat reduced. It will continue to thicken more upon standing. Turn off the heat and allow it to set for 2–3 minutes. This serves 4–6 as a main course.

Chicken Cordon Bleu

Pound whole boneless skinless chicken breasts between two sheets of waxed paper to produce the thin scallops needed for this recipe. Try to get them down to about ¼" thick for best results, but watch out for tearing. Using a heavy rolling pin for the pounding works as well as anything. As with all recipes utilizing breast meat, be careful not to overcook your chicken or the meat will become tough.

2 whole skinless boneless chicken breasts, prepared as above

4 thin slices of good quality ham (4 oz.)

1 T. Dijon mustard

1 T. honey

2 long thin rectangles Swiss *or* Jarlsburg cheese (4 oz.)

½ c. flour

½ t. salt

½ t. paprika

1 t. parsley flakes

2 eggs, beaten with 2 T. water

1 c. fine dry bread crumbs

2 T. butter

2 T. olive oil

Mix together the flour, salt, paprika, and parsley; set aside. Combine the Dijon and honey; spread evenly on the inside of each pounded chicken breast. Place 2 slices of the ham over the honey-mustard mix on each breast, keeping the edges of the ham within the edges of the chicken. Place the cheese slightly to one side of center and roll the chicken tightly closed, starting with the side the cheese is on. Dip the chicken into the seasoned flour mixture, into the beaten egg, and finally into the bread crumbs. Sauté in the hot olive oil and butter over medium heat until browned on all sides and the chicken meat runs clear when pierced with a fork. Serve with rice pilaf or mashed potatoes and a green vegetable. Cut the whole breasts in half to make 4 servings total.

Crispy-Baked Chicken

This recipe incorporates the flavors of another classic stuffed chicken dish, chicken Kiev. In the original, herbed butter is hidden within the wrapped chicken breasts. Because the seasonings go on the outside in this variation, it's a quick and easy preparation.

4 skinless boneless chicken breast halves
¼ c. butter, melted
4 T. olive oil
¼ t. garlic powder
2 T. fresh minced parsley
2 T. snipped chives
½ t. paprika
1 c. fine dry bread crumbs
¼ c. grated Parmesan cheese

Combine the melted butter, olive oil, garlic powder, and herbs. Dip each chicken breast to thoroughly coat on all sides. Combine the Parmesan cheese, paprika, and bread crumbs. Coat the chicken evenly with the crumbs and place in an oiled baking dish. Pour any remaining butter mixture over the tops of the chicken. Bake at 375°F for approximately 45–50 minutes, until nicely browned and juices run clear when pricked with a fork. This is good served with baked potatoes and some nice fresh peas or asparagus; serves 4.

Chicken Stir-Fry

Lime is the citrus of choice here, combining with ginger, garlic, sesame oil, and soy sauce to give this stir-fry its special tang. Although I think this tastes best made with chicken, you

156

may vary it by using beef, shrimp, or even tofu. Brown rice is my preferred accompaniment to this dish.

Marinade

3 T. soy sauce
1 t. sesame oil
2 T. peanut oil
Pinch of hot pepper flakes
1" piece of ginger root, peeled and grated
2 T. lime juice
2 lg. cloves garlic, peeled and minced
2 T. brown sugar
1 lb. boneless skinless chicken breasts cut in strips
1 bunch scallions, sliced (1 c.)
2 c. thinly sliced carrots
2 c. broccoli florets
2 c. snow peas *or* green beans
1 lg. red bell pepper, seeded and cut into strips
2 T. peanut oil for stir fry

Optional

Baby corn
Fiddleheads
Cashews

Stove-top chicken meals with lots of appeal include stir-fry (shown here with fiddlehead ferns added) and chicken fingers with cranberry-orange dipping sauce sure to please the younger set.

Combine all marinade ingredients. Pour over the chicken, coating it well. Store in the refrigerator, covered, for at least 1 hour. If you make this a day ahead, it's even better. When ready to prepare, have your brown rice cooked in advance, as the actual stir-fry won't take very long at all. Heat the peanut oil in a large skillet or wok over high. Add the drained chicken, reserving the marinade. Stir-fry it quickly for a few minutes, adding the carrots and scallions after a couple of minutes. Stir-fry a couple of more minutes and then add the broccoli, snow peas or beans, and reserved marinade. Continue cooking for a couple more minutes, stirring frequently. Add the red pepper strips and the corn, if using, about a minute before you're ready to serve. Mound the brown rice onto each plate and pour the stir-fry over. Add a few cashews for garnish, if you wish. This makes about 6 servings. Note: Always parboil fiddleheads as per previous instructions, if using them.

Chicken Fingers with Cranberry-Orange Dip

Just about everybody loves chicken fingers. They're surprisingly easy to make at home, and unlike some of the preformed, fatty products available commercially, they are both delicious and nutritious. I've made these fairly bland to go along with the dip. However, you can add extra seasonings to your heart's content. Try Italian herbs and a little grated Parmesan cheese to go with spaghetti marinara or a little lemon pepper seasoning to accompany chicken-flavored rice. Cut whole boneless chicken breasts into long, thin strips for this or simply buy the chicken precut. One pound will equal about 8 strips or 2 a piece.

1 lb. boneless skinless chicken strips
¼ c. flour
1 t. salt
¼ t. poultry seasoning
¼ t. onion powder
½ t. paprika
¼ c. corn or canola oil

Rinse the chicken in cold water, leaving the surface slightly damp. Combine the flour, salt, paprika, and onion powder in a small bowl. Heat the oil in a large, heavy skillet over medium high. Dredge the chicken pieces in the flour mixture, covering well on all sides. Place in the skillet and cook for approximately 2–3 minutes per side, turning once or twice. You want your chicken to be golden brown but not dried out. Serve with cranberry-orange dip, honey mustard, or barbeque sauce.

Cranberry-Orange Dip

While cranberries are in season, pick up a few extra bags and put them in the freezer. When you need some for recipes such as this, just remove what you need and reseal the rest in a freezer bag. They should be good to use for up to a year.

½ c. cranberries
½ c. and 1 T. orange juice
1 t. grated orange rind
1 t. finely shredded fresh ginger
2 T. honey
2 T. sugar
⅛ t. salt
1 t. cornstarch

Combine the cranberries, honey, sugar, and ½ c. orange juice in a small saucepan. Bring to a boil, lower heat, and cook, uncovered, for about 5 minutes. Add the grated rind and shredded ginger. Blend until fairly smooth; the cranberries will give the sauce some texture. Return to the saucepan. Stir together the cornstarch and remaining orange juice until smooth. Add to the pan and bring back just to boiling; remove from heat. Serve dip warm or cool. This makes about ½ cup of dip.

Dandelion Jelly

Away back in my misspent youth, I attempted to concoct some dandelion wine. I was using a very old recipe, and evidently from the results, it was not a very good one. And so, since then I've stuck to less-fermented fare. If you're looking for an unusual preserve to impress your friends with, look no further. The most complicated aspect of making dandelion jelly is separating the yellow flower head from the leafy green portion holding it in place. Although time-consuming, it is absolutely imperative if you wish to produce a palatable jelly. Plan on picking about 1½ quarts of dandelion flowers to yield 2–2½ cups of golden petals. Holding each blossom with one hand, use a clean pair of scissors to snip the base away and then pull off the remaining circlet of green leaves from the base of the blossom. This is time-consuming, so you might wish to watch a good show on television or listen to some relaxing music while you're doing it. If you're quick, this procedure might take an hour—possibly more, depending on your dexterity and the size of the blooms.

2 heaping c. dandelions, petals only
3 c. water
5 c. sugar
2 T. lemon juice
1 box powdered pectin
A few drops yellow food coloring (optional)

Place the dandelions in a heatproof glass bowl, jar, or 2 qt. measuring cup. Pour the boiling hot

water over the dandelions and allow this mixture to steep overnight at room temperature (place a cover over it when it has cooled enough to no longer steam). Carefully pour the liquid through a wire sieve that has been lined with either a coffee filter or a double layer of cheesecloth. Measure 2½ cups and place in a large stainless steel saucepan. Add the lemon juice and pectin, stirring to dissolve, and bring to a boil, skimming the surface as necessary. Add the sugar and a few drops of yellow food coloring; although I don't generally use much artificial coloring in my food, in this case it adds a nice bit of color. Continue to stir and boil until the mixture sheets from a spoon, i.e., a little of the hot liquid begins to adhere to itself enough to almost spread into a sheet when it is slowly poured sideways from the spoon. If you have a candy thermometer, it should register about 220°F at this point. Skim again as necessary and pour the boiling hot jelly into hot sterilized jars; seal with sterilized lids and process in a boiling water bath for 10 minutes. Remove to cool on a padded, level surface, making sure all the lids have sealed properly. For short-term use, pour into a clean nonplastic bowl or glass jar and refrigerate to use within a month. This makes 8 or 9 half pints of jelly.

Who would think even a bunch of dandelions could be turned into a golden jar of jelly?

159

Sweet Violets

Our springtime lawn and meadow have areas covered with purple and white violets in full bloom. As our daughter Amanda was born in May, her childhood birthday cakes often featured fresh-plucked violets for decoration. If you'd like to enjoy the violet flowers in a less transitory capacity, why don't you try candying them?* Although many recipes call for brushing the violets with lightly beaten egg white and sprinkling with sugar, I use a sugar syrup followed by a dip in superfine sugar. The flower petals will curl up in the hot liquid, but the finished product carries no chance of contamination from the egg whites and most likely will last a bit longer as well.

1½ c. sugar
½ c. water
50–100 fresh–picked violets

Whirl ½ c. of the sugar in a blender until it becomes very fine. Although you may buy superfine sugar separately if you wish, I find this method easy and inexpensive. Set the sugar aside in a small bowl. Meanwhile, combine the ½ cup of water and remaining cup of sugar in a small, heavy saucepan. Cook over medium heat, stirring, until the sugar dissolves. Insert a candy thermometer, if you have one, and cook until the syrup "spins a thread" when slowly dripped from a spoon. This will register 215–220°F on your candy thermometer. You may either dip the violets by their stems (which will be removed later) or remove as much of the green from the violet as possible before dipping and use a couple of forks or a pair of metal tweezers to dip the flowers first in the hot syrup and then in the superfine sugar. Shake off excess and place each to cool and dry on waxed paper spread over a cooling rack. Chances are, you'll have some sugar and dipping liquid leftover; use them to sweeten beverages or sift the sugar to remove lumps and use it in baking. Remember to remove as much of the green portion of the flower as possible; it will give your candied violets an unpleasant bitter taste otherwise. Store them in a small airtight container in a cool, dry location.

*Please don't confuse our wild lawn and woodland violets with the houseplants known as "African violets"; the latter are not edible!

While we're at it, let's not forget tiny purple and white violets, just waiting to make one of nature's more pure confections.

"Make Hay While the Sun Shines . . ."

DURING MY CHILDHOOD, the month of June brought two significant events: the end of school for the summer and haying. Actually, to be more accurate, it brought first-cut haying, as opposed to second or possibly even third cut. Grasses and plants mature in a cyclical fashion, so hay cut in June could well be of a different makeup than that harvested in late July or August. Graduated haying signaled a shift in farming practice from the early twentieth century, when frequently only one cutting was done in late summer, after the hay crop had matured and dried in the field. This made for lower yield and less nutritional value but, at the time, was accepted practice. I didn't really wonder about such things when I was a kid; I just remember hearing the whine and groan of ancient farm trucks circling the seventeen-acre pasture across the road from our house. As they trailed after the tractor hauling a baler thumping out rectangular bales of hay, older neighborhood kids would haul the bales over to each truck in turn, hefting them up over the sides to whoever was perched up top stacking them.

I knew once he'd hayed his own large farm fields, our neighbor Ray would eventually drive his tractor over to the small pasture behind our house, cutting, tedding, winnowing, and eventually baling the hundred-plus bales that would feed our animals over the upcoming winter. Once he'd finished the process, we'd hustle to get all the bales safely under cover in our goat barn before any June thunderstorms rolled our way. Predictably there would always be a few bales that would fall apart in the field, the twine around them not quite tight enough to hold the hay firmly in place. I used to think gathering up these partial bales was the easy part of the job—no more aching fingers and shoulders from grasping and hauling the tightly packed full-sized hay bales. That was until the time I had gathered one of those partial bales in my arms and was halfway back to the barn when the tail of a garter snake slid out of it and over my forearm. As the rest of the snake proceeded to smoothly follow its wayward tail over my arm, that particular bundle of hay and I parted ways in a speedy fashion.

My neighbor Rodney cuts grass in the field across the road, making hay while the sun shines.

With the many farm critters benefiting from hay harvested in June, how fitting that June is also National Dairy Month. It's the perfect time to be contemplating all the delicious milk-based dishes to be made courtesy of our friends the cows, goats, and sheep. If you'd like to adventure on past the requisite puddings and milkshakes, why don't you try your hand at cheese making? Especially with some of the soft varieties, making your own cheese may just be easier than you think. If you must rely on store-bought milk, there will be a few cautionary tales along the way; our system of pasteurization helps make the milk safer for consumption but not always such a reliable source for cheese making. If you're lucky enough to live in a rural area, as I do, sources of milk suitable for cheese making may be easier and more economical to come by. You will need a few pieces of specialized equipment, such as a reliable cheese thermometer, which will register at a lower temperature than common candy or meat thermometers. If you decide to become really adventuresome and try to make hard cheese, the process becomes more complex. I've included more explicit directions as needed with each individual recipe.

June

Farmer or Pot Cheese

Time: ½ hour preparation time, approximately 1 day to set curd, another 12 hours for draining.

Farmer or pot cheese is easier to make than hard or cured cheeses. If you have your own fresh milk supply, you may wish to double or triple this recipe. The buttermilk or lemon juice is necessary for curd formation when using pasteurized milk. If you're using ultrapasteurized, currently the most common commercially sold milk, I would suggest the acidity of the lemon juice for better results.

2 qt. milk, fat content your choice
¼ c. lemon juice
or ½ c. buttermilk

Rural oversight committee: synchronized cows keeping tabs on the neighborhood.

Place the milk in a stainless steel bowl or saucepan that has been set in a larger pan of hot water. Heat the milk to 180°F. Stir in the buttermilk or lemon juice and remove both pans from the heat, with the smaller pan still semisubmerged in the water. Cover and allow the mixture to stand for up to 24 hours. You will be able to tell when this is ready because the solid white curd will separate from the liquid whey. Drain the mixture through a cheesecloth that has been set in a colander. Allow the curd to drain for about 4 hours in the colander. Rinse it gently with cool water, then bring up the corners of the cheesecloth, and tie them tightly to make a hanging bag. Allow the cheese to drain for another 6–8 hours, until it is fairly firm. Starting with ¼ teaspoon, stir in salt to taste. You may now add herbs or other seasonings as you wish. Refrigerate your farmer cheese, covered, and use within 3–4 days.

Boursin Cheese Spread

This rich-herbed cheese spread is a snap to make with your own fresh farmer cheese and a bit of butter. Fresh herbs from your garden are an added bonus. In this recipe, the amounts given for parsley and chives are geared toward fresh herbs while the rest indicate dried. If you have access to fresh varieties of the other herbs listed, double the amount of each used.

1 recipe (1 c.) unsalted farmer cheese
½ c. butter, salted or unsalted
2 cloves garlic, crushed
1 T. minced chives
1 T. parsley
½ t. marjoram
½ t. basil
½ t. black pepper
½–1 t. salt
¼ t. dried thyme

Cream the butter until it is quite soft. Stir in the farmer cheese and the rest of the ingredients, beating it smooth. Check for seasonings. Serve at once or mound in a small bowl and refrigerate, covered, up to 3 days. Serve with crackers, breadsticks, or rustic bread. This makes about 1½ cups of spread.

Fresh cheeses such as farmer's cheese require no aging process. Their curd is very fine.

Paneer (Panir) or Queso Blanco

Approximate time: Preparation about 30 minutes, draining time 1 hour initial plus 8–12 hours.

Paneer and queso blanco are fresh white cheeses that are very similar in makeup and flavor, even though they originated in very different parts of the world. Each is produced in a manner similar to farmer cheese, although the temperatures utilized are higher. The loose curds are pressed to form a solid, which may then be crumbled or cut into cubes. Neither of these cheeses melt when exposed to heat and can therefore be browned in a little hot oil to enjoy plain or when added to other ingredients. The determining factor between them is the temperature the milk is heated to before adding the coagulating agent, in this case lemon juice. For queso blanco, the milk is heated to just under boiling, whereas for paneer it actually comes to a full boil.

½ gallon milk
¼ c. lemon juice
½ c. hot water, optional, for paneer

Place the milk in a stainless steel saucepan. For queso blanco, it is helpful to have a cheese thermometer so that the milk reaches the optimal temperature without actually boiling. Over medium heat, stirring occasionally to prevent scorching, heat the milk to 200°F for queso blanco or to a full boil for paneer. Remove from the heat and gradually stir in the lemon juice. Allow the hot mixture to sit for about 15 minutes, stirring occasionally, to ensure the curds and whey have totally separated. When this has occurred, the whey will appear an almost-clear light yellow as opposed to milky or opaque. Adding just a bit more lemon juice will facilitate separation if need be. If you are making paneer and would prefer a slightly softer cheese, stir in the ½ c. of hot water at this time. Pour the mixture into a sieve lined with a double thickness of fine cheesecloth. Allow to drain thoroughly for about an hour. Twist the cheesecloth around the curds to further extract liquid. Place the still-wrapped cheese on a plate, with another heavy plate weighting it down. Refrigerate 5–6 hours or overnight. Remove from the cheesecloth, wrap in plastic or waxed paper, and plan to enjoy within two weeks. This makes about one-half pound of cheese.

Queso Blanco Soup with Blue Corn Tortilla Chips

This easy and colorful soup makes a simple summer lunch or the first course for a more substantial meal. If blue corn tortilla chips are not readily available, plain yellow ones may be substituted. As the summer progresses, you may well be able to harvest most of the ingredients fresh from your own garden. Admittedly, here in Vermont I'll probably never be able to grow my own limes and avocados; however, for this soup they're worth purchasing from "away."

½ c. diced red onion
1 t. minced jalapeño
1 t. minced garlic
2 T. olive oil
1 c. diced tomato
1 c. diced summer squash
½ t. salt
½ t. cumin
½ t. oregano
3½ c. chicken broth
1 avocado, peeled and diced
Fresh cilantro
Lime wedges
Queso blanco, diced or crumbled
Blue corn tortilla chips

Sauté the onion, garlic, and jalapeño in the olive oil until tender but not browned. Stir in the tomato and squash; stir and cook a minute or two longer. The squash should be just tender crisp. Add the broth and seasonings. Simmer for about 10 minutes to blend the flavors. Divide the soup between 4 serving bowls. Sprinkle each with the diced avocado, fresh cilantro leaves, and the crumbled queso blanco. Add a squirt of fresh lime. Garnish with blue corn tortilla chips to crumble in; serve at once. The soup itself may be made in advance and reheated; add the garnishes fresh at serving time.

*Queso blanco soup with blue
corn tortilla chips will brighten
up anyone's day.*

171

Cottage Cheese

Time: Initial preparation about 15 minutes, 12–16 hours curd formation, final preparation 1 hour.

Adding a small amount of rennet to your cottage cheese base will help it form a thicker curd. You may make it without, although the cheese will more resemble farmer cheese. Rennet tablets are available at some specialty shops and health food stores and are also widely available online. The rennet used here is cheese-making rennet, which is scored into four equal segments. If you have junket rennet tablets, which are smaller and less effective, you would probably use an entire tablet. You also need a reliable cheese thermometer, cheesecloth for straining, a colander, a 2 qt. saucepan, and stainless steel bowl or another pan large enough to use as a double boiler for slow heating with the first pan.

2 qt. milk, fresh or reconstituted instant nonfat
¼ c. cold water
¼ rennet tablet *or* ¼ c. buttermilk (I recommend rennet)
Salt to taste
Cream, optional

Dissolve the rennet in the cold water. Heat the milk over low heat to 80°F; be careful not to overheat it. Stir in the rennet or buttermilk, cover the pan, and set aside for 12–16 hours, until a curd has formed. Using a knife with a long blade, cut gently through the mixture to form ½" cubes. Fill the large bowl or pan with hot tap water (about 110°F). Place the pan with the cheese curd into the larger container, adding water if need be to bring it up to the level of the milk inside. Slowly heat the water to raise the curd temperature up to 110°F. I do this by using the lowest heat setting on the smallest burner on my gas stove. If you're heating slowly enough, this will take about half an hour. Maintain the curds at this temperature for about 20 minutes, stirring occasionally to ensure even heating. I leave the heat on for the first 5–10 minutes and then turn off the burner and allow the temperature to maintain through retained heat. It's all right if the mixture gets up to around 115°F while the heat is still on, but you don't want it any higher or your curd will toughen. Once the mixture has completed the heating process, pour into the cheesecloth-lined sieve and drain the whey, gently lifting the corners of the cheesecloth to help the process without compressing the curds too much. Once drained, fill your large container with cold and fresh water and briefly submerge the sieve, cheesecloth, and cheese, swirling to rinse all the whey from the curds. Drain well again, pour the curds into a bowl, and season to taste with salt. Start with ¼ teaspoon and add accordingly. If you prefer a creamed cottage cheese, stir in about ¼ cup of cream. You are now ready to enjoy your cottage cheese.

Garden Veggie Cottage Cheese

Now that you've made your own cottage cheese, you can also have the fun of adding "extras" to it—just like you'd buy in the store, only better! Try bits of diced fruit stirred in or on the side, or whip up this vegetable version, good with crackers, stuffed in a tomato, or all by itself.

1 recipe cottage cheese
1 T. fresh parsley *or* cilantro, minced
¼ c. diced carrot
¼ c. diced celery
¼ c. diced radishes
¼ c. diced red bell pepper
2 T. minced scallions *or* chives
¼ t. fresh-cracked black pepper

Combine all ingredients in a medium bowl, stirring gently to combine. Refrigerate to blend the flavors. Store leftovers, covered, to use in 3–4 days.

Finely diced vegetables combine with cottage cheese to make garden veggie cottage cheese.

Spinach Pie

Here's a simple and tasty dish utilizing ingredients bountiful in spring and summer: spinach, scallions, eggs, and cheese. If you don't have fresh spinach, a box of thawed frozen spinach works very nicely for this recipe. Spinach pie makes a great main course or side dish, but may also be cut in smaller pieces for snacking or appetizers.

4 scallions, trimmed and sliced
4 T. butter
1 sm. or ½ lg. clove garlic, peeled and minced
2 T. flour
3 eggs
1 c. cottage cheese: 8 oz.
2 c. shredded cheddar or Jack cheese: 8 oz.
¼ t. nutmeg
¼ t. salt
¼ t. Tabasco sauce
10 oz. finely chopped cooked spinach

Over low heat, melt the butter and gently sauté the scallions and garlic until they are wilted but not browned. Remove from the heat and set aside. Beat together the eggs, seasonings, and flour until smooth. Stir in the cottage cheese, shredded cheese, and the cooked spinach, making sure the latter is well drained. Pour into a well-buttered pie tin and bake at 350°F for 35–40 minutes, until slightly puffed and set in the center. Serve warm or at room temperature for ease of slicing; refrigerate leftovers. This makes 4 main dish servings or up to 8 side dish servings. It's quite tasty for breakfast, as well.

Cream Cheese

Time: About ½ hour preparation and then approximately 1 day draining time.

Cream cheese is another relatively easy-to-make fresh cheese. Again, it will take about one full day to complete, although most of this time is spent by the cheese mixture just hanging out forming curd. This will produce about a pound of cream cheese. Although regular rather than ultrapasteurized half and half will give you the best results, I have been able to successfully make cream cheese using a combination of Organic Cow ultrapasteurized half and half and Kate's cultured buttermilk (regular pasteurization). These are both local New England brands; you may wish to experiment with what is available locally to you. In general, the cheese will take a little longer to produce using ultrapasteurized dairy products.

2 pints pasteurized (not ultrapasteurized) half and half
¼ c. buttermilk
¼ rennet tablet
2 T. water
½ t. salt

Place the half and half in a medium-large stainless steel saucepan. Heat slowly until the liquid measures just 100°F on an instant-read thermometer. Don't overheat it; this is important, as higher temperatures might "kill" the rennet. Immediately remove the half and half from the heat. Dissolve the rennet in the cool water. Stir the buttermilk and the rennet into the cream mixture. Cover the pan and allow it to set, undisturbed, for between

18–24 hours, at which time there will be a nice thick creamy topping over the entire surface. Pour this mixture into a small meshed wire sieve that has been lined with enough dampened cheesecloth for a double layer with extra hanging over the edges. Drain the whey, eventually twisting the ends of the cheesecloth together to form a draining bag. Allow the cheese to drain for about an hour, refrigerated; at this point, it will probably have the consistency of sour cream. Pour it into a bowl, add the salt, and then scrape the cheese back into the rinsed cheesecloth bag. You may then either replace it in the strainer or place it on a plate and weight it down with a heavy plate. It can then drain in the refrigerator for another day, if you wish. Allow it to drain for another 12–24 hours for best consistency.

Pineapple-Date Dip

Here's a nice way to use your cream cheese. This fruity dip is equally tasty with carrots, apple slices, strawberries, or whole-grain crackers. It will thicken somewhat upon standing, as the dates slowly absorb more liquid. Store any leftovers, covered, in the fridge. It should last up to a week.

1 lb. regular or light cream cheese
½ c. chopped walnuts
½ c. chopped dates
8 oz. can crushed pineapple in juice

Beat the cream cheese in a small mixer bowl until it is soft and creamy. Beat in the pineapple with its juice. Fold in the nuts and dates. Serve with desired fruits and/or crackers. Because the dip is initially fairly soft, it may also be used at this point as a low sugar frosting for a variety of fruit- or spice-type cakes. Be sure to refrigerate your cake if using pineapple-date dip as frosting.

Banana Bread

Banana bread is yummy any time of the year, but it's especially tasty spread with your own homemade cream cheese. This recipe makes a nice moist loaf that slices well and keeps up to a week in cool, dry conditions. This banana bread also freezes quite nicely; separate the individual slices with small sheets of waxed paper or aluminum foil and store well wrapped to enjoy within a month, a bit at a time.

½ c. corn oil
1 c. sugar
2 eggs
3 bananas, mashed
½ t. nutmeg, optional
2 c. flour
1 t. baking soda
½ t. salt
½ t. baking powder
¼ c. milk
½ t. vanilla
½ c. chopped walnuts
1–2 T. rum, optional

In a large mixer bowl, combine the mashed bananas, oil, sugar, and eggs. Beat them until smooth. Alternately mix in the combined dry ingredients and the combined milk, vanilla, and the rum, if using. Pour the mixture into a greased and floured 9" × 5" loaf pan. Bake at 350°F for up to an hour, or until the top is golden brown, cracked, and the inner parts of the cracked area are no longer sticky to touch. If in doubt, insert a toothpick or wooden skewer, which should come out clean or with only a few crumbs clinging to it. Cool the banana bread in the pan for about 10 minutes and then turn it out and allow it to finish cooling on its side on a mesh rack. This recipe makes one loaf and is easy to double if you wish more.

175

Clotted Cream

Approximate time: About ½ hour heating time, 12 or more hours for thickening.

Traditional clotted cream, an English specialty, is the thick, buttery crust that rises to the top of gently heated cream. Devonshire cream refers to a type of clotted cream from a specific region in England. Clotted cream is very rich, with a butterfat content of 55 percent. Although many clotted cream recipes call for raw milk for the best results, it can be made from pasteurized or even ultrapasteurized cream with a little patience. I've tried making it a few different ways; I think the stove-top method is the easiest.

Stove top. Heat 1 or 2 c. heavy cream in a small saucepan to 82°F. This requires a cheese thermometer, available online or through specialty shops. Allow it to sit at room temperature about 12 hours and then refrigerate for 12 more. (You shouldn't cover the cream while it is sitting, although a piece of cheesecloth draped and fastened over the top will help keep marauding insects or any stray particles of dirt from contaminating your product.) At this point you may carefully skim the thickened yellow clotted cream from the top. If you are using ultrapasteurized cream, you may need to refrigerate the pan for an additional 12–24 hours to allow more separation. Store the clotted cream in a covered jar and use within 4 days.

Classic Scones

Scones served with clotted cream and a dab of strawberry jam or orange marmalade must surely be one of the British Isle's finest contributions to humankind. There are so many lovely ways to vary your scones, limited only by personal taste and your imagination. This is a classic version, utilizing dried currants in the batter.

1¾ c. flour
6 T. sugar
1 t. baking soda
½ t. salt
6 T. cold butter
1 t. grated lemon zest
¾ c. buttermilk
½ c. dried currants

Combine the flour, sugar, baking soda, and salt in a medium mixing bowl. Cut in the butter or crumble it in with your fingers until it's the size of small peas. Beat together the egg and buttermilk and stir lightly into the dry ingredients along with the lemon zest. Scoop the batter into 8 equal mounds on a parchment or waxed paper–lined baking sheet. A metal ice cream scoop with the little sliding inset works well for this, if you have one. Bake on middle upper shelf in a 375°F preheated oven for 15–20 minutes, until they are puffed, golden brown, and firm to touch. Serve warm or at room temperature with your choice of butter, clotted cream, and/or jam.

Crème Fraîche

Approximate time: About 15 minutes preparation plus 12 hours for thickening.

This French specialty is a cross somewhere between sweet and sour cream. It's as delicious as a dessert topping, and also adds a nice accent to many soups. The buttermilk or sour cream starter will enable even ultrapasteurized cream to thicken, although if you have access to regular pasteurized cream, it is preferable for this recipe. Crème fraîche will store up to 10 days, refrigerated and covered.

2 c. heavy cream
2 T. buttermilk *or* ¼ c. sour cream

Place the cream in a small saucepan and heat it to 85°F. Stir in the buttermilk or sour cream and pour the mixture into a glass bowl or bottle. Cover and allow it to stand at room temperature for about 12 hours, until it is quite thick. Refrigerate, covered, for up to 10 days.

Mozzarella Cheese and Ricotta Cheese

Approximate time: Plan on about 2 hours of fairly intense cheese making.

When we talk about mozzarella cheese, we're beginning to enter the world of More Complicated Cheese Making. Because it's a fresh cheese, it can still be made fairly quickly, but it does require more steps and complexity for a satisfactory finished product. You'll note I've indicated two cheeses in the recipe heading; that's because ricotta cheese is essentially a by-product of the mozzarella-making process and is one of the easiest cheeses you'll ever make! Plan on about 2 hours the first time you try these; you'll probably become more efficient with practice. This doesn't mean you'll be hanging out at the stove throughout the process; it's just that truly good things are well worth waiting for.

1 gallon whole milk
2 t. citric acid
¼ rennet tablet
¾ c. nonchlorinated water
1 t. sea salt *or* cheese-making salt (noniodized)
1 T. cider vinegar (optional)

Place the milk into a very large (minimum 6 qt.) stainless steel cooking pot. Dissolve the citric acid in ½ c. of the cold, nonchlorinated water and stir it thoroughly into the milk. Insert your cheese-making thermometer and gently heat the milk, stirring occasionally, to between 88° and 90°F. While the milk is heating, dissolve the rennet in the remaining water. Once the correct temperature has been reached, turn off the heat and gently but quickly stir the dissolved rennet into the warm

This cubed curd was cut from a block of semicoagulated milk solids and will go through other steps on the way to becoming semihard or hard cheese, either fresh such as mozzarella or aged such as cheddar. Here mozzarella cheese is being pulled by hand, giving it its characteristic stringy texture.

milk. Leaving the thermometer right in the milk, cover the pan and allow it to hang out, undisturbed, for 5 minutes. At this point the milk should have made the separation process into solids and liquid. Cut through the curd gently with the cheese thermometer itself (I have a long one that works well for this purpose), your spoon, or a long, thin knife. Make a crisscross pattern, about 1" either way; just don't overwork the mixture at this point. Over medium-low heat, again heat the cheese-to-be, gently stirring it occasionally for even heating. Once it has reached 110°F, again turn off the heat. Now stir with the spoon for 4–5 minutes; this is the point where the curds will attain their characteristic stringy texture. Have your cheese-cloth-lined colander set in a large stainless steel or glass bowl (I place them in the kitchen sink). Once the stirring process is complete, carefully pour the curds and whey into the bowl, lifting the cheese-cloth and pressing it just slightly to remove most of the whey. Place the curds into a microwavable bowl; I use a 2 qt. glass measuring cup for this step. Stir in the sea salt just until it's well bended.

Heat the cheese for 1 minute, which will make it appear soft and "melty." Work it with your hand to evenly distribute the heat and again microwave it for another 30 seconds. Pull it with your fingers; it should be nice and stringy at this point. If need be, you can microwave for another 30 seconds; my microwave seems to heat it sufficiently after the initial two heating periods, but each one is different. Be cautious when handing the cheese

at this point; it will be hot, although it's perfectly all right to sample some if you wish! Gently knead until it's nice and malleable and then form it into your desired shapes: one large ball, several smaller ones, a braid, or even small "strings" of cheese. Submerge it in ice water for a quick chill; the texture may suffer otherwise. Now wrap in plastic and refrigerate until you're ready to enjoy it!

Once your mozzarella is safely chilling, pour the whey back into the large heating pan. Insert the thermometer and heat it to approximately 202°F, although anywhere between 200°F minimum to 210°F will do the trick. Obviously, temperature control is easier for ricotta, so you may feel free to warm it at a higher burner heat than used for the mozzarella. Once it's reached the magic number, remove it from the heat and allow it to cool down to about 140–150°F. Adding 1 T. of vinegar during the cooling process will increase the curd production. Gently pour it back through the cheesecloth-lined colander you already have set up for straining the mozza-rella. The solids left this time are your ricotta; you should have about 6 oz. or so. It will take longer to drain the ricotta than the mozzarella because the curd formation is much finer; please don't try to hurry the process. Place the drained ricotta into a bowl, cover, and refrigerate to use within a week. You may add a pinch or two of salt, if you wish. Just don't add too much; ricotta has a delicate flavor. The leftover whey may be used for bread making, for feeding to whatever chickens or pigs you might have wandering around the backyard, or if you're all cheesed out at this point, simply discard it; it's already served its purpose nobly!

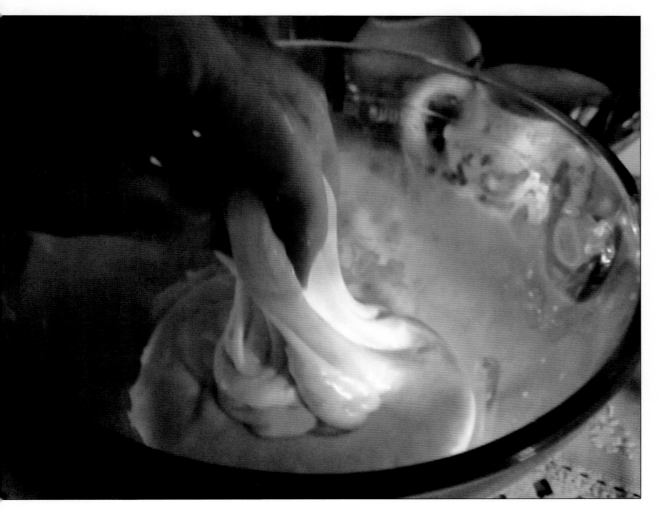

White Pie

My mom used to make herself little "white pies" for her supper after my dad had died, and she was cooking for one. In that instance, she used premade individual pizza crusts and commensurately fewer ingredients. As I recall, she added a bit of crumbled feta to her white pie, which would be a nice addition if you'd like a little extra tang. The addition of whey to the homemade crust used here gives it a nice springy texture from that little added shot of protein.

1 c. whey or water
1 t. salt
1 t. sugar
1 T. dry yeast
2 c. bread flour
¼ c. olive oil, divided
2 plum tomatoes, sliced
¼ c. diced red onion
1 lg. clove garlic, minced
½ t. dried oregano
½ c. pitted kalamata olives, optional
Fresh ground black pepper
Fresh ground sea salt
½–1 c. ricotta cheese
½ lb. mozzarella cheese, shredded or sliced

Combine the lukewarm whey and/or water with the sugar and salt. Add the yeast, stirring until it is dissolved. Allow the mixture to work for about 5 minutes, at which point the yeast should be starting to form bubbles. Stir in 1 T. of the olive oil and the flour. You will have an almost–batterlike dough. Generously oil a pizza pan, a 12" round cake pan, or a 9" × 13" rectangular pan. Gently spread the pizza dough evenly over the surface of the entire pan, using a bit more of the olive oil on your fingertips to help prevent sticking. Warm the onion, garlic, and oregano in the remaining 2 T. of the olive oil. To assemble, spread the ricotta cheese evenly over the dough, grinding some salt and pepper over the top. Sprinkle on the shredded mozzarella. Top with the sliced tomatoes and the onion mixture. Sprinkle on a little more salt and pepper. Bake at 450°F for 20–25 minutes, until bubbly and brown.

White pie uses both mozzarella and ricotta cheeses to make a tasty light summer supper.

Cheese Curds

Cheese curds are formed as part of the hard cheese-making process. Rather than pressing the curds and allowing them to ripen into cheddar, they are salted and eaten as is. Although they are now becoming more readily available in grocery stores nationwide, nothing really beats a nice fresh cheese curd. Use the cheddar cheese recipe below, simply deleting the pressing and curing steps involved. Store your cheese curd, covered, in the fridge for up to a week or so.

Fresh cheddar cheese curds may be pressed into hard cheese or used fresh for such treats as poutine.

Poutine

Poutine is a specialty comfort food from our friends in neighboring Quebec. It generally consists of french fried potatoes and cheese curd topped with hot gravy. Although I've seen versions utilizing beef gravy, it's my understanding that veal- or chicken-based gravy is the more authentic coverall. This gravy is richer than many because it has a velouté (cream sauce style) base of extra butter and flour. If you prefer, make the gravy a day ahead and heat up just in time for the fries.

Gravy

1 chicken thigh *or* 1 veal chop (cheap cut is fine)
1 small onion, chopped
1 stalk celery, sliced
1 small carrot, chopped
1 t. salt
1 t. oil
¼ t. paprika
¼ t. black pepper
4 c. water
¼ c. each butter
¼ c. flour

Heat the oil in a medium, heavy saucepan over low heat. Add the chicken or chop, placing the chopped vegetables all around. Cover and cook over medium heat until the meat is well browned on one side. Stir the vegetables, turn the meat, and continue cooking until everything is a deep golden brown. This is an important step in producing a rich brown gravy for your *poutine.* Pour in the 4 cups of water and add the salt, pepper, and paprika. Increase the heat until the mixture boils, turn it back to medium low, and cook gently for about an hour. At this point the liquid should have

reduced to about 2 cups and have a rich color and aroma. Strain the broth through a fine sieve, discarding the vegetables. If you wish, pick the meat from the bones and use for sandwich filling. Melt the butter over low heat, stirring in the flour and cooking for a minute or two. Whisk in the broth all at once and bring to a boil, whisking until it is smooth and thickened. Keep warm until ready to use or cool and refrigerate for another day.

French Fries and Curds

4 medium russet-type potatoes
Corn oil for frying
1 c. cheese curds

This is essentially the same french fries recipe as used for fish-and-chips in March, just slightly different proportions. Scrub and trim the potatoes, cutting them into long, thin matchsticks about ¼" in diameter. Soak them briefly in cold water, draining and patting them dry just before frying. Heat 2" of the oil in a large, heavy skillet; if you have a candy and frying thermometer, clip it to the side. It should heat to about 375–400°F. Fry the potatoes in small-enough batches so that they are in a single layer. Once browned, remove to a baking sheet and keep warm in a 200°F oven while cooking the rest. When the potatoes are all fried, you are ready to assemble your *poutine.* Sprinkle the curds over the french fries in the baking pan. Pour the gravy over all and allow to heat in the oven for 2–3 minutes, until the cheese just starts to melt. Serve at once. This serves 4 with plenty of gravy.

Ginseng Valley Cheddar Cheese

My kitchen window gazes out at Big and Little Ginseng Mountains at the western end

of the valley. Nestled in their shadow is Lilac Ridge Farm, its herd of Holstein and Brown Swiss dairy cattle the perfect purveyors of organic milk. Cheddar cheese is the most complicated of the cheese recipes listed here, but it is manageable if you're able to give a little extra time and attention to detail. It requires a stainless steel pan for the milk, a large metal pan or bowl for use as a double boiler during the heating and ripening processes, cheese wax for dipping, rennet, a cheese press,* and a packet of mesophilic starter. Although it is possible to produce hard cheese without mesophilic starter, using it will give you a better product. I am able to obtain mine through my local cheese-making supply store. It's also easy to order it online. I recommend the New England Cheese Company as a source: www.cheesemaking.com. If you're really excited about making your own cheese, this site also offers recipes and invaluable instruction as well as a wide range of supplies.

1 gallon whole milk (*not* ultrapasteurized)
1 pkt. mesophilic starter
2 t. sea salt (not iodized) *or* cheese making salt
¼ cheese-making rennet tablet
¼ c. cool water (not chlorinated)

Heat the milk gently over hot water until it reaches 88–90°F. For the first two phases of making your cheese, the pan of milk will remain in the tepid water. Add the powdered mesophilic starter, stirring gently to dissolve. Cover the milk and allow it to sit, undisturbed, for about 45 minutes, maintaining the 88–90°F temperature throughout. I find that it pretty much stays at the same temperature for the allotted time on retained heat; if it begins to drop too low, turn one burner on low for just a few minutes until the temperature level is back where it belongs. Be careful not to overheat it. Dissolve the rennet in the cool water and gently stir it into the warmed milk. Continue to retain it at 88–90°F for another 30–45 minutes, until the curd is formed. At this point you should be able to gently draw one clean finger up through the curd mixture and have it fall away smoothly. Remove the curd mixture from the water while you heat the water to between 105–110°F; turn off the heat. Place the pan holding the curds back into the heated water and *slowly* heat it, gently stirring occasionally, until the mixture reaches 102°F. This process should take about half an hour; don't try to rush it. The slow heating process will allow the curds to shrink and become denser. Now remove the pan from the water and allow it to hang out another 15 minutes, stirring gently every five minutes or so. Carefully pour the warm curds into a colander lined with several thicknesses of quality cheese-making cheesecloth. Allow it to drain in a quiet, warm place (I leave it in my kitchen sink) occasionally twisting the bag to facilitate drainage, for 1 hour. Empty the curds into a large bowl, gently breaking them up into bite-sized pieces with clean fingers. Work the 2 teaspoons of salt into the curds. If you prefer to use the curds fresh, they are now ready to be bagged in plastic and refrigerated. For hard cheese, rinse the cheesecloth well, twisting it to damp-dry. Place the curds back in several thicknesses of the cheesecloth. For the simplest method of pressing your cheese, simply weight down the twisted cheesecloth bag between two untreated wooden planks. I find using a small cheesecake rim, oiled to prevent possible rusting, works nicely if you'd like a nice round piece of cheese. In

this instance, I place the bag of curds in the cheesecake rim and place the rim on a rack that is in turn is balanced over a larger pan to catch the whey as it drips. I weigh the top down with my half-gallon glass measuring cup, filled with water, or with a 5–10-pound bag of sugar or flour in it. Press the cheese on one side for about ½ hour. Remove it from the cheesecloth long enough to flip it over, replace it in the rim, and continue to press. Repeat this on both sides after an hour on each side. Finally, simply leave the cheese, still pressed and draining, for 12-24 hours or overnight. Increasing the weight at this point will help facilitate the process, although the initial pressing weight should be fairly gentle. The more weight you have on the cheese, the shorter time it will take to remove the whey. If pressing between two pieces of wood, simply flip it over at the time increments mentioned. Once you have pressed the cheese to your liking, allow it to stand uncovered in a protected place at room for 6–8 hours, flipping it occasionally, to develop a hard crust. Chill for an hour or so to facilitate the waxing process. Finally dip it in melted cheese-making wax (paraffin may be substituted, although it's not the best choice). Melt the wax very carefully; it's extremely flammable! *Never* melt wax over direct heat; use a double boiler or a dish placed over hot water. Dip smaller cheeses using tongs, one-half at a time, allowing the wax to set before adding two more layers. Age the cheese, turning it at intervals, in a room where the temperature does not exceed 70°F (cooler is better, but the fridge is too cool; about 55–60°F is optimal). This process will take a minimum of two months; be patient!

Here curds have been pressed into a small wheel of fresh cheese. After waxing, it will be aged for several months to produce cheddar cheese.

Macaroni and Cheese

Macaroni and cheese ranks right up near the top in the comfort foods category. Even though it's a kid-friendly dish, there's no reason why adults can't enjoy it too, especially with the addition of good, sharp cheddar cheese to the creation.

2 c. elbow macaroni
3 T. butter
3 T. flour
½ t. paprika (optional)
2 c. milk
1 t. salt
½ t. dry mustard
½ t. onion powder
¼ t. Tabasco sauce
½ lb. shredded sharp cheddar cheese (2 c.)
1 c. fine bread crumbs

3 T. butter
¼ c. grated Parmesan cheese

Cook the macaroni in salted boiling water according to package directions until it is just tender, about 6–8 minutes. Meanwhile, melt the butter in a medium saucepan over low heat, stirring in the flour, salt, mustard, onion powder, and Tabasco sauce and then the milk, whisking or stirring constantly to prevent lumping. Bring just to a boil, cooking until it's thickened and bubbly. Remove from heat and stir in the cheese until it melts. Combine the cheese sauce with the cooked, well-drained macaroni and place in a buttered casserole. Top with the bread crumbs which have been tossed with the melted butter and Parmesan cheese. Add a sprinkle of paprika to the top, if you desire. Bake at 350°F about 30 minutes, until bubbly and browned. The amount of servings you get will depend on the size and appetites of the people involved in consuming it; it should serve at least 4–6.

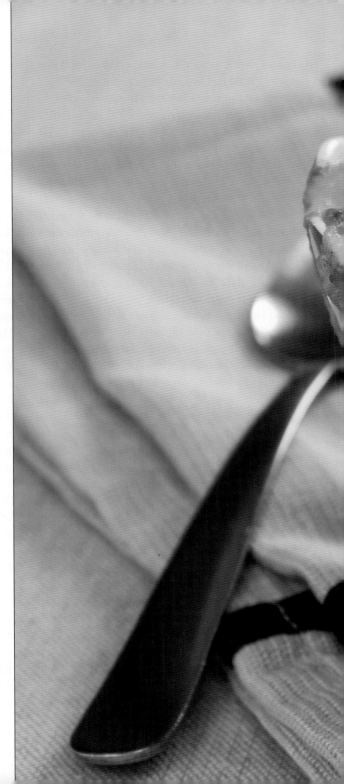

Cheese Strata

There are as many variations on cheese strata as there are types of cheese and bread with which to make it. For this simple cheese strata sandwich Swiss or cheddar cheese between slices of French bread, baking the whole in a savory egg custard. It's good for breakfast or brunch and with the addition of a green salad or vegetable makes a satisfying supper as well.

8 baguette-sized or 4 larger slices of French-style bread
6–8 oz. Jarlsburg or Swiss or cheddar cheese, sliced or shredded
   3 T. butter
   2 c. milk
   4 eggs
   ½ t. each salt
   ½ t. dry mustard
   ¼ t. white pepper
   ¼ t. nutmeg

Butter each bread slice on one side only. If using the large slices, cut each in half. Use the remaining butter to generously grease an 8" or 9" square baking pan or casserole dish. Beat together the egg, milk, and seasonings until well blended. Place the bread, unbuttered-side up, in the baking dish. Pour the egg mixture over the slices, rotating them as necessary so that they evenly absorb the liquid. Sandwich the cheese in between every two slices of bread, buttered sides out. At this point the strata can be covered and refrigerated for a few hours (up to overnight) or baked immediately. Place in a 350°F oven until puffed and golden, about 45 minutes. Serve warm. This makes about 4 servings.

Sautéed Snow Peas

June is generally when the first snow peas, also known as sugar pod or edible pod peas, begin to ripen. Although some varieties of sugar snap peas utilize both the pods and mature peas within, snow peas are eaten only for their pods, while the peas within are still immature. They're grand in stir fries and such but are also pretty tasty all on their own. Sautéing the snow peas allows them to retain their bright green color and crisp tender character.

   ½ lb. fresh snow peas (3–4 good handfuls)
   2 T. olive oil
   1 T. soy sauce
   1 T. sugar

Remove the strings and stems from the snow peas. Place the olive oil in a medium-sized heavy skillet (I prefer cast-iron) or wok. Heat the oil to moderately hot; stir in the snow peas. Sauté for a few minutes, until they turn bright green and possible begin to brown a bit. Add in the soy sauce and sugar, sauté a minute longer, and serve to 3 or 4 people.

Strawberry Time

June air is mellow with the scents of new mown hay, freshly mowed lawns, and freshly turned soil. It's also strawberry time in Vermont—a season to glory in those sublime crimson berries that never taste quite as good as when they're fresh picked from the bed. Pies, jams, and shortcakes are sure to follow close behind.

Fresh Strawberry Shortcake

New Englanders prefer biscuits to sponge cake for shortcake—hence, the name "short," as in buttery. Here the biscuit dough is made sweet and soft and then baked in a round tin to cut in wedges. Nothing quite compares to fresh strawberry shortcake with real whipped cream. It's in a class by itself.

   1 qt. strawberries, hulled and sliced
   ½ c. sugar, or to taste
   1 c. heavy cream
   ¼ c. sugar

Shortcake
   1¼ c. flour
   ¼ c. sugar
   2 t. baking powder
   ¼ c. butter, melted
   ½ c. milk

Combine the strawberries and sugar in a medium bowl. Allow them to sit while preparing the shortcake; this will allow time for the strawberries to "juice up." Combine the melted butter and milk in a medium mixing bowl. Stir in the combined dry ingredients until everything is just mixed; don't overbeat. Pour into a buttered 9" round cake pan, smoothing it evenly. Bake at 375°F until golden brown and baked through, approximately 25 minutes. A toothpick inserted into the shortcake's center should come out clean or with just a few crumbs clinging to it. Using a small cold bowl, combine the heavy cream and sugar, beating them together until the cream just holds fairly stiff peaks. I prefer to serve the short-cake while it is still hot out of the oven. Carefully cut it into eighths, removing the individual wedges to serving plates and splitting them open. Spoon the strawberries evenly over the cut surfaces of each. Add a dollop of the fresh whipped cream to the tops of your shortcake servings and enjoy! Some people have been known to save extra servings for breakfast the next day.

Strawberry-Glazed Pie

For years I made a tasty variation of this using half a package of "wild" strawberry gelatin powder. However, this version utilizes only the fruit itself—equally tasty and all natural.

1 baked 9" pie shell
1 qt. fresh strawberries
1¼ c. sugar
¼ c. cornstarch
Dash salt
½ pkg. unflavored gelatin powder (1 t.)
1 c. cold water
1 t. lemon juice
Whipped cream

Wash and hull the strawberries, setting aside ½ –¾ c. of the less than perfect ones. Gently dry the rest by patting them with paper towels and refrigerate them until you're ready to assemble the pie. Place the reserved berries and ¾ c. of the water in a blender or food processor and puree them until you have a smooth liquid. Combine the pureed strawberries, sugar, cornstarch, and salt in a medium saucepan. Cook and stir over medium-low heat until it thickens and bubbles. I find using a slotted spoon or whisk helps to keep the mixture smooth. Meanwhile, soften the gelatin in the remaining ¼ cup of cold water. Once the hot mixture has come to a full boil, remove it from the heat and stir in the gelatin until it is totally dissolved. Stir in the lemon juice. Allow this mixture to cool slightly by placing the pan into a large bowl of cold water. Try for room tempera-ture, which will still be pourable but also cool enough to not cook or degrade the raw berries. Gently combine the whole-hulled berries with the glaze, coating them evenly. Pour the mixture into the baked, cooled pastry shell. Refrigerate the pie for at least 2 hours to set the glaze. Serve with fresh whipped cream. This pie is at its best the first time it's served, although you can refrigerate leftovers for a day or two if need be.

Strawberry-glazed pie is a celebration of fresh strawberries.

Sopapillas with Strawberry Apple Dipping Sauce

Sopapillas are essentially little fried biscuits, a delicacy with origins in Mexico. Their name translates as "sofa pillows" because of the manner in which they plump up while frying. Although sopapillas don't contain sugar, they are traditionally served with honey and are also tasty with powdered or cinnamon sugar or maple syrup. The strawberry apple sauce provides a cheery crimson contrast to the little fried breads and a bright flavor for dipping. This recipe makes about 1½ dozen sopapillas, depending on their sizes. It is extremely easy to double, triple, or quadruple this recipe, depending on how many you want and how long you wish to stand frying them!

1 T. butter, melted
½ c. milk
½ t. salt
1 c. flour plus extra for forming dough
1½ t. baking powder
Corn oil for frying

Begin heating about 1½" of oil in a heavy cast-iron skillet over medium heat. Combine the melted butter and milk in a large mixing bowl. Stir in the combined dry ingredients until to form soft dough. Allow the dough to rest a few minutes in order for the flour to adequately absorb the liquids. Lightly pat the dough out on a well-floured surface, folding and turning it a few times but keeping the overall texture quite soft. Pat the dough to a uniform ½" thickness and cut it into 1" squares. Once the oil has heated to approximately 350–365°F, add the little pillows about 9 or 10 at a time, depending on the size of your skillet. Although I sometimes utilize a candy thermometer to check the temperature of the oil, other times I simply heat it for about 10 minutes over medium heat. The sopapillas will plump up and turn golden on one side. If you're lucky, they will obligingly flip themselves over; otherwise, use a fork or slotted spoon to help them along. Once they are deep golden brown on both sides, remove them to a paper towel–lined tray to cool. Pile into a paper towel–lined bowl or basket and enjoy them warm or at room temperature.

Sopapillas with strawberry apple dipping sauce will get your day off to a dandy beginning.

Strawberry Apple Dipping Sauce

If you have some less-than-perfect strawberries or perhaps a few that are getting a little too old to enjoy whole, try utilizing them in this sauce. The chopped apple mellows it out and adds pectin for consistency. This may also be poured over pancakes, waffles, French toast, or even ice cream.

1½ c. hulled, diced strawberries
1 c. sugar
1½ c. cored, diced unpeeled apple
1 T. lemon juice

Combine the strawberries, apple, and sugar in a medium-sized heavy saucepan. Bring to a full boil over medium heat, stirring occasionally. At a full boil, the entire surface of the mixture will be bubbling briskly. Remove it from the heat and allow it to cool to room temperature. Stir in the lemon juice. In a blender, puree the sauce until it is fairly smooth; the apple peel and strawberry seeds will give it a little texture. Serve the sauce warm or chilled for dipping or pouring. This makes about 2 cups of sauce; refrigerate any leftovers.

Strawberry-Fruited Salad Greens

If you're lucky, you'll have some fresh lettuce or spinach out in your garden waiting to be picked. A combination of the two is even better. I've never measured the quantity of greens used for this salad, generally just washing and tearing up a nice heaped serving for each salad bowl.

Leaf lettuce *and/or* baby spinach, torn into bite-sized pieces
3–4 fresh strawberries per serving
2 T. glazed nuts per serving
Optional: a few pieces of diced mozzarella or queso fresco per serving

Heap the greens of choice into serving bowls, or if you prefer, combine them in a larger serving bowl. Sprinkle the sliced strawberries and glazed nuts over the top, adding the diced cheese if you wish. Just before serving, drizzle with orange mint dressing. For a little variety, add in a bit of diced mango and serve your salad with lime poppy seed dressing.

Glazed Nuts

1 c. pecans or walnuts
1 T. butter
1 T. light corn syrup
2 T. brown sugar
½ t. salt

Combine the butter, corn syrup, brown sugar, and salt in a small saucepan. Bring just to a boil. Stir in the nuts and cook, stirring, until the syrup has dehydrated and the nuts are glazed. Be careful not to burn them. Pour the nuts out onto a waxed paper–lined cookie sheet to cook thoroughly, pulling them apart if they clump together.

Orange Mint Dressing

½ c. orange juice
1 T. honey
1 T. balsamic vinegar
¼ t. salt
⅛ t. freshly ground pepper
2 T. olive oil
1 T. chopped fresh mint leaves, loosely packed

Whisk together everything but the mint leaves to combine well. Just before pouring over the greens, add the mint. This makes about ¾ c. of dressing and generously dresses 4 large salads.

Lime Poppy Seed Dressing

Lime poppy seed dressing adds a bright touch to any fruit salad. Try it with pineapple and citrus sections for a delicious breakfast or brunch treat.

3 T. sugar
3 T. lime juice
½ t. salt
¼ t. onion powder
½ c. corn oil
1½ t. poppy seeds

Blend together the sugar, salt, lime juice, onion powder, and oil until everything is well incorporated and the mixture is thick. Stir in the poppy seeds and serve at once or chill, covered, for later use. This makes approximately ¾ cup of dressing.

Chocolate-Dipped Strawberries

Sometimes simple pleasures are the best. The only two ingredients necessary for this one are fresh whole strawberries and some quality chocolate. You need bulk chocolate for this recipe, not chips. The chips have lecithin added as a stabilizer, which might be good for chocolate-chip cookies but isn't so great for melting. I prefer the Callebaut brand, which I purchase in bulk at my local food co-op, although any good-quality chocolate will do. Watch out for anything with too-high cocoa solids content; they will prevent the chocolate from liquefying properly when it melts. I find real white chocolate, which contains cocoa butter but no cocoa solids, melts the best of all, but beware of those pesky imitation "white" concoctions made with palm oil; they won't give the same result and don't even taste particularly good.

About 36 large strawberries with stem ends attached
½ lb. bulk dark chocolate
½ lb. bulk milk chocolate
½ lb. bulk white chocolate

Wash the strawberries and gently pat each one dry with paper towels. Place ⅓ on each of three waxed paper–lined baking sheets. Chop each kind of chocolate into small chunks and set aside. I use a small double boiler for melting my chocolate. If you don't have one, use a medium saucepan and a metal or glass bowl that will fit the top of the pan without falling into the water. Fill the pan of choice about ½ full and bring the water to a boil. Reduce to a simmer and place the boiler top or bowl, filled with the white chocolate, over the water. Stir the chocolate occasionally until it just melts smooth. Removing the bowl from the double boiler or pan, dip the first third of the strawberries into the melted chocolate, swirling to coat evenly. Holding each strawberry by its stem or hull is the easiest way to facilitate dipping. Place each dipped berry on the waxed paper and set aside in a cool place once completed. Place any extra melted chocolate into a small bowl or plastic sandwich bag to use for decorating the berries once all are dipped. Next place the milk chocolate in the bowl, repeating the melting and dipping proce-

dure. Finish with the dark chocolate. If at any time the chocolate begins to harden too much for easy dipping, simply place the bowl back over the simmering water for a minute or two. It is important to maintain a low, even temperature for the melting process, because overheating the chocolate will cause it to harden, at which point further exposure to heat will only harden it further. Once the berries are all dipped, snip a little hole in one corner of each plastic bag and squeeze decorative stripes of contrasting chocolate over the dipped

strawberries. If the chocolate in the bag seems a bit too hard, soften it by dipping briefly into hot water prior to snipping the corner. You may also drizzle the remaining melted chocolate over the strawberries from a spoon if not using bags, although the results will be harder to control. Make sure to keep the chocolate-dipped strawberries in a cool place until they are ready to be enjoyed! They are best eaten as soon as possible after the chocolate has hardened.

What could be more tempting than a platter of fresh strawberries covered in rich chocolate?

Coconut Custard Pie

Custard pies in general are notorious for their soggy crusts. Some recipes even call for slipping the cooked custard filling into the baked pie shell after the fact, although that seems like a great deal of effort for such a humble little pie. This version uses a slightly different approach to the whole situation by including flour and butter in the custard, allowing the "crust" to separate from the filling during the baking process. If you prefer a plain custard pie, simply omit the coconut or do as I sometimes do—sprinkle half the top with coconut and the other half with nutmeg.

4 eggs, beaten
¾ c. sugar
2 c. milk
1½ t. vanilla
½ c. flour
¼ t. salt
¼ c. butter, melted
1 c. flaked coconut
¼ t. grated nutmeg

Combine all the ingredients except the coconut and nutmeg in a medium mixer bowl and beat until smooth. Pour the mixture into a deep buttered 9" pie plate that has been placed on a baking sheet. Sprinkle the coconut and nutmeg over the top and carefully slide into a preheated 425°F oven. Bake for 10 minutes, reduce the heat to 350°F, and continue baking for about 20 minutes longer, until the filling is mostly set and a knife inserted near the center comes out clean. Cool thoroughly before cutting. This is especially good topped with a little whipped cream. Be sure to refrigerate leftovers.

Sunday Sponge Cake

Sponge cake is a quintessential country dessert, utilizing lots of farm fresh eggs for its light texture and golden color. The key to its elevation is adequate beating of the egg whites, forming a light and airy batter that rises in the heat of the oven. Variations on sponge cakes are used in everything from trifles to tiramisu; even those little "cream"-filled snack cakes have a sponge cakelike base. Don't feel you need to wait for Sunday to enjoy this; it's good any day of the week.

7 extra-large eggs, separated
½ t. salt
½ t. cream of tartar
1½ c. sugar
1½ c. cake flour
1 t. vanilla
2 T. lemon juice *and* 2 T. water
or ¼ c. orange juice

In a large mixer bowl, beat the egg whites with the salt and cream of tartar until foamy. On high speed, gradually beat in 1 c. sugar, until it forms thick and glossy peaks; set aside. In a narrow medium bowl, beat the egg yolks on high speed with the remaining sugar and the vanilla until they are thick and lemon colored. Lightly beat in the flour and orange juice or combined lemon juice and water. Pour the yolk mixture over the whites and fold the two mixtures gently and thoroughly together, being careful not to over blend. Pour into an ungreased tube pan; bake at 350°F about 45–50 minutes, until the top springs back when the cake is touched lightly. Cool upside down; inverting the pan over a narrow neck glass bottle works well. Run a knife or metal spreader around the edges of the pan to loosen and then turn the sponge cake out of the pan. Sprinkle with confectioner's sugar, if desired. This is especially yummy served with fresh sliced strawberries and whipped cream. This cake will make around 16 servings and will store well at room temperature, covered, for 3–4 days.

Bride's Cake

June being the traditional month of weddings, we couldn't let it go away without including a classic white cake recipe. It uses plenty of egg whites, as does the white butter cream frosting that frosts and decorates it. There are multiple uses for the egg yolks you'll have left, from custard and crème brûlée to homemade mayonnaise. So go ahead, indulge and enjoy; this cake is perfect for bridal showers, birthdays, or even small weddings (or larger ones if you wish to expand your recipes several times over).

1 c. unsalted butter, softened
2 c. sugar
3 c. cake flour
1 t. salt
3 t. baking powder
1 c. milk
2 t. vanilla
½ t. almond extract
2 t. grated orange *or* lemon zest
6 egg whites

Cream together the butter and sugar until they are light and fluffy. Beat in the flavorings. Alternately mix in the combined flour, salt, and baking powder and the milk, beginning and ending with the flour mixture. Lastly, beat in the egg whites, until the batter is smooth and creamy. Divide it evenly between three 9" round cake pans, smoothing the tops. Bake at 350°F for about 30 minutes, until the tops are light golden brown and spring back when touched lightly. Cool in the pans for 10 minutes before gently running a knife or spatula around the edges of each and turning the cake layers out to finish cooling on wire mesh racks. When they have fully cooled, fill and frost as desired.

Bride's cake, here taking advantage of a variety of luscious summer berries to produce a spectacular ending to any festive summer meal.

White Butter Cream Frosting

Use the best-quality butter you can find for this recipe; flavor is everything! And as with all recipes in this book, never try to substitute margarine, especially here; not only will the flavor be off, but so will the texture. An accurate candy thermometer is strongly recommended for making butter cream of any sort; it's possible to make it without one, but more consistent and easier with. Although most butter cream recipes use only unsalted butter, I've used a 2:1 ratio of unsalted to salted for the little extra flavor the salt adds; just be sure to use mostly unsalted, or it will become too salty. This recipe produces about 3 cups, enough to generously frost your cake with some left for decorating. Be sure to refrigerate any cake frosted with real butter cream; the eggs and butter make it very perishable.

1½ c. sugar
¾ c. water
1 T. light corn syrup
4 lg. egg whites
2 t. vanilla
1 c. unsalted butter
½ c. salted butter

Place the egg whites in a medium deep mixing bowl. In a small, heavy saucepan, combine 1 c. sugar, the corn syrup, and the ¾ c. water. Stir it over low heat until the sugar is dissolved. Clip the candy thermometer to the side of the pan, increase heat to medium high, bring to a boil, and cook without stirring until the syrup registers 238°F on the candy thermometer. If you're not using a thermometer, a few drops of the hot syrup dropped into cold water will form a soft ball. While the syrup is heating, beat the egg whites to soft peaks. Gradually add the remaining ½ c. of the sugar, beating the mixture to stiff peaks. Once the syrup has reached the correct temperature, pour it in a steady stream over the beaten egg whites, beating constantly until it is thoroughly incorporated and the mixture is stiff and glossy. Chill the meringue mixture until it is cool. Beat the butter in a medium mixing bowl until it is light and fluffy. Beat in the chilled meringue and the vanilla until the frosting is just creamy and smooth. For best results, have your cake ready to frost as soon as the butter cream is ready, as this frosting must be refrigerated and the chilling process will cause the butter in it to harden.

Nothing Tastes Sweeter Than Peas on the Fourth of July

HAVING PEAS RIPE for the picking by the Fourth of July has long been a standard for the industrious gardener in this little corner of the world. In order to sample the sweet green legumes by Independence Day, the garden must be turned and peas planted in April, a time when snow frequently still covers the ground. Thanks to the advent of sugar pod varieties, which tend to ripen earlier, this goal has become a little easier to attain. However, I must admit it's still the sweet baby peas harvested from the pod to which I aspire. Location is often as important as aspiration where gardening is concerned. The main garden frequently remains far too muddy for tilling in April, the threat of a submerged rotor tiller hanging blackly overhead. However, there's a little strip of land on the east side of the house, dry and drained, that as a rule is more than happy to be turned over on a significantly earlier date. Thanks to this obliging little garden, we really have been able to enjoy our peas by the Fourth of July.

Speaking of Independence Day, what better time to fire up the grill, toss together a few salads, and maybe even crank out a batch or two of homemade ice cream? Did someone say S'mores . . . ? How about concocting them from your own homemade marshmallows and graham crackers? July heralds the true beginning of garden bounty as well, and July recipes reflect that bounty. Broccoli, spinach, chard, and lettuces are all waiting to be picked, and strawberries are quickly morphing into black and red raspberries and jewellike red currants. And let's not forget how all those garden and fruit tree blossoms now ripening into vegetables and fruit were pollinated, either. On a sunny July afternoon, it's easy enough to hear the industrious humming of honeybees as they set about collecting nectar for their honey and pollinating blossoms at the same

time. Annual and perennial flowers in full bloom only help them in their endeavors. Throughout the month, the bees' industry will reward us with garden and orchard bounty for our summertime pleasure and, if we're lucky, to preserve for the winter as well.

Peas on the vine waiting to be picked— fresh peas give notice summer has really arrived.

July

Curds and Whey vs. Curds and Cream

Although in cheese making it's all about curds and whey, there is another sort of curd that's especially tasty this time of year. If you've ever been lucky enough to enjoy an English cream tea, you probably know what I'm talking about. Fruit curd is a rich, buttery spread to enjoy on scones, crumpets, biscuits, or even pancakes. It's especially delicious when paired with Devon cream or crème fraîche.

Lemon Curd

Lemon curd seems to be the standard by which all other curds are measured. It's very versatile, lending itself not only to a topping at breakfast or brunch but also as a cake or tart filling. If you're feeling frugal, you may substitute thawed frozen lemon juice (but please not the stuff that comes in those little plastic lemons on the produce section shelves). You might also try 1 t. of pure lemon extract in place of the zest.

2 egg yolks
1 whole egg
¾ c. sugar
¼ c. fresh lemon juice
2 t. grated lemon zest
6 T. unsalted butter

Whisk together in a small, heavy saucepan the egg and yolks, the sugar, and the lemon juice. Cook, whisking frequently, over medium heat until the mixture thickens and just starts to bubble. Remove from the heat, add the lemon zest, and whisk the butter in one tablespoon at a time, until it

is all incorporated. Cool the curd to room temperature and store, covered, in the refrigerator.

Raspberry Curd

Raspberries produce a rosy-colored curd. Try some on pancakes or French toast. This recipe works equally well with berries picked fresh from your garden or with those waiting in your freezer for just such an occasion.

1 c. red raspberries
¾ c. sugar
2 egg yolks
1 whole egg
1 T. lemon juice
6 T. unsalted butter

Place the raspberries in a small saucepan over medium heat. Crush them with a fork to release the juices; the purpose here is to heat them enough to release the juices without cooking them. Once they are nicely mashed and juicy, strain them through a wire mesh sieve to remove the seeds and excess pulp. You should end up with about 4 T. of thick raspberry juice. Combine the raspberry juice, lemon juice, egg yolks, egg, and sugar in a small, heavy saucepan, whisking well to combine. Stir over medium heat until the mixture just comes to a boil. Remove from the heat and whisk in the butter, about a tablespoon at a time. Cool to room temperature and then refrigerate, covered. This will make about 1 cup of curd.

The bees will be happy to spy our neighbors' green garden in full bloom.

Summer Strawberry Raspberry Jam

For this summer jam, I crush and freeze my strawberries in advance. Do this by removing the hulls and reducing the berries to a rough saucelike consistency (but not a puree!) by pushing down on them with a heavy sharp pastry cutter or chopping them fine with a sharp knife and mashing with a fork. Even the raspberries may be quick frozen and measured out just for this, although the freezing process may cause them to expand slightly. All that this means is that you might need 4½ cups instead of 4 to yield the 2 cups of crushed raspberries you need for this recipe; or again, crush and measure in advance. Raspberries are soft enough to easily crush with a fork or spoon. By temporarily preserving the berries at their peak of freshness, I then have a superior product to combine with the first green apples of summer, generally ready around the end of July or beginning of August. This recipe doesn't use commercial jelling products, so close attention to temperature and technique are important.

1 qt. raspberries, crushed to yield 2 c.
1 pt. strawberries hulled and crushed to yield 1 c.
5 c. sugar
1 t. citric acid *or* ¼ c. lemon juice
1 c. finely diced green apple with peel

Combine all the ingredients in a 2 qt. heavy stainless steel saucepan. Clip your candy thermometer to the side, if you're using one. Stirring constantly, bring the mixture to a full boil over high heat. Reduce the heat to medium and continue to cook, stirring occasionally, until the jam sheets from a spoon, or until the thermometer registers 220°F. (Note that for every 1,000 feet of altitude you live above sea level, the jelling temperature will reduce by 2°F.) Some folks seem to think simply heating berries and sugar to 220°F will make you jam, but they are sadly mistaken; this will only produce runny, overly sweet berries. The citric acid and apple are both components that help the jam to jell properly, as will heating it to a proper temperature. You'll be able to see when it's ready because the texture of the liquid dripping off the side of the spoon will become somewhat viscous, the drops adhering into a flat sheet when it's slowly dripped—hence, the term "sheeting." Just remember the full jelling effect won't occur until the jam is cool, so don't try to attain that texture while cooking or you'll end up with a burned, unappealing mess. Pour the hot jam into jars as and finish per "Preserving Guidelines"—processing in a boiling water bath for 10 minutes, allowing them to cool and checking for proper seal. This recipe will yield about 6 half pints or a dozen quarter pints of jam. Feel free to set a little aside in a bowl for "tasting," if you wish.

Cream Scones

Scones make a perfect pairing with curd, even better with a bit of clotted cream thrown in for good measure. If you prefer slightly less decadent fare, enjoy them with fresh-made jam. Cream scones are an especially delicate variation on this classic quick bread. The easiest way to form these scones is by patting three equal portions of dough into circles about 5" in diameter, brushing the tops with cream and sprinkling with pearl sugar (regular granulated does fine if you don't have pearl sugar). Next cut each circle into 4 wedges. I do this directly on the baking sheet, gently separating the wedges just slightly before popping the whole thing in the oven. Cream scones are also frequently cut into heart shapes; in this instance, pat the dough about 1" thick and cut with floured cookie cutter, brushing with cream and sprinkling with sugar before gently removing to baking sheets.

2 c. flour (for a lighter scone, try 1 c. each all-purpose and cake flour)
¼ c. sugar
¼ c. firm unsalted butter
1 t. vanilla, optional but tasty
1 T. baking powder
½ t. salt
1 egg

¾ c. cream
Extra cream for brushing tops
Sugar or pearl sugar for sprinkling tops

Combine the flour, sugar, baking powder, and salt in a medium mixing bowl. Using a pastry cutter or two knives, cut in the butter until the mixture resembles coarse meal. Stir together the egg, cream, and vanilla with a fork until they are well blended. Pour the cream mixture over the dry ingredients and mix lightly until just well blended. Turn out onto a smooth surface (I just use the baking sheet) and knead 8–10 times before patting out dough and shaping as above. Bake on an upper rack in a 375°F oven until they are light golden brown, approximately 15–20 minutes. The baking time will be longer for rounds cut in wedges and shorter for individual hearts. Serve warm or at room temperature. If these are more scones than you can eat in a day or two, simply wrap label and freeze to use within a month.

Raspberry Almond Muffins

These sweet. rich muffins taste almost like something you'd buy in a pastry shop. They are tasty for breakfast, brunch, coffee, or tea break—even dessert! Pearl sugar is a coarse granular sugar frequently used when baking Scandinavian sweet breads. It is increasingly easy to purchase, but if you can't find it, granulated sugar will do for the topping.

⅓ c. butter, melted
¾ c. milk
½ t. almond extract
1 egg
⅓ c. sugar
2 c. flour
3 t. baking powder
½ t. salt
¼ c. good-quality raspberry preserves
2 T. pearl (coarse) sugar
¼ c. slivered almonds

Combine the melted butter and egg to mix well. Add the milk and the almond extract. Stir in the combined dry ingredients. Divide evenly between 12 buttered or paper-lined muffins cups. Make a slight indent in each muffin and top with 1 t. of the raspberry jam. Sprinkle the muffins evenly with the pearl sugar and slivered almonds. Bake on an upper rack in a preheated 375°F oven for about 20 minutes, until golden brown and firm on top when lightly touched. Enjoy these muffins warm or cold but be aware that the preserves will be very hot for about 5 minutes.

The Flight of the Honeybee . . . Finding a Bee Tree

Honeybees are mighty amazing little critters. They also happen to be the state insect of Vermont. As our state flower is red clover, this combination works out rather nicely for the production of Vermont's "other" sweet treat, clover honey. Because honeybees produce and store honey in their hives, folks have been busy figuring out how to harvest that honey for thousands of years. An added bonus of the honeybees' industry is beeswax, produced by certain members of the hive through special abdominal vents, and valuable in its own right for use in candles, natural lip balms, as a protective covering for cheese, and even as a type of modeling clay. Honeybees, whether domestic or wild, send out scouts to hunt for important nectar sources, which they do through both sight and smell. They also use the sun for direction. The scouts, upon arriving back at the hive, will then "dance" for the other bees, indicating through their motions and buzzing how far away the nectar source is and in which direction. Wild honeybees generally nest in hollow cavities of aging trees, where they will stockpile their sweet golden liquid. Unlike domestic hives, a wild honey tree may hold several years' accumulation of honey—a real bonanza for anyone lucky enough to claim it. When I was growing up, I was told a person finding a wild honey tree in Vermont could legally claim the honey within it for harvest, even if the tree was on someone else's land, providing that person was skilled and industrious enough to track down the tree in the first place and then have the courage to fight off the honeybee colony for their spoils. One summer when the kids were little, we followed a flying trail of honeybees to a large half-dead tree deep in the woods behind our house. We could see them swarming in and out of a hole near the top of the truck; we'd finally found our honey tree! However, as I've mentioned, finding a honey tree and then having the skill and will to actually harvest that honey can be two different things. I didn't relish either trying to cut down the tree or the thought of fighting off all those newly enraged bees for their honey, so our discovery, while exciting, remained just that. Still, it is fun to remember.

Honey Graham Crackers

Using a pizza or pastry wheel makes cutting these in squares that much easier. You may also wish to try cutting a few into different shapes with cookie cutters, brushing with milk and sprinkling with a little colored sugar for a fun and slightly healthier variation on a cookie.

1½ c. all-purpose flour
1 c. whole-wheat flour
½ c. packed brown sugar
¼ c. granulated sugar
½ t. salt
1 t. baking soda
1 c. unsalted butter
¼ c. honey
¼ c. milk
Milk for brushing tops of crackers
Optional: cinnamon sugar for topping crackers

In a large mixing bowl, combine the flours, sugars, baking soda, and salt. Cut or crumble in the cold butter with a pastry cutter or your fingers until the mixture resembles coarse cornmeal; there should still be little lumps of butter visible, but they should be fairly fine. Combine the milk and honey and pour over the flour and butter mixture, mixing with a fork until the wet and dry are just combined. Divide the dough into two equal portions, wrap airtight and refrigerate at least 2–3 hours; 2–3 days is fine. For longer periods, freeze the dough to use within a month. When you're ready to bake your grahams, roll out a portion of the chilled dough on a lightly floured board to about ⅛" thickness. Cut into 3" squares, place on ungreased baking sheets, and prick the top of each cracker several times with a fork. If desired, brush lightly with milk and sprinkle with cinnamon sugar (1 t. cinnamon to 2 T. sugar). Bake on the upper shelf of a 350°F oven for 10–12 minutes, until they are golden and slightly puffed. Watch closely so they don't burn. This makes about 4 dozen or so, depending on their size.

Honeybee Custard Cake

This rich, sweet coffee cake is glazed with honey and almonds. It may be enjoyed for breakfast, brunch, a midmorning snack, or even for dessert. Try making the dough and the custard filling the evening before and refrigerating overnight for ease of preparation in the morning. If you prefer a little less fuss, simply prepare the cake and forego the custard filling; it's quite nice all by itself.

Cake

¾ c. milk
⅓ c. sugar
2 eggs
6 T. butter
1 T. dry yeast
2 c. bread flour
¼ t. salt
¼ t. Fiori di Sicilia
or 1 t. each vanilla and grated orange rind
2 T. honey
2 T. sugar
2 T. butter
½ c. toasted, slivered almonds

Custard

1 c. milk
1 c. cream
6 egg yolks
2 T. cornstarch
½ c. sugar
1 t. vanilla
¼ t. almond extract

Glaze

¼ c. butter
¼ c. sugar
¼ c. honey
1 T. water
⅓ c. slivered almonds

Prepare the custard cream. Combine the sugar and cornstarch in a medium-sized heavy saucepan. Whisk in the milk and cream until liquid and dry is totally incorporated. Cook over medium heat, whisking frequently, until the mixture comes to a full boil. Meanwhile, beat the egg yolks in a small bowl to combine. Add a small amount of the hot milk, stirring well, to temper the egg yolks. Quickly whisk the yolks into the hot mixture and, continuing to whisk, heat to boiling one again. Remove from the heat and whisk in the flavorings. Allow to cool completely, stirring a few times the first 5 minutes or so and then covering the custard cream with a piece of waxed paper to prevent a skin from forming in the top. Refrigerate until ready to use.

For the cake batter. Melt the butter in a large, heavy saucepan over low heat. Stir in the sugar, milk, and eggs, whisking smooth and heating until just lukewarm. Remove from the heat and stir in the yeast to dissolve. Beat in the salt and flour; you will now have a fairly stiff batter. Allow it to rest for about 15 minutes before pouring it into a buttered ring pan, smoothing it evenly. Place in a warm place to rise for about ½ hour. Bake at 375°F for 25–30 minutes, until golden brown and hollow sounding when tapped. Cool upright for about 5 minutes before turning out of the pan and completing the cooling process. Using a long serrated knife, evenly split the cake in two horizontally. When you assemble the cake, the "top" will become the base and the rounded portion formed by the ring pan will become the top.

Honeybee coffee cake may be enjoyed as a decadent breakfast treat or for a sweet summer dessert.

Split the cooled cake and prepare the glaze. Melt the butter in a small saucepan; add the honey, sugar, and water. Bring to a full rolling boil. Carefully spoon about ¼ c. of the mixture over the bottom layer of cake. Place the cake in the fridge to cool the glaze. Pipe or spread the custard cream evenly around the bottom layer and add the top

layer. Add the almonds to the remaining honey glaze and bring it back to boiling; maintain at a full boil for 1 minute. Allow it to cool slightly before spooning evenly over the filled coffee cake. If it's too hot, it will begin to melt the filling, in which case place the cake in the freezer for about 5 minutes. On the other hand, don't cool it completely or it will become too sticky to glaze evenly.

Honey Shrub

My mother was a great advocate of the restorative properties of honey and cider vinegar. Shrubs were originally a cool summer drink combining vinegar, water, and a sweetener—refreshing in a presoda and iced tea world. Red clover, Vermont's official state flower, produces a golden light honey that's just perfect for shrub. This drink is simple and bracing, although possibly somewhat of an acquired taste. The weaker of spirit may prefer to substitute lemon juice for the cider vinegar; I'm sure our forbearers wouldn't object.

> 1 T. honey (preferably clover)
> 2–3 t. cider vinegar
> Pinch of ground ginger (optional)
> 8–12 oz. cold water

Combine all the ingredients in a tall glass, stirring vigorously. Add some ice cubes for the maximum cooling effect. Sip and savor.

Fresh Green Pea Soup

Although we tend to think of pea soup as a dish prepared from dried split peas, fresh or frozen green peas make a lovely green soup with a delicate flavor you can't replicate with the dried. It also takes considerably less time to make and is a good way to use up those post–Fourth of July peas you might not have captured quite at their peak of freshness. This soup is especially tasty chilled.

4 c. fresh or frozen thawed green peas
4 c. chicken stock *or* vegetable stock *or* water
½ t. salt or more if using water
2 T. butter
2 t. sugar
½ c. diced onion
¼ t. white pepper
1 T. fresh mint leaves
Crème fraîche *or* sour cream

Cook the onion in the butter until the onion is tender but not browned. Add the peas, salt, pepper, sugar, and broth or water and bring to a boil. Cook just until the peas are tender, about 5 minutes. Puree small batches at a time in a food processor or blender, remembering that hot liquids are more prone to escape from these devices than cooler ones. For an especially smooth soup, pour the pureed mixture through a strainer; this will produce a thinner, slightly less abundant amount of soup. A food mill might also work well for

Cool and smooth fresh green pea soup may be enjoyed with or without a dollop of cream.

producing a smoother soup. If you'd prefer a little extra fiber, just keep it as is. Return to the pan and stir in the minced mint leaves. Serve warm or chilled with a dollop of crème fraîche or sour cream swirled on the top of each helping. This serves 6–8.

Cheese Broccoli Turnovers

Cheese broccoli turnovers are an outgrowth of my family's affection for broccoli with cheese sauce coupled with my desire to create another savory finger food, the better to showcase homemade puff pastry. They are delicious as a fancy appetizer, an accompaniment to soups or salads, or even as an unusual breakfast treat. The turnovers may be prepared in advance and frozen, unbaked, in sealed freezer bags (freeze them on baking sheets first to retain their shape). Simply place the frozen turnovers on ungreased baking sheets and proceed as for fresh ones, adding about 10 minutes baking time per sheet.

1 recipe puff pastry ("January")
2 c. diced broccoli
1 T. butter
1 T. flour
¼ t. salt
¼ t. nutmeg
¼ t. dry mustard
⅛ t. white pepper
1 T. snipped fresh chives
⅓ c. milk
2 oz. cream cheese
3 oz. (¾ c.) shredded sharp cheddar cheese

Steam the broccoli until it is just tender but still bright green, about 2–3 minutes. Remove from the heat, drain, and set aside. Make a roux of the butter and flour in a medium saucepan by melting the butter and stirring in the flour and the dry seasonings. Add the milk, chives, and cream cheese, whisking briskly; the mixture will be very thick. Remove it from the heat as soon as it starts to bubble. Stir in the cheddar cheese until it melts and everything combines smoothly. Lastly, stir in the broccoli. Transfer the mixture to a small bowl, cover, and refrigerate until you're ready to make your turnovers. You can make this a day or two in advance if you wish; it should be cold when you're filling the turnovers. Although this amount is quite close to what you'll need to fill 20–24 small turnovers, which is what the pastry recipe will yield, you may have a bit of leftover filling. This is good spread on buttered toast and broiled for just a minute or two, or used as a filling for a grilled sandwich. For constructing the turnovers, roll the pastry dough thin and cut into 3" × 3" squares. Place about 1 t. of cooled filling on each, folding the dough over into a triangle and sealing the slightly moistened edges. If desired, brush with milk and sprinkle with poppy or sesame seeds. Cut a small slit in the top of each. Bake in the upper third of a preheated 425°F oven until puffed and golden brown, about 15–25 minutes.

Ham-and-Broccoli Quiche

Quiche is a great summertime supper—easy to prepare and easy to reheat. It's versatile enough to enjoy for breakfast, brunch, or lunch as well. Take advantage of plentiful fresh broccoli to concoct this tasty and healthful egg tart.

1 unbaked pastry shell
3 eggs
½ c. dry milk powder
1 c. water
½ c. cream
¼ t. nutmeg
¼ t. Tabasco sauce
½ t. salt
½ t. onion powder
½ t. dry mustard
2 c. diced fresh broccoli—steamed until just tender, drained, and cooled
4 oz. diced ham: about 1 c.
4 oz. diced Gruyère cheese: about 1 c.

Combine the eggs and seasonings in a medium bowl. Beat the eggs with a whisk or large fork until the whites and yolks are totally integrated. Mix together the dry milk and water until it forms a smooth slightly thick liquid. Add this mixture along with the cream to the eggs, again stirring until totally bended. You want a smooth golden mixture, but not one that has been beaten so much that there is froth. Place in order the broccoli, ham, and cheese into the unbaked pastry shell, distributing them evenly. Place the pie plate in the middle of a preheated 425°F oven. Carefully pour the egg mixture over the filling ingredients. Bake at 425°F for 10 minutes. Reduce heat to 350°F and bake for 25 minutes longer, until the top is light golden and is slightly puffed. Remove to a cooling rack and allow it to cool for at least 10 minutes before serving. This will serve 4, although with a salad and bread it might be stretched to 6. Refrigerate any leftovers promptly. It's easy to reheat individual pieces in the microwave for about 1 minute before serving, or they may be eaten chilled.

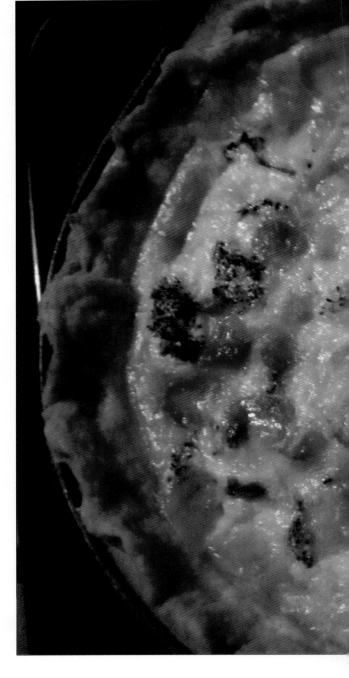

This ham-and-broccoli quiche just hits the spot for brunch or a light summer supper.

Garden Greens with Brown Butter Sauce

Garden greens are a little different kettle of greens than the wild greens available earlier in the year. Chard, beet greens, and kale are all hearty garden greens with a more rich and mellow flavor than the little guys bursting forth in spring. Although I don't generally raise collard or turnip greens, I'm thinking they'd be tasty prepared in this manner as well.

1 lg. bunch of garden greens, well washed (about 4 c. chopped)

Brown Butter Sauce
¼ c. butter
1 T. molasses
1 T. soy sauce
2 T. cider vinegar
A few drops Tabasco sauce

Pick the greens over and wash them well with cold water. If they are young and tender, they may be left whole; if very large, coarse chop them, stems into fine pieces and leaves larger. Place them in a large covered pan or Dutch oven with about a cup of water and bring to a boil. Allow the greens to steam for about 5 minutes, until they are tender but still retain their bright colors. While they are cooking, prepare the brown butter sauce. Melt the butter in a small saucepan. Stir in the remaining sauce ingredients and heat for a minute or two to bend the flavors. Drain the greens well and serve them with the sauce. They are especially good with pork chops or barbecued ribs.

Summer Bean Salad

My brother and sister-in-law, Marshall and Veronica, live near our town's main parade route and have frequently hosted "after-parade" family picnics. One of their many specialties at these gatherings would be a big bowl of colorful and crunchy bean salad. Bean salads make a wonderful accompaniment to just about any cookout meal or summer picnic. Try varying the types of beans you use or substitute whole kernel corn for one of the bean varieties. This is also a great way to use up leftover cooked beans.

2 c green beans
2 c. yellow beans
2 c. lima *or* kidney beans
½ c. cider vinegar
½ c. corn oil
1 t. salt
¼ c. sugar
¼ c. honey
1 t. paprika
1 t. mustard seeds
½ t. celery seeds
1 small red onion, diced
1 stalk celery, diced
½ red, green, or yellow bell pepper, diced

Cut the beans into manageable pieces, probably no more than 2" long. If necessary, parboil them in a little salted water until they are tender crisp, about 8–10 minutes. Drain them well; however, it's not necessary to chill them. Combine the beans in your favorite salad bowl along with the onion, celery, and bell pepper. Whisk or shake together the vinegar, oil, salt, honey, sugar, paprika, mustard seeds, and celery seeds until

Perfect for your Fourth of July celebrations, summer bean salad and shimmering red, white, and blue salad are easy to make ahead, giving you time to enjoy your holiday.

everything is somewhat emulsified. Pour immediately over the bean mixture, stirring to coat well. Although you may serve the salad immediately, it's better when allowed to chill out in the fridge for a few hours or overnight to blend the flavors.

Red, White, and Blue Salad

Three cheers for the Fourth of July! And three cheers for this colorful jellied fruit salad—a perfect accompaniment to your patriotic barbecue. Cooking with plain gelatin powder is easier than you might think and can produce eye-catching results. Use fresh or best-quality (frozen rather than bottled) lemon and lime juice for best flavor and results.

1 pint fresh strawberries
1 c. fresh blueberries
2 pkg. unflavored gelatin powder
1 c. cottage cheese

4 oz. cream cheese
¼ c. lemon
¼ c. lime juice
¾ c. sugar
3 c. water
Pinch of salt

Soften the gelatin in ½ c. cold water. Meanwhile, bring 1 c. of water to a boil in a medium saucepan. Remove from the heat and stir in the gelatin, sugar, salt, and the lemon and lime juices until the sugar and gelatin are fully dissolved. Add the remaining 1½ c. of cold water, stirring well.

Pour 1 c. of this mixture into a 4-cup gelatin mold. Very lightly oiling the mold or spraying it with nonstick cooking spray will help your salad to unmold more easily later. Place the thin layer of gelatin in the refrigerator or freezer to firm up slightly; watch closely so it doesn't totally gel. Refrigerate the remaining mixture as well to chill just until it resembles raw egg whites when stirred. Rinse and hull the strawberries—depending on their size, halve, quarter, or leave them whole if small. Rinse the blueberries as well. Arrange about ¾ c. of the nicest-looking strawberries and ½ c. of the blueberries on the partially set gelatin layer. If

you've quick set it in the freezer, now is the time to move it to the fridge so it doesn't end up freezing solid! Chop the remaining strawberries into small pieces. In a medium mixing bowl, beat the cream cheese until it is soft and smooth. Fold in the remaining gelatin mixture, the cottage cheese, and the remaining strawberries and blueberries and pour carefully over the layer already in the mold. Refrigerate for approximately 2 hours, until the salad is firmly set. When you're ready to serve, dip the mold for a few seconds in hot water up to the level of the gelatin mixture and immediately turn out on the serving plate. This serves about 8.

Sweet-and-Sour Slaw

Perhaps you have some little green cabbages maturing in your garden. They're at their most flavorful and nutritious when harvested and eaten nice and fresh. This slaw can be prepared a day in advance, covered, and left in the refrigerator until serving time; it actually improves the flavor. Honey or sugar may be used, as you wish.

¼ c. sugar *or* honey
¼ c. cider vinegar
¼ c. water
1 t. salt
½ t. paprika
½ t. onion powder
¼ t. celery seeds
¼ t. black pepper
½ c. corn oil
Shredded cabbage: about 4 c.
Green pepper, diced

Heat together all the ingredients except the corn oil, cabbage, and green pepper. Bring them just to boiling, then remove from the heat, and add the corn oil. Cool slightly and pour over the cabbage and pepper. This would probably coat 4 cups of cabbage combined with green pepper to taste quite nicely.

BLT Salad

If you're lucky, July will bring the first juicy ripe tomatoes for you to enjoy. If you're even luckier, you'll still have some respectable lettuce or other salad greens to enhance your enjoyment. Unfortunately, the same July heat that ripens tomatoes tends to turn cool-loving greens such as lettuce bitter and cause them to bolt (grow stems and start flowering). I have no qualms about investing in a nice head of commercially grown iceberg lettuce to form the base for this salad; better the lettuce than the tomatoes!

Crisp lettuce *or* mixed salad greens
Fresh tomatoes cut in wedges, *or* cherry tomatoes
3 slices bacon per person, cooked crisp
2 slices preferred bread per person
1 T. olive oil per person
Herbed buttermilk dressing (next)

Heat the olive oil in a heavy skillet over medium high heat. Cut the bread into cubes; add them to the hot oil, turning occasionally until they are golden. Allow the croutons to cool while preparing the rest of the salad. Chop or tear the lettuce into large individual salad bowls. Add tomatoes and crumbled bacon to each. Top with the croutons and drizzle herbed buttermilk dressing over all just before serving, or allow each person to dress his or her own.

Herbed Buttermilk Dressing

This dressing is fairly thin; it contains none of the stabilizers used in many commercially produced dressings. Because it's a fresh dressing, you'll want to use it within a couple of weeks. A hint for a longer shelf life: the most perishable part of this dressing is the buttermilk; check the "sell by" date prior to purchase. Buying the freshest there is should help keep your dressing fresh longer as well.

1 c. buttermilk
½ c. mayonnaise
½ t salt
1 sm. or ½ lg. clove garlic*
1 T. fresh *or* 1 t. dried parsley
1 T. fresh *or* 1 t. dried minced chives *or* scallions
¼ t. coarse ground black pepper
¼ t. dried *or* ¾ t. fresh snipped dill weed

Whisk together the mayonnaise and buttermilk until smooth. Gently stir in the remaining ingredients until everything is nicely blended. Store your dressing, covered, in the refrigerator. This will make about 1½ cups of dressing.

*The flavor of the garlic may be quite pronounced initially; allowing the dressing to mellow for a day or two in the fridge will make it less pungent.

Potato Salad

Potato salad is another summer staple; a good way to use up the last of the stored potatoes, if you're lucky enough to still have some, or made even tastier with tiny new potatoes just dug. Most potato salads include a mayonnaise dressing, although in some instances a vinaigrette type may be used. If you'd like to try a vinaigrette marinade, I would recommend the dressing Provençal used in the Salade Niçoise for this purpose. Simply marinate warm chunks of cooked potatoes in the dressing, adding bits of minced red onion and/or celery, if desired. Serve as is, or chill overnight to more fully develop the flavors.

Green Beans Provencal

This is an open-ended recipe in that you can marinate quite a few green beans or only a few in the amount of dressing made here. The herbed salad dressing is also nice on green salads, or use it for the Salade Niçoise recipe below. And although they would probably no longer be considered Provencal, green beans cooked in this manner are also quite tasty marinated in the easy French dressing listed earlier.

¼ t. rosemary
¼ t. thyme
¼ t. salt
¼ t. marjoram
¼ t. basil
¼ t. tarragon
¼ c. white wine vinegar
or lemon juice
or 2 T. of each
½ c. olive oil
1 clove garlic, minced
1 T. snipped fresh chives
Fresh green beans, strings removed if necessary

Snap or cut the beans into 2" sections or leave whole, as desired. Cook them briefly in boiling salted water to cover until they are just tender but still bright green, about 10 minutes. If you already have cold cooked green beans left over from an earlier meal, you're one step ahead. In either instance, marinate the still-warm or chilled beans in just enough dressing to lightly coat them. Allowing them to marinate for a few hours or overnight improves the flavor saturation.

When preparing creamy potato salad, I like to enhance the flavor with olives and the texture with sour cream.

4 medium-sized red-skinned potatoes, cooked in the skin until just tender
1 stalk celery, diced
2 T. snipped chives
2 T. minced fresh parsley
1 T. fresh-snipped dill weed
½ t. salt
¼ t. fresh ground pepper
¼ c. sliced green-pimento stuffed olives
2 hard-cooked eggs, optional
¾ c. mayonnaise, or to taste
½ c. sour cream
Paprika if desired

Allow the potatoes to cool to room temperature before cutting them into 1" cubes. If using potatoes with tender skins, don't bother to peel them; the skins add color and texture. Place in a large bowl and add everything but the mayonnaise, sour cream, and eggs. Allow the salad to chill, which will start the flavors blending. Once it is thoroughly cold, stir in the mayonnaise, sour cream, and the peeled, diced hard-cooked eggs, if you're using them. Garnish the salad with a sprinkle of paprika and/or more of the fresh herbs, if desired.

213

Salade Niçoise

The origins of this tempting main dish salad are from Nice, in the south of France—hence, the name Niçoise. It combines tuna, potatoes, and haricots vertes (green beans) with eggs, olives, and a savory herbed dressing. Add fresh salad greens and wedges of ripe red tomatoes to round out the color, flavor, and nutritional value of this meal-in-a-salad. Although anchovies are also considered traditional to Salade Niçoise, I choose to omit them. However, if you're an anchovy fan, by all means include a few of the little rascals. Tuna canned in olive oil is used in a traditional Niçoise, but if you prefer to grill up a small piece of fresh tuna instead, I won't prevent you.

1 recipe dressing Provencal, made with lemon juice
1 t. Dijon mustard
1 T. drained capers
6 oz. can tuna packed in olive oil
2 hard-cooked eggs
1 lg. or 2 smaller potatoes—red, blue, or purple skinned
½ lg. or 1 smaller tomato, *or* a few cherry tomatoes
¼ c. Niçoise olives or halved kalamata olives
1 handful, about ⅛ lb., fresh young green beans
Mixed salad greens *or* leaf lettuce
Anchovies, optional

Prepare the dressing as directed, whisking in the mustard and capers. Cook the potatoes in boiling salted water until they are just fork tender; remove them from the cooking water to cool. I add the whole, stemmed green beans to the same water, although you may cook them separately if you wish. After coming to a boil, the beans need cook only about 5 minutes so that they're still bright green and just crisp tender. Remove the beans to cool also; the beans and potatoes are best served at room temperature for this salad, although chilled is fine if you wish to prepare them in advance. To assemble, neatly center the drained tuna on a 12" serving platter. Arrange the potatoes, beans, and greens symmetrically around the tuna. Garnish with tomato and egg wedges; sprinkle with the olives. If you're using anchovies, now would be a good time to drape a few artistically over the salad. Drizzle on the dressing and serve at once to two folks with robust appetites or 3–4 less hungry. Crusty bread or rolls make a nice go-with.

Salade Niçoise gives a Mediterranean flavor to your menu; it's colorful and delicious.

Easy French Dressing

Summertime is salad time, so be sure to have lots of delicious dressings on hand to complement all those fresh fruits and vegetables. Easy French dressing works well with either; toss it with tender lettuce and baby radishes for an early summer treat, or try drizzling over thin slices of honeydew or cantaloupe for a new take on melon.

2 T. lemon juice
2 T. sugar
¼ t. onion powder
½ t. salt
½ t. paprika
6 T. olive oil

Combine the lemon juice, sugar, salt, paprika, and onion powder in a small bowl and whisk well to dissolve all the seasonings. Gradually whisk in the olive oil, beating vigorously, until the mixture is smooth and thickened. Refrigerate any leftovers, covered. This makes a little more than half a cup of dressing.

215

Marinated Flank Steak

This marinade is perfect for the rather tough cuts of steak you never quite know how to prepare. The marinade adds flavor and tenderness to the meat for a delicious and economical meal. This steak may be grilled or pan fried. In the latter case, pour the remaining marinade over the steak about 2 minutes before it's done, turning at least once, so that the sauce will cook to a safe temperature and further glaze the steak without burning. Depending on the thickness of the steak, it may take 4–5 minutes per side in a hot skillet coated with a little olive oil. Leftovers go into the fixings for another cool summer salad.

2 lb. flat boneless steak
½ c. orange juice
¼ c. red wine vinegar
¼ c. olive oil
¼ t. fresh ground black pepper
2 cloves garlic, minced
½ t. oregano
½ t. rosemary
½–1 t. salt, to preference

Combine all the marinade ingredients, which would be everything except the beef, whisking them to blend well. Using the sharp tip of a knife or tines of a heavy-duty fork, puncture the surface of the steak multiple times on both sides. Place it in a nonreactive container, such as glass or plastic, as close in size to the steak as possible. If it makes the process easier, you may cut the steak in two or more pieces in order to fit it in snugly. Pour the marinade over all, turning to coat all surfaces evenly. Cover and refrigerate the steak, turning at least once in the process, for 1–2 days in order to suffuse it with flavor and adequately tenderize it. When you're ready to grill, place the steak on a preheated medium-high grill, cooking it approximately 10 minutes per side for medium rare. Brush the steak with the marinade several times during the cooking process, until it has all been utilized. The one safety reminder here is to use the last of the marinade well before the grilling process has ended so that any raw meat juices in it cook thoroughly. Allow the steak to rest about 10 minutes before slicing thinly at a diagonal angle. This amount of steak serves up to 8 as it is. If you prefer, slice only half of it and refrigerate the rest to use another day in steak-and-barley salad. In this manner, you can feed 4 for one hot meal and up to 8 with the salad.

Marinated flank steak provides two hearty meals from one grilling, as a main course one day and a hearty salad the next.

Steak-and-Barley Salad

This hearty salad is cool enough for the hottest summer night. I've been fortunate enough to discover a purple hulled variety of barley, which is just magnificent in this recipe, although really any good, respectable barley will do. Add some fresh melon or a dish of sorbet for a refreshing end to your meal.

1 lb. cold grilled flank steak, above, thinly sliced
1 c. barley
2½ c. water
2 T. snipped fresh chives
1 additional recipe marinade (above)
1 c. sliced asparagus *or* green beans, raw or cooked and chilled
1 medium zucchini, diced
1 lg. tomato, diced, *or* 1 c. cherry tomatoes

If you intend to divide the steak into two meals, it may be easier for you to simply prepare a double batch of the marinade initially, using half for the marinating process and refrigerating the remainder for the salad. Plan to make your salad within 2–3 days of cooking the steak to ensure freshness. The cooking time for the barley may vary according to what type you use. I prefer organic purple barley, unprocessed, which takes between an hour and an hour and a half to cook. Place it in a medium saucepan with a tight-fitting lid, add the water, and bring to a boil. Reduce the heat and simmer, covered, until it is tender but still somewhat chewy. Add the snipped chives to

the second batch of marinade. Pour about ¼ c. of this mixture over the thinly sliced steak, stirring to coat well, and allow it to chill in the refrigerator to further flavor the meat. Stir the diced raw zucchini and another ¼ c. of the marinade into the hot cooked barley. If you are using raw asparagus or green beans, add them as well; if using chilled leftover veggies, as I often do, wait until the next step. Once the barley mixture has cooled to room temperature, refrigerate it to chill thoroughly. Stir in the marinated beef strips, the beans, or asparagus (if using precooked), the tomatoes, and any remaining marinade. Allowing the salad to mellow in the fridge for a few more hours will enhance the flavor. This is especially nice served with good crusty bread or rolls.

Barbecued Chicken

"White" barbecue sauce is the traditional one for chicken around this house, so named because it contains no tomatoes. Reminiscent of the sauce frequently used at church and volunteer fire department fund-raising barbecues, it's tangier and less sweet than a tomato-based sauce. Set a little aside for dipping the cooked chicken in while eating; it can be slightly addictive!

Sauce

½ c. cider vinegar
½ c. water
¼ c. butter
¼ c. corn oil
½ t. dried thyme
2 T. Worcestershire sauce
1 t. paprika

½ t. onion powder
1½ t. salt
2 t. honey
¼ t. celery salt
¼ t. Tabasco sauce
3–4 lb. chicken, cut in barbecue-sized pieces

Combine all the sauce ingredients in a small saucepan. Bring to a boil, reduce the heat, and simmer for about 5 minutes. Remove from the heat and cool completely. When ready to barbeque, heat your grill to medium high. I prefer to place the chicken pieces on lightly oiled squares of foil for the initial cooking process. Grill them covered, just of center of the heat (if using a gas grill) for about 35–45 minutes, basting once or twice with some of the sauce. To complete cooking and to give a nice finish to the skin, place the chicken directly on the grill, turning frequently and basting with more sauce, until the outside is crisp and brown and the meat tender. When pricked with a fork, juices should run clear. Remove from the grill and serve with any extra sauce. Potato salad, corn on the cob, tossed salad and/or baked beans all sound like good ways to round out this meal. Potato chips might not be such a bad idea, either.

Easy Barbecue Pork Sandwiches

You don't even need a grill to make these easy to concoct and eat sandwiches. If you do have a gas grill and the weather is hot, simply use the burner on the side for cooking and help keep the house cool. Serve your barbecue pork sandwiches with a nice platter of vegetables

and dip, and corn on the cob or potato salad for a relaxed summer supper.

1 lb. stew pork
2 T. corn oil
1 med. onion
1 lg. clove garlic
1 T. chili powder
1 T. cider vinegar
2 c. water
2 T. brown sugar
¼ c. ketchup
Hamburger buns (or hot cooked rice)

Make sure the pork is cut into uniform cubes about 1" square to facilitate even cooking. Heat the oil in a medium-sized heavy saucepan. Add the pork and brown it well over medium-high heat. Add the onions and garlic, cooking a minute longer. Combine all the remaining ingredients and pour over the meat mixture in the pan. Bring to a boil, lower the heat, and simmer, covered, until the meat is very tender, about 1 or 1½ hours. Add small amounts of water as necessary to prevent burning, but don't overdo it; you want the sauce to cook down somewhat. Once everything is nice and tender, pull the pork into shreds with two forks, if desired. Serve over hamburger buns. For a change, try the pork over hot cooked rice instead; it won't be a sandwich, but it will still be tasty! This serves 4.

Hot Dogs and Sauce with Rice

If you ever have one of those lazy summer days when you don't really feel like cooking but want to produce something more impressive than a frankfurter in bun, try this. This is a very kid-friendly recipe and great for potlucks. It's simple and tasty, easy enough to prepare on the burner of an outdoor grill if you're so inclined. Add some fresh veggies from the garden as sides and you're good to go.

1 lb. franks, sliced into ½" pieces
2 T. butter *or* oil
1 small onion, thinly sliced
⅓ c. packed brown sugar
¼ c. ketchup
1 T. vinegar
1 T. prepared mustard
1 c. water
2 c. water
1 c. rice
1 T. butter

Bring the rice, 1 T. butter, and 2 c. water to a boil in a medium covered saucepan. Reduce the heat and simmer the rice until it's fluffy and soft, about 20 minutes. Meanwhile, prepare the hot dogs and sauce. Heat the 2 T. butter or oil in a large, heavy skillet. Add the sliced franks and brown them over medium heat. Add the sliced onion about halfway through the browning process, allowing it to soften and lightly brown as well. Add the brown sugar, ketchup, mustard, vinegar, and 1 c. water, bring to a boil and cook the mixture a few minutes over medium-high heat, until the sauce has reduced somewhat. Serve the hot dogs and sauce over the hot cooked rice. This serves 4–6, depending on appetites and sizes of the people involved.

I Scream, You Scream . . .

We all know the old childhood chant for ice cream. Summer is ice cream time, and homemade ice cream is a special summertime treat. Ice cream has a long and storied past. Although Nero sent slaves into the mountains for ice so that he could concoct a type of fruit and honey sorbet, according to some sources, dairy-based ice cream (as in yak milk) actually originated in China several millennia ago. Whatever its true origins may be, it remains one of the most popular desserts in the world. Here are three variations, two made the traditional way and one for those requiring no special ice cream machine; each one tasty, I think you'll agree.

Chocolate Frozen Custard

I prefer my chocolate ice cream somewhat mellow as opposed to the exceedingly dark concoctions some folks have produced. My hubby Bruce tells me the flavor of the frozen custard in this recipe reminds him of those little frozen fudgy treats on a stick you can buy by the package.

2 c. milk
1 c. sugar
¼ c. unsweetened cocoa powder
6 egg yolks
Dash salt
¼ c. semisweet mini chips or grated chocolate
2 c. heavy cream
Additional mini chips or chopped chocolate, optional

Combine the cocoa powder, salt, and sugar in a heavy sauce pan, whisking to combine the fine powder with the more granular sugar; this will help it integrate more smoothly with the liquids in the recipe. Whisk in the egg yolks and then the milk. Cook, stirring frequently, over low heat until the custard reaches 165°F or coats a spoon, as mentioned in the vanilla frozen custard recipe. Immediately stir in the grated semisweet chocolate or mini chips, stirring to melt them. Chill the custard thoroughly before combining with the heavy cream. If you wish, add in up to another ½ cup of mini chips or grated chocolate. Freeze according to individual ice cream freezer guidelines, or follow the steps above for pan freezing. This will make about 2 quarts of ice cream.

French Vanilla Ice Cream

The ingredients in French vanilla ice cream are very similar to those in frozen custard recipes, in that the liquid base is enriched with egg yolks. This produces a golden·ice cream with a creamy flavor and texture. The basic recipe lends itself nicely to addition of seasonal fruits or other such goodies. An ice cream maker is strongly recommended for making creamy ice creams and sherbets. The continual stirring motion integrates air into the freezing liquid, giving them their characteristic smooth and creamy texture. It is possible to make them without, although the texture may suffer somewhat. I've included directions for "freezer freezing" below.

2 c. milk
1 c. sugar
6 egg yolks
Dash salt
1 T. vanilla
2 c. heavy cream

Combine the milk, sugar, egg yolks, and salt in a heavy saucepan, whisking to blend them thoroughly. Cook, stirring frequently, over low heat until the custard mixture reaches 165°F, or until it "coats a spoon." You will notice a significant change in consistency when it reaches this point. Immediately remove from the heat and chill completely. If for some reason the custard has heated a little too much and is beginning to appear curdled, place the pan in a bowl or larger pan of cold water and beat the custard vigorously for a minute or two. It is imperative that the custard be ice-cold before proceeding to the next step. Add the vanilla and heavy cream to the chilled custard. At this point you will be freezing your soft custard according to the directions of your individual ice cream maker. If you don't have one, pour the custard into a 9" × 13" baking pan and freeze it until the edges are partially frozen. Scrape into a mixer bowl and beat the mixture smooth. Pour back into the pan and repeat this procedure at least two more times. Each time the custard should have a thicker, creamier consistency. After the final beating, pour it into your desired storage container and allow it to freeze solid. This makes 1½ to 2 quarts.

Mint Mallow Ice Cream

Although I try to give equal garden space to both my peppermint and spearmint plants, the spearmint inevitably takes over, running rampant over my hapless peppermint and any stray chives foolish enough to get in their way. I therefore spend a fair amount of time each summer pulling and redistributing spearmint plants and probably using them far more than my preferred peppermint for this very reason. Either of these mints or a combination of both will work for this recipe, in which the fresh mint leaves are heated with milk and cream to infuse them with their flavor. It's not such a bad idea to begin the infusing process the day before, both for the best flavor and most effective chilling time. I use homemade marshmallows in this ice cream, although purchased mini-marshmallows will work just fine. Because the ice cream is thickened with whipped cream and egg white meringue, it is direct frozen rather than using an ice cream maker.

1½ c. milk
1½ c. heavy cream
2 c. packed fresh mint leaves
1 T cornstarch
3 eggs separated
1c. sugar divided
⅛ t. salt
2 c. homemade marshmallows, cut fine
1 c. semisweet chocolate mini chips (optional)

Combine the cream and half the mint in a small saucepan; combine the milk and remaining mint in a second and bring each to just under a boil. Remove from the heat and allow them to steep, covered, until lukewarm. Place them in the refrigerator to finish chilling overnight. Pour the cream into a fine meshed wire sieve placed over a small mixing bowl, allowing it to drain thoroughly and pressing the mint leaves with the back of a spoon to facilitate the process. Place the bowl of cream, covered, back in the fridge. Strain the milk mixture into a medium saucepan, again pressing to extract as much milk as possible. Into the cold milk whisk the cornstarch, ⅓ c. of the sugar, salt, and egg yolks. Whisk thoroughly to blend well and then cook the mixture over medium heat until it thickens and bubbles, stirring constantly to prevent sticking or burning. Chill the custard over cold water to room temperature and place the covered pan in the fridge to chill completely. Place the egg whites in a large heat proof mixing bowl and begin whipping them until they hold soft peaks. Meanwhile, combine the remaining ⅔ c. sugar with ⅓ c. water in a small saucepan. Bring to a full boil and allow it to boil for 3 minutes. With the mixer running, pour the hot sugar syrup in a thin stream over the beating egg whites. Continue to beat them at medium high speed for another 2–3 minutes, until stiff glossy peaks form. Gently pour the meringue mixture into a bowl, cover, and refrigerate until it is very cold, at least an hour. Once all three mixtures have chilled thoroughly, fold them together in a large bowl, adding the marshmallows and the chocolate chips if desired. If you wish, add a few drops of green food coloring. Immediately turn into a half gallon freezer container, smoothing the top slightly. Cover and freeze solid before serving.

Homemade Marshmallows

If you've never tried homemade marshmallows, you don't know what you're missing. The flavor and texture border on the sublime— a far cry from those puffy little nuggets you find hanging out in plastic bags on the bottom shelves of grocery store candy aisles. Add them to the mint mallow ice cream base, combine them with homemade graham crackers and chocolate for amazing S'mores, or just pop them in your mouth; they won't disappoint!

3 T. unflavored gelatin powder (3 pkg.)
½ c. cold water
2 c. sugar
¾ c. light corn syrup
½ t. salt
½ c. water
1 T. pure vanilla extract
Confectioner's sugar or toasted coconut

Soften the gelatin in the ½ c. cold water in a large heatproof mixer bowl. Meanwhile, combine the sugar, corn syrup, remaining ½ c. water, and the salt in a heavy medium-sized saucepan. Heat over medium high, stirring, until the sugar dissolves and the mixture begins to boil. Clip a candy thermometer to the side of the pan and cook, without stirring, to 244°F, which is just the beginning of what is referred to as "medium ball" stage. Turn the mixer, with a whipping attachment, to medium speed. Immediately pour the hot syrup over the dissolved gelatin in the mixing bowl, increase the speed to medium high, and beat the mixture for 15 minutes. At this point it will be thick, fluffy, and white. While it is beating, prepare a 9" × 13" pan by lightly oiling or coating with nonstick spray and then sprinkling it with confectioner's sugar or toasted coconut. Beat in the vanilla and immediately pour it into the prepared pan, smoothing the top. Sprinkle either confectioner's sugar or toasted coconut over the top to evenly coat the surface.

Nothing beats the flavor and texture of homemade marshmallows, shown here dusted with confectioner's sugar or coated with toasted coconut for a special treat.

Fudge Walnut Brownies

All-American brownies are one of our most universally loved treats. Who could imagine a school bake sale without them? Homemade brownies can make an already yummy dessert classic even better. Try these with a scoop of homemade ice cream for a cool summer delight. The corn syrup in this recipe will ensure dense, chewy brownies that store well.

½ c. butter
½ c. corn oil
2¼ c. sugar
¼ c. light corn syrup
½ t. salt
2 t. vanilla
1¼ c. flour
4 squares unsweetened chocolate
1 c. chopped walnuts
4 eggs

Melt together the butter, chocolate, and oil. Stir in the sugar, salt, and vanilla. Beat in the eggs, 2

at a time. Stir in the flour and then the chopped walnuts. Spread in a greased and floured (or cocoa sprinkled) 9" × 13" pan. Bake at 350°F for 30–35 minutes, until the top is shiny and slightly firm to touch; don't overbake. Cool slightly before cutting into bars; this makes 24.

Raspberry–Chocolate Chip Cheesecake

What's not to love about raspberries and chocolate held together in a creamy cheesecake? Raspberry–chocolate chip cheesecake is a perfect summer dessert, capturing raspberries at their brightest. As an added bonus, it's easy to prepare in advance. Let it hang out in your refrigerator until it's time to impress everyone!

Puree

2 c. fresh or frozen red raspberries
¼ c. water
Crust:
1 wrapped pkg. (⅓ box) chocolate (not chocolate-coated) graham crackers
Or 1 c. homemade graham cracker crumbs *plus* 2 T. unsweetened cocoa powder
¼ c. sugar
¼ c. butter, melted

Filling

3–8 oz. pkg. cream cheese
1 c. sugar
1 T. cornstarch
¼ c. raspberry puree
3 eggs
¼ c. cream
1 c. mini chocolate chips
1 t. natural raspberry flavoring (don't use imitation; just omit)

Cream Topping

1 c. heavy cream
1 c. sour cream
½ c. confectioner's sugar
1 t. vanilla

Raspberry Glaze

½ c. raspberry puree (or remainder)
¼ c. sugar
1 t. cornstarch

Combine the raspberries and water in a small saucepan and cook, crushing with back of spoon, until mixture comes to a boil. Blend or process until smooth and then pour the mixture through a wire sieve to get rid of most of the seeds. This makes about ¾ cup of puree; set aside ¼ c. for the filling and use the remainder to make the glaze. Add water to the remaining raspberry puree to equal ¾ cup total. Combine with the sugar and cornstarch in a small saucepan. Bring to a boil over medium heat. Remove from the heat and cool completely. Crush the crackers to fine crumbs and combine with the cocoa powder, if you're using it. Stir in the sugar and butter and pat into the bottom of a buttered 10" springform pan. Beat the cream cheese and sugar in large mixer bowl until smooth and creamy. Beat in the eggs, one at a time, and the cornstarch. Mix in ¼ c. of the raspberry puree, flavoring and cream until everything is well combined. Fold in the mini chocolate chips. Pour over crust and bake in a 350°F oven about 45–50 minutes, until middle no longer quivers when you shake the pan. Gently run the blade of a knife or a spatula around the edge of the springform pan; this will help prevent the top from cracking while it's cooling. Allow the cheesecake to cool at room temperature for about an hour and then refrigerate until it's thoroughly chilled. Slide a spatula around the edge of the springform pan and release the clasp to remove it. Place the cheesecake with its base on a serving plate. Beat the heavy cream to soft peaks, adding the sugar and vanilla. Fold in the sour cream. Frost the cheesecake with the cream topping. To decorate the cheesecake, pour the glaze from a pastry bag with a fine tip or a plastic sandwich bag with one corner snipped into concentric circles on top of the cheesecake. Using a toothpick or knife tip, lightly draw out from the center of the circle and then in toward the center of the circle, alternating all around the cake. This will form a kind of webby design. Garnish with raspberries and cream, if desired. This serves 12–16.

Chocolate Raspberry Torte

Probably because they're so perishable, commercially purchased fresh raspberries aren't as affordable as many other fruits and berries. If you're able to pick your own or purchase at a farm stand, you'll be rewarded with a superior product and more reasonable price tag. Better yet, perhaps there's a little corner of your lawn just yearning to nurture a few red raspberry bushes. With adequate water, a bit of fertilizer, and an annual thinning and trimming, you'll be rewarded with an abundance of the delicate little fruits.

1 recipe chocolate layer cake (page 30)
½ c. classic red raspberry sauce (below)
1 t. cornstarch
1½ c. fresh raspberries
½ c. semisweet chocolate bits
½ c. milk chocolate bits

1½ c. heavy cream
4 oz. semisweet chocolate
Easy buttercream frosting (below)
1 T. corn oil

Easy Buttercream

6 T. salted butter
6 T. unsalted butter
1 t. vanilla
3 c. confectioner's sugar
2 T. cream

Bake the cake in two 9" round cake tins. Cool 10 minutes in the tins, turn out on racks, and finish cooling thoroughly before using. Meanwhile, heat the heavy cream in a small saucepan until it just boils. Remove from the heat and stir in the semisweet and milk chocolate chips until they are all melted. Refrigerate the cream until it is quite cold. Combine the ½ cup of cold raspberry sauce and 1 t. of cornstarch in a small saucepan and bring to a boil; remove from heat and chill this as well. For the buttercream frosting, combine the butter and vanilla in a medium mixing bowl, creaming them together until smooth. Gradually beat in the confectioner's sugar alternately with the cream. (This will make enough frosting for the outside of a 9" layer cake, as used here. If you'd like to utilize this recipe at some point to fill and frost a cake, increase each of the ingredients by half.) To assemble the torte, place one cake layer, bottom-side up, on preferred serving dish. Whip the chilled chocolate cream until it's thick and fluffy and spread it evenly over the cake. Top with 1 c. of the raspberries and the raspberry sauce. Place the top cake layer, top-side down, on the filling, pressing gently. Frost the entire cake with the buttercream, reserving a little to pipe decoratively around the edges, if you desire. Decorate the torte with the remaining raspberries and the piped buttercream; refrigerate until serving time. This makes a lovely big cake, which will serve a number of people. You may cut and wrap individual pieces to freeze for later, if you wish.

Chocolate raspberry torte makes the end of your summer meal extra special.

Raspberry Cream Pie

Sweet, fresh-picked red raspberries, still warm from the sun, are one of life's less common pleasures. Aside from eating them out of your hand, raspberry cream pie is one of the nicest uses I can think of for such delights.

9" baked, cooled pastry shell
4 oz. cream cheese
½ t. vanilla
¾ c. heavy cream
¾ c. confectioner's sugar
2 c. fresh or unsweetened frozen raspberries
½ c. sugar
1 pkg. unflavored gelatin
½ c. cold water
¾ c. heavy cream
¾ c. confectioner's sugar
¼ c. sugar

Beat the cream cheese until fluffy in a small mixing bowl. Gradually add the confectioner's sugar and vanilla and then whip in the cream until the mixture is thick and creamy. Spread this into the baked pastry shell and chill. Dissolve the gelatin in the cold water. Combine the ½ c. sugar and the berries in a saucepan and cook over moderate heat until they just begin to boil, stirring frequently. Stir in the gelatin mixture and bring back to a boil. Remove from the heat and cool the mixture in the pan in a bowl of ice water, until it mounds when dropped from a spoon. Don't let it thicken too much, as you will next be pouring it over the cream filling layer in the pastry shell. Once the fruit filling has been evenly spread over the cream filling, allow it to chill for around an hour. When ready to serve, whip the ¾ c. of heavy cream with the ¼ c. sugar until soft peaks form. Pipe through a pastry bag or dollop it decoratively around the edges of the pie. This makes 8 servings.

Classic Red Raspberry Sauce

Growing up in a Scandinavian American household, I was exposed to lots of raspberries: fresh, in jams, in puddings, and in syrup form. Probably because of that exposure, smooth raspberry sauce is one of my favorite things; its uses are many and varied. Besides forming an integral part of this torte, check out some other easy recipes at the end of this one.

2 c. raspberries, either fresh or frozen unsweetened
¼ c. sugar
1 T. raspberry liqueur, optional

Place the raspberries and sugar in a small saucepan. Bring the mixture slowly to a full boil over medium heat, occasionally crushing the berries with a back of a spoon to bring the juices out. Stir in the raspberry liquor. If children are going to be consuming the sauce and you're concerned about the alcohol content, either add the liquor at the beginning of the cooking process so that the heat will cook it away, or simply omit it altogether. Pour the berries into a fine-wire mesh sieve and strain them through, pushing the pulp

Sweet and juicy, crimson red raspberries provide us with a plethora of summer pleasures.

with the back of a spoon. This step is important both for the texture and volume of the sauce. When it's been adequately strained, you should have about 1 cup of glowing red, naturally thickened raspberry sauce. I don't mind a few seeds in mine, although if you prefer it super smooth, you may wish to strain it again; the second straining should go much faster than the first. This recipe is extremely easy to double, triple, or quadruple, in case you're expecting a crowd for raspberry sundaes. It freezes easily too; pour into small resealable containers, label, and freeze for a rainy day. Red raspberry sauce has many uses—pour it over ice cream, cake, or custard; swirl it in a bowl with fresh whipped cream or yogurt; or try one of the refreshing drinks below.

Raspberry Spritzer

2 T. red raspberry sauce
8 oz. sparkling water
Red raspberries frozen in individual ice cubes, optional

Combine the sauce and sparkling water in a tall glass, adding plain or raspberry-filled ice cubes to taste. Try varying the recipe with flavored waters and different garnishes, adding a lemon slice to lemon, lime to lime, or a ripe red cherry to black cherry flavor sparkling water. A cool treat on a hot summer day.

Raspberry Slushy

This is a little bit like the slushies you can purchase at many convenience stores. The difference is the all-natural ingredients and delicious flavor; there's nothing like the real deal!

2 c. crushed ice
2 T. red raspberry sauce
¼ c. orange juice *or* pineapple juice *or* lemonade

Combine all the ingredients in a blender. Puree them at high speed until the mixture is thick and smooth. Enjoy this by sipping it through a straw.

Raspberry Ice Cream Soda

When I was growing up, Brattleboro still had a couple of drugstores sporting their own soda fountains. It was quite a treat to visit one of these and order an ice cream soda. At the Hotel Pharmacy, the proprietor himself would occasionally measure out the syrup and light cream, which would be stirred in a bulb-shaped soda glass, fizzed up with seltzer, and topped with a coordinating scoop of ice cream.

2 T. red raspberry sauce
½ c. milk *or* half and half
Sparkling water
1 scoop vanilla *or* raspberry ice cream

Mix together the sauce and milk or half and half in a large glass. Gently pour in the sparkling water to within about an inch of the top. Add a scoop of ice cream, a long-handled spoon, and a bendy straw. Yum!

Outdoor Adventures and the Abundant Garden . . .

BEFORE THE ADVENT of air-conditioning and effective fans, second-floor bedrooms could become quite stifling in the heat of an August night. My mother, a great believer in the healthy properties of fresh air, solved this problem by moving us, beds and all, out to the back porch for the summer months. There was no screening on the porch, making the mosquito's job that much easier, and the occasional skunk or other peculiar-smelling night wanderer was able to pass through unhampered as well.

Being out in the clear night air also enabled us the better to hear faint percussion from the miniature cannon an eccentric old farmer a few hillsides over purportedly had set up to frighten the raccoons out of his sweet corn. Concerned with the raccoons' persistence, he'd cleverly set it up to go off every hour or so . . . at least until the complaints started streaming in to my dad and other officers down at the town police station.

Ah, those were the days. However, positives generally outweighed the negatives in these nocturnal adventures. Fireflies glimmering in the evening woods, bats fluttering in the soft mauve pink of a predawn sky—those images are what remain in my mind far more than the misadventures of mosquitoes, skunks, and old farmers setting off explosions of questionable efficacy. By the end of the month, autumn's tang was definitely working its way back into the early-morning air, making those wool blankets from the Army & Navy store mighty warm and inviting. Because the porch faced east, we were also provided a good inducement to be up and about by full sunrise; no need for an alarm clock out there! And in August, up and about is a good thing;

The garden soaks up the sunshine of an August day. It seems as though everything is suddenly ripening at once.

August is also when the blueberries begin to fully ripen, adding another splash of color to our culinary palate.

summer's bounty is overflowing. It's the month when all those seeds so hopefully planted in May have matured into a plethora of vegetables and flowers. It's also when the lazy gardener will rue not having weeded or mulched a little more assiduously earlier in the season, as the weeds will more than obligingly cover every square inch of unguarded turf. However, going on the assumption that we've all been very conscientious about such things, it's time to haul out the preserving kettles and clear last season's leftovers from our freezers, for the time of harvest is upon us.

August

Wild Blueberry Muffins

One of Bruce's coworkers lives on a hillside over in Sullivan, New Hampshire. His front lawn is covered with high-bush wild blueberries, and for several years when our kids were little, we'd head over as a family to pick berries there. Wild blueberries are one of nature's true delicacies—smaller and tangier than their domestic counterparts. I especially love them for making muffins and pancakes. If you're lucky enough to have access to wild blueberries, I hope you'll enjoy them this way too.

¼ c. butter, melted
1 egg
1 c. milk
½ c. sugar
2 c. flour
3 t. baking powder
¼ t. salt
2 T. sugar
½ t. cinnamon
1½ c. fresh or frozen thawed wild blueberries

In a medium mixing bowl, whisk together the melted butter, egg, and milk. Stir in the combined flour, ½ c. sugar, baking powder, and salt until the wet and dry ingredients are just combined. Gently stir in the blueberries. If you're thawing frozen berries, run them under cool water for just a minute or two and allow them to drain well before adding to the batter. Divide the batter evenly between 12 buttered or paper-lined muffin cups. Combine the 2 T. sugar and the cinnamon and sprinkle them evenly over the tops of the muffins. Bake on the upper shelf of a 400°F oven

Wild blueberry muffins rely on nature's bounty to provide the tiny sweet fruits that give them their special texture and flavor.

for about 20–25 minutes, until the tops are rounded and golden brown and the muffins are firm to touch. Place the muffin tin on a wire rack to cool, tipping the muffins out after about 10 minutes. Serve these warm or at room temperature; store extras in the muffin tins, lightly covered with foil or plastic wrap. This makes 12 muffins.

Calico Muffins

This is the time of year for calico muffins. The first apples are ripening, early carrots are ready to pull, and as always in August, there is more zucchini than we generally know what to do with! The vegetables and fruit are grated and added to the batter, giving these muffins their characteristic multiflecked "calico" appearance.

1 c. shredded carrot
1 c. shredded zucchini
1 c. shredded apple (no need to peel)
1 c. sugar
¾ c. corn oil
2 eggs, beaten
1 t. baking soda
¾ t. salt
1 t. cinnamon
1 t. vanilla
1 t. grated orange zest
2 c. flour
½ c. shredded coconut
½ c. chopped walnuts

Whisk together the sugar, corn oil, eggs, vanilla, and orange zest. Add the shredded carrots, zucchini, and apple. Stir in the combined dry ingredients until well blended; this produces a fairly stiff batter. Divide the batter between 18 lined or well-greased muffin cups. Bake on an upper shelf of the oven at 375°F until golden and springy to touch, approximately 15–20 minutes. These are moist

and keep quite well if wrapped tightly and protected from heat. You can also individually wrap in plastic and freeze; use within one month for best taste.

Corn Pancakes

Fresh corn pancakes spread with blackberry jam or crabapple jelly make a tasty August breakfast. A side of maple bacon can only improve such things. If you happen to have an ear or two of corn leftover from a previous meal, wrap and store it in the fridge for up to 3 days. Simply cut it off the cob with a serrated knife when you're ready to make pancakes. Canned or thawed frozen corn may (sigh) be substituted if need be.

1 c. flour
1 T. sugar
1 T. baking powder
1 t. salt
1 egg
1 T. corn oil
1 c. milk
¾ c. cooked fresh corn

Whisk together the egg, milk, and oil. Add the dry ingredients, whisking until smooth. Lastly, stir in the corn. Have your griddle so hot that a drop of water skitters across the surface. Oil it lightly and drop on three equal spoonfuls. Cook until bubbles form all across the pancakes' surface. Flip them to the other side, allowing approximately the same amount of cooking time for the second side. The corn sometimes slows down the cooking process, so make sure your centers are done all the way through before removing. You can make these whatever size you prefer; I generally get about 12 pancakes from this size batch. Serve hot with butter and blackberry jam or crab apple jelly. For a savory alternative, try serving them with fresh tomato sauce instead.

Crab Apple Jelly

Rosy crimson crab apple jelly is surely one of the most naturally beautiful jellies you can produce and is also one of the easiest. One of my coworkers compares the flavor of crab apple jelly to flowers, which may be a rather close approximation. Finding the correct crab apples for your purpose may be the most challenging part of the whole operation. For a number of years my mother had a Dolgo crab apple tree on the front lawn, later replaced by another out by the side of our old goat barn. If you can find this particular tree and have the space for it, you will be rewarded by fragrant white flowers in the spring, beautiful crimson fruit in late summer, and a plentiful source for making fine jelly. Unlike many fruits, apples and crab apples already have high pectin content, especially in their skins. For optimal results, pick the crab apples while they're still quite firm and slightly under ripe.

8 c. crab apples, washed well in cold water
4 c. water
3 c. sugar

Place the clean crab apples in a large nonreactive pan. Some folks prefer to remove the stems and blossom ends of the crabapples before placing them in the water. I don't generally and have found that as long as my fruit is fresh and clean, this is not a problem. Bring the fruit and water to a boil and simmer, covered, for 20–30 minutes. Strain the juice through several thicknesses of cheesecloth, allowing plenty of time for draining without squeezing the bag, which will produce the clearest jelly. Plan on at least an hour for this procedure; longer is even better.

You should now have around 4 cups of crab apple juice. Discard the pulp; it's great in the compost bin. Combine the 4 c. of crab apple juice and 3 c. of sugar in a large stainless steel saucepan. Bring the mixture to a boil, skimming occasionally if need be. Maintain the mixture at a full rolling boil until it sheets from a spoon when a little of it is poured out sideways. This will register around 220°F on a candy thermometer. Immediately pour through a funnel into hot, sterilized jelly jars, bringing the liquid to within ½" of the top. Add lids and rims, screwing them on fairly tightly. Process the jelly in a boiling water bath for 10 minutes. Carefully remove to a padded level surface to cool; you should hear the lids pinging down as they seal. Once they have cooled completely, you can leave the rims on or remove them, as you wish. This makes about 5–6 half pints, or twice as many quarter pints.

Rustic Bread

Here's the perfect accompaniment to your platter of spaghetti or for that meatball grinder you've been dreaming about. If you prefer, divide the dough into 4–6 sections and form into grinder rolls instead of 1 long loaf; adjust the baking time down just a bit.

1 c. very warm water
1 t. sugar
2 t. salt
1 T. olive oil
1 T. yeast
2¼ c. bread flour

Place the water, sugar, and 1½ t. salt in a large mixing bowl. Sprinkle on the yeast, stirring to dissolve. Beat in 2 c. of the flour. Cover the dough with a damp dish towel and allow it to rise

Crab apples hanging crimson on the tree are harvested and boiled whole to produce the juice which in turn forms the basis for jewellike crab apple jelly.

in a warm place for 1 hour. Knead in additional flour to make a nice springy dough. Form into a long, thin loaf and place on a greased baking sheet that has been sprinkled lightly with cornmeal. Cut four diagonal slashes on the top with a sharp knife. Combine the remaining ½ t. salt with ¼ c. hot water. Allow the bread to rest for

15 minutes while the oven is preheating to 425°F. Every 5 minutes, brush the top lightly but liberally with the salt water. Bake on an upper oven rack for approximately ½ hour, until the loaf is lightly browned and sounds hollow when tapped. Place on a cooling rack; serve warm or cool.

239

Love Apples

Tomatoes, one of the most universally loved and utilized vegetables, are technically a fruit (due to their seeds being held within the body). Originally cultivated by the Aztecs, tomatoes eventually made their way to Europe, where the initial response was lukewarm at best. Whether they were referred to as "love apples" (*pommes d'amour*) due to their internal resemblance to other fruits of passion such as apples, figs, and pomegranates, or simply as a clever marketing ploy, tomatoes eventually surged to the forefront of culinary stapledom. How nice to know they're not only adaptable to a wide range of recipes but also good for us, containing both the antioxidant lycopene and loads of vitamin C. Tomatoes are so eager to be consumed in so many delicious ways, so who could resist them? Enjoy them now, before the weather starts dipping much below 50°F; tomatoes are tender plants that don't do well in autumn's chill. There are ways to extend your growing season should you desire. Most obvious is a thin covering of newspaper or old sheets to protect your plants from early frosts, taking them off in the morning. If you have a plant or two in an aboveground planter, simply move them in at night when it gets too chilly. It's also possible to bring an entire plant or two in (roots and all), hang upside down where they won't dry out too much, and allow the partially ripe tomatoes to finish the process indoors, although this is a less-than-exacting approach and a rather space-consuming one. Perhaps better to ripen your green tomatoes on the windowsill or simply to fry them up for a summertime treat.

Fried Tomatoes

There's a reason folks frequently use green tomatoes for frying; they're not as juicy as fully ripe ones and therefore less apt to start leaking all over the frying pan. I've used slightly under-ripe tomatoes, which do just fine too. In any event, you'll want the big round slicing tomatoes rather than the plum-shaped sauce and paste tomatoes. I've never attempted to fry the tiny cherry or grape tomatoes; I think their abundance of skin would get in the way of any real enjoyment.

¾ c. flour
¼ c. cornmeal
1 t. salt
¼ t. pepper
¼ t. crumbled basil
1 egg, beaten with ½ c. water
Tomato slices, about ¼" thick
Corn oil for frying

Combine the flour, cornmeal, salt, pepper, and basil in a small bowl. Beat the egg and water together in another small bowl. Dip each tomato slice in the dry mixture, the egg and water, and again in the dry mixture. Heat about ½" of corn oil in a cast-iron or heavy frying pan until it's a medium-high temperature. Place the tomato slices in the hot oil and fry, turning once, until each is golden brown on both sides. Drain on paper towels and serve hot.

Tomato Paste

If you raise plum tomatoes, you might like to make up a few batches of tomato paste. It forms an easy base for spaghetti, soup, or pizza sauce and can even be used to make homemade ketchup. Immerse whole plum tomatoes in boiling water for 20–30 seconds, remove, and plunge in cold water until they're cool enough to handle. Slip the skins off, cut in half, and scoop out the seeds. Blend or process the peeled and seeded tomatoes until smooth. Place the smooth

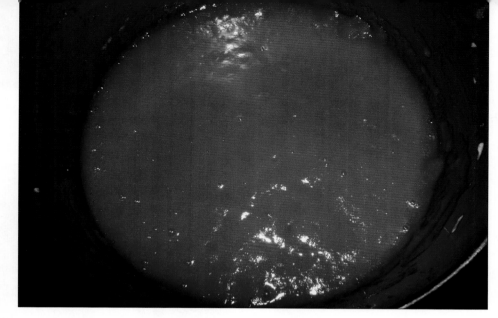

Ripe paste tomatoes are peeled, seeded, cooked, and pureed to make tomato paste.

pulp in a heavy nonreactive saucepan. Bring to a boil and then cook over low heat, stirring occasionally, until it has reduced down to the consistency of tomato paste. A pound of plum tomatoes, about 6–8 depending on size, will yield about ¾ cup of paste. Drop by tablespoons or quarter cups onto a wax paper–lined baking sheet and freeze overnight. Seal the paste in ziplock bags, labeled with date and contents.

Fresh Tomato Sauce

Tomato sauce is the consistency of marinara, but with fewer of the herbs and spices. It makes a nice basis for various sauces or soups. It can also be served, as above, with corn pancakes or as an accompaniment to egg or meat dishes.

8–10 c. seeded peeled chopped tomatoes, about 2 lb.
1 lg. onion peeled and chopped: 1 c.
1 lg. carrot peeled and diced: 1 c.
2 stalks celery, cut in 1" slices: 1 c.
1 t. salt
1 T. honey *or* sugar
¼ t. pepper

Combine the tomatoes, celery, onion, and carrots in a large nonreactive saucepan. Bring to a gentle boil and cook, covered, over medium-low heat for approximately ½ hour, until all the vegetables are tender and the sauce slightly reduced. Blend or put through a food processor, food mill, or sieve. I recommend sieving the sauce after blending for a smoother product. At this point, you should have approximately 4 cups of sauce. Stir in the salt, pepper, and honey or sugar.

Fresh Tomato Marinara

Yum—who doesn't like a nice big plate of spaghetti? Classic red marinara sauce is even better when prepared using your own fresh tomatoes or those readily available at farmers' markets and roadside stands this time of year. This sauce is also easy to make using whole frozen plum tomatoes. Defrost them in the microwave and slip the skins off before blending as above. If you have fresh herbs, substitute 3 to 4 times as much as for the dried, mincing them before adding to the sauce.

12 plum tomatoes: about 6 c. or 1½ lb.
2 T. olive oil
½ lg. onion, chopped: ½ c.
2 cloves garlic, peeled
1 stalk celery, chopped, optional
1 carrot, chopped
1 t. salt
½ t. dried basil
½ t. oregano
¼ t. black pepper *or* red pepper flakes, depending on preference
2 bay leaves
½ c. dry wine, optional

Peel tomatoes, if desired, by plunging briefly into boiling water and then in cold until they're cool enough to handle. The skins will then slip right off. Combine all the vegetables in a blender or food processor and blend until smooth. Combine with the olive oil in a large, heavy saucepan. Add the seasonings and wine and bring to a boil. Reduce the heat to medium low and simmer, uncovered, for about ½ hour, until the sauce is reduced by a third, or until it reaches the desired consistency.

Italian Meatballs

These savory little meatballs are equally good paired with marinara and spaghetti, or made into a hot Italian grinder. Make extras if you'd like to freeze some for another day.

1 lb. ground beef
½ t. garlic powder
½ t. onion powder
1 t. salt
1 t. parsley
¼ t. pepper
¼ t. nutmeg
1 egg
¼ c. fine bread crumbs
½ c. water
2 T. grated Parmesan or blended Italian cheese
Olive oil for sautéing

Combine everything but the olive oil, blending thoroughly. Form the mixture into 16 small meatballs. Heat approximately 2 T. of the olive oil in a large, heavy skillet and sauté the meatballs, covered, over medium heat. Turn them once; they will probably cook through in 8–10 minutes. Once they are cooked through, add to your marinara sauce. If you prefer to freeze some, I would recommend quick freezing the uncooked meatballs on a cookie sheet and then wrapping them in a double layer of foil or plastic wrap. Plan to use them within a month or two.

Taco Salad

When Bruce and I were first married, taco salad was riding a wave of popularity, at least here in Vermont. Geographically located so much closer to Canada than Mexico, it took awhile for all that tasty south-of-the-border cooking to wend its way northward, although it was well worth the wait once it arrived! Home-seasoned taco meat is easy to prepare and has the added advantage of containing just what you wish; no unwanted or hidden fillers. Add lettuce, tomatoes, shredded cheese, and your choice of condiments for a tasty and balanced summertime supper.

1 lb. ground beef (or chicken or turkey)
1 T. chili powder
1 t. cumin
1 t. salt
½ t. black pepper
½ t. oregano
1 T. dried onion flakes
¼ t. garlic powder
½ t. paprika
¼ c. water
Shredded cheddar *or* Jack cheese
Sour cream
Lettuce, cut or torn into bite sized pieces
Salsa of choice
Tomatoes cut in wedges
Sliced avocados, sprinkled with lime juice, *or* guacamole
Taco chips
Diced onions, optional
Bell peppers, optional
Olives, optional
Salad dressing of choice

In a medium cast-iron skillet, slowly brown the ground meat over medium heat, breaking it up fine. Stir in all the seasonings to coat the meat well. Add the water, bring to a boil, and cook for a minute or two, until the mixture has reduced down to a nice consistency. Pile taco chips and cheese of choice onto a serving large tray or bowl, or divide among individual bowls. Spoon the hot meat over the tops, adding vegetables and toppings of choice. Serve at once. This should make 4 generous servings.

Farmers' Market Pizza

For several years when our children were young, I vended baked goods at the Brattleboro Area Farmers' Market. Always eager to utilize seasonal produce, I found this pizza a great way to combine the garden's bounty into a flavorful treat. Here's where you can get lazy or creative. When making the pizza "off-season," it's much easier to simply use half a small can of tomato paste combined with three parts water and simmered with the other ingredients rather than the fresh tomatoes listed below. If you've made your own paste, use 4–6 tablespoons, depending on how thick it is and how thick you'd like your sauce. Fresh tomatoes in season give a wonderful flavor and texture that's hard to replicate; however, if you've frozen the home-made paste, the flavor is also quite nice.

Crust

1 c. very warm water
1½ t. salt
1 t. sugar
1 T. dry yeast
1 T. olive oil
¾ c. whole wheat flour
1½ c. bread flour
Extra olive oil for oiling pan
Cornmeal for sprinkling on pan

Sauce

8 fresh plum tomatoes, seeded and chopped
½ t. salt
½ t. minced garlic
¼ t. black pepper
2 T. olive oil
¼ c. diced onion
½ t. oregano

Topping

½ lb. mushrooms, sliced
2 c. small zucchini slices
Red bell pepper rings
or any desired fresh veggies
Onions, optional
Broccoli, optional
Artichokes, optional
2 T. olive oil
½ t. salt
¼ t. red pepper flakes
2 sprigs fresh basil with stems removed cut fine, optional
8 oz. shredded mozzarella cheese
8 oz. shredded cheddar cheese

For the dough, combine the warm water, sugar, salt, and oil in a large bowl. Stir in the yeast until dissolved. Add the wheat flour, stirring well. Stir in enough bread flour to make a stiff batter, kneading in extra flour to form a soft dough. Allow to rest in the bowl while you prepare the sauce and toppings. Prepare your sauce next: combine all ingredients in a heavy saucepan and cook over medium heat approximately 15 minutes, until the tomatoes are cooked and flavors well blended. The mixture shouldn't be too juicy. For a smoother sauce, puree briefly in a blender. (If using tomato paste, you'll probably only need about 5 minutes cooking time.) Heat the olive oil in a heavy skillet. Add the vegetables and seasonings except for the basil. Gently cook the zucchini, mushrooms, and pepper rings until crisp tender, adding the basil just at the end of cooking time. Set aside while forming the crust. If you are using slightly denser vegetables such as artichokes, you will need to remove all inedible parts and precook before sautéing. You may use either a large round pizza tin or a 10" × 15" baking sheet. In either case, spread a little olive oil over the surface, dusting on a bit of cornmeal as well. Gently spread and push the dough all the way to the edge, leaving the sides a little higher than the center. Spread the sauce over the dough, add the shredded cheeses in an even layer, and finally top with the veggies and basil. Bake on a middle shelf in a preheated 450°F for approximately 10–15 minutes, until the cheese is bubbly and the crust golden brown underneath and cooked through. If you use a 12" round pan, the layers will be thicker, and it may take a bit longer to bake.

Fresh Dilled Cucumbers

This sweet, sour, and salty dill brine can be used more than once, especially handy when cucumbers are ripening daily. If you love pickles but don't want to get caught up in the complications of processing them, this is the recipe for you; easy to use any time of the year.

¼ c. cider vinegar
¼ c. sugar
¼ c. water
1 t. salt
¼ t. black pepper
Chopped fresh or dried dill weed
Thinly sliced cucumbers, skin left on if home-grown

Combine the sugar, vinegar, and water in a small saucepan. Bring to a simmer, stirring to dissolve the sugar completely. Remove from heat and add the salt, pepper, and dill weed. You could use about a teaspoon of dried dill or just snip a small bunch of the fresh to add, avoiding any large stems. Once the mixture has reached room temperature, transfer it to a stainless steel or glass bowl, or better yet to a small glass jar with a lid. Add as many thin cucumber slices as you can fit and still have each covered by the liquid. Refrigerate at least a couple of hours; more is better. I like to run the tines of a fork lengthwise down the whole cucumber before slicing it; your slices will then have a decorative edging that looks more complicated than it was to make! As I've mentioned, you can replenish more slices as needed, fishing out the older ones when they get too limp or pale. This recipe is also easy to double or more if you're looking to make a lot of these all at once.

Dill Dip

While we're on the subject of dill and cucumbers, here's a dip that is the perfect complement to the cucurbitataceae (try saying that three times fast!) in your garden. How convenient that they usually ripen at the same time, as one flavor is so well attuned to the other. This dip also tastes great with other veggies, as well as crackers, chips, and breadsticks.

1 c. sour cream
1 c. plain yogurt
2 t. salt
½ t. pepper
1 t. dried *or* 1 T. snipped fresh dill weed
2 t. dried *or* 2 T. snipped fresh chives
2 t. dried *or* 2 T. snipped fresh parsley

Combine all ingredients in a small bowl, stirring to combine well. Allowing this to mellow in your fridge for an hour or so improves the flavor; be sure to use a container with a cover or a film of plastic wrap or aluminum foil to maintain freshness. Plan to use this within a week. If it seems to be getting a little stiff, stir in a tablespoon or so of milk.

Creamy Cabbage Slaw

This is especially nice as an accompaniment to grilled or barbecued meats and poultry. It's easy to make and is a good way to use up some of that fresh cabbage from your garden.

½ c. sour cream
½ c. mayonnaise
1 T. grainy brown mustard
1 T. sugar
¾ t. salt
Approximately 6 c. finely shredded cabbage

Combine all the dressing ingredients in a medium bowl. Stir in the cabbage to coat it well. Serve at once or refrigerate, covered. This makes enough for several servings or for more than one meal, whichever comes first.

Roasted Corn on the Cob

Summer just isn't summer without some roasted corn on the cob. Here are two variations, each easy to cook on the grill or over a wood fire. In either case, open wide and say, "Yum!"

Ears of corn either in the husk or husked
Butter
Salt
Pepper
Foil for husked ears
Lime juice, optional
Cilantro, optional
Chili powder, optional

For corn in the husk, remove the outer layers, leaving the more delicate pale husks near the kernels. Also pull out as much of the silk as you can. Slide the inner husks back around the ears and submerge the corn in cold water for 15 minutes. For husked corn, spread each ear with a bit of butter, adding salt and pepper to taste. If you wish, add a bit of cilantro and/or chili powder. Roll each husked ear in a double thickness of aluminum foil, twisting the ends to seal. In either instance, place the corn directly on a preheated (about 350°F) grill; cover and cook, turning about every 5 minutes, for a total of 15–20 minutes. The ears should be steaming hot and bright yellow; some of the kernels should also be nicely browned. Serve at once with butter, salt, pepper, and seasonings to taste. (A squeeze of lime juice adds a nice tart contrast.)

Grilled Chicken with Peach Maple Glaze

This is a comparatively delicate grilling recipe; the flavors are lighter and sweeter than many. It showcases the bright flavor of fresh-picked ripe peaches mellowed with maple syrup. Due to the high sugar content of the glaze and delicacy of the chicken breast meat, I recommend cooking the chicken on foil. This will help ensure moist, delicious chicken that is nicely glazed but not burned.

2 lb. chicken, cut up (2 large breast halves each cut in half work well)
2 fresh peaches peeled and diced: 1 c.
¼ c. maple syrup
1 t. grated fresh ginger
1 t. soy sauce
1 T. butter
1 T. lemon juice
2 T. olive oil
Salt to taste
Pepper to taste

Pour the olive oil onto a double thickness of aluminum foil, folded up at the edges, adding a few grinds each of salt and pepper. Swirl the chicken, skin-side down, through the oil to coat it. Grill over medium-low heat, covered, for half an hour. Meanwhile, prepare the glaze. Combine the peaches, ginger, lemon juice, butter, and soy sauce in a small saucepan. Bring to a boil; reduce heat and simmer for about 10 minutes, to thicken slightly.

Remove from heat and use to glaze the chicken. Gently turn the chicken pieces over; they should be golden brown on the grilled side. For the remaining half-hour cooking time, baste the skin side of the chicken with the peach maple glaze approximately every 10 minutes. The glaze should be somewhat bubbly and golden, but not burned. This chicken is very tasty with sweet potato fries, grilled corn on the cob, and creamy cabbage slaw. It serves 4.

Grilled chicken with peach maple glaze is paired here with roasted corn for a classic midsummer's meal.

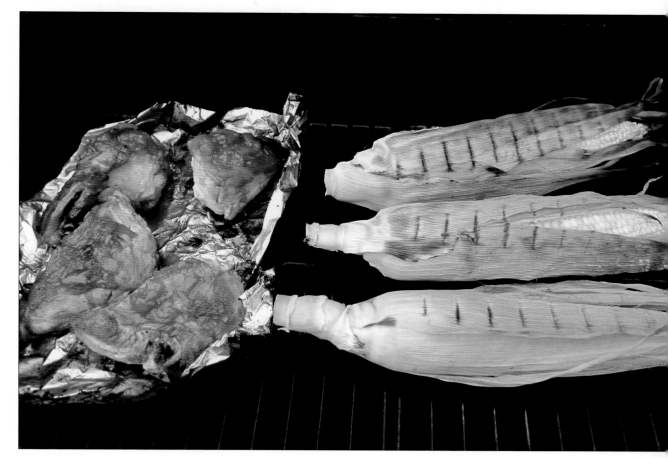

Pork Ribs with Honey Maple Barbecue Sauce

Another yum! Barbecued pork ribs just hit the spot for an August cookout. Make your sauce a few days in advance if you prefer; store in the fridge to allow the flavors to mellow. This is another recipe that's very easy to double or triple depending on how many pounds of ribs you have and how many folks are coming to dinner.

2 lb. meaty pork ribs, cut into serving-sized pieces
Salt
Pepper
Canola, corn, *or* olive oil
¾ c. tomato paste
1½ c. water
2 t. salt
2 T. vinegar
2 T. maple syrup
2 T. honey
1 T. corn oil
¼ t. celery salt
¼ t. hot pepper flakes
1 T. instant minced onion *or* ¼ c. diced fresh

Combine all the sauce ingredients in a medium saucepan. Bring to a boil over medium heat, stirring frequently to prevent burning. Reduce the heat and simmer, stirring occasionally, for about 5–10 minutes, until it thickens slightly. Remove from the heat to use at once or refrigerate for later use. When you're ready to grill, season the pork ribs with salt and pepper and brush or sprinkle them lightly with oil. Place directly over a medium-low flame and cook them, covered, turning occasionally, for about 45 minutes. I find using an oiled metal cooling rack works nicely for this purpose. Brush the ribs with some of the sauce and continue cooking them, basting and turning, for another 15–20 minutes, until they are tender, browned, and nicely glazed, but still moist. Serve any extra sauce on the side. Sides such as potato salad, pasta salad, baked beans, corn on the cob, and/or coleslaw all go nicely with these, as do a pan of rolls or some corn bread. This amount of ribs should serve 4 nicely.

Picadillo

I've been making this variation of a Cuban recipe for years. The combination of sweet, savory, and salty flavors is a real crowd pleaser. Although ground beef is traditional, you may try substituting ground turkey or chicken if you prefer, remembering the flavor will be somewhat different. I've even made it using soy-based meat substitute, which isn't bad, either.

1 lb. lean ground beef
1 lg. onion, chopped
2 cloves minced garlic
1 small *or* ½ large green bell pepper, chopped
1 medium tomato, chopped
⅓ c. raisins
⅓ c. sliced pimento stuffed olives
½ c. dry white wine
1 t. salt
½ t. pepper
Hot cooked rice

Combine the ground beef, onion, and garlic in a large, heavy skillet. Cook and stir over medium-high heat until the meat loses its pinkness and the onions are softened. Add the green peppers, tomatoes, salt, and pepper and cook for another 5 minutes. Stir in the raisins, olives, and wine; cook for another couple of minutes; and serve over hot cooked rice. This will serve 4–5.

This picadillo recipe is a unique combination of sweet, savory, and salty flavors.

Spanish Rice

My mother, Evelyn, frequently made a variation of this in August, when peppers, onions, and tomatoes were all ripe in the garden. How convenient that summer squash and corn were ripe as well; they're both good accompaniments to this dish. I'm not sure just how "authentic" it might be, but it is quite tasty.

6 slices bacon, halved crosswise
1 lg. onion, chopped: 1 c.
1 med. green pepper, chopped: 1 c.
1 c. uncooked rice
½ t. cumin
½ t. salt
6–8 fresh tomatoes, peeled and chopped

In a large, heavy skillet, lightly cook the bacon on 1 side only and remove from pan. Sauté the onion and green pepper in the bacon fat for a minute or two, adding the rice, tomatoes, cumin, and salt and breaking up the tomatoes with a spoon. Bring to a boil, then top with bacon, cover, and simmer on low heat about 20 minutes, until liquid is absorbed and rice is tender. You might need to add a little water. My mom used to transfer the rice mixture to a casserole, top with the bacon and bake, uncovered, in a 350°F oven. In this case, I'd say bake it for about ½ hour. I prefer the stove-top version because having the oven on in August isn't always all that enjoyable, although the bacon is tastier when baked rather than steamed. This serves 4.

Ropas Viejas

This is another savory dish of Cuban origin: beef cooked until it's so tender it separates into "ribbons" combined with sliced peppers, onions, and tomatoes. Ropas viejas translates to "old clothes" because the colorful strips of vegetables and meat resemble a bundle of raggedy old clothing.

2 lb. flank steak *or* beef for pot roasting
2 T. olive oil
1 lg. onion, sliced
2 cloves garlic, crushed
1 carrot, sliced
1 stalk celery, sliced
1 t. cumin
1 T. fresh *or* 1 t. dried oregano
2 t. salt
½ t. pepper
6 c. water
1 bay leaf

In a Dutch oven, brown the meat in the olive oil over medium-high heat. Add the onions, garlic, carrot, and celery and brown a minute or two longer. Add the salt, pepper, cumin, oregano, bay leaf, and water. Bring to a boil, reduce heat, and cook, covered, for 1½ to 2 hours, until the meat is very tender. Remove the beef to a cooling platter until it can be comfortably handled. Meanwhile, increase the heat under the braising liquid and allow it to reduce until it equals about 2 cups. Once the meat is cool enough to handle, tear it into 2–3" strips with two forks or your fingers, discarding any fatty pieces or gristle. Set aside while preparing the sautéed vegetable mixture.

2 T. olive oil
1 lg. onion, sliced
½ t. cumin
½ t. salt
2 lg. *or* 3 small bell peppers—different colors, seeded, and sliced
4 medium tomatoes (about 1 lb.) sliced into wedges
1 T. fresh *or* 1 t. dried cilantro
1 T. capers
1 T. lime juice

Pour the olive oil into a large, heavy skillet. Sauté the onions in the olive oil over medium heat until they just begin to turn tender. Add the bell peppers, salt, cumin, and cilantro, turning and sautéing 2–3 minutes longer. Stir in the tomatoes, beef, capers, lime juice, and strained, reduced cooking liquid. Heat everything together for another 2–3 minutes, until it is hot and cooked to your liking. Serve over white or yellow rice with crusty bread if you wish; the juices are delicious to sop up. This serves 6–8 easily.

Ropas viejas, another dish with Latin American roots, is a savory variation on pot roast.

Veggie Tempura

Almost any fresh small vegetable lends itself well to tempura. For the most satisfying results, plan to include at least three kinds; the August garden contains a plethora. Tempura batter is lighter by nature than many other deep frying dips; a combination of flour and cornstarch helps approximate flour specific to tempura frying, which may not be readily available. Be sure the water used in the batter is icy cold; this prevents the batter from becoming sticky, which in turn ensures the tempura itself doesn't absorb too much of the frying oil along the way. Although the tempura veggies can be served simply with salt and pepper on the side, the dipping sauce is more traditional and adds a nice touch.

Corn or vegetable oil for frying
½ c. flour
½ c. cornstarch
1 egg yolk
1 c. ice water
Extra flour for dipping

Desired Vegetables

Broccoli
Summer squash
Zucchini
Green beans
Peppers
Onions
Carrots
(Approximately 8 c. total)

Dipping Sauce

½ c. soy sauce
1 T. grated fresh ginger
½ c. minced scallions
2 T. sugar
2 T. white wine vinegar

Combine all the dipping sauce ingredients and allow them to mellow together while making the tempura. If you wish your sauce a little less intense, add a bit of water with the other ingredients. Heat about 2" of oil in a heavy skillet (cast iron for even heat distribution). The temperature should be around 350–375°F throughout the frying period. Cut the vegetables into uniform pieces—fairly thin for denser ones such as carrots. Combine the cornstarch and flour in a medium bowl. Whisk in the egg yolk and ice water until you have a thin smooth batter. Dip the veggies a few at a time into the tempura batter, shaking off extra, and submerge them in the hot oil. Fry them until they are light brown and slightly tender; perhaps 4–5 minutes, depending on the vegetable and heat of the oil. Continue to fry a few at a time until used up your veggies and/or run out of batter. Serve the tempura hot with the dipping sauce for dipping to 4 vegetable-inclined folk.

Mom's Dill Pickles

I happen to be the mom in question here; my own mother preferred pickling beets and crab apples to cucumbers. This is a simple and delicious recipe, which makes crunchy, salty, sour pickles—just the way I like them. It makes approximately 8 pints; however, if I only have enough cukes to make 2–3 pints at a time, it's really no problem. The weight of the cucumbers given is for guesstimating purposes only; I cut the amount I have on hand to size, fit them into the jars before icing them to see how many

pickles I'll be making on that day, and gauge my other ingredients accordingly. Extra pickling brine may be kept in a noncorrosive, covered container for a week or two, until you're ready to make your next batch of pickles. If you're done pickling, it also makes a tasty condiment for french fries or fried fish.

4 lb. well-scrubbed, fresh baby pickling cucumbers
2 c. cider vinegar (5 percent acid)
6 c. water
1/3 c. noniodized white sea salt *or* pickling salt

For Each Pint

1 scant t. mustard seed
2 sprigs or heads of fresh dill
2 small cloves of garlic, or 1 lg. clove, halved

If you have slightly larger cukes or a combination of sizes, cut them so that all the pieces are as uniform as possible. Soak the cucumbers in a large container of ice water for at least 2 or up to 8 hours. Meanwhile, clean and sterilize pint pickling jars, keeping them hot until filled. Prepare the pickling brine by bringing to a boil the cider vinegar, sea salt, and water. Place ½ of the garlic and ½ of the dill in the bottom of each hot jar. Tightly pack in the drained cucumbers, adding the rest of the garlic and dill and the mustard seeds on top. Pour the boiling brining solution to within ½" of the top of the jar. Screw on the lids and process in a boiling water bath for 15 minutes. Carefully remove and allow the jars to cool on a buffered surface, such as clean dish towels over the top of the table, until they are no longer hot. Make sure each seal has popped shut. Store them for about 6 weeks to develop the flavor before enjoying your pickles.

Bread-and-Butter Pickles

This recipe makes about 5 pints. I prefer little onions from my garden for their delicate size. If your onion slices are too large in diameter, you may wish to halve them crosswise. Likewise, make your pepper strips petite for best results; about 2" long and julienned fine will be about right.

4 lb. medium cucumbers
1 c. thinly sliced onions
1 lg. garlic clove, halved
½ c. julienned green peeper
¼ c. pickling *or* noniodized sea salt (use white for purity)
3 c. sugar
1 t. turmeric
1 t. celery seed
1T. and 1t. mustard seed
2 c. white vinegar (5 percent acid)
3–4 c. ice cubes or crushed ice

Thoroughly wash cucumbers and cut into ¼" slices. In a large bowl, combine the cukes, onions, garlic, and salt; cover with the ice, mix well, and allow the mixture to stand for 2–3 hours, until the ice cubes have just melted down and everything is cold and crispy. Drain off the liquid and remove the garlic. Combine the sugar, spices, and vinegar and bring just to a boil. Add the cucumber mix and cook for 10 minutes. Pack in clean, hot pint jars, pouring liquid over and leaving ½" headroom. Adjust lids and process in a boiling water bath for 15 minutes. Allow to cool and check for seal as per dill pickles.

Fresh cucumbers are packed into jars with herbs, spice, and hot brine to be processed and enjoyed later as dill pickles or bread-and-butter pickles.

Ground Cherries

Ground cherries are a sweet member of the tomatillo family. When fully ripe, the dry, papery husks will each disclose a single deep yellow fruit with a flavor somewhat reminiscent of pineapple. The seeds are rather finicky to start; I find they require a heating pad and grow lights for an extended period to fully germinate. I've had the best luck with seeds called Aunt Molly's Ground Cherries from Veseys Seeds of Prince Edward Island, Canada. There seem to be a few more varieties available recently, sometimes called Pineapple Tomatillos, although for now I believe I'll stick to a proven product. Ground cherries make a delicious treat simply eaten fresh, may be added to fruit salads, made into pies or cobblers, and even frozen (simply spread the husked fruits on a baking sheet and transfer to sealed freezer bags when frozen). For an unusual take on these little fruits, try making them into tangy sweet salsa. It's especially tasty with grilled chicken, pork, or salmon.

Ground Cherry Salsa

Sungold cherry tomatoes are a delightfully sweet variety that complements the flavor of the ground cherries in this recipe. If you don't have sungolds readily available, substitute another sweet variety of cherry or grape tomato instead. The choice of bell peppers is also up to you; I recommend red, yellow, or orange as opposed to green for their mellow flavor.

1 c. yellow cherry tomatoes, quartered
1 c. ground cherries, halved
¼ c. diced bell pepper
¼ c. diced red onion
1 t. minced jalapeño, or to taste
1 T. minced fresh cilantro
2 T. lemon juice
1–2 T. honey
½ t. salt, or to taste

Combine all ingredients in a small nonreactive bowl. Allowing them to mellow for a little while improves the flavor. This is best served within 1–2 days; leftovers may be pureed into a kind of golden gazpacho, if you wish. It makes a nice accompaniment to grilled chicken or fish.

Just Peachy . . .

Peaches are a valuable part of American agriculture, being one of the most widely grown fruits in the United States, right behind grapes, apples, oranges, and strawberries, according to recent government sources. They contain a variety of nutrients, including vitamins C and A, potassium, B-complex vitamins, and a whole lot of minerals. Peaches also are rich in antioxidants and flavonoids. Perhaps their only downside is that they are so perishable, not storing nearly as well as apples or oranges. And while a just-picked, fresh peach is my idea of ambrosia, the hard- and under-ripe

Juicy golden peaches blushed with color are as delicious to eat as they are beautiful to behold.

peaches we're frequently relegated to buying in the grocery store certainly are not. I've been heartened by the gradual introduction of varieties to augment the old standby Reliance, historically the only peach hardy enough to produce fruit in our Northern climate. Still, we remain somewhat at the mercy of each winter's cold as to whether the forming buds will be able to withstand subzero temperatures and actually produce fruit the following summer. Once the little pink blossoms appear in the spring, barring a wayward late frost, we're again on our way to a summer of peach bliss. Although canning peaches is a traditional method of preservation, for the amount I produce, freezing works just fine. After briefly immersing the peaches in boiling water, I plunge them in cold water, slip the skins away from the fruit, cut each peach in half, removing the pit, and then quick freezing them on baking sheets. Tossing with a bit of lemon juice or ascorbic acid helps the peaches to retain their color without browning. Seal in plastic bags and your summer bounty becomes a year-round treat.

Peach or Mango Chutney

Here's what you want to serve with all those lamb recipes from last April. Mangoes can easily be substituted for the peaches in this recipe, making it easier to prepare year-round.

2½ c. peeled, diced peaches or mango (2 lb.)
¼ c. diced onion
¼ c. diced red bell pepper
½ c. raisins
1–2 T. peeled, minced ginger root
Juice (2 T.) and grated peel of 1 lemon
¼ c. cider vinegar

½ c. sugar
1 clove garlic, minced
¾ t. salt
A pinch of chili pepper flakes, or to taste

Combine all ingredients in a medium, heavy stainless steel saucepan. Cook over low heat, stirring occasionally to prevent sticking, for about ½ hour, until the mixture is thick and golden. This is a tasty accompaniment for a variety of Indian dishes and is also good served with crackers and cream cheese. It may be frozen by placing in small seal-top containers; plan to use by the time you're ready to make more.

The vibrant colors of summer are captured in this pan of fruit chutney simmering on the stove.

Peach Preserves

Use about half slightly under-ripe peaches and half ripe and juicy for the best results in this recipe. A little touch each of fresh lemon and ginger root add a nice flavor. As with most of the jam recipes in this book, commercial pectin is not necessary for making a batch of tasty jam; in this case, the under-ripe peaches and lemon juice combine to help the preserves gel nicely. If you're not sure about processing technique for jams and jellies, take a peek at the preserving guide (page xii).

4 c. peeled, diced peaches
4 c. sugar
1 t. minced ginger root
1 t. grated lemon zest
2 T. lemon juice

Combine all ingredients in a large, heavy stainless steel saucepan. Stirring occasionally, bring to a full boil, skimming as necessary. Adjust heat to medium high and continue cooking, stirring frequently, until the mixture sheets from a spoon and/or it registers 220°F on a candy thermometer. Immediately pour into hot sterilized jelly jars and seal. Process in a boiling water bath for 10 minutes, remove, and allow the jars to cool on a flat-padded surface. Check to make sure all the jars have sealed. This will make approximately 9 quarter pints or 4½ half pints of peach preserves.

Fresh Peach Cake

Although this is technically a cake, the slow baking and high fruit and sugar content make it moist and spongy in consistency, with a crunchy sugar and walnut topping. If you dice and freeze less-than-perfect, fresh peaches in measured batches, it will be easy and economical to thaw some for this peachy dessert whenever you'd like it.

1 c. sugar
1 egg
3 c. juicy diced peaches
1½ c. flour
1 t. baking soda
¼ t. salt
½ t. each vanilla
½ t. cinnamon
1 c. chopped walnuts
1 c. lightly packed brown sugar

Beat together the sugar and egg until they are light and fluffy. Stir in the peaches and vanilla to blend well. Beat in the combined flour, baking soda, cinnamon, and salt until everything is just well mixed. Pour into a generously buttered 9" × 9" pan. Sprinkle the walnuts and brown sugar evenly over the top. Bake in a 325°F oven for 45 minutes. Serve warm or cool with whipped cream or vanilla ice cream. This serves at least 10–12; because it's so rich, smaller servings are a distinct possibility.

Grilled Peach Melba

Use fairly firm but juicy peaches for this easy-to-grill-and-eat recipe. A metal cooling rack and small squares of heavy-duty foil aid in the grilling process. The proportions given will serve 2 and are very simple to expand for as many as you'd like. These make a great accompaniment to brunch or dinner, served warm or at room temperature. Hot off the grill, they make a yummy summer dessert— even better when served with a scoop of your favorite ice cream (think vanilla, raspberry, or peach).

1 large peach
1 T. raspberry *or* strawberry-raspberry jam
1 t. peach *or* raspberry liquor
1 t. butter
2 t. sugar

Cut the peach in half, carefully removing the pit but leaving the peel intact. Place the metal cooling rack over the grill rack, with the flame set to high. If using charcoal, make sure it's burned sufficiently to exude an even, fairly intense heat. Place 1 or 2 squares of heavy-duty aluminum foil per peach directly on the rack, adding the butter to the middle and allowing it to melt. Make your foil squares big enough to encompass the peach halves with a little extra to turn up around the edges. Place the peach halves cut-side down in the melted butter, swirling them around to coat evenly. Turn them cut-side up and sprinkle evenly wit the sugar. Next, grill for about 3–4 minutes, cut-side down, on the foil to blend the butter and sugar. Pull the foil to one side and grill the peaches, still cut-side down, directly on the metal rack for another 3–4 minutes, lifting and turning at an angle once or twice for even grilling. Finally, place the peaches, skin-side down, back on the foil, again placing the foil on the hot rack. Top with the combined jam and liquor, close the grill or cover the peaches, and grill for another 3–4 minutes, until the filling is heated through and the extra filling has formed a buttery syrup with the juices on the bottom of the foil. Carefully remove from the heat and serve as above.

Grilled peach melba is just waiting for a scoop of ice cream to complete a luscious summertime dessert.

261

Fresh Blueberry–Glazed Pie

Blueberries are another New England native fruit, and a mighty fine one at that. For such tiny things, they pack a real punch of flavor and nutrition. Although wild blueberries make almost any dish better, this is one blueberry dessert for which I prefer larger cultivated blueberries. They stand up better to the blueberry glaze, making a shiny and inviting statement to blueberry lovers young and old. A dollop of whipped cream flavored with vanilla or a pinch of cinnamon rounds out the presentation.

1 qt. (4 c.) fresh blueberries
1 c. sugar
¼ t. salt
3 T. cornstarch
½ pkg. unflavored gelatin powder
1½ c. water
2 t. lemon juice
1 baked 9" pastry shell
Fresh sweetened whipped cream

Place 1 cup of the berries in a blender along with 1¼ cups of the water, sugar, salt, and cornstarch. Blend them together until you have a fairly smooth liquid; it doesn't have to be perfect. Place this mixture in a medium saucepan and bring to a full boil, cooking and stirring until it has thickened somewhat. Meanwhile, soften the gelatin in the remaining ¼ cup of water. As soon as the blueberry glaze has thickened, remove it from the heat and immediately stir in the gelatin until it is totally dissolved. Stir in the lemon juice. Cool the mixture to room temperature or a little cooler by placing the pan into a larger pan or bowl of cold water; adding ice will aid the process. Gently stir the remaining blueberries into the glaze until everything is coated, and pour it into the baked, cooled pastry shell. Allow it to chill for at least 2 hours. Serve with sweetened whipped cream. This serves 8.

Fresh blueberry–glazed pie is even better with a dollop of whipped cream.

Blueberry Pie

An old New England tradition is having a piece of pie for breakfast. Aside from being absolutely delicious, we now know blueberries contain loads of antioxidants and other good things. So, I guess you could consider a piece of blueberry pie, perhaps accompanied by a glass of cold milk, as a healthy start to your day! If in doubt, simply save it for dessert; that vanilla ice cream hanging out in your freezer was just waiting to top something anyway.

4 c. blueberries (wild if you can get them)
1 c. sugar
¼ t salt
¼ c. flour *or* 3 T. cornstarch
¼ t. grated nutmeg
½ t. grated lemon rind
2 crust pastry milk

Combine all the filling ingredients in a large bowl and stir gently to combine well. Pour them into a pastry-filled 9" pie plate. Brush the edges of the lower crust lightly with milk and top with the upper crust. Brush the top lightly with milk and sprinkle it with sugar if desired. Use a fork or sharp knife to prick or cut a decorative design in the top; this will allow steam to escape while the pie is baking. (If you're using frozen berries, allow the unbaked pie to sit at room temperature for a little while if you have time; otherwise, the edges of the piecrust may overbrown before the filling is done.) Bake at 425°F for 10 minutes. Reduce heat to 350°F and continue baking until the crust nicely browned and the filling bubbles, about 45 minutes. Make sure the whole pie is bubbling, not just the outer edges, or your filling will be somewhat runny. Place a cookie sheet under the pie tin, on the next rack down, to help catch any possible spills from the filling leaking over the edges of the tin. Cool the pie before cutting for best results. This serves 8–10.

Crumb Topping

If you'd prefer a crumb topping rather than the upper pastry crust for your pie, try this one. It's easy to prepare and, with minor flavoring adjustments, can be used with a wide range of pies. Place one rolled pastry crust in a 9" pie plate, bringing the edges up evenly and fluting them, before adding the fruit filling and crumb topping.

1 c. flour
¼ c. sugar
¼ c. butter, melted
¼ t. desired flavoring: cinnamon, nutmeg, or ginger
Or ¼ t. vanilla, lemon, or almond extract

Stir all the ingredients together until the mixture forms crumbs. (If using extract, mix this with the butter before adding the flour and sugar for even flavor distribution.) Sprinkle the crumbs evenly over the top of the filled pie. Bake as directed above.

Blueberry Cake

Blueberry cake brings back memories of visits to Jim and Olive Hayes, friends of my parents who lived up on a mountain in Guilford, Vermont. They cooked on a woodstove, lighted their house with kerosene lamps, and pumped their water through a hand pump situated in the kitchen sink. In later years, a gas stove and lamps were added, although Jim and Olive remained true individualists all their lives. Olive was a wonderful cook, who frequently utilized the bounty of their large garden and numerous berry patches to produce the most delicious dishes. Her blueberry cake was one of my favorites. I'm not sure what recipe Olive followed when making blueberry cake, so I'll give you mine instead.

2 c. flour
1 c. sugar
2 t. baking powder
¼ c. butter
1 c. milk
1 egg
1 c. or more of fresh (or frozen) blueberries

Combine all ingredients except the egg and blueberries and beat until smooth and creamy. Add the egg and beat well again. Fold in the blueberries and pour into a 9" × 9" greased and floured pan. Bake at 350°F for 35–40 minutes, until golden brown and firm to touch. Cut in 9 squares and serve with lemon nutmeg sauce.

Lemon Nutmeg Sauce

2 c. water
½ c. sugar
1 T. cornstarch
Dash salt
¼ c. lemon juice
2 T. butter
¼–½ t. fresh grated nutmeg
¼ t. pure lemon extract *or* 1 t. grated lemon zest

Combine the water, sugar, cornstarch, and salt in a medium saucepan. Cook over high heat to a full boil. Remove from heat and stir in the lemon juice, butter, lemon zest or extract, and nutmeg. Serve warm or room temperature over blueberry cake. If saving more than a day, cover the sauce and refrigerate.

Marie's Chocolate Zucchini Cake

If you've ever raised zucchini, you're probably aware that at times there really can be too much of a good thing. One pleasant way to rid yourself of some of that excess is to turn it into something unexpected, such as this rich chocolate cake.

4 lg. eggs
1½ c. sugar
1 c. corn oil
2 c. all-purpose flour
½ c. dark cocoa powder
¼ t. salt
2 t. baking soda

2½ c. shredded zucchini
2 t. grated orange zest
½ c. semisweet chocolate mini chips

Beat the eggs at high speed, gradually adding sugar until mixture is thick and ivory colored. Stir together the dry ingredients. At low speed, quickly add the oil and vanilla to the mixture and then the dry ingredients. Fold in the zucchini and orange zest lightly so the batter retains its lightness. Pour into two greased and floured 9" round cake pans (or a 9" × 13"). Sprinkle the chips evenly over the tops. Bake at 350°F for 30–40 minutes, until top is firm when lightly touched. Cool in pans for 10 minutes, and then if you wish to make a layer cake, turn the round cakes out of pans to complete cooling and follow the directions below. If baked as a rectangle, cut in squares to serve as is, or top with ice cream, whipped cream, frozen yogurt, or orange sherbet. For special occasions, try filling and frosting your zucchini cake as follows.

Zucchini Cake for Special Occasions

Melt ¼ c. orange marmalade and glaze the tops of the layers. Spread with fresh orange butter cream cheese frosting (see below) and top with fresh fruit; strawberries and kiwi are especially nice for this.

Orange Butter Cream Cheese Frosting

2 sticks unsalted butter: 8 oz.
½ block (4 oz.) cream cheese

1 lb. confectioner's sugar
2 t. grated orange zest
2–4 T. orange juice

Beat the butter and cream cheese in a medium mixing bowl until creamy. Gradually add the confectioner's sugar alternately with the orange juice. Stir in the orange zest. This makes a generous amount of frosting, plenty for spreading and some for decorating too. When prepared in this manner, Marie's chocolate zucchini cake will easily serve 16 or more.

Orange Chiffon Cake

My quintessential August dessert is a slice of orange chiffon cake topped with fresh peaches and whipped cream. This makes a large cake, probably divisible into 16 good-sized servings. As you'll note below, there are several ways to enjoy orange chiffon cake, each one quite tasty. Feel free to sample them all!

2¼ c. cake flour (stirred or sifted)
1¾ c. sugar
1 T. baking powder
1 t. salt
½ t. cream of tartar
½ c. corn oil
5 large eggs, separated
3 additional egg whites
1 T. grated orange rind
¾ c. orange juice

Beat the egg whites in a large mixing bowl at medium speed until frothy. Add the cream of tartar, increase speed, and beat until it forms stiff peaks. While the whites are beating, combine the flour,

Orange chiffon cake pairs deliciously with fresh seasonal fruit and ice cream.

sugar, baking powder, and salt in a large bowl. Make a well in the center and add in order the oil, egg yolks, peel, and juice. Whisk the mixture until smooth and then fold it into the beaten egg whites just until the two are well combined. Keeping the mixture light and airy is the key to making a high-, fine-textured chiffon cake. Bake in ungreased 10" tube pan in a preheated 325°F oven until cake springs back to touch, about 65–70 minutes. This may seem like a long time, but please don't under bake your cake or it will fall, which would be a very sad chiffon cake indeed. Invert the pan onto a funnel or neck of bottle for at least 3 hours (in a pinch, use a wire cooling rack) until the cake is entirely cool. Run knife or spatula between cake and tin to loosen. Although an ungreased tin is imperative for proper rising (the batter clings to the side as it bakes, enabling it to reach the top of the pan), I have found removal can sometimes be tricky; judicious use of a large flat knife and metal spatula usually help my cause. If it gives you too much trouble, you might try lightly oiling and flouring the *bottom only* of the tube pan to facilitate removal.

You may glaze this with a mixture of 2 T. orange juice and 1 c. conf. sugar, frost with a butter cream icing, or leave as is and enjoy with sweetened peaches or strawberries and whipped cream or ice cream.

Lemon variation: Substitute lemon peel for orange. Use ¼ c. lemon juice and ½ c. water in place of orange juice. Proceed as above.

An Apple a Day... the Abundant Orchard

OF THE MANY pleasures contained on our little piece of land, I believe I enjoy the orchard most. There are only about a dozen apple trees, two scraggly rows separating the east boundary of our main garden from the meadow behind. The trees are mostly antique varieties, planted thirty or forty years ago by my late mother. I don't know what became of Mother's records indicating which trees were planted where, so each year is a guess-and-by-golly procedure when it comes time to harvest and cook them. Some are relatively easy to identify: a big rangy tree near one end produces Yellow Delicious, while its neighbor to the south appears to be a Roxbury Russet, the skins cloaked in a veneer of soft brown. The end tree of each row produces bright red McIntosh or Cortland apples, respectively. In the middle is a big old tree that always over-abundantly produces large yellow apples striped red, while behind it another produces equally large ones tinged soft yellow—perhaps one is a pound sweet? Further along are Rhode Island Greening and the more mundane Red Delicious.

Because we don't spray our trees, the skins are less than perfect, although the flesh for the most part is surprisingly uncompromised. I wonder if the hardiness of these older varieties plays a part in their resistance to pests, or if the number and variety of trees makes them somehow less susceptible? I must admit, they don't winter terribly well, so I usually slice and freeze a number for later use or make them into applesauce before freezing in pint containers. September into October is prime harvesting time for our apples, as well as pears from the one tree that manages to survive alone over by the Ames Hill Brook. By November, alternate frosty nights and warming days have begun the decaying process, although weather alone isn't responsible for the state of our crop. We share our orchard in all seasons with a number of woodland friends.

Our summer visitors include colorful songbirds flitting through the branches, ferreting out insects living in the bark, or later pecking at the ripening fruit itself. I've been delighted to spot the brilliant red flashes of scarlet tanagers, black and vermillion of redstarts, and the intense blue of diminutive indigo buntings. Occasionally a pair of

A tree full of red apples silhouetted against a sky of blue signals fall is on the way.

Baltimore orioles will choose to nest nearby, the male's brilliant orange-and-black plumage only slightly more intense than the lady oriole's yellow trim. We have a virtual stampede of both red and gray squirrels racing back and forth regularly year-round. I still haven't determined if they actually eat the apples or just enjoy utilizing the intermeshing branches as a safe conduit from their squirrel homes in the woods south of the garden over to the birdfeeders on our side lawn.

My favorites are the whitetails who visit our orchard and the meadow behind it year-round. Spring and summer they scrounge only occasional nibbles from the low-hanging apple branches. Vernal preferences run more toward the young raspberry and blackberry bushes they greedily sample before bedding down in the relative security of the small field behind our house. However, in late summer and fall, priorities change. The thick grass under the apple trees begins to show signs of disturbance as sharp hooves dig out fallen apples. These drops, entangled in the very stalks that cushioned their fall, are quickly uncovered and consumed. Half-eaten apples jostle cheerily with those not sampled, soon softening into brown slurry for the unwary to slip upon. That's all right with me, though. Deer in the wild don't live particularly easy existences. If our little corner of the world provides them with some sustenance and passing happiness, then let them enjoy it, I say. We've more than enough to share.

September

Applesauce

Homemade applesauce is one of Mother Nature's comfort foods. It's easy to prepare, easy to store, and lends itself to many delicious recipes, if ever you tire of eating it as is. It's my favorite way to utilize all the dropped apples in our orchard that are mostly still fine but have acquired a few bruises on their journey from the tree branch to the ground below. Start with any combination of apples you desire, making sure they're washed clean of dirt that might have accumulated along the way. I like to use a variety in the same batch, for the richness of flavor and texture. I also keep a few of the reddest peels on for color. This is an individual preference and may also depend on what kitchen implements you have. If you have one of those nifty conical devices with the little holes in it, you simply force your cooked apples through, leaving the peels behind. If you've only a few skins to sort out, you could remove by hand or leave them in for the "health benefits." I frequently put everything into my blender and let that do the trick; you'll have tiny bits of skin, but they're hardly noticeable. Or if you prefer, peel your fruit before stewing it and the problem is solved at the offset. Here are some general guidelines for proportions when making homemade applesauce.

3 c. peeled, cored, quartered apples
1 c. water
½ c. sugar, or to taste
Grated nutmeg
Cinnamon

Place the apples and water in the smallest saucepan they'll comfortably fit into and still have some room for expansion while cooking. Cover, bring to a boil, reduce heat to a gentle boil, and cook until tender, about 15 minutes. I prefer to let the cooking water evaporate down in the process so that there's no need for draining, which removes flavor and nutrients. Stir or blend until smooth as you like, or put through a strainer, as above. Adding sugar is a personal preference; you may wish to add none at all, dependent on the sweetness of the apples and how you intend to use them. I prefer to add nutmeg only to my applesauce or occasionally a little each of nutmeg and cinnamon. Again, it's a matter of personal preference. If I have extra, I simply place it in pint plastic seal-top containers, label, and freeze. Applesauce may also be canned.

Hot Mulled Cider

Hot mulled cider is tasty for breakfast, lunch, or dinner, not to mention at any variety of autumnal festivities. Although you can produce an acceptable alternative using apple juice, it's never as good as cider pressed fresh from the orchard. This recipe produces a single serving—easy to multiply as you wish. The cranberries are optional, although especially nice around Thanksgiving.

1 c. apple cider
2" stick of cinnamon
3 cloves
2 whole allspice berries
1 t. chopped candied ginger
1" piece fresh orange peel
3 fresh cranberries

Place all ingredients in a small, heavy saucepan. Heat to just under boiling. Maintain the heat at a simmer for about 15 minutes to adequately blend flavors. Beware of heating for too long, as the cider will eventually evaporate and you'll end up with a more concentrated product.

Parmesan Pastry Pinwheels

These delicate buttery little pinwheels are a snap to make. They utilize puff pastry dough, which I like to make up in advance and store in my freezer. They are the puff pastry equivalents to pie crust cookies, in that I save the edge scraps from making turnovers to use in making these. Try them with the chicken salad Véronique, which you'll find a little later on, as an accompaniment to soup, an appetizer, or even as a slightly decadent breakfast treat.

Puff pastry scraps (or cut whole pieces to size)
Grated Parmesan cheese
Seasoned salt
or fresh ground salt and pepper
Sesame seeds *or* poppy seeds

Allow the scraps of dough to thaw just enough to be malleable. Unwind them and cut to uniform size, strips about ½" × 8". Sprinkle generously with Parmesan cheese and seasoned salt, or with cheese, salt, and pepper. Sprinkle them with sesame or poppy seeds, if desired. Roll each pinwheel into a loose circle and place on an ungreased baking sheet, pressing down some to flatten and expand slightly. Bake on the upper rack of a 425°F oven for about 8–10 minutes, until the pinwheels are golden brown and bubbling. Gently remove each pinwheel to a wire cooling rack. These are best served warm.

Scandinavian Mushroom Turnovers

Here comes another recipe for puff pastry; I do dearly love it! These savory little triangles are inspired by the flavors of my childhood; I learned to appreciate the many uses of dill and sour cream at an early age. And once you've made a batch of these turnovers, you'll have a perfect excuse to use up the pastry scraps in Parmesan pastry pinwheels!

1 or 2 recipes puff pastry ("January")*
½ lb. mushrooms, diced
1 T. olive oil
¼ c. diced leek (white part only) *or* onion
¼ t. salt
¼ t. nutmeg
⅛ t. white pepper
½ t. dried dill weed
1 t. Dijon mustard
2 t. flour
½ c. sour cream
1 c. diced Havarti cheese

Sauté the diced leek or onion and mushrooms in the olive oil in a large, heavy skillet over medium heat until they are tender and most of the moisture has evaporated; do not brown them. Remove from the heat and stir in the flour, dry seasonings, and the Dijon mustard. Allow this mixture to cool to room temperature and then stir in the sour cream and Havarti cheese. Place the mushroom mixture in a small bowl, cover, and refrigerate until chilled, or up to a couple of days; it should be cold when filling your turnovers.

*This amount of mushroom filling will be enough for two recipes of puff pastry, with possibly a bit extra. Try spreading the filling on toast points or crackers if you have leftovers.

This mixed tray of mini spinach, broccoli, and mushroom turnovers is ready for a party.

Mushroom Soup

My son-in-law Dale is from northern Vermont. Each late summer his family heads into the woods of Lamoille and Orleans counties in search of chanterelles. These delicious golden mushrooms with their delicately fluted caps and apricot scent are highly desirable restaurant fare. Sounds like a fun adventure, doesn't it? But beware to any who don't know their mushrooms as well as Dale and his relatives; look-alikes lurk around every corner in the Vermont woods. Some are not nearly as tasty as chanterelles, and others can be downright toxic. Never try harvesting your own mushrooms in the wild unless you have an excellent field guide, an expert to train you, or preferably both!

4 oz. mushrooms, sliced or rough chopped
2 T. butter
2 T. flour
½ t. salt
¼ t. grated nutmeg
⅛ t. each thyme
⅛ t. white pepper
2 c. milk
¼ c. sour cream

White button-type mushrooms are fine for this recipe, although you may vary them according to your taste. Sauté the mushrooms slowly in butter for about 5 minutes, until slightly softened. Stir in flour and seasonings and cook 5 more minutes. Stir milk in all at once; heat slowly until mixture just comes to a boil. Stir in the sour cream and serve at once. This makes 2–3 servings, but is also easy to double.

Stuffed Mushrooms

Another delicious way to serve mushrooms is stuffed and baked. Dale's special trick for preparing stuffed mushrooms is to place a little piece of cheese in the bottom of each mushroom cap before filling them. These are equally delicious with added sausage or clams, or vegetarian style just with cheese. Use the filling of your choice or invest in some extra mushrooms and try all three!

Sausage

8 oz. button-type mushrooms
8 oz. Italian sausage
¼ t. garlic powder
1 t. dried cilantro
3 T. olive oil
½ c. dry bread crumbs
¼ c. grated Parmesan cheese

Clam

8 oz. button-type mushrooms
1 can minced clams and broth
1 clove minced garlic
½ t. tarragon
1 t. parsley
2 T. melted butter
2 T. olive oil
2 t. lemon juice
¾ c. dry bread crumbs
¼ c. grated Parmesan cheese
1–2 oz. Gruyère cheese

Veggie

8 oz. button-type mushrooms
1 c. bread crumbs
2 T. olive oil
2 T. butter
2 T. diced onion
2 T. diced red bell pepper
¼ c. grated Parmesan cheese
1 clove garlic, minced
¼ t. rosemary
¼ t. thyme
1–2 oz. Colby, Jack, or cheddar cheese

Oil a 9" ×13" pan with 2 T. of the olive oil. Rinse the mushrooms, remove the stems, and save for soup or other uses. (If you're making veggie stuffed, you may wish to mince the stems and add them to the other filling ingredients.) Place the hollow caps in the baking sheet. Place a small cube of the desired cheese in each mushroom cap. Combine all the other ingredients, mixing well. Mound the mixture firmly over the top of each mushroom. Bake at 375°F for 30–35 minutes, until nicely browned, the meat is fully cooked, and the cubed cheese is melted.

Late-Summer Gardens . . .

There are still plenty of vegetables to be harvested from the garden in September, especially those with a longer growing season. Tomatoes, corn, and summer squash are now interspersing with winter squash, second plantings of cold weather favorites such as broccoli and cauliflower, and beans that are no longer harvested for their pods but rather for the dried legumes within. If we're lucky, frost will hold off until October, extending the growing season and resultant harvest.

Scalloped Tomatoes

Scalloped tomatoes lend themselves well to either fresh or whole frozen tomatoes. If using fresh, immerse them for about 30 seconds in boiling water, cool quickly in cold water, and the skins will peel right off. If using frozen, either microwave or quickly heat the whole frozen tomatoes until they are just partially thawed, at which time you will be able to remove their skins easily as well. If you're relegated to using canned, use the juice and all but omit the salt.

6–8 medium tomatoes, prepared as above
½ sleeve saltine crackers, crushed: 1 c.
½ t. onion powder
½ t. salt
¼ t. pepper
½ t. oregano
¼ c. butter, melted
¼ c. grated Parmesan cheese

Combine the cracker crumbs, salt, pepper, oregano, and onion powder. Stir in the melted butter. Pour about half of the cracker crumb mixture into a well-buttered casserole dish. Arrange the tomatoes on top and sprinkle the remaining crumbs over them. Sprinkle on the Parmesan cheese and bake in a 375°F oven for 35–40 minutes, until the top is browned and the tomatoes bubbly. This serves 4–6.

Baked Stuffed Summer Squash

This dish is easy to make with or without meat. I prefer it with a little sausage added, although you may substitute ground beef or one of the vegetarian ground meat substitutes if you prefer. It's a great way to use some of the overabundance of certain squashes the late-summer garden always seems to provide us.

2 summer squash or zucchini, each 6–8" long
½ lb. pork sausage, ground beef, *or* meat substitute
¼ lb. (1 c.) shredded cheddar cheese
¼ c. diced onion
1 c. diced fresh tomatoes
4 slices French-style bread, torn in pieces: 2 c.; or 1 c. cooked brown or white rice
2 T. olive oil
½ t. oregano
½ t. salt
¼ t. each cumin
¼ t. pepper

Cut each squash in half lengthwise. Place the halves, cut-side down, in a shallow pan with ½" of water. Cover and bring to a boil; simmer the squash for about 5 minutes, until they're barely tender. Remove from the pan and allow to cool a little. Scoop out the seeds and fiber from the center, leaving a thin shell all around. Place the seeds (which should be small and tender) and inner squash fiber into a medium-sized mixing bowl and chop them fine. Add the sausage, ground beef, or meat substitute (broken into small pieces); shredded cheese; diced onion and tomatoes; bread or rice; oregano; cumin; salt; and pepper—mixing very well. Mound the mixture evenly into the hollowed-out squash shells. Place the stuffed halves, cut-side up, in an oiled baking dish and drizzle the olive oil evenly over all. Bake in a 375°F oven for 50–60 minutes, until the filling is browned on top and slightly puffy. Carefully remove from the baking dish and serve 1 per person.

Dad's Succotash

The roots of succotash go back into Native American cooking lore. The canned lima beans and corn masquerading as succotash when I was growing up were nowhere near as appealing as is this garden-fresh variety made using equal parts of corn and shell beans (substitute fresh or frozen lima beans if you wish). My dad, Bill, was so taken by this recipe the first time we made it that he set out to produce an even larger amount the next time around. Somewhere during its production, he got a little carried away; he never quite seemed to even out the amounts of corn and shell beans, constantly adding a bit more of one or the other. Eventually he ended up with 11 cups of each, which resulted in a prodigious quantity of succotash. I was in nurse's training at the time and didn't get home very often. What should greet me when I did but the same pot of succotash I'd left there a month earlier? Suffice to say, enthusiasm was somewhat dulled thereafter.

2 c. corn cut from the cob
1½ c. fresh shell beans or lima beans
4 slices bacon or salt pork, diced
1 medium onion, chopped
2 bay leaves
¼ t. thyme
½ c. light cream
Salt to taste
Pepper to taste

Fry together the bacon or salt pork and onion until just browned. Add the beans, bay leaves or thyme, and enough water to just cover. Bring to a boil and reduce heat to a simmer. Cook until almost tender, about ½ hour. Add the corn and simmer another 15 minutes or so. Most of the liquid should have cooked away by now. Remove the bay leaves and add the cream along with the thyme, salt, and pepper. This may be eaten either as a main course or side dish.

Minestrone Soup

Making a big pot of minestrone is a great way to use up ever-so-many vegetables from your late-summer garden. This particular recipe is based more on Northern Italian cuisine; you will note rice is used rather than pasta, and there are some potatoes included as well. It makes a fairly thick soup, richly flavored but not over the top in calories. Feel free to add a bit more broth or water if you'd like more soup base, adjusting seasons accordingly. Also, the amount of tomatoes used here gives a nice but not pronounced background flavor; if you're a fan of tomato-y minestrone, dice in a few more of those, as well.

4 c. chicken stock

2 c. water

1 lg. onion, diced

2 stalks celery, diced

½ c. dried beans

2 cloves garlic, crushed

2 oz. (4 slices) bacon, diced

2 T. butter

2 T. olive oil

2 bay leaves

1 t. crushed rosemary

1½ t. salt

½ t. pepper

½ t. basil

2 lg. carrots, very thinly sliced: 2 c.

1 c. diced potatoes

4 plum tomatoes *or* 2 lg. slicing tomatoes, peeled, and diced

1 lg. *or* 2 small zucchini, diced: 2 c.

3 c. shredded cabbage

1 c. peas

1 c. cooked white rice

or ½ c. uncooked white rice and 1 c. water

Combine the bacon, olive oil, onions, celery, and garlic in a large, heavy saucepan. Cook over medium-low heat for about 10 minutes to wilt down but not brown. Add the beans, broth, 2 c. water, bay leaves, rosemary, basil, salt, and pepper. Bring to a boil, reduce heat, and simmer, covered, for about 1½ hours. Add the rice, 1 c. water, carrots, and potatoes; bring up to boiling; reduce heat; and simmer another ½ hour. Add in the cabbage and zucchini; simmer for an additional 20 minutes. Just before serving, stir in the peas and allow everything to heat through nicely. This is excellent served with homemade pizza, although it's hearty enough to eat as is with crusty bread. This makes quite a bit, about 4 quarts. Freeze extra, if you wish, to use within a month or so.

Homemade Potato Chips

These are easier to make if you have a food processor capable of thinly slicing your potatoes. A slicing implement called a mandolin also works well. Beware if you're hand slicing; remember to use a guard in between the slicing implement and your fingers lest you end up in the local hospital emergency room getting stitches, as I did one fine summer's eve. At any rate, try to make your potato slices as thin and uniform as possible for the best finished product. Homemade fried potato chips are a real treat, whether you choose to make them from fresh-dug white potatoes or to be adventuresome and try some made with sweet potatoes.

1 medium potato per person, scrubbed
Corn or other vegetable oil for frying
Ice water
Sea salt
A bit of crumbled rosemary, optional

Pour about 2" of oil into a heavy skillet or frying pan, or use an electric fryer if you prefer. Preheat the oil to 350°F. While it is preheating, slice your potatoes as above; there's no need to peel them unless you need to remove blemishes. Submerge the slices into a large bowl of ice water for at least 5 minutes. When you're ready to fry, pat the potato slices dry on a clean dish towel or paper towels. Carefully place a single layer at a time in the hot oil, stirring gently to separate them. Allow them to brown to your preference, usually for about 5 minutes. Remove from the hot oil with a slotted spoon and place on a paper towel–lined baking sheet or rack to cool. Sprinkle them with sea salt, adding a bit of crumbled rosemary if you wish. This is an open-ended recipe, making as many or few chips as you wish. Be sure if you're frying them in batches to allow the oil adequate time to heat back up to 350°F each time.

Grape Gelatin Ring

September is prime grape-ripening season, whether wild or cultivated. Your choice of purple, red, or white grape juice forms a shimmering ring in this recipe. It's based on a wine gelatin recipe I discovered years ago, but tastes better, I think. It's also family friendly, but sophisticated enough for adult palates as well, should you like an unusual addition to your next "company" menu.

3½ c. grape juice; I prefer to reconstitute frozen concentrate
2 pkg. unflavored gelatin powder
2 T. lemon juice
¼ c. sugar
1" × ½" × ¼"–wide piece of fresh peeled ginger root, optional
Pinch of salt
Fresh grapes for garnish

Place 3 c. of the grape juice along with the ginger root in a medium saucepan and bring to just under boiling. In the meantime, soften the gelatin in the remaining ½ c. of cold grape juice. Once the grape juice in the pan has heated sufficiently, remove from the heat and stir in the softened gelatin, sugar, lemon juice, and salt until everything is well dissolved. Pour into a lightly oiled 4 c. jelly mold, or just into a bowl if you prefer. Allow to set for at least 2 hours in the refrigerator before unmolding by dipping into hot water just up to the rim and quickly turning out onto a serving platter. Garnish with clusters of grapes and other fruit as desired. This makes 8 half-cup servings.

Grape gelatin ring adds a nice touch to harvest season dinners.

Fox Grape Jelly

Fox grapes are small wild grapes indigenous to New England. They grow in my backyard, climbing over the side of our old goat barn and twining high in the branches of the ash tree that has overtaken one corner of the building. These grapes are also commonly found in the New England woods. A rite of passage for many country kids is finding the perfect large grapevine swing from which to practice acrobatic skills. Fox grapes are a Concord-type grape and, as such, are excellent for making juice and jelly. When extracting juice from grapes, it's important to remember they contain a substance called tartaric acid. The juice should be allowed to stand overnight so that the tartaric acid crystals can settle to the bottom of the bowl or jar. The juice can then be decanted, leaving the crystals behind. You may wish to repeat this procedure more than once; although the crystals are harmless, they are rather crunchy and detract from the texture of your finished product.

3–4 lb. of stemmed rinsed grapes: about 2 generous quarts
3 c. water, divided
2 c. diced tart apple with peel
3½ c. sugar
1 t. citric acid *or* 2 T. lemon juice

Place the grapes and 1½ c. water in a large nonreactive kettle. Heat them slowly to just under boiling, crushing them well with a potato masher or sturdy pastry cutter. Allow them to simmer for about 5–10 minutes to draw out the juices, but don't boil; they burn easily, and you also don't want your liquid to evaporate. Place a large sieve, lined with a double thickness of jelly-making cheesecloth, over a glass or nonreactive bowl or large glass measuring cup. Carefully pour in the grapes and allow them to drain thoroughly. I leave mine in the refrigerator overnight. Squeeze the bag to extract the maximum amount of juice, but don't be too zealous about it. Once the juice has had a chance to stand undisturbed for at least 24 hours, carefully pour it into another container as described above, leaving the tartaric acid crystals in the bottom. Repeat this procedure once for the best results. Now measure your juice; you should have about 3 cups. If you need to add a tiny bit of water, that's OK, but if the measurement is too short, consider either reducing the other ingredients in the recipe proportionately or juicing a few more grapes, if you have them. Combine the diced apple with the remaining 1½ c. water in

Fox grapes on the vine and in a bowl will soon be fox grape jelly.

a small saucepan. Bring to a boil, reduce the heat and simmer, covered, for about 10–15 minutes. Drain the apple mixture through a double layer of jelly-making cheesecloth into small bowl or 1 cup measure. You should have 1 c. of concentrated juice. If the amount is short, add a small amount of water to the drained apple pulp, reheat to boiling, and strain again. Once you are ready to make your jelly, prepare your jelly jars as described in the preserving guidelines. Combine the 3 c. grape and 1 c. apple juices in a medium-large nonreactive saucepan. Add in the sugar and the citric acid or lemon juice. Stirring occasionally, bring the mixture to a full rolling boil. Continue to boil briskly, stirring occasionally to prevent boiling over the edges, until the mixture sheets from a spoon or reaches a temperature of 220°F (2°F less for every 1,000 feet above sea level you might live). Pour the hot jelly into hot sterilized jelly jars and process according to the preserving instructions included in the "Preserving Guidelines" (10 minutes submerged in a boiling water bath). Once processed, remove to a dry clean towel to cool completely and finish sealing (the jar tops will pop down and stay there). This makes approximately 5 half pints or 10 quarter pints of jelly.

Chicken Salad Véronique

The term "Véronique" generally indicates grapes have been added to a fish or poultry dish; one of the classics is sole Véronique. Most frequently used are seedless green grapes, although I've occasionally substituted a juicy red grape with nice results. This salad is a handy way to use up roasted chicken. Combined with the grapes, celery, pecans, and a creamy tarragon dressing, it makes a refreshing late-summer supper. You may vary the amount of grapes according to personal taste.

3 c. diced skinless chicken breast meat
2–3 c. seedless grapes
2 stalks sliced celery: 1 c.
½ c. chopped pecans
1 t. dried crumbled tarragon
½ c. mayonnaise
½ c. sour cream

Combine the chilled chicken, grapes, celery, and pecans in a medium serving bowl. Stir together the mayonnaise, sour cream, and tarragon. Pour over the salad and mix lightly to combine well. Serve at once or refrigerate, covered, until serving time. It's especially tasty with hot rolls, crusty bread, or Parmesan pastry pinwheels. This serves 6.

Chicken salad Véronique is a cool and creamy use of chicken and grapes. It's shown here with Parmesan pastry pinwheels and a side of mixed beans.

Hot Tuna Sandwiches

Another nice treat for when the days begin to alternate between the warmth of summer and cool of fall is the humble hot tuna sandwich. These loaded little buns can easily be cooked on your grill, wrapped in foil, although if you prefer popping them in a hot oven, that will do the trick as well. Because they contain cheese, I use a rather thin layer of tuna salad for balance; use more or less, according to personal preference. Try them with homemade potato chips for a real treat. Slices of fresh ripe tomatoes taste great on these, or skip the tomatoes and serve them up with garden fresh minestrone. Or, if you really like tomatoes, do both!

4 to 6 hamburger buns
2–6 oz. cans water pack tuna, drained
2 T. minced celery
4 T. mayonnaise
2 t. lemon juice
Optional: a few sprinkles instant minced onion
4 to 6 slices Swiss, cheddar, *or* American cheese
Optional: 4 to 6 large thin slices fresh tomato
Salt
Pepper

Combine the flaked tuna, mayonnaise, lemon juice, and celery, mixing well. Divide the mixture evenly between the buns. Sprinkle each with a few onion flakes, if desired. I like to do this individually as some folks in my family like the onion and others don't. Add the tomato slices (if you're using them), a sprinkle of salt and pepper, and top each with a slice of cheese and the top of the bun. Wrap loosely in foil, sealing at the seam. (Hint: if I'm making some with onion and some without, I turn the foil shiny side out for one type and dull-side out for the other.) Grill them over medium heat, turning once, for about 5 minutes, or until the sandwiches are heated through and the cheese melted. Or place in a hot (425°F) oven for about the same amount of time.

Jacob's Dish

This meatless main course forms the basis for a yummy vegetarian meal. Its unusual title is a biblical reference to the "mess of pottage" for which Jacob supposedly sold his birthright. Consisting of lentils and rice seasoned with butter, olive oil, and lots of onion, it's a salty and savory foil for any number of late-summer vegetables.

1 c. white rice
½ c. gray lentils
1 lg. onion, diced: 1 c.
2 t. salt
3 c. water, divided
2 T. butter
2 T. olive oil

Combine the lentils and 1 c. water in a small saucepan. Cover the pan tightly, bring to a boil, and reduce the heat so that the mixture just simmers. Allow the lentils to cook until the water has evaporated, about 15 minutes. Meanwhile, in a large saucepan combine the butter and olive oil. Add the rice, onion, and salt and sauté the mixture over medium-high heat for about 5 minutes, stirring frequently, to soften but not brown the onions and to give the rice a slightly opaque appearance. Add the remaining 2 cups of water and bring the rice to a boil. Give it a stir, tightly cover the pan, reduce the heat to a simmer, and allow the mixture to cook until the rice has absorbed all the water, about 15 minutes. Add the lentils to the rice, stirring well to blend thoroughly. Serve at once, accompanied by vinegar-dressed cooked greens or a nice tossed salad. Later in the fall, butternut squash mashed with brown sugar, butter, and a little mixed spice (cinnamon, nutmeg, ginger) makes a nice go-with. This should serve 4–6, depending on the appetites involved.

Swedish Meatballs

As with hot tuna sandwiches, meatballs are a nice interim dish, perfect for when summer begins creeping toward fall and days may be more or less warm, depending on nature's whimsy. Mashed potatoes are the logical choice to accompany Swedish meatballs, although rice or noodles also go nicely. Add in a green or yellow vegetable and a nice tart fruit sauce such as cranberry or lingonberry, a Scandinavian fruit that is now increasingly available for eating and even growing in the United States.

1½ lb. lean ground beef or equal parts beef, pork, and/or veal
1–2 slices bread, preferably rye, torn in pieces:
1 c. packed pieces
½ c. milk
2 eggs
1¼ t. salt
¼ t. white pepper
½ t. allspice
¼ t. nutmeg
1 medium onion, finely diced, or ¼ c. dried onion flakes
2 T. butter
2 T. flour
2 c. of desired liquids for gravy, as in recipe

If using fresh onion, I prefer to heat it gently with just a bit of water until it has become slightly tender. Combine the onion, bread, milk, and eggs in a large mixing bowl. Stir and mash it with a spoon to break up the bread. Add the remaining ingredients except for the butter and flour and mix well with a wooden spoon or your hands until the mixture is nice and smooth. Melt the butter in a large, heavy skillet over medium heat. Form the mixture into balls or patties and fry gently in the butter until done through. Covering the pan helps facilitate the cooking process. Remove to a serving plate and add the flour to the pan drippings. Stir in veggie cooking liquids, beef broth, and/or equal parts milk and water and cook to thicken. Serve with mashed potatoes and a side of cranberry or lingonberry sauce. This makes approximately 2 dozen meatballs, depending on the size you choose, and 6–8 servings as a main course, more as part of a buffet.

Pork Medallions with Blackberry Cream Sauce

Take advantage of fresh August blackberries for this recipe. It may be prepared with frozen berries off-season, if need be. This has evolved into one of my favorite recipes over the years; a variation was even served at Tim and Abbey's wedding. It was originally inspired by the British cooking show Two Fat Ladies, *in which Jennifer prepared a (very distant) cousin of it using venison.*

1 lb. pork tenderloin, cut crosswise into 8 medallions
¼ c. flour
¼ t. ground ginger
¼ t. salt
1/8 t. white pepper
2 T. butter
2 T. olive oil
1 c. chicken broth
¼ c. cream
1 c. blackberries
½ c. blackberry merlot *or* grape juice
¼ c. blackberry jam

Flatten the medallions slightly and dredge them in the flour mixture. Sear them on both sides in the butter and olive oil in a large cast-iron skillet over medium-high heat. Turn with tongs or a spatula rather than piercing with a fork. Once they are uniformly browned, add the chicken broth, cover, and cook about 5 minutes; then uncover; and let it reduce by half. Remove the medallions to a serving platter. Add the cream to the pan, swirling and cooking for about a minute longer. Meanwhile, combine the blackberry jam and wine or apple juice in a small saucepan and bring to a boil. Pour the cream gravy and the blackberry sauce over and around the medallions and top with the blackberries. Serve with mashed potatoes and a green vegetable or two. Even some corn thrown in as a side dish isn't such a bad idea! This recipe is also really good with red raspberries and jam instead of blackberries. It will serve 4.

September is also blackberry season, sweet tart berries that can enhance both the main course and dessert.

Blackberry Crème Brûlée

If you're lucky enough to have fresh black-berries, this recipe is a lovely way to enjoy them. It's not difficult, but does require a bit of advance planning, as the blackberry custard must be thoroughly chilled before applying and browning the sugar topping. Making the custards a day in advance or in the morning of the day you plan to serve will allow you ample time to enjoy them. You'll also need a small kitchen torch for browning the tops. For goodness' sakes, do not try to use a blowtorch! You could end up incinerating yourself and the custards! If you don't have one, you can try browning the brûlées under the broiler, watching carefully, although I'm afraid the results won't be quite as nice. They're fancy enough for company, but please don't feel you must wait for guests to enjoy these summer treats!

1¾ c. heavy cream
5 T. sugar
6 egg yolks
2 T. blackberry brandy, blackberry wine, *or* Chambord
1 c. fresh blackberries, ½ pint
4 T. sugar

Place the cream in a medium, heavy saucepan and bring to just under boiling. Meanwhile, beat together the 5 T. sugar, the blackberry wine or liquor, and the egg yolks until they are well blended. Add a little of the hot cream to temper the mixture, whisking briskly. Combine the egg mixture with the rest of the hot cream in the pan and continue to cook it, stirring constantly, until it coats the surface of a metal spoon lifted through it; this is a temperature of about 170°F. You want to cook the mixture sufficiently without allowing it to come to a boil, which might cause it to curdle. Meanwhile, distribute the blackberries evenly between 4 6-oz. custard cups. (If using my own berries, I don't bother to wash them, but I do wash commercially purchased berries just before I use them as a safeguard against any nasty little pathogens that might possibly be lurking therein.) Pour the hot custard over the berries in each custard cup. Place the filled cups in a 9" ×13" baking pan, filling it about halfway up the sides of the custard cups with very hot water. Bake in a preheated 325°F oven for 35–45 minutes, until the custards are mostly set. Remove them from the water bath and place on a clean dry surface to cool to room temperature, about ½ hour. Chill for at least another 2 hours, or overnight. When you are ready to serve your blackberry brûlées, sprinkle to remaining 4 T. of sugar evenly over the tops of the 4 custards. Using a small kitchen torch, brown the top of each until it bubbles and turns a deep even golden brown. Serve at once.

Apple Pie

Let's head back to the orchard; apple pie is an American classic. You can't really do much better for a homey, delicious dessert. Use your choice of standard piecrust or for a twist cheddar cheese piecrust (add a bit of shredded cheese after cutting together the butter and flour). I prefer using a mix of apples for best flavor and texture. Some firmer ones, such a Rome, keep their shape well, but I also like adding some Macs or Cortlands for their deli-cious flavor. Depending on their size, this will take 6–8 apples.

1 recipe preferred piecrust
6 c. peeled, cored, and sliced apples
¾–1 c. sugar, depending on apples' tartness and personal taste
1 t. cinnamon
½ t. fresh grated nutmeg
¼ t. salt
2 T. flour
Milk or cream for glazing top crust
1–2 T. sugar for sprinkling on top crust

Roll out ½ of the chilled piecrust and fit loosely into a 9" pie plate. Place the sliced apples in a large bowl, sprinkling with remaining ingredi-ents. Stir to combine thoroughly using a large spoon or your clean hands. Pile this into your pie plate and brush the edge of crust with a little water or milk for binding. Roll out and top with upper crust. I often cut an apple outline into the top crust before fitting it over the apples, being careful to leave some uncut crust in the outline so that the whole shape doesn't just fall out! Trim extra crust from the edges if there is a lot of overhang and fold the top crust down over the bottom, pinching to seal. Either crimp the edges or press with a fork or spoon to complete sealing and form a decorative trim. Brush the top with a little milk or cream and sprinkle with sugar or cinnamon sugar. Bake at 375°F for 50–60 minutes, until the crust is golden brown and the apples are tender and just bubbling in the center of the pie. Remove to a cooling rack. Serve warm or at room temperature. Apple pie will keep a day or two at room temperature, loosely covered. For a longer period of time, it should be refrigerated to prevent drying out or spoilage. Chances are you won't need to worry about that anyway!

Homemade apple pie, dusted with cinnamon sugar, is all set to pop in the oven.

Apple Crunch

"Apples with crunchy topping" was one of my mother's favorite apple recipes. It's not a particularly fussy recipe, pretty much allowing you to make as much or little as you wish. The topping contains oatmeal, brown sugar, and butter, giving it an almost butterscotch-y flavor. Once it's baked, I prefer topping it with half and half or milk, as opposed to ice cream or richer fare. Your conscience will dictate your choice, I'm sure.

4–5 apples—peeled, cored, and sliced
½ c. butter
½ c. flour
½ t. cinnamon, optional
¾ c. brown sugar
¾ c. rolled oats

Place the apples in a lightly greased 9" cake tin or equivalently sized casserole dish, patting them down a bit. Combine the flour, oats, sugar, and the cinnamon if desired in a medium mixing bowl. Melt the butter and pour it over the dry ingredients, mixing well. Crumble this mixture evenly over the apples, covering as much of the surface as possible. Bake in a 350°F oven for 30–40 minutes, until the apples are tender when pierced with a fork. Serve warm or cool with choice of topping. It's also tasty just the way it is!

Apple Brown Betty

Apple brown Betty is another humble but delicious apple dessert. You can use any sort of bread you'd like for this, as long as it lends itself to a sweet dish. It's a great way to get rid of odds and ends of crusts and such. This is even less exacting than apple crunch; you simply make
as many layers as you'd like. Here are some proportions to make a medium-sized dish.

4–5 apples—peeled, cored, and sliced
4–5 slices of bread, torn into bits
¾ c. sugar
1 t. cinnamon
¼ c. orange juice
2 T. melted butter

Combine the cinnamon and sugar in a small bowl, mixing well. In a buttered baking dish, place a thin layer of bread. Top with a layer of apple slices and a generous sprinkling of cinnamon sugar. Repeat the layers, ending with a final layer of bread sprinkled with cinnamon sugar. Drizzle with the orange juice and butter. Bake in a 350°F oven for approximately 45 minutes, until the apples are tender. Serve warm or cold with half and half or whipped cream.

Marlboro Pie

This is based on a very old recipe commonly referred to as "Marlborough pie." I use the simpler spelling in honor of my neighbor town to the west; Marlboro, Vermont, home for many years to my Aunt Edith and Uncle Russell Hertzberg. The pie itself is somewhat similar to a pumpkin pie, although applesauce is used rather than pumpkin. The flavors are a bit more delicate as well. For a fancier version, melt a bit of crab apple or currant jelly to glaze the top of the cooled pie and garnish with dollops of whipped cream and red-skinned apple slices. Dipping the slices in a little lemon juice will help prevent discoloration.

½ recipe piecrust
2 eggs, beaten
1½ c. thick applesauce
1¼ c. milk
¼ c. cream
¾ c. sugar
1 T. cornstarch
½ t. each cinnamon
½ t. nutmeg
¼ t. salt
¼ t. ground cloves
1 t. grated lemon zest

Preheat oven to 425°F. Roll the crust out to fit loosely in a 9" pie pan. Fold the edges under and press up into high flutes to help prevent spills. Combine the eggs, applesauce, sugar, spices, cornstarch, salt, and lemon zest. Whisk to combine well. Stir in the milk and cream. Place the pie pan on a cookie sheet or baking tin. Carefully pour the filling in and place the pie on the middle shelf of the preheated oven. This is probably the most challenging part of making the whole pie! Bake at 425°F for 10 minutes. Reduce heat to 350°F and bake for approximately 45–50 minutes longer, until the apple custard seems set in the center and the surface is uniformly lightly browned. Allow to cool completely before serving. Refrigerate as soon as it's cool enough. This is an easy pie to make the day before you wish to eat it.

Gingerbread with Apple Cream

Gingerbread is another old-fashioned classic country dessert. It's delicious served warm with fresh whipped cream and also satisfying served in plain slices, cold, with a glass of milk. This time of year, for a little change, why not try it with apple cream: a fluffy blend of whipped cream and applesauce.

⅓ c. sugar
¼ c. corn oil
½ c. light molasses
1 egg
1¼ c. flour
1 t. baking soda
¼ t. nutmeg
½ t. ginger

½ t. cinnamon
½ t. salt
1 t. grated orange or lemon zest, optional
¾ c. hot tap water

Combine sugar, oil, molasses, and egg in a medium mixing bowl, whisking to combine well. Add the combined dry ingredients, including the citrus zest if included, whisking again to a smooth stiff batter. Lastly, stir in the hot water; batter will now be thin. Pour into a greased and floured 9" cake pan and bake in a 325°F oven approximately 30 minutes, until the top springs back when touched lightly. Serve warm or cool with whipped cream, lemon sauce, or apple cream.

Gingerbread with apple cream is another fall treat worth eating.

293

Apple Cream

1 c. heavy cream
⅓ c. sugar
1 t. vanilla
1 c. cold applesauce

Whip the cream with the sugar and vanilla until it holds soft peaks. Fold in the applesauce until everything is just well combined. Serve over pieces of warm or cool gingerbread.

Sunflowers

Noting says summer garden quite like a row of towering yellow sunflowers looking down on the rows of beans and tomatoes. By the time September rolls around, some of those sunflowers will have produced a head full of seeds. With the recent popularity of ornamental sunflowers, it's important to remember many of them do not produce viable seeds for snacking on. If you wish to raise your own sunflowers for the seeds, take note of the varieties you purchase, making sure they're the seed producers and not just pretty in a vase. Cut the flower heads at the curve on the stem once the petals have shriveled and seeds have matured and allow them to dry completely in a sheltered spot before removing the seeds from the flower head. Now comes the challenge; hulling your seeds! Some newer varieties make this step easier, but the technique remains the same: slit or crack the outer shell to remove the tender seed from within.

Sunflower Seed Granola

The biggest challenge I face in reaping a viable sunflower seed harvest is outsmarting the little critters who wish to enjoy them as well. Keeping a close eye out on the ripening flower heads and nabbing them before the birds and squirrels get the same bright idea is the September game plan for success. Use plain old-hulled seeds for this, not roasted or salted; they're readily available in most grocery stores this time of year if you haven't raised any of your own.

3 c. rolled oats
¼ c. corn oil
1 t. vanilla
½ c. sun butter
½ c. packed brown sugar
½ c. flaked coconut
¾ c. hulled sunflower seeds

Optional

½ c. banana chips
½ c. chocolate mini chips
½ c. raisins

Combine the oil and sun butter in a large saucepan or stainless steel mixing bowl. Warm them over low heat, stirring frequently, until the

Big, bold, and yellow, sunflowers brighten the garden and provide nutritious seeds for snacking or baking.

sun butter melts and the mixture is smooth. Stir in the brown sugar and vanilla to amalgamate well. Stir in the rolled oats, coating them completely. Turn the mixture onto a large waxed paper–lined baking sheet. Bake in a slow (300–325°F) oven for 20 minutes, stirring twice. Stir in the sunflower seeds and coconut and continue baking another 10 minutes, stirring once. Turn off the oven and allow the granola to cool slowly, about another half hour, before removing to cool completely. Once it is entirely cool, stir in any desired add-ins. Store your granola airtight; zip-type plastic bags work well for this. I personally think adding fresh sliced bananas and a splash of milk to a bowl of sunflower seed granola is a grand way to start the day.

Sun Butter Swirl Brownies

Sunflower seeds may just have the potential for turning into the northern peanut. Although they're a seed rather than a legume, they can be utilized for many of the same purposes. Sun butter, which is a creamy spread made from ground sunflower seeds, is becoming more widely available. If you haven't yet had an opportunity to try it, this recipe will provide you with a good incentive. In this case the sunflower seeds were commercially produced, although you could try roasting your own by combining them with a small amount of oil (1–2 t. per cup of seeds), sprinkling with salt and toasting in a moderately slow oven (325°F) for about 20 minutes.

½ c. butter, softened
1½ c. sugar
2 oz. unsweetened chocolate
3 eggs
1½ t vanilla
½ c. flour
½ c. sun butter
½ c. salted sunflower seeds, optional

Melt together the chocolate and butter, either in the microwave or over low heat on top of the stove. Beat in 1 c. of the sugar, 1 t. of vanilla, and 2 of the eggs. Lastly, stir in the flour. Pour this mixture into a buttered and floured 8" or 9" square pan. In a small bowl, beat together the sun butter, ½ c. sugar, ½ t. vanilla, and the remaining egg until the mixture is smooth. Dollop this on top of the brownie batter in the pan and swirl the two batters together lightly to marbleize. Sprinkle the sunflower seeds evenly over the top, if desired. Bake on the middle shelf of a 350°F oven for 30 minutes. Allow the brownies to cool approximately 10 minutes before cutting into 16 bars. Serve them warm or at room temperature.

Sunny Honey Sundaes

Ice cream sundaes originated in the days when it wasn't considered proper to imbibe soda and other such intemperate beverages on the Sabbath. Since hot fudge or butterscotch sauce dribbled over dishes of ice cream, topped with whipped cream and a cherry, contained no soda whatsoever, they were considered fair game for a Sunday treat. Thanks to the "healthful" ingredients in sunny honey sundaes, you could probably even concoct them for Sunday brunch. However, don't feel constrained; feel free to enjoy these tasty sundaes any day of the week.

1 pt. vanilla or chocolate frozen custard ("July") or other favorite ice cream
¼ c. honey
¼ c. sun butter
2 T. milk
½ t. vanilla
¼ c. sunflower seed granola
½ c. heavy cream
2 T. sugar
½ t. vanilla
4 cherries, optional

Combine the honey, milk, and sun butter in a small saucepan. Place over low heat, stirring constantly, until the mixture is thoroughly combined and warmed through; don't overheat. Stir in ½ t. vanilla. Place the cream, sugar, and remaining ½ t. vanilla extract in a small bowl and whip them to soft peaks. Divide the frozen custard or ice cream evenly between 4 parfait glasses or bowls. Top each equally with the honey sauce and granola. Add a dollop of whipped cream to each and top with a cherry, if desired. Serve to 4 deserving people.

Sunflower Crinkles

I wish chocolate-covered sunflower seeds were more readily available in this area; they're a great add-in to granola and cookies. Actually, they're pretty tasty as a snack all by themselves too. If you don't happen to have easy access to them either, they can be ordered via the Internet, or in the case of these cookies, simply substitute an equal amount of your favorite mini chocolate chips.

6 T. unsalted butter
⅔ c. sun butter
1 t. vanilla
½ c. sugar
½ c. brown sugar
1 egg
2 T. milk
1 c. flour
⅔ c. whole wheat flour
1 t. baking soda
½ t. salt
¾ c. chocolate-coated sunflower seeds

Cream together the butter and sun butter until smooth, adding in the vanilla, brown and granulated sugar. Add the milk and egg, again beating until smooth and fluffy. Finally stir in the flours, baking soda, and salt. At this point the dough should be of a good texture for rolling between your hands into balls. Form it into approximately

3 dozen balls (about 1 T. of dough each). Place the sunflower seeds or chocolate chips in a small dish or saucer. Push one side of each dough ball into the seeds to just coat and invert each onto an ungreased cookie sheet. You may need to firm the seeds or chips into the tops of the cookies a bit so they don't slide off; flattening the cookie slightly works just fine. Bake on the upper rack at 375°F for 9–10 minutes, until the cookies are puffed, light golden, and the surfaces appear crinkled. Cool for a minute on the sheets before removing with a spatula to wire cooling racks. If you don't wish to bake all your cookies at once, simply place in the freezer right on the baking sheet until they are frozen. Either cover the sheet with foil or gently transfer the unbaked cookies to sealed plastic bags, to use within a month or so. Add an extra couple minutes of baking time if the cookies are frozen when you bake them.

Banana Cupcakes

Banana cupcakes are delicious, kid-friendly little desserts any time of the year. They're especially tasty frosted and then topped with chocolate-covered sunflower seeds. If you prefer, the batter may also be baked in two or three 9" round tins; reduce the oven temperature to 350°F and bake for 25–35 minutes; cool for 10 minutes in the pans before turning out onto cooling racks. Banana cake holds a certain amount of nostalgia for me; when Greg was in first grade, I baked him a banana birthday cake in the shape of a train, complete with steam locomotive. As I recall, the cotton batting "steam" held air born with florist's wire was quite splendiferous.

1 c. mashed bananas, about 3 medium
2 t. vanilla

1½ c. sugar
½ c. corn oil
⅓ c. buttermilk*
2¼ c. cake flour
3 eggs
1 t. salt
1 t. baking powder
1 t. baking soda

Beat together the bananas, vanilla, oil, and sugar. Add the combined flour, baking powder, baking soda, and salt along with the buttermilk; beat again on medium speed until smooth. Lastly, beat in the eggs, again on medium speed, until you have a nice smooth batter. In order to have cupcakes of a uniform size, I portion out the batter using a small release-type ice cream scoop. You could use any type of measuring implement that works for you; the paper lined or greased and floured muffin tins should only be about ½ full. Bake the cupcakes on the upper third of a preheated 375°F oven for about 18–20 minutes, until they are puffed, golden, and spring back when touched lightly. Allow to cool in the tins for 5–10 minutes before removing to racks to cool completely. Frost and decorate as desired. This recipe makes 2½ dozen reasonably sized cupcakes, perfect for kids and for adults who don't wish to overindulge.

*Buttermilk is readily available in the dairy case, although in a pinch you could substitute ⅓ c. milk soured with 1 t. lemon juice or vinegar.

Plum Ketchup (Dipping Sauce)

Once upon a time my parents had a plum tree planted on the little strip of land between the north side of the house and the Ames Hill Brook. Plums have a bit of a hard time where we live, as many require Zone 5 or warmer conditions to thrive. Finicky southern Vermont sometimes masquerades as Zone 5, but when you least expect, it slips away into twenty-five-degree-below-zero Zone 4 weather, sometimes ending the most promising plum tree's production. However, that little plum tree did manage to hang on for several years, perhaps being one of the few hardier varieties available. I remember the little plums fondly, bright red skins splitting open to disclose juicy golden flesh. Every yellow jacket from miles around would be clustered near any dropped ones, eagerly ingesting as much of the sticky sweetness as the late-summer warmth would allow. For this recipe I prefer a dark plum, such as black friar, for both flavor and the deep-purple color it imbues to the ketchup, although you are welcome to experiment with whatever varieties may be available to you.

3 c. pitted diced plums (not peeled)
½ c. sugar
¼ c. cider vinegar
1 t. cinnamon
1 t. grated fresh ginger root
½ t. mace *or* nutmeg
⅛ t. anise seed
⅛ t. ground cloves
¼ t. salt
1 t. instant minced onion *or* 1 T. grated fresh onion, optional

Combine all ingredients in a medium stainless steel or glass saucepan (non-aluminum). Heat them slightly to start the juices flowing. Pour into a blender and puree until smooth. Return the mixture to the saucepan and simmer over medium-low heat until it is slightly thickened, about 10–15 minutes. Serve warm or cold; store leftovers in the fridge for up to 2 weeks or freeze in small containers to use a little later.

Dark purple plums combine with sugar, vinegar, and spice to give plum ketchup eye appeal and rich flavor. It's especially tasty as dipping sauce for chicken tenders.

Plum Dandy Cupcakes

When I was growing up, there were a number of 4-H clubs in and around Brattleboro. On occasion, our club would get together with some of the others for a combined meeting. At one in particular, a leader by the name of Mrs. D. brought what I considered at the time to be some truly amazing cupcakes. They were spice cake with vanilla frosting, and each one was stuffed with part of a canned plum. Although Mrs. D. and her recipe have since passed on, her memory lingers, as does a facsimile of those long-ago cupcakes, recreated here using fresh plums.

¼ c. unsalted butter
½ c. packed brown sugar
¼ c. granulated sugar
¼ c. sour cream
1 egg
½ t. cinnamon
¼ t. grated nutmeg
¼ t. allspice
¼ t. salt
⅛ t. ground cloves
⅛ t. lemon extract
1 c. all-purpose flour
½ t. baking soda
6 small plums (prune plums), halved and pitted*

Beat the butter with the sugars until light and fluffy. Beat in the sour cream, egg, and lemon extract. Stir in the combined dry ingredients until the batter is smooth; it will also be quite thick. Divide it evenly between 12 cupcake paper-lined muffin cups. Lightly press ½ of an unpeeled plum, skin-side up, into the top of each portion of batter. Bake on a middle or upper oven rack at 375°F for 18–20 minutes, until the batter as puffed and golden around the plums and firm to touch. Cool the cupcakes in the pan for about 10 minutes before turning them out to cool completely. You may simple sprinkle them with confectioner's sugar, although I think they're much improved with Portsmouth Icing. This makes 12 cupcakes.

*If you don't have access to small plums, use 3 larger ones, quartered.

Portsmouth Icing

If memory serves me, I first came across a recipe for Portsmouth frosting in an old Fanny Farmer Cookbook, *one of my early standbys, many years ago. I don't remember too much about the original other than that it utilized milk and butter melted together as a base. The frosting this recipe produces is dense and smooth, almost like a fondant candy filling.*

2 T. butter
2 T. milk
½ t. vanilla
2½ c. confectioner's sugar

Heat the milk and butter in a small saucepan until the butter melts and the mixture is steaming. Turn off the heat and stir in the vanilla and confectioner's sugar. The icing will appear smooth but somewhat runny. Working quickly, swirl some of the icing on each cooled cupcake. It will harden once it cools; if it begins to harden before you're done, simply heat the remaining icing for a few seconds, until it is of spreading consistency again.

Use smaller prune plums for plum dandy cupcakes if you can find them; otherwise, quartered larger plums will do just fine.

Bringing in the Harvest . . .

BY OCTOBER, THE garden is winding down for the year. It's time to finish digging potatoes, pull beets and carrots, and gather up the rest of the winter squash and pumpkins. This is perfect timing; Halloween is just around the corner, with Thanksgiving soon to follow!

First, the garden requires a little TLC: pulling up plants and stalks, getting a last tilling in, perhaps sowing winter rye, to add a little green nourishment to the soil over the winter months looming ahead. I admit to occasionally leaving some plants and stalks for the winter birds to pick at. There are still hearty vegetables hanging out there, of course; broccoli and kale turn sweeter in the autumn cold, and brussels sprouts are just coming into their own. Perhaps if you managed an extra planting of them, you'll even have some fall peas to savor!

Late-sown leaf lettuce or mesclun mix to add variety to the habitual fall coleslaw. Let's not forget the little guys who winter over: garlic waiting to reach maturity under a blanket of straw and parsnips that will turn sweeter in the winter cold. On the garden's edges, chives and mint are dulling down, ready to sleep under a blanket of snow. Rhubarb has already quietly gone dormant, while the annual herbs have succumbed to early frost.

That's all right, though, because the autumn kitchen has just shifted into high gear! Pie pumpkins, after having their seeds scraped out for boiling and roasting, are set to steam tender. Once slightly cooled, the flesh easily separates from the thin outer layer of skin. The two then go their separate ways: the skin to enrich the compost pile, the flesh directly into the blender, pureed smooth with just a touch of the cooking liquid. Now you're ready to freeze for future reference, or to turn your pumpkin puree into any number of pumpkin-y delights.

Golden October light shines on our neighbors' farm, while color creeps into the mountains up the valley.

October

Jolly Jack Cheese Dip

Who says Halloween has to be all about sweet stuff? Although its base is cheese rather than pumpkin, a hollowed-out pumpkin shell is used as the serving bowl for Jolly Jack cheese dip. (Line the pumpkin first with foil or plastic wrap if you wish for ease of cleanup.) This tasty dip just fits the bill for autumnal festivities, no matter the ages of the participants.

8 oz. yellow cheddar *or* Colby cheese, shredded

2 T. flour

8 oz. regular or light cream cheese

2 T. butter

2 T. diced celery

2 T. diced red bell pepper

¼ cup finely chopped green onion

½ t. salt, or to taste

½ t. dry mustard

½ cup dairy sour cream

1 cup milk

Few drops Tabasco sauce

Small hollowed-out pumpkin(s) if desired

Assorted breadsticks and crackers for dipping

Raw veggies for dipping

Melt the butter in medium saucepan over low heat. Stir in celery and onions; cook until slightly tender but not browned. Add red bell pepper, salt, mustard, and flour; cook; and stir a minute longer. Stir in milk all at once, increase heat slightly, and cook and stir until thickened. Stir in sour cream, cream cheese, and cheddar or Colby cheese until just melted. Add Tabasco sauce to taste, more salt if necessary (check to season). To serve, pour into a warm (not cooked) hollowed-out pumpkin or 3–4 minipumpkins, and serve immediately. (If made in advance, cover in microwaveable bowl and refrigerate and then heat in microwave just before serving. As settings may vary, follow the one that seems to fit the bill best.) Jolly Jack dip is good with raw or blanched broccoli, cauliflower, snow peas, carrots, etc., and breadsticks or crackers. It's also tasty as a topper for baked or mashed potatoes or hamburger patties.

Jolly Jack cheese dip is a fun way to celebrate fall.

Roasted Pumpkin Seeds

Although some folks simply bake their pumpkin seeds and then sprinkle them with salt, I prefer a two-step cooking process. Boiling the seeds in salted water prior to baking helps soften the hulls and allows the salt flavor to penetrate more efficiently than simply salting the surfaces. The drained seeds are then baked to a golden brown, perfect for snacking on any old time. You may prepare as many or as few seeds as you wish using this method.

Fresh pumpkin seeds, as much of the flesh scraped away as possible

Salted water at a ratio of 1 t. salt per cup of water

Oil or nonstick cooking spray

Place the pumpkin seeds with salted water to cover generously in an appropriately sized saucepan. Bring to a boil over high heat, reduce the heat, and gently boil, uncovered, for 15 minutes. Allow the mixture to cool to room temperature or cooler for as little as ½ or up to 24 hours. Strain the water off through a wire mesh sieve, shaking to remove as much moisture as possible. Discard the water and distribute the seeds in an even single layer on one or more lightly oiled or sprayed baking sheets. Bake on the middle or upper racks of a preheated 350°F oven for about ½ hour, stirring the seeds once or twice as they bake. The seeds will turn a nice golden brown when they've baked long enough. Cool the seeds on the baking sheets before storing in sealable plastic bags or dishes. Seeds prepared in this manner should store well for several months if left in a cool, dry location.

Pumpkin Bread

I've intentionally made this recipe just a bit lighter than many I've seen. The juice gives a little extra moistness and flavor that otherwise would need to be accounted for with more sugar and butter.

¼ c. melted butter
½ c. corn oil
1½ c. sugar
4 eggs
1 c. orange *or* apple juice *or* cider
1¾ c. pumpkin pulp (1 can if you don't have your own)
4 c. flour
2 t. baking soda
2 t. cinnamon
1 t. nutmeg
1 t. ginger
1 t. salt
1 c. raisins, walnuts *or* pumpkin seeds, optional

Combine the butter, oil, sugar, and pumpkin in a large mixing bowl. Beat together until smooth, adding the eggs and juice gradually. Combine the dry ingredients and add all at once, beating on low until the flour mixture is well incorporated. Fold in fruit, seeds, and/or nuts as desired. Pour into 2 greased and floured 9" × 5" loaf pans. Bake in a preheated 350°F oven approximately 1 hour, until he tops are brown and shiny and a toothpick comes out clean. It is common for the tops of loaves such as this to crack; another way to test for doneness is to lightly touch the batter showing in the cracks to determine if it's solid rather than sticky. Cool on racks 10 minutes in the pans and then turn out and lay the loaves on their sides to finish cooling completely. Loaves this size will generally fit nicely into 1-gallon-size plastic storage bags. They may also be wrapped in plastic wrap or aluminum foil. Although these keep well for up to a week at cool room temperature, you can also label and freeze one or more to use within a month or two.

Hazelnut Harvest Granola

This spicy sweet granola not only tastes good, but it's also a treat to look at! The bright colors of the dried fruits resemble little autumn leaves drifting through a pile of granola goodness.

3 c. rolled oats
¼ c. unsweetened pumpkin *or* butternut squash pulp

½ c. brown sugar
¼ c. corn oil
1 t. each cinnamon
1 t. grated orange rind
½ t. nutmeg
¼ t. salt
¼ t. ground cloves
½ c. chopped hazelnuts
¼ c. dried cranberries
¼ c. snipped dried apricots

Combine the pumpkin or squash, oil, brown sugar, salt, and spices in a large bowl, whisking to combine well. Stir in the rolled oats until they are completely coated with the mixture. Turn out onto a lightly oiled baking sheet and bake on a middle or upper shelf of a 350°F oven for 20 minutes. Stir the granola, redistributing the edges, and sprinkle the hazelnuts over the top. Bake for another 20–25 minutes, stirring once or twice, until the mixture is lightly browned and a bit of it feels crisp and dry when slightly cooled; be careful not to burn. Remove from the oven and stir in the dried fruits. Allow to cool thoroughly before bagging or storing airtight. This makes about 5 cups of granola. It stores well if kept cool and dry.

Squash Gems

Squash gems are technically a muffin, although the flavor and texture are more a combination of fruit bread crossed with a doughnut. Nutmeg, lemon, and cinnamon flavor these sweet little quick breads. Next time you're cooking some butternut squash, mash it before adding the seasonings and reserve ½ a cup of the plain mashed squash. Refrigerate it for up to a week to use when baking squash gems.

½ c. unseasoned mashed butternut squash
1 c. and 2 T. sugar, divided
6 T. butter, divided
1 egg
¾ c. buttermilk *or* sour milk*
1 t. baking soda
1¾ c. flour
½ t. salt
1 t. nutmeg
1 t. cinnamon
1 t. grated lemon zest *or* ¼ t. pure lemon extract

Whisk together the squash, 2 T. of the butter, melted, ¾ c. sugar, buttermilk, egg, and lemon zest or extract. Stir in the flour, baking soda, nutmeg, and salt until just well blended. Divide evenly between 12 well-buttered muffin cups and bake on the upper rack of a 375°F oven for approximately 20–25 minutes, until they are nicely risen, light golden brown, and spring back when lightly touched. Loosen the muffins and allow them to cool in the tin for about 5 minutes. Meanwhile, melt the remaining 4 T. of butter. In a separate small bowl, combine the remaining 6 T. of sugar and 1 t. of cinnamon. Dip the tops of the warm muffins in the butter to coat each well and then in the cinnamon sugar, again coating each generously. These are at their best when served while still warm, but also save well for a day or two. Once they have cooled, place them back in the muffin tins and cover the tops with aluminum foil. This makes a dozen muffins.

*Cultured buttermilk is available in many grocery stores, or you can reconstitute powdered. If you don't have any, add 1 t. lemon juice or vinegar to ¾ c. regular milk to sour it.

Almost a cross between a muffin and a doughnut, squash gems have a light spicy flavor all their own.

Cranberry Bread

This is based on a recipe I discovered years ago that utilized cooked cranberry sauce as opposed to raw cranberries. I've revised it several times and still prefer it to any other. Although you may use canned whole-berry cranberry sauce, I generally just scoop out a little from a batch of homemade.

2 c. flour
1 t. baking soda
½ t. salt
¾ c. sugar
2 eggs
⅔ c. milk
¼ c. melted butter
1 c. whole cranberry sauce
1 c. chopped walnuts
1 T. grated orange zest (optional)

Combine in a large bowl the eggs (slightly beaten), milk, butter, cranberry sauce, nuts, and the zest if using. Next, combine the dry ingredients and stir into the mixture in bowl. Pour into a greased and floured 9" × 5" loaf pan. Bake in a preheated 350°F oven for about 1 hour, until the top is cracked, shiny brown, and set to touch. Due to the high-moisture content of this bread, it's a little trickier to test using a toothpick than some others, but generally, if one is inserted, it should come out clean as well. Cool in the pan for about 10 minutes and then turn it out to finish cooling on its side on a cooling rack. Wrap and store as you would for pumpkin bread.

Buttermilk Biscuits

Buttermilk biscuits have a tangier flavor and more golden appearance than regular baking powder biscuits. You may either use fresh buttermilk or a combination of dried buttermilk powder and water. By keeping the dough soft, you'll have light, tender biscuits with a slightly springy texture, good with butter and/or honey.

2 c. flour
1 t. baking powder
1 t. baking soda
½ t. salt
6 T. cold butter
2 t. sugar
½ scant c. buttermilk
or 6 T. water and ¼ c. buttermilk powder

Combine the flour, sugar, salt, baking powder, and baking soda in a large mixing bowl. Stir in the buttermilk powder, if you're using dry buttermilk. Cut in the cold butter, using a pastry cutter or two knives, until the mixture forms coarse crumbs. With a fork, stir in the water or just under ½ c. of buttermilk. This should form a very soft dough; allow it to stand for just a minute, which will allow it to firm up enough for you to handle it more easily. Turn the dough out onto a generously floured baking sheet and lightly press and fold it over until it forms a cohesive layer about 1" thick. Cut this into 12 even squares, or if you prefer round biscuits, cut them out with a round cookie cutter or floured top of a drinking glass, reusing any scraps. I have some aluminum glasses that work nicely for this purpose. The important thing to remember when making biscuits is to handle the dough as little as possible and use a light hand for a light product. Bake the biscuits right on the same in, on the upper shelf of a preheated 400°F oven for about 10 minutes, until they are golden brown and firm to touch. This will make about 12 biscuits, depending on their size.

Anadama Bread

This classic New England bread supposedly derived its name from a pithy comment made by a sea captain upon returning home to discover his wife, Anna, was nowhere to be found. Spluttering angrily at the lady in absentia, he gathered together cornmeal, molasses, and a few other foodstuffs to produce the original version of the hearty bread we call anadama.

½ c. molasses
½ c. yellow cornmeal
¼ c. butter
2 t. salt
2 c. cold water
2 pkg. dry yeast: 1½ T.
¼ c. warm water
5–6 c. bread flour

Combine the molasses, cornmeal, butter, salt, and the 2 c. water in a medium saucepan. Bring to a boil, stirring constantly to keep the cornmeal from sticking and lumping. Remove from the heat and cool to lukewarm. Meanwhile, soften the yeast in the ¼ c. warm water. Add this to the lukewarm mixture along with 2 c. flour. Please note that you must cool the cornmeal/molasses mixture adequately; if it's too hot, it will kill the yeast and you'll have two hard, flat loaves of bread. It should be lukewarm to touch, about 130°F. Once the yeast and flour have been incorporated, knead in additional flour to make a smooth elastic dough. Let it rise in a warm, moist place until double in bulk, about 45 minutes. Punch the dough down and form it into two loaves. Place each in a greased 9" × 5" loaf pan, seam-side down, and allow it to rise until the dough reaches the tops of the pans. Bake at 350°F until the tops are nicely browned and the loaves sound hollow when tapped; start checking after about ½ hour. Butter the tops while still hot and turn out of the pans on their sides onto racks to cool.

Vermont Cheddar Onion Bread

Get yourself some good sharp cheddar cheese for this recipe. It makes bread that is at its best still warm from the oven, if you can manage to slice it without compressing the loaf too much. It's also very tasty toasted and is a good accompaniment to any number of soups and stews.

8 oz. shredded cheddar cheese
½ lg. onion, minced: ½ c.
2 T. snipped fresh chives, or 1 T. dried
2 t. salt
¼ c. sugar
2 T. butter
2 pkg. dry yeast: 1½ T.
2 c. hot water
5–6 c. bread flour

Toast the minced onion in a hot skillet over medium-high heat until it is lightly browned. Combine the onion, cheese, chives, sugar, butter, salt, and hot water in a large mixing bowl. Stir it to partially melt the cheese. Once it has cooled to lukewarm, dissolve the yeast in this mixture. Allow it to work for a few minutes, until it begins to bubble. Stir in 2 c. of flour to make a soft dough. Gradually knead in enough more flour to make a smooth, elastic dough. Let it rise in a warm, moist place until it has doubled, about 45 minutes to 1 hour. Punch the dough down and form it into 2 loaves, placing each seam-side down in a buttered 9" × 5" loaf pan. Let it rise again until the dough reaches the tops of the pans. Bake at 350°F until golden brown and hollow sounding when tapped, about ½ hour to 40 minutes. Butter the tops while hot and turn the loaves out of the pans onto their sides to cool on racks.

Twice-Baked Potatoes

Plain-baked potatoes are a treat to me, as long as the potatoes are good quality to begin with. Start with a nice russet-type potato, scrubbed and pricked a few times with a fork. Bake at 350°F for up to an hour, depending on the size of your potatoes. If you want them a little faster, try microwaving them between 5 and 10 minutes first to reduce your baking time. Once they're baked, enjoy with butter or sour cream, or turn them into twice baked for a special treat.

2 large *or* 4 small russet-type potatoes
¼ c. milk
¼ c. sour cream
1 T. chopped chives *or* minced scallion
½ t. dried dill weed
½ t. salt
¼ t. pepper
2 T. butter
¼ c. shredded cheddar cheese
2 slices bacon, cooked and crumbled, optional

Bake the potatoes until they are soft. Remove from the oven and, holding with a clean dishtowel, cut the larger potatoes in half lengthwise, or cut a thin lengthwise slice from the top of each smaller potato. Scoop out the cooked potato into a medium bowl, leaving about a shell about ¼" thick. Place the potato skins in a small baking dish. Mash the potatoes with the milk, 1 T. of the butter and sour cream. Stir in the seasonings, the bacon if using, and the cheese. Pile the potato back into the shells. Dot the tops with the remaining butter and sprinkle lightly with paprika. At this point you can either cover the potatoes and refrigerate for up to a day, or pop them back into a 400°F oven for about 15 minutes, until they are slightly puffed and browned. If you are reheating them, plan on about ½ hour baking time. This serves 4.

Scalloped Ham and Potatoes

My folks kept a crock of salt pork brining in a cool north-facing closet (you'll find out more in "November"). When the salt pork was ready, my mother thought up any number of ways to utilize it. One of her answers to the conundrum was a multilayered casserole of precooked potatoes and ham, intermingled with whole kernel corn, sliced onions, and flour. She poured milk over everything and topped it off with thin slices of salt pork. I must admit, the salt pork was probably my favorite part of the entire dish. This is one of those nostalgia recipes that wouldn't win any awards at the cordon bleu; the flour tends to remain a somewhat separate entity. Yet over the years, I've come to rather enjoy it that way. Amounts can vary, depending on how many leftovers you have and who you're planning to feed with them.

Cooked ham, in small thin slices
Cooked potatoes, sliced thin
Whole kernel corn, canned or frozen, thawed
Thinly sliced onions
Flour
Salt
Pepper
Butter
Thinly sliced salt pork *or* bacon *or* butter
Milk

Butter a casserole dish of desired size. Place a layer each of potatoes, ham, corn, onions in order. Sprinkle each layer with about 1 T. of flour and salt and pepper to taste. Make about three layers, ending with an extra layer of potatoes, salt, and pepper. Pour enough milk over all until it barely reaches the top. Dot it with butter and top with the salt pork or bacon, if desired. Bake in a 350°F oven for up to an hour, until it is browned and bubbly and the meat on top is nicely cooked.

Ragout of Roots

Although many of us prefer the sweet, nutty-flavor parsnips develop by wintering over in the garden, they are also widely harvested in the fall. The combination of three roots in this recipe blend to produce a mellow ragout, perfect with everything from roast chicken to pork chops.

1 c. finely diced rutabaga
1 c. finely diced carrots
1 c. finely diced parsnips
3 T. honey
2 T. butter
½ t. salt
¼ t. ginger
⅛ t. cloves
⅛ t. pepper

Place in order the rutabaga, carrots, and parsnips in a medium saucepan. Add the salt and water to barely cover. Bring to a boil, reduce the heat, and cook the vegetables for about 20 minutes, until they are tender. Drain any remaining liquid, saving for soups or gravy if desired. Add the honey, butter, and spices and stir to combine. This makes 4–6 side servings.

Maple Butternut Squash

Butternut squash is a versatile and delicious vegetable. It's comparatively easy to grow and will store quite well in a cool, dry but not cold area. It's tasty in everything from soups to pasta dishes, but I still like it best mashed with a little butter and maple syrup.

1 medium butternut squash—peeled, seeded, and cut in chunks
¼ c. each butter
¼ c. maple syrup
½ t. salt
¼ t. pepper
¼ t. grated nutmeg

Once it's cut up, you'll probably have about 3–4 cups of squash. Place it in a medium saucepan with water to barely cover it. Bring to a boil, reduce the heat, and boil gently, covered, until it's tender, about 20 minutes. Drain any excess cooking liquid; if you're making gravy, this is an excellent way to use the liquid rather than throwing it down the drain. Add the butter, maple syrup, and seasonings to the squash and mash until it's as smooth as you wish. Servings depend somewhat on the size of the squash and the enthusiasm of the appetites involved.

Baked Acorn Squash

Acorn squash are now available in more diminutive sizes than once they were. They are just right for baking with either a sweet or a savory filling. I prefer a little sweet with mine. You can go the maple syrup route, which is never a miss, or try something a little more complex.

2 small acorn squash, cut in half and seeded
2 T. butter

¼ c. brown sugar
2 T. orange juice
¼ t. salt
Pinch of black pepper
Sprinkle of cinnamon, optional

Place the squash cut-side down in a 9" × 13" baking pan. Add water to come up about ½" depth. Cover the pan loosely with foil and bake at 350°F for about 30 minutes, until the squash is slightly soft but not cooked all the way. Meanwhile, combine all the other ingredients in a small pan, heating until the butter is just melted. Remove the foil and carefully turn the squash over. Divide the filling evenly between the four halves, brushing a little bit up the sides. Return to the oven and continue baking for another 15–20 minutes, until the squash is tender and starting to glaze. You may wish to increase the oven temperature slightly near the end. Remove the squash carefully so as not to spill the filling; serves 4.

Roasted Brussels Sprouts

Before we enter the amazing world of Cabbage 101, let's give a nod to its petite cousin the brussels sprout. Shaped like little miniature cabbages, brussels sprouts grow in a spiral around a sturdy central stalk. They are very cold hardy, withstanding frosts that would cause less stout-hearted vegetables to wither up and die. I've even harvested perfectly respectable (and delicious) brussels sprouts from under half a foot of snow. Simplicity is the trick here; roasting the sprouts brings out their natural, nutty sweetness. If you wish, add just a splash of balsamic vinegar right before serving them.

1 lb. brussels sprouts: 3 c.
3 T. olive oil
½ t. sea salt
Few grinds black pepper

Roast the sprouts on an open baking sheet on an upper rack in a 375°F oven for 20–25 minutes, until the outsides are nutty brown and the sprouts are tender when poked with a fork. This makes 4 satisfying servings.

Cranberry-Apple Coleslaw

Cranberries are a popular fall fruit, although if you don't live in the northern United States it may be a bit harder to find fresh ones. Cranberry coleslaw is tasty with everything from fish to meat loaf. It's especially nice as an accompaniment to chicken or turkey dishes. This recipe utilizes sweetened dried cranberries, an increasingly popular commodity. Try some of the flavor-infused varieties (such as orange or cherry) if you wish.

4 c. shredded cabbage, green, red, *or* a combo
1 c. walnuts *or* pecans, coarsely chopped
1 medium apple—washed, cored, and chopped (don't peel)
½ c. dried cranberries
2 T. honey *or* maple syrup
½ c. mayonnaise
¼ c. cream
¼ c. orange juice

Combine the cabbage, nuts, apple, and cranberries in a serving dish. Stir together the honey or maple syrup, mayonnaise, cream, and orange juice until smooth. Pour the dressing over the salad, tossing them together until everything is well combined. Cover and refrigerate any leftovers; this makes a good amount of slaw.

Braised Red Cabbage

As with many of my autumn recipes, this one has Scandinavian roots. Perhaps it's the long cold winters both New England and the Nordic countries share that encourage us to produce lots of tasty meals from the heartiest fruits and vegetables. This dish features a tangy combination of red cabbage and apples, with just a hint of vinegar, sugar, and spice. It's a nice accompaniment to dishes such as roast pork or pork chops, Swedish meatballs, or chicken.

4 c. shredded red cabbage
2 c. diced tart red apples, skin on
2 T. butter
1 T. sugar
1 T. cider vinegar
¼ t. salt
¼ t. allspice
⅛ t. cloves

Combine all the ingredients in a medium nonreactive saucepan along with about ½ cup of water. Cover and bring to a boil over high heat. Reduce the heat to medium low and continue to cook until the cabbage is tender and the water mostly evaporated, about 10 minutes. This serves about 6 as a side dish.

Homemade Sauerkraut

This is a good time of year to think about making your own sauerkraut. Cabbage is plentiful and temperatures are cool enough to allow for a good fermentation process; summer heat doesn't always bode well for homemade sauerkraut. Cabbage that has been exposed to frost will have a higher sugar content, which also aids in the fermentation process. The fresher the cabbage, the better sauerkraut you'll produce. Use either a gallon-sized ceramic crock or a food-grade plastic bucket to hold the shredded cabbage. You will also need a ceramic plate or nontreated wood round cut to size to weight the salted cabbage down with; otherwise, it may not form the juices necessary to the process, and you'll end up with spoiled brown cabbage. Preclean your brining container and lid by washing with clean, soapy water and rinsing with boiling water. Once your sauerkraut has cured to the optimal stage, refrigerate it in a covered container for a longer shelf life. Don't use sauerkraut that has darkened; it's definitely past the first blush of youth. It is also possible to can sauerkraut. Bring the cured kraut to a boil, place in clean hot jars, and process in a boiling water bath—10 minutes for pints or smaller, 20 minutes for quarts. Make sure all lids have sealed properly; see "General Guidelines" for further details.

2 heads fresh green cabbage (5 lb.)
3 T. noniodized canning or sea salt

Salt Water, if Necessary

Use a ratio of 1 c. water to 1 t. salt; boil and cool before using

Remove the core and any tough or wilted outer leaves from the cabbage. I weigh mine after this step is completed; an accurate weight is important for the salt to cabbage ratio. Shred the cabbage fairly fine using a large grater, mandolin, food processor, or simply a knife and cutting board. Layer it in the clean crock with the salt, starting with the cabbage and ending with the salt. Weight the mixture down with a clean ceramic plate or untreated wooden disk that has had a sealed plastic bag of water or several clean small stones placed on top. Set the crock aside in a cool, dry place and allow the cabbage to work for 2 days. Remove the top and stir the mix to make sure juices have formed and the cabbage is brining evenly. Add a small amount of salt water if the top of the cabbage isn't covered with the brine, just to cover. Replace the weighted lid and continue the fermentation process for a total of 2 weeks to 6 weeks, stirring the cabbage every couple of days. In general, sauerkraut should be fermented at temperatures below 75°F and above 55°F— too low and it won't ferment properly; too high and you run a greater risk of spoilage. The higher the temperature, the less time will be required to complete the process. Lower temperatures may require up to 6 weeks. Please note that because this is a fermenting process, you're going to be aware of the smell, a good reason to find a little corner of your house that's somewhat out of the way for your crock. You'll know the process is complete once bubbles have stopped forming and rising to the surface of the sauerkraut. Once the flavor has developed to your liking, place the sauerkraut in plastic or noncorrosive covered containers and place in the fridge to enjoy at leisure, or can as above. The amounts given should produce about 2 quarts of sauerkraut.

Cabbage, cut fine and then salted in the crock, brines slowly into homemade sauerkraut.

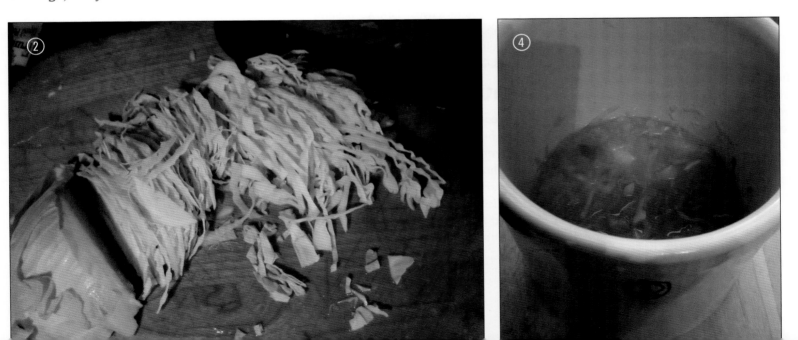

Kohl Dolmer (Stuffed Cabbage)

There are variations of stuffed cabbage to be found in almost all northern European countries. My Grandma Kall used to stuff an entire cabbage with the rice and meat mixture. A simple brown sauce is a frequent accompaniment to kohl dolmer. I prefer to stuff individual cabbage leaves, and also to add a tangy sweet tomato sauce for them to braise in.

6–8 blanched cabbage leaves
2 T. corn or canola oil
1 lb. ground beef
1 t. salt
1 c. cooked rice
1 t. parsley flakes
½ t. cinnamon
¼ t. pepper
½ onion, diced: about ½ c.
1 egg
½ can tomato paste: about 4 T.
2 T. soy sauce
2 T. molasses

Choose a large head of cabbage with outer leaves that seem fairly loose. Core the cabbage and immerse it, leaves down, in a large pan of boiling water. After about 15 seconds, turn the cabbage over for another few seconds. Lift the cabbage out and submerge briefly in cold water. You should be able to remove the leaves, one by one, by peeling back gently at the upper edge of each. Carefully trim some of the thick spine on each leaf so that it is close in thickness to the rest of the leaf and remove the leaf at its base. Reimmerse the head as necessary. Any leftover cabbage can be chilled and used for other cooking or salad purposes. Save about 3 cups of the cabbage blanching water for the next step. For the filling, combine all ingredients except the tomato paste, soy sauce, and molasses. If you wish, you can precook the onion in a tablespoon or so of water until it's just crisp tender. Mound the meat mixture on the cabbage leaves, gauging how much filling by the size of the leaf. Fold over the side edges first, then the base, and finally the upper leaf end. This should make a fairly well-sealed packet. Heat the oil in a large cast-iron skittle over medium heat. Add the cabbage packets, folded-side down first, and brown for about 5 minutes per side. You can tie the packets first with cotton kitchen string or thread if you prefer, although I find if I've left sufficient overhang of the leaves this step isn't necessary. Carefully place the leaves folded-side down again and pour about 2 cups of the cabbage blanching water over them. Braise over medium-low heat, covered, for about ½ hour. Combine the tomato paste, soy sauce, and molasses with another ½ c. of the blanching water and pour over the stuffed cabbage leaves. Braise, basting occasionally, for about 15 more minutes. I like to serve these with either cooked carrots or green beans. This serves 4–6.

Cauliflower Soup

In her later years, my mom was especially fond of cooking herself up a big pan of cauliflower soup. It reminded her of the cabbage soup of her childhood, I think. I happen to love cooked cauliflower pretty much any way I can get it, and this dish is no exception. It's filling without being too heavy and just hits the spot on a chilly autumn day.

1 qt. chicken *or* vegetable broth
2 stalks celery, sliced
¼ t. white pepper
1 lg. head cauliflower cut in small florets, or about 4 c. frozen
1 lg. onion, chopped: 1 c.
2 T. butter
1 c. light cream
½ t. grated nutmeg

Melt the butter in a soup kettle or Dutch oven and add the onion and celery, sautéing until softened but not brown. Add the broth and cauliflower and bring to a boil. Lower the heat and simmer until the cauliflower is very soft, about 20 minutes. At this point, I would puree at least half the soup to thicken it and make a smoother texture; how thorough you are with this step is up to you. Add the cream, white pepper, and nutmeg to the soup and heat to just below boiling before serving. Make about 2 quarts.

Carrot Ginger Soup

This is a good project for a rainy or snowy day. It takes a little while but is well worth the effort. Once you've made your own homemade soup, you won't want "store-bought" anymore.

1½ lb. carrots, washed and cut into small pieces
1 lg. sweet potato, peeled and cubed
1 lg. onion, peeled and cut in chunks
2–3 stalks celery, sliced coarse
2 T. olive oil
1 t. salt
½ t. each pepper
½ t. grated nutmeg
1" piece of fresh ginger root, washed and grated
4 c. water
3 c. orange juice

In a large, heavy skillet or Dutch oven, slowly brown the vegetables in the olive oil. This could take a good ½ hour over low heat, but you needn't worry about hovering over it. Aside from an occasional stir to redistribute, this will take care of itself. Add the seasonings and water, cover and bring to a boil. Reduce the heat to medium low and simmer until everything is nice and tender. Allow to cool somewhat, and then puree in small batches along with the orange juice. If too much water has evaporated during the cooking process, you may need to add a bit more until it seems the right consistency. After blending, it may be poured back in your large cooking pan to serve either warm or cool. Makes a generous amount, although this can easily be frozen; pour into snap-top containers, cover, label, and freeze.

Country Corn Chowder

During my childhood, corn chowder was generally made with diced salt pork, which my mother would pull out of the large crock of brine set off in a dark cold corner of a north-facing closet. I don't brine salt pork anymore and over the years have perfected my own chowder recipe using bacon. If you happen to have your own salt pork crock hanging around, or would prefer to try making this with commercially produced salt pork, by all means give it a whirl. This is definitely one of my "standby" recipes; the number of times I've made it over the years must surely number in the high hundreds by now.

4–6 slices bacon, diced: 4 oz.
1 lg. onion, chopped: 1 c.
1–2 stalks celery, diced: 1 c.
2–3 carrots, diced: 1½ c.

2 c. ½" cubed potatoes
2 t. parsley flakes
¾ t. salt
¼ t. pepper
1 c. water
3 c. milk
2 T. butter
2 cans cream-style corn or 3 ½ c. cut from the cob

Dice the bacon and cook over low heat in a heavy 4 qt. soup kettle or Dutch oven until crisp and brown. Remove and set aside. Drain some of the bacon fat, leaving approximately 2 T. in the pan. Add the onion and celery and cook about 5 minutes, until tender crisp but not browned. Add the carrots, water, salt pepper, and parsley and cook 5 more minutes, covered. Add the potatoes and cook, covered, another minute, at which point the potatoes should be just tender and the water mostly absorbed. Stir in the milk and corn; I sometimes add a little dried milk powder for added richness. If using fresh corn, bring to a simmer and cook about 5 minutes prior to adding the butter. If using canned corn, simply add the butter at the same time and simmer until the butter is melted and everything nicely heated through. Add the cooked bacon, stir, and serve with crackers. I prefer Pilot crackers if you can find them; otherwise, saltines will do just fine. This makes approximately 2 qt. of chowder, enough for a couple of hearty meals. It reheats very well at a medium-low setting.

Butternut Apple Soup

Butternut squash and apples make a winning combination in this smooth, sweet, and savory soup. It makes an especially nice accompaniment to grilled ham-and-Swiss sandwiches, although it's also quite tasty all by itself. It will serve several people with hearty appetites, or a few folks with more for another day.

1 small butternut squash—peeled, seeded, and cubed: 3 c.
4 medium apples—peeled, cored, and quartered: 3 c.
1 small onion, peeled and chopped: ½ c.
1–2 stalks celery, chopped: ½ c.
¼ t. crumbled rosemary
Salt
White pepper
1 T. maple syrup
½ t. cinnamon
¼ t. nutmeg
¼ t. ginger
¼ c. cream, optional

Place squash, apples, onion, and celery in a medium-sized heavy cooking pan. Add water to cover and bring to a boil. Reduce heat to medium low and cook, covered, until the vegetables are soft. Cool slightly and puree until smooth. Return the puree to the pan and add everything else except the cream. Start with about ½ t. salt and ¼ t. pepper; adjust according to your personal taste. It's much easier to add seasoning at the table than it is to try and mellow down an over salted or seasoned dish after the fact. Reheat to just under boiling. Stir in the cream if desired and serve. If desired, you may store the seasoned puree in the fridge for a day or two in advance of serving, heating and adding the cream at the last minute.

Kale Soup

Once you've harvested your dried beans, tomatoes, onions, and kale from your fall garden, you're ready to make kale soup. What better way to end a day of outdoor fall activities than to be greeted by a fragrant steaming bowl of this classic? Add a crusty loaf of homemade bread or a pan of golden cornbread, sit back, and enjoy.

½ c. dried kidney beans *or* other red beans
1 c. water
1 c. chopped onion
1 c. chopped carrot
2 T. olive oil
3 c. diced fresh tomatoes *or* a 14.5oz.can of diced tomatoes*
2 sm. *or* 1 lg. clove garlic, peeled and minced
1 lb. linguica (Portuguese sausage) sliced thin
2 c. ½" dice potatoes
3 c. chopped cabbage
1 bay leaf
Pinch of red pepper flakes
1 t. salt
1 T. cider vinegar
1 bunch kale: 1–1½ lb.
6 c. water

At least an hour or up to a day in advance, place the dried beans and 1 c. of water into a small saucepan with a tight fitting lid. Bring to a boil, then remove from the heat, and allow them to stand, covered, for at least an hour. Place the oil in a heavy 4 quarts soup pot or Dutch oven. Over medium heat, sauté the onions, carrots, and garlic until wilted but not browned. Stir in the linguica and cook another 5 minutes, stirring occasionally. Add in the beans and any cooking liquid, the bay leaf, salt, red pepper flakes, vinegar, and 6 cups of water. Bring to a boil, reduce the heat, and simmer, covered, for about an hour. Add in the cabbage and potato, bring to a boil and simmer for about 10 minutes. Meanwhile, energize yourself by stripping all the tender leaves from the rinsed bunch of kale, tearing them into 2"- to 3"-sized pieces. Discard the tough stems or put them aside for vegetable stock. Add the kale leaves into the soup, stirring to integrate them, and allow the mixture to again come to a boil. Simmer for an additional 10–15 minutes, remove the bay leaf (or at least don't eat it!) and serve. This makes quite a large quantity of kale soup—yummy for chilly autumn evenings. Once it has cooled, you may freeze some if you wish to use within a couple of months.

*I prefer salt free tomatoes for this recipe; adjust salt to your taste if using regular canned tomatoes.

Chili with Meat

One of the nice things about chili is how versatile it is. Although I used ground meat in my chili, you could alternatively use chunks of your favorite meat, browning it first and allowing it to simmer slowly, tenderizing along the way. This is one of my favorite recipes for using whole frozen tomatoes. They impart a nice, fresh garden flavor to the chili, and because everything cooks down together, there's no need to worry about them holding their shape.

1 c. dried red beans
1 lb. lean ground beef, pork, *or* turkey
1 lg. chopped onion: 1 c.
2–3 cloves garlic, minced
1 red bell pepper, seeded and chopped
2 t. salt
1 T. chili powder
1 t. cumin
2 T. cider vinegar
½ t. Tabasco sauce, or to taste
1 lg. can of tomatoes or 6–8 fresh/frozen, thawed, and peeled

Boil the beans in water to cover for 1 minute and set aside, in the liquid, while preparing the rest of the dish. Cook the ground meat in a large skillet until it loses its pinkness, adding the onions, garlic, and red pepper. Cook until the veggies are tender but not browned. Stir in the seasonings and tomatoes, breaking them up with a spoon. Add the beans and their cooking liquid. Simmer the chili over medium-low heat for about an hour, stirring occasionally and adding a bit of water if needed to prevent sticking. The chili should be fairly thick, although the tomatoes may burn if it becomes too dry. Serve topped with shredded cheddar or Jack cheese, accompanied by corn bread, garlic bread, or corn chips.

Garden Chili

Chili is hearty and satisfying on a chilly fall night. If you love your veggies, you'll love this meatless version, made with lots of garden-fresh produce.

1 c. dried red beans
1 lg. sweet potato
2 T. corn oil
2 c. whole kernel corn

1 lg. onion, diced: 1 c.
1 green bell pepper, seeded and chopped
2–3 cloves garlic
2 t. salt
2 T. lime juice
1 T. chili powder
1 t. cumin
A pinch of red pepper flakes
1 lg. can of tomatoes or 6–8 fresh/frozen, thawed, and peeled

Boil the beans in water to cover for 5 minutes; set aside to soak in the liquid. Peel and chop the sweet potato into ½" cubes. Heat the oil in a large, heavy skillet over medium heat. Add the sweet potatoes, onion, garlic, and green pepper and sauté for about 5 minutes, until the veggies are tender. Add all the seasonings, the beans in their cooking liquid, the corn, and the tomatoes. Bring to a boil, reduce heat, and simmer for about a half to three-quarters of an hour, until everything is tender. Serve with shredded cheese, if you wish, and desired bread or rice.

A cast-iron skillet of garden chili bubbles on the stove, ready to be enjoyed with corn bread, garlic bread, or hot cooked rice.

321

Mom's Meat Loaf

This recipe reflects the traditional Scandinavian flavors I was raised with. I guess the "mom" here refers both to my mother and me; her for the original idea and me for the revisions I've made. Baked or mashed potatoes go nicely with this.

1 lb. ground beef
½ c. milk
1 egg
1 medium onion, minced
2 slices bread, torn into pieces: 1 c. lightly packed
1 t. salt
½ t. ground allspice
¼ t. grated nutmeg
½ t. pepper
1 T. Worcestershire sauce
1 T. fresh *or* 1 t. dried parsley flakes

Place the torn bread in a large mixing bowl, pouring the milk over it to soak briefly. Add the rest of the ingredients and mix well to combine. Use either a wooden spoon or your clean hands to mix the most efficiently. Place in an ungreased 9" × 5" loaf pan. Bake in a preheated 350°F oven for approximately 1 hour, until nicely browned and cooked through (juices will run clear if you pierce the middle with a sharp knife or fork). If you're in a hurry, push the meat loaf apart in the center before baking to make two halves. I frequently serve this right out of the pan. If you prefer to remove it to a serving platter, allow it to rest for about 5 minutes, run a knife around the edges, and gently tip it out, or simply cut slices while in the pan and remove them to the platter that way. This makes 4 nice servings.

Mom's meat loaf shares the plate with a baked potato, scalloped corn ("January"), cranberry compote ("November"), and maple butternut squash.

Collops

Round steak is a lean and flavorful but rather tough cut of meat. This recipe for collops comes from sunny California, courtesy of my brother and sister-in-law, John and Naomi Wheelock. They've been West Coasters for a good many years now but still have an old-fashioned recipe or two up their sleeves. The word "collops" refers to thin slices of meat and is probably of Swedish origins, although the recipe here actually has Scottish roots, occasionally utilizing lamb or venison in place of the beef. For a more traditional take, you may substitute a bit of diced suet for the butter, an option John and Naomi included in the original. I've adjusted the salt down slightly for my taste, although their version calls for the greater amount; personal preference will dictate.

1 lb. round steak
1 lg. onion, chopped: 1 c.
1–1½ t. salt
½ t. pepper
2 T. flour
2 T. butter *or* diced suet
2 t. Worcestershire sauce
1½ c. water

Slice the steak very thin and then cut it into about 1" dice. This is easier to do if you allow the steak to partially freeze first—maybe an hour in the freezer while you're doing something else. Once it's been diced, place it and the onions in a medium bowl or plastic bag and toss them with the flour. Preheat the butter in a large, heavy frying pan until it's quite hot but not burned; add the meat and onion mixture and fry, turning and breaking it up, until everything is nicely browned. Add the water, Worcestershire sauce, salt, and pepper, stirring to blend thoroughly. Bring to a boil and then lower the heat and simmer, stirring occasionally, for about 15 minutes. At this time you should have a nice gravy to go with your meat; add a bit more water if necessary. Mashed potatoes and toast points are the traditional accompaniments to collops, although buttered rice will also do. Serve to 4 folks looking for a bit of comfort food.

Brunswick Stew

If you consider squirrel hunting to be part of your repertoire, this is the recipe for you. Personally, I've never eaten squirrel meat, although I'm sure the little critters squabbling over the corn and seeds at our bird feeders would provide tender morsels were I so inclined. However, I'd rather just watch their antics than consume them. Fortunately for all concerned, the Brunswick stew recipes I've come across all indicate you can exchange a chicken or two for the squirrel meat, so to each his or her own! It's still a savory combination of tastes and textures, ready to curb the heartiest appetites. I've find some recipes overflowing with barbecue sauce entirely too sweet; to me this one is "just right."

3 lb. chicken, cut up; *or* 2 squirrels, cleaned and dressed
3 slices bacon, diced; *or* 2 T. oil
1 lg. onion, chopped: 1 c.
2 c. diced red-skinned potatoes
6–8 peeled, diced tomatoes
1½ c. whole kernel corn
1½ c. fresh or frozen lima beans
1 T. Worcestershire sauce
1½ t. salt
½ t. pepper
½ t. marjoram
2 T. brown sugar
2 T. cider vinegar
¼ t. Tabasco sauce

In a large, heavy skillet with a cover or a Dutch oven, cook the diced bacon over medium heat until it is brown and has rendered out its fat. Remove the bacon bits from the pan and set aside. Season the chicken or squirrel on both sides with the salt and pepper. Brown the pieces, skin-side down first, in the bacon fat or oil. Once it is golden on one side, turn it over and add the chopped onion while the meat finishes browning on the other side. Stir in the tomatoes, marjoram, brown sugar, vinegar, Worcestershire, and Tabasco sauce. Bring the mixture to a boil and simmer, covered, over medium-low heat until the meat is almost tender, about 20–25 minutes. Stir the mixture and add in the potatoes, bacon, corn, and lima beans. Cover again and boil gently about 20 minutes longer, until the potatoes are tender and the meat thoroughly done. Buttermilk biscuits go nicely with this stew. It will serve 6 nicely.

Brunswick stew accompanied by buttermilk biscuits makes a hearty autumn supper.

Pumpkin Pie

Why wait until Thanksgiving to enjoy pumpkin pie? The pumpkins are ripe, the air brisk, appetites whetted. And thanks to canned pumpkin puree, we're now able enjoy the fruits of this mellow orange gourd year-round.

1½ c. homemade *or* canned unsweetened pumpkin pulp
¾ c. sugar
⅔ c. powdered dry milk
1 c. water
2 eggs
1 t. cinnamon
½ t. ginger
½ t. salt
¼ t. cloves
¼ t. nutmeg
½ c. heavy cream
1 unbaked 9" pastry shell, made with high-fluted sides

Combine the pumpkin pulp, eggs, sugar, salt, and spices in a medium-sized mixing bowl. Whisk together until the eggs are fully beaten into the other ingredients and everything is well incorporated. Combine the powdered milk and water in a small bowl until smooth. Gently stir the milk and cream into the pumpkin mixture. Carefully pour the filling into the pastry shell; if using home pureed pumpkin, I always pour it through a wire mesh sieve, stirring and pushing solids to extract the most goodness. This small step screens out any fibrous material and gives you a superior creamy filling. Bake at 425°F for 10–15 minutes (meaning it's not a huge deal if the oven doesn't reduce at the 10-minute mark on the dot, just in that general vicinity). Reduce the heat to 350°F and continue baking for an addition 45–50 minutes, until the filling is set through. Remove from the oven and cool on a rack for an hour before completing the cooling process in the refrigerator. This makes 8 nice servings, topped with whipped cream and perhaps a sprinkle of diced candied ginger if you're feeling festive. Be sure to refrigerate any leftovers.

Pie pumpkin in the garden will soon be pumpkin pie on the table.

Oatmeal Jammies

You don't need to wear your pajamas while enjoying these cookies, although they do make a pleasant bedtime snack, coupled with a glass of milk. Vary the jam filling according to taste, or try a few different fillings for a rainbow of color and flavor.

1 c. butter
1 c. sugar
1 c. packed brown sugar
2 eggs
1½ t. vanilla
1 t. baking soda
1½ c. flour
3 c. rolled oats

Favorite jelly/jam: strawberry, raspberry, apricot, etc.

Cream the softened butter together with the sugars until smooth. Beat in the eggs and vanilla until the mixture is light and fluffy. Stir in the flour, baking soda, and rolled oats. Form the mixture into 1" balls and place on greased and floured cookie sheets. Press with your finger to make an indent in each top. Add a small dollop of jam, about ½ t. in each. Bake on an upper rack at 375°F for approximately 18 minutes total. Allow the cookies to cool slightly before carefully removing to cooling racks to complete the process; the hot jam will make the cookies a bit fragile while hot. This makes about 3 dozen cookies.

Gingersnaps

October just seems like a good time for gingersnaps, an old-fashioned comfort cookie. These ginger cookies are not too strongly flavored so that the sugar sweetness and butter

essence come through. They may be baked until either soft and chewy or crispy crunchy, as you desire.

2 c. flour
2 t. ginger
1 t. cinnamon
2 t. baking soda
½ t. salt
¾ c. butter
1 c. sugar
1 egg
¼ c. molasses
Sugar to roll dough in

Cream the butter and sugar; beat in the egg and molasses. Blend in the combined dry ingredients until well incorporated. Form teaspoons of dough into round balls, roll in sugar, and place about 2" apart on ungreased cookie sheets. Bake at 350°F about 10–12 minutes. Less baking time will give a chewier cookie. This makes about 4 dozen small cookies.

Jumbo Chocolate Chip Cookies

These cookies come out almost as big as the ones you see in the bakery. They're yummy for special trick-or-treaters or just a special treat for you.

1 c. butter
1 c. sugar
1 c. packed dark brown sugar
2 t. vanilla extract
2 eggs
1 t. salt
1 t. baking soda

2¾ c. flour
2 c. semisweet chocolate chips
1 c. chopped walnuts, optional

In a large mixing bowl, cream the butter, sugars, and vanilla until smooth. Beat in the eggs until well blended. Stir in the combined flour, salt, and soda. Lastly, add in the chocolate chips and the nuts if you're using them. Form the dough into 2" balls and place them on greased and floured cookie sheets, leaving about 2" of space around each cookie. Bake on the upper rack of a 375°F oven for 12 minutes (don't overbake). Allow them to cool for a minute or two and then gently loosen with a spatula and place on cooling racks. This recipe will yield about 2 dozen cookies.

Green Mountain Popcorn Balls

If you have some trick-or-treaters you know especially well, why not surprise them with homemade popcorn balls? Vermont is the Green Mountain State, and one reason our mountains are so green are the plethora of maple trees dotting their slopes. It seems only fitting popcorn balls benefiting from a hint of maple syrup should be named in honor of them.

16 c. popped corn, placed in huge buttered metal bowl
2 c. sugar
½ c. light corn syrup
¼ c. maple syrup
⅞ c. water
1 t. salt
1 t. vinegar
2 T. butter
1 t. vanilla

Combine everything except butter and vanilla in a heavy metal saucepan, stirring until dissolved. Insert candy thermometer and cook over medium high heat to 255°F, swirling pan occasionally. Be careful, for this has reached the *wicked* hot stage! Immediately remove from heat and stir in butter and vanilla until smooth and golden. Pour quickly but carefully over popcorn, stirring to coat evenly with a large metal or wooden spoon. Continue to stir it around in the bowl to coat evenly for a few minutes, until cool enough to safely handle. Butter your hands and form into balls while still fairly hot; if you wait too long, the syrup will already have hardened and you'll have candied popcorn, not popcorn balls. Allow to cool completely on waxed paper–lined baking sheets or cooling racks. This makes 16 3" popcorn balls. Once they've cooled sufficiently, wrap individually in waxed paper, plastic wrap or foil—add some decorative ribbon ties on if you wish.

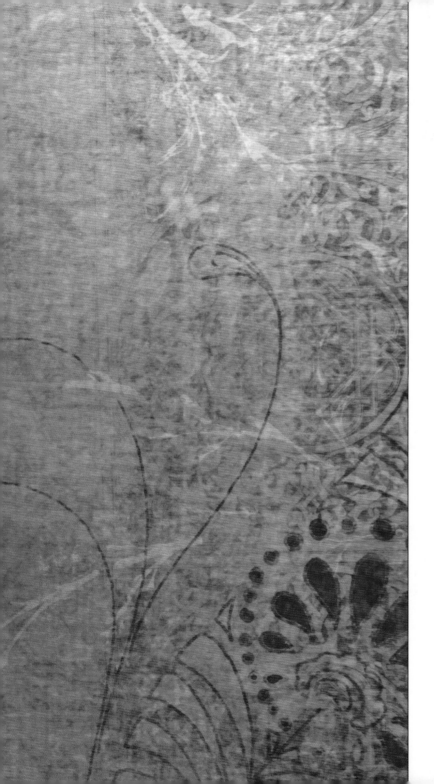

"Over the River and Through the Woods . . ."

SURELY ALMOST EVERYONE recognizes the words to Lydia Maria Childs's classic Thanksgiving poem set to music; it's been around since 1844. The horse-drawn sleigh may have given way to all wheel-drive vehicles, and Grandma may be watching Macy's Thanksgiving Day parade rather than slaving over a woodstove, but the sentiment remains the same. Thanksgiving isn't only America's favorite holiday, but it's also a great family day. And whether it's spent north, south, east, or west, it's a time to savor and be thankful for the fruits of our labors and the bounty of the harvest. It just makes plain, gray November seem to go by a little bit faster, anticipating that special Thursday near the end of the month.

November is a chance to showcase the vegetables, fruits, and nuts we've harvested and preserved throughout the year. And perhaps it's also a chance to savor home-grown and home-cured meats, if you've the room and the disposition for raising a few turkeys or pigs. Whatever you fancy, it always seems to taste a little bit better when you've prepared it yourself.

The frost is already on the pumpkin in this harvest display welcoming everyone home for the holiday.

November

Evelyn's Oyster Stew

Just as turkey means Thanksgiving dinner to so many of us, oyster stew remains my favorite "meal before." My mom used to make it for breakfast during the holidays, when oysters were available in the stores around Brattleboro. Some recipes for oyster stew are quite rich and elegant, with so many ingredients it's a wonder you can taste the oysters at all. Mother Evelyn made a different kind of stew: just oysters, water, milk, and a little butter. It's simple and pure, and still one of my favorite holiday treats.

8 oz. fresh oysters
1 c. water
1½ c. rich milk (or add a dash of cream)
2 T. butter
Dash of salt
Oyster crackers

Bring the oysters, their liquid, and the water to a gentle boil in a medium saucepan. Cook until, as Mother would put it, the edges curl, about 3–4 minutes. Add in the milk, butter, and a dash of salt, if you wish. Heat gently until the butter melts; simmer a few minutes longer for richer flavor, but be careful not to let it boil again. Pour it gently into 2–3 bowls half filled with oyster crackers. The crackers will absorb the broth if allowed to stand a minute or two, which is my favorite way to eat oyster stew. Enjoy!

New England's Own Cranberries

Cranberries are one of New England's native fruits and are grown commercially here, especially in Massachusetts. Fresh cranberry sauce may be prepared either whole-berry style or in a smoother variation. Each is relatively easy to prepare and will keep well for several days if refrigerated. Buying bags of whole fresh cranberries in season and popping a few in the freezer for later use will extend your time frame for enjoying such things well past November. Cranberries are a great source of vitamin C and are also packed full of antioxidants, so feel free to enjoy!

Whole-Berry Cranberry Sauce

Whole berry is the easiest to prepare of cranberry sauces and arguably a bit healthier than jell, as the skin and berries left "whole" add a bit more texture and fiber to the presentation.

2 c. whole cranberries, rinsed and picked over
¾ c. water
¾ c. sugar

Combine all ingredients in a small saucepan. Bring to a boil over medium heat, reduce heat to low, and simmer for about 8–10 minutes, until the sauce is thickened but still bright red. Serve warm or chilled; makes about 2 cups.

Cranberry Jell

This is a bit sweeter than traditional cranberry sauce. Adding orange juice along with the sugar and water imparts a nice fresh flavor. For an extrasmooth product, I suppose you could strain the pureed sauce through a wire mesh sieve, although I think it's just fine the way it is.

3 c. (1 pkg.) fresh cranberries, rinsed
1½ c. sugar, or to taste
1 c. orange juice
1 c. water

Combine the rinsed, picked-over cranberries in a medium nonreactive saucepan along with the sugar, water, and orange juice. Bring to a boil, reduce the heat somewhat, and continue to boil gently for about 10–15 minutes, until the sauce begins to jell. Cool slightly before pouring into a blender or food processor and blending until smooth. Pour into a decorative bowl and chill thoroughly before serving. This makes about 4 cups of jell.

Autumn-Harvest Cranberry Compote

This is a refreshing change from traditional cranberry sauce: a mix of cranberries and raspberries with apples and pears. It retains the texture of the fruit and a nice light flavor. The mildness of the apples and pears bring a natural sweetness without too much added sugar. Optional add-ins may include chopped walnuts for texture and crystallized ginger for an added zing.

1 c. cranberries and
1 c. raspberries
½ c. sugar
¼ c. water
1 c. chopped apple, skin on
1 c. chopped pear, skin on
2 T. lemon juice
½ c. chopped walnuts, optional
2 T. diced, crystallized ginger, optional

Combine the fruit, sugar, lemon juice, and water in a medium saucepan. Bring to a boil and cook over moderate heat, stirring occasionally, for about 10 minutes. At this point the sauce will have thickened slightly but still retained its bright color and texture. Add the walnuts and ginger, if desired. Serve warm or chilled; makes about 4 cups of sauce.

Pretty to look at and delicious to taste, autumn-harvest cranberry compote adds a bright spot of flavor to almost any meal.

Aunt Esther's Lemon Cream Jell

Perhaps you'd like a little change from cranberry sauce to go with your turkey. My Aunt Esther Wheelock frequently brought a decorative glass dish filled with her lemon cream gelatin to family Thanksgiving dinners. She shared her recipe with me, which makes for a nice remembrance of her every time I make it. Although Aunt Esther used packaged lemon gelatin mix for hers, I prefer fresh lemon instead. For the amount of juice and zest needed, plan on two small lemons or a single nice large one. Esther always used it as a side salad, but it's also rich and sweet enough for dessert, if you prefer.

15 oz. can fruit cocktail in light syrup
2 t. grated lemon zest
6 T. lemon juice
⅛ t. salt
¾ c. sugar
2 pkg. plain gelatin powder
6 oz. cream cheese
¾ c. heavy cream, whipped
Optional: 1 c. seedless grapes, halved

Drain the fruit cocktail, reserving the syrup; you should have about half a cup. Combine the syrup with enough water to equal 1¾ cups. Place ½ cup of this liquid in a small bowl, sprinkle the gelatin powder over it, and stir well to combine. Allow it to stand and soften while heating the remaining liquid to boiling in a medium saucepan. Meanwhile, stir together the lemon juice, lemon zest, salt, and sugar. Stir first the gelatin and next the lemon sugar mixture into the boiling hot liquid, stirring until everything is dissolved. Remove from the heat and allow it to stand about 10 minutes, until it is warm but not hot. In a medium mixing bowl, beat the cream cheese until fluffy. Gradually add the warm lemon gelatin mixture to the cream cheese, beating thoroughly and occasionally scraping down the sides of the mixing bowl. The cream cheese will be integrated into the gelatin and the top will appear frothy. Place it in the refrigerator for about 15 minutes, until it is cold but not starting to set. Whip the cream to soft peaks and fold that, along with the drained fruit cocktail and the grapes, into the lemon jell. Pour into desired serving dish and refrigerate at least 2 hours before serving.

Honey-Mashed Rutabaga

Rutabagas are the yellow turnips with purple tops, larger and more formidable than wimpy little white turnips. Some folks refer to rutabagas as "Swedes"; the Swedish term for Sweden roughly translates as "Land of the Rutabagas." Bruce and I both love rutabagas; for us, it wouldn't be Thanksgiving without them. It seems a shame, but rutabagas are one of those old-fashioned vegetables that don't garner the respect they once did. I think the trick to enjoying their flavor is to enhance it a bit; here the golden sweetness of honey adds a little highlight you're sure to enjoy.

4 c. peeled, cubed rutabaga
1 t. salt
¼ c. milk
2–4 T. honey
2–4 T. butter
¼ t. white pepper

Because rutabaga is so dense, it takes longer to cook than most vegetables. Cut it into fairly small dice; no more than 1" cubes would be my recommendation. Place it in a medium saucepan, adding the salt and enough water to just cover it. Cover the pan, bring to a boil, reduce the heat slightly, and boil gently until the cubes are quite tender, about ¾ of an hour. Drain it well and add 2 T. each of the butter and honey, pepper, and milk. Mash until the mixture is creamy; taste and add a bit more honey, butter, or salt only if you think it needs it. Serve nice and hot; this will serve approximately 6.

Baked Sweet Potatoes with Sugar-'n'-Spice Butter

Being of a Northern culinary persuasion, I still prefer mashed white potatoes with my Thanksgiving turkey. However, many folks consider sweet potatoes an integral part of the feast, and with good reason! Sweet potatoes are another nutritional powerhouse that just happen to taste delicious—a winning combination. They're wonderful mashed or candied, but taste pretty darned good baked too. Make them even tastier with the judicious addition of a little butter, sugar, and spice.

1 small or ½ larger sweet potato per serving
¼ c. butter
1 T. honey
1 T. brown sugar
¼ t. cinnamon
¼ t. grated orange rind
Pinch of nutmeg or mace
Pinch of cayenne pepper

Bake the sweet potatoes along with the pork chops, at 375°F for about 45–50 minutes. If the potatoes are large and don't seem to be cooking as fast as the pork, you can microwave them on high for 2–5 minutes, until they are tender. They may even be left in the microwave for a few minutes, keeping hot on retained heat, while you're plating the rest of your meal. While the sweet potatoes are baking, prepare the sugar-'n'-spice butter by creaming the softened butter with the honey and brown sugar. Beat in the remaining ingredients until the butter is smooth and creamy. Serve a dollop over each hot split sweet potato.

Let's Talk Turkey . . .

America's favorite Thanksgiving fare is a true American native. The North American wild turkey, *Meleagris gallopavo*, is one of only two species of wild turkey in the entire world. Its cousin, *Meleagris ocellata*, lives in a relatively small area around the Yucatan Peninsula in Central America. There are five subspecies of *gallopavo*, of which the most numerous is *sylvestris*, the Eastern wild turkey. When Europeans first traveled to the Americas, turkeys roamed in great bands throughout the countryside. Unfortunately, overhunting and loss of habitat brought the turkey uncomfortably close to extinction by the beginning of the twentieth century. Thanks to the Pittman-Robertson Act of 1937, and extensive reintroduction programs, wild turkeys again roam the United States, their numbers grown from only about 30,000 in the 1930s to over 7 million today. The turkey we're so fond of eating is descended from a domestic Mexican subspecies that was brought back to Spain in the early 1500s. Same ancestry, but bred into a bird of an entirely different demeanor than its wild cousins. Benjamin Franklin wanted the turkey to be our national bird rather than the bald eagle. Who could blame him? The turkey is an American original loved and devoured by almost everybody. Still though, can you imagine a turkey proudly straddling our national seal? Food for thought indeed.

Roast Turkey

The instructions here are for a 15-pound turkey, although ingredients are easy enough to adjust for different sizes. I prefer to roast my turkey at a slightly higher temperature than many instructions call for and have never had it turn out anything but tender and juicy. Methodology is what's important here—coating your bird well with a lubricating agent such as bacon or butter, and roasting it covered until near the very end, at which point a briefly uncovered rendezvous with a hot oven turns the skin to a crisp brown. I also prefer to stuff my turkey before roasting; the stuffing adds flavor and moistness to the turkey, which returns the favor to the stuffing. However, you must be careful not to undercook your bird; the stuffing must be properly heated through to a safe temperature. Prompt removal of any extra stuffing is also an important step to safely enjoying leftovers.

15 lb. turkey, neck and giblets removed
6 strips bacon
¼ c. butter
2 t. parsley flakes
1 t. paprika
½ t. thyme
Salt
Pepper

Stuffing

14–16 slices stale or toasted bread
½ c. butter
1 T. poultry seasoning
1 lg. onion, diced: 1 c.
2–3 stalks celery, diced: 1 c.
Water or low-sodium broth to moisten

First prepare your stuffing. If you have had the ambition and freezer space, you will have been saving odds and ends of bread for just this purpose. If not, no problem; one loaf of most types of bread should fit the bill nicely. I prefer bread with some texture to it, such as a nice oatmeal loaf, although you're limited only by personal preference here. I frequently fit all the slices onto a large cookie sheet and bake them a few minutes, either the night before or the morning of preparation, while preheating the oven for the turkey. You can also briefly toast each in a standard toaster,

although this can be time-consuming. I do think the toasting process adds an extra depth of flavor to the stuffing. Melt the butter in a 4 qt. pan or Dutch oven over medium-low heat. Add the onion and celery and cook, stirring occasionally, until they become tender but not brown. Meanwhile tear the bread into pieces and mix it with the poultry seasoning. Add 2 cups of water or broth to the celery/onion mixture and stir in the bread. You will now decide how much more liquid you wish to add to your stuffing; some prefer a moister stuffing, while others like it more crumbly. Once

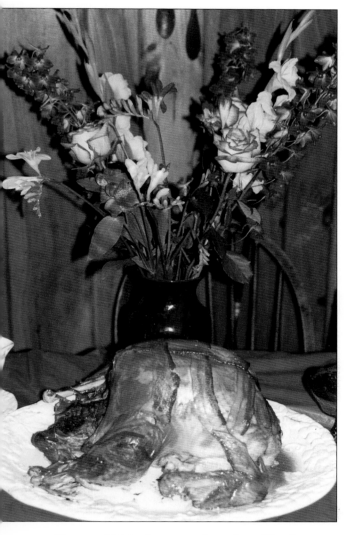

These wild turkeys captured on film by Bruce are true American natives. They provide much leaner fair than their domestic cousins.

it's moistened to your preference, remove from the heat and prepare the turkey.

Rinse the turkey with cold water and drain. I don't worry about patting it dry, although some recipes may call for this. Place 2 strips of bacon in a large roasting pan and position the turkey on top of it breast-side up. Add the neck to one side. Stuff both cavities loosely, as the filling tends to expand during cooking. Tuck the neck skin under the bird and tuck the drumsticks into the loop of skin near the tail, if it's intact. Combine the melted ¼ c. of butter with the herbs and seasonings and brush over the entire surface of the turkey. Drape the remaining bacon strips over the breast and drumsticks. Cover the turkey with the vented top of the roasting pan. If for some reason you don't have a top, make a tent of heavy-duty foil instead. Covering the turkey during this phase of cooking will help ensure a moist, tasty bird. Roast in a preheated 350°F oven for about 20 minutes per pound. For approximately the last half hour, increase the heat to 425°F, and uncover the turkey to finish roasting. The turkey will be deep golden brown, and the skin will be crispy as opposed to moist appearing when it is done; a fork inserted near the thigh joint will cause clear juices to run. Allow the turkey to rest in the pan

for 15–30 minutes, which allows the juices to remain in the bird rather than running all over the serving platter. It's also a nice time to finish up all the side dishes you're serving with the turkey.

Once the turkey is removed to the serving platter, it's time to make the gravy. I frequently add leftover vegetable cooking water to the pan drippings for more flavorful and nutritious gravy; just don't overwhelm the base with them. I like to heat this mixture in the roasting pan for a minute or two to scrape up all the savory brown goodness left from the roasting process, discarding the neck once this is accomplished. You may also either pour or use a bulb syringe to transfer the juices to another cooking pan prior to this step, if your roasting pan is not stove-top worthy, although by all means add some hot liquid and swish it around if it helps loosen up any bits of goodness. Around 3–4 cups of extra liquid would be sufficient for this size bird. At any rate, either measure or guesstimate the total amount you subsequently have, adding 1 T. flour whisked into a small amount of cold water for each cup of gravy base. Cook and stir over high heat until it is lovely and bubbly, adding salt and pepper to taste only if necessary. Strain through a wire mesh sieve if need be for a nice smooth gravy and serve hot.

Turkey Divan

Turkey divan is another one of those delicious dishes that has too frequently been corrupted by canned cream-of-something soup. Mind you, I occasionally use cream soups myself, but as with the advent of so many convenience foods we've sometimes allowed ourselves to forget what the "original" tastes like. In this case, it's well worth revisiting. Putting aside a little turkey stock in advance will give you just the right amount for this recipe, although prepared chicken broth substitutes nicely.

1 lb. leftover sliced turkey breast
¼ c. butter
¼ c. flour
1½ c. milk
1 c. chicken or turkey broth
2 egg yolks
½ t. dry mustard
1 t. salt
¼ t. pepper
½ c. shredded cheddar cheese
¼ c. grated Parmesan cheese
3–4 c. lightly cooked broccoli florets, well drained
Thinly-sliced French bread, buttered

Melt the butter over low heat. Add the flour and seasonings, cooking for a minute over low heat. Add the milk and broth all at once, increase heat and bring just to a boil. Reduce heat again and add the well beaten egg yolks and the cheddar cheese, stirring just until the cheese melts; do not boil. Remove from the heat. Place the bread slices, buttered-side down, in a greased casserole or baking pan. Layer the turkey and broccoli, topping with the sauce. Sprinkle with the

Parmesan cheese and bake in a preheated 375°F oven for 35–45 minutes, until the top bubbles and browns slightly. Serves 6.

Turkey Mole

This dark, spicy Mexican sauce is a nice contrast to the traditionally milder Thanksgiving flavors. I've tried to balance the complexities of a good mole with products readily available further north. Again, I'd recommend white meat, although in a pinch dark will do. If you happen to have chicken floating around instead, it will substitute very nicely.

Turkey Base

3–4 lb. turkey; breast or thighs
½ t. onion powder
½ t. garlic powder
½ t. paprika
1 T. salt
6 c. water
2 T. corn oil

Sprinkle the turkey evenly with the onion and garlic powders and the paprika. Brown in the oil, covered, in a Dutch oven over medium heat until the turkey is golden brown on both sides. Add the salt and the water. Bring to a boil, lower the heat to a simmer, and cook, covered, for about an hour, until the turkey is cooked through and tender. Remove the turkey from the broth and allow it to cool separately while preparing the rest of the sauce. If you prefer, the turkey and broth can be refrigerated overnight, then separated out, and utilized for the mole the next day.

Sauce

4–6 dried ancho chilies
½ c. sliced almonds *or*

¼ c. each sliced almonds and *pepitas* (pumpkin seeds)
6 T. corn oil, divided
2 T. sesame seeds
¼ t. anise seeds
¼ t. ground cloves
¼ t. ground allspice
¼ t. black pepper
½ t. cumin
½ t. cinnamon
½ t. oregano
1 medium onion, peeled and chopped
4–6 cloves garlic, peeled and chopped
1 slightly green banana, peeled and chopped
1 lb. tomatoes, peeled and chopped
½ c. raisins
¼ c. packed brown sugar
2 squares unsweetened chocolate
1 c. crushed corn tortilla chips
½ c. dry bread crumbs

Place the ancho chilies in a small saucepan along with 2 c. of the turkey broth. Bring to a boil, reduce the heat and simmer for about ½ hour, until the chilies are tender. While the chilies are cooking, prepare the rest of the sauce. In a medium cast-iron skillet, sauté the almond in 2 T. of the corn oil until they just begin to brown. Add the sesame seeds and all the spices, stirring over medium heat a minute or two longer until they are warm and fragrant. Remove them from the pan and set aside. In the same pan, again add 2 T. of oil, the onions, and garlic, and cook over medium heat until they begin to brown. Add the banana and chopped tomatoes and continue to cook, occasionally mashing the vegetables down with a spoon, until the tomatoes and onion are tender. Add the raisins and remove the pan from the heat. Strain the liquid from the cooked chilies, reserving it, and remove and discard the stems and seeds from them. Add broth to the chili cooking liquid to total 4 cups. In a blender, combine approximately half each of the spice/nut mixture, the veggie/fruit mixture, and the broth. Blend until smooth. Repeat with the remaining mixtures, combining them all in a large saucepan. Brown the bread crumbs slowly in the remaining 2 T. of corn oil. Bring the mole mixture slowly to a boil and then stir in the grated chocolate, brown sugar, crushed tortilla chips, and the bread crumbs. Allow it to simmer and thicken for about 5 minutes. Serve over the sliced or cubed turkey, accompanied by cooked rice. This will make a least 6–8 servings. Extra mole sauce may be sealed in a small container, labeled, and frozen to be used with a couple of months.

Oriental Turkey Soup

Since we've already established turkey to be a Native American bird, this title seems a bit of a misnomer. However, the flavor of the turkey blends well with the other ingredients and will provide you with a nice little contrast from more traditional post Thanksgiving fare. Options for the turkey-broth base include your choice of a cooked or raw turkey thigh, or a meaty turkey carcass including whatever odds and ends of the Thanksgiving bird might still be hanging around.

1 turkey thigh, about 1 lb. or the rough equivalent of leftovers
1 large onion, chopped
1 lg. carrot, chopped
2 T. peanut or corn oil
Optional: paprika and salt
12 c. water
1½ t. salt
1½ t. soy sauce
2–3 lg. cloves garlic, peeled and halved
¼ t. red pepper flakes
1–2 t. grated fresh ginger root
1 lg. star anise
5 oz. can of water chestnuts
1 lb. ground turkey
1 t. salt
1 t. grated ginger root
1 egg
½ t. garlic powder
1 bunch scallions, sliced
1 bunch bok choy, chopped
1 c. julienned carrots
8 oz. snow peas, halved lengthwise
Crispy Chinese noodles

If using a raw turkey thigh, season the skin with a bit of salt and paprika. Pour the oil into a Dutch oven set over medium heat. Place the turkey skin-side down, in the heated oil, adding the chopped carrot and onion around the edges. Reduce the heat to medium low, cover the pan, and brown slowly, turning the turkey once and stirring the vegetables as needed. If you are using leftover cooked turkey, brown only the vegetables, adding in the turkey once they are dark golden. Now add the water, garlic cloves, 1–2 t. ginger, star anise, salt, soy sauce, and red pepper flakes. Increase the heat to high until the mixture begins to boil. Again reduce the heat to medium low and allow it to simmer until the turkey is very tender, about an hour. While it is cooking, combine the ground turkey, the drained, diced water chestnuts, 1 t. salt,

1 t. ginger, the egg, one scallion, diced, and garlic powder, mixing well. Form into small meatballs; set aside (refrigerate if for longer than ½ hour). Once the turkey is sufficiently cooked, strain the mixture, putting the broth back in the Dutch oven and discarding the vegetables and spices. Pick the cooled turkey meat from the bones and add it back into the broth. Bring the broth back to boiling and gently add in the turkey meatballs, simmering them for about 10 minutes. I use a measuring teaspoon to form them, which will give you small uniform meatballs. Add the chopped and sliced bok choy, carrots, snow peas, and scallions. Bring the soup to a boil, to just tender cook the veggies. Serve it at once, topped with crispy Chinese noodles. This makes quite a bit of soup—enough for a crowd or some to freeze for another day.

For an intriguing twist on turkey leftovers, how about concocting a pot of Oriental turkey soup?

Turkey Burgers with Sweet Potato Fries

If you prefer your turkey ground rather than roasted, here's the recipe for you! Turkey burgers are easy to prepare, nutritious, and another little reminder of how versatile and delicious this bird can be. Add the tang of cranberry mayonnaise and the mellow crunch of sweet potato fries for a satisfying light meal.

1 lb. ground turkey
2 T. minced onion
2 T. minced celery
1 t. salt
½ t. poultry seasoning
¼ t. pepper
2 T. oil
4 hamburger or bulky buns, toasted
4 slices tomato, optional
4 leaf lettuce leaves, red or green
¼ c. finely shredded red cabbage
4 slices mild cheddar cheese, optional

Sweet Potato Fries

2 sweet potatoes: about 1 lb.
Corn oil for frying
Salt
Pepper

Cranberry Mayonnaise

½ c. cranberry-orange dipping sauce ("May")
½ c. mayonnaise
1 t. grated horseradish, optional

Combine the dipping sauce, horseradish, and mayonnaise, stirring to blend well. Refrigerate until serving time. This is also good with ham or meat loaf sandwiches; or use the dipping sauce as a spread by itself. Trim the sweet potatoes, removing any irregularities. Peel or not, as you wish. Cut them lengthwise into ¼" sticks. Chill them briefly in ice water while heating 2" of oil in a large, heavy skillet over medium-high heat. Allow the oil to heat up to between 375°–400°. Drain the potatoes, patting them dry with paper towels, and fry them a few at a time until they are golden and tender. Transfer them to a paper towel–lined baking sheet, sprinkle lightly with salt and pepper, and place them in a 200°F oven to stay warm while preparing the rest of the fries.

Combine the turkey, onion, celery, and seasonings, mixing lightly. Form into 4 thin patties and fry in the 2 T. hot oil over medium heat until they are lightly browned on both sides and cooked through. If you're using cheese, top the cooked burgers with a slice each and allow them to hang out, covered, in the skillet with the heat turned off; the cheese should melt from the retained heat. Brown the hamburger buns in a little butter, or broil them until just golden. To assemble, place a burger on each bun, topping with tomato, cabbage, and lettuce. Place a generous swirl of cranberry mayonnaise on the upper bun half before sandwiching everything together. Serve the extra cranberry mayonnaise alongside for dipping the fries in. Add some homemade dill pickles and enjoy a meal for 4!

Roast Duck with Autumn Berry Sauce

In my childhood, our neighbor around the corner was an elderly bachelor who mostly made his living raising poultry and sheep. He also augmented his income by running a trap line along the Ames Hill Brook and off in the swampland adjacent to his property. One year in particular, he had a run of luck with his traps at the same time he had planned to butcher off some ducks he was selling to grace holiday tables. Thrifty New Englander that he was, he skinned the mink from his traps with the same knife he then used to butcher his ducks. Although minks have sleek and lovely pelts, they also have scent glands that are not pleasing to smell, let alone taste. Suffice to say, his customers did not remain loyal. Fortunately, duck purchased from a supermarket, butcher, or farmer more conscious of hygiene than my late neighbor can be a classic fall treat, so don't be afraid to try it! It's one of the easiest birds to roast, since the fat in its skin makes the duck self-basting. The richness of the meat pairs well with a slightly tart berry sauce.

4–5 lb. duckling, giblets and neck removed
1 t. salt
1 small onion, chopped
1 small apple, chopped

If the duck is frozen, allow it to thaw approximately 2 days in your meat keeper, 2–3 hours before you plan to begin roasting it, rinse it well with cold water, removing any extra clumps of fat adhering to the underside of the skin. Pat the duck dry with paper towels and puncture the skin multiple times with a skewer, knife tip, or sharp fork. This will enable the fat to more freely render while it's roasting. Stuff the duck with as many apple and onion chunks as will fit. Sprinkle it with salt, place it in the roasting pan, and allow it to stand, uncovered, in the refrigerator until ready

Autumn berries are cooked into a spicy sweet sauce to accompany roast duck.

to cook. The salt will begin to draw out moisture and help the duck's skin to crisp up a little better while roasting. Preheat the oven to 375°F and place the uncovered duck in the roasting pan on a middle shelf. Roast it for approximately 30 minutes per pound, basting it occasionally in its own juices, until the internal temperature registers 170°F, or until juices run clear when a knife or fork is inserted into the duck's thigh. The skin should appear browned and crispy. Remove the duck from the roasting pan and allow it to rest for about 15 minutes before carving.

Autumn Berry Sauce

This sauce is also good served with chicken, turkey, pork, or rabbit. The salt is optional, although you may prefer that hint of it with the meat. If you do omit it, this sauce is also quite nice with pancakes or French toast.

1 c. blueberries, preferably wild
½ c. cranberries
1 c. orange juice
¼ c. honey
1 T. diced candied ginger
¼ t. allspice
¼ t. salt, optional
2 t. cornstarch
2 T. water

Frozen fruit works just fine for this recipe; another great time to enjoy the largesse from your summer's labor. Combine everything except the cornstarch and water in a small saucepan. Cook over high heat until it comes to a boil. Reduce the heat and boil gently for five minutes, until the cranberries have all popped and the sauce has slightly thickened. If you'd prefer a smoother sauce, carefully place in the blender and run it until smooth. Be cautious if the liquid is too hot; you don't want an exploding blender!

Return the sauce to the cooking pan and stir in the combined cornstarch and water. Bring to a boil once more and then remove from the heat. This can be served warm or chilled, although it will pour easier when warm.

345

A Dissertation on Salt Pork

November is butchering time in Vermont. The weather is finally cold enough to safely hang the carcasses a few days without the possibility of the meat spoiling, a necessary step in the procedure. Domestic turkeys and pigs, frequently destined for the Thanksgiving table, may also share freezer space with lamb, beef, or even venison if there's a hunter in the family. When I think of November in the country, my mind wanders back to salt pork. Each year at butchering time a large white crock would take its place in the uninsulated closet situated on the north side of my parents' house. Within its dark interior, slabs of white fat streaked with ribbons of pink flesh floated in a brine of liquid salt. The piglets taking up residence in the pen near our back brook each spring bore little resemblance to the hundred-plus-pound porkers lounging there by mid-November. It was then that thoughts of butchering would begin. Having nurtured our porcine companions all summer with the finest pig feed, garden produce, and table scraps, it seemed only appropriate to also assist them in the journey from their role as cohabitants of our land to that of gracing our table as succulent roasts and chops. Although their short lives were arguably lazy and comfortable, they still made the ultimate sacrifice to feed us well. Commodity or not, it was our responsibility to treat them as humanely as possible during the process. The actual slaughtering usually fell to my older brother, father, and/or husband, along with a few neighbors or friends. Each porker would be dispatched with a quick shot to the head and submerged in a claw foot bathtub full of water heated by a pile of burning logs underneath. The bristles would be scraped off using sharp knife blades. Once valuable organs such as liver and heart had been removed and put aside, the carcass would be split down the backbone. The halves would then be hooked through a hind-leg tendon and hung to cure. Butchering would commence a few days later, one side at a time being brought to the metal-topped kitchen table to be separated into its various components, wrapped, labeled, and frozen. That is when both the salt pork crock and the smokehouse would begin their yearly ritual as well. I won't attempt to detail the many uses of the many parts of the average pig. Most forms of curing and smoking are better left to professionals, who for a set fee will provide you with hams and bacon to your heart's content. I've included a few recipes, in case you're feeling adventurous. You'll find maple-cured bacon, salt pork, and cherry-smoked ham directions below and those for Easter ham in April. Sausage is a different case entirely, easy to prepare without curing. If you really want sausage links, you'll need to invest in casings, which are sold either natural, such as lamb intestines, or synthetic, such as cellulose. You'll also need a sausage stuffer, which is a considerable investment. Or you can just whip up a batch or two of sausage when you feel in the mood, using fresh or frozen ground pork.

Brood sows such as those shown here (accompanied by a friendly rooster) are much larger than the young pigs my family butchered each fall.

Vermont Country Sausage

A classic fat-to-lean ratio for sausage is 40 percent fat to 60 percent lean. All that fat is what gives the sausage its moist texture and crispy exterior when fried. However, it's also what makes sausage not the healthiest food on the menu. I usually try for a 30:70 ratio, which still isn't particularly lean, but at least gives some of the flavor and texture you're looking for in a good sausage. Any less fat and you end up with a rather tough ground-pork patty. Some recipes call for the addition of ground suet (beef fat) to even out the ratio, although I haven't attempted such things.

1 lb. ground pork
1½ t. salt
1 t. dried sage
½ t. powdered ginger
½ t. dried thyme
½ t. dried sage
½ t. black pepper
2 T. maple syrup
2 T. water

Combine all ingredients in a large bowl, mixing them very well. I prefer to use my hands for this. The mixture can then be wrapped and refrigerated to blend flavors, for just a few hours or 2 to 3 days. When you're ready to cook, form the mixture into thin patties and fry over medium-low heat in a heavy cast-iron skillet. Alternatively, form the sausage meat into a flat, wide rectangle and cut it into finger-sized pieces about 1" × 1" × 4" long. The meat may also be crumbled into breakfast strata or meat pones.

Meat Pone

Corn pone is a type of corn bread most often made without eggs, resulting in a somewhat flat and crusty product. Meat pone, at least as my mother prepared it, used regular cornbread batter, which was then poured over a mixture of ground meats and seasonings. My mom was a great fan of meat pone, making it on multiple occasions. She used a can of condensed tomato soup, partially diluted, rather than tomato sauce. Either one will work nicely.

1 recipe corn bread (below)
½ t. salt
¼ t. pepper
½ lb. ground beef
½ lb. pork sausage
1 med. onion peeled and diced: ¾ c.
1 sm. green pepper seeded and chopped: ¾ c.
Tomato sauce ("August") *or* condensed tomato soup

Corn Bread

½ c. flour
½ c. yellow cornmeal
¼ c. sugar
2 t. baking powder
½ t. salt
¼ c. corn oil
1 egg, beaten
¾ c. milk

Crumble the meats into a large, heavy skillet. Add the chopped onion and green pepper and cook, stirring occasionally, until the meat loses its pink color and the vegetables are softened. Stir ½ c. of tomato sauce and the salt and pepper into the mixture and pour it evenly into a 9" × 9" pan.

Prepare the cornbread: Combine the wet ingredients in one bowl and the dry in another. Stir them together lightly, just until they are well blended. Pour evenly over the meat mixture; it will form a thin coating. Bake in a 375°F oven for about 25 minutes, until the cornbread is golden brown and a toothpick or wooden skewer inserted near the center comes out clean. Cut into squares and serve hot with tomato sauce. If using condensed soup, reconstitute it by about half with water before using.

This square of meat pone is all set to provide a simple yet hearty autumn supper.

Italian Sausage

This sausage is relatively mild. As with the country sausage above, I've used a fairly high ratio of salt to meat for that "classic" sausage flavor. If you prefer less sodium in your sausage, feel free to adjust accordingly.

1 lb. ground pork
1½ t. salt
2 t. paprika
½ t. fennel seeds
¼ t. red pepper flakes
2 T. orange juice
2 T. water

Pound together the fennel seeds and red pepper flakes, either with a mortar and pestle or under waxed paper with a rolling pin. Stir in the salt and paprika, combining well. Mix together the ground pork, seasonings, orange juice, and water until everything is fully combined. Wrap the sausage in plastic wrap and refrigerate for at least a few hours, or up to 3 days to blend the flavors. This is great in marinara sauce, as a filling for stuffed mushrooms, or to top off a pizza.

Cherry-Smoked Ham

Fruit or nut trees provide mellow smoke for giving ham its characteristic flavor. I begin with a boneless rolled pork shoulder for ease of preparation. A bone in shoulder is much larger, necessitating more brine, longer brining and smoking time, and most likely a challenge in finding a container (and refrigerator) large enough to hold it. If you're ambitious enough to bone and roll your own, tie it securely with kitchen string, or better yet use prewoven string mesh, available in some kitchen and specialty stores. Because I cure pork into ham for the quality of ingredients and flavor rather than as a method of preserving, I don't use nitrates or nitrites in the process. Therefore, treat your ham as uncured meat; if you purchase the pork, pay attention to "sell by" dates, preferably getting meat that is good for at least a week or more after purchase. Obviously, if you're lucky enough to have your own, it's going to be nice and fresh to begin with. Because prefrozen meat doesn't absorb the curing ingredients in the same manner as fresh, it's better to brine and smoke immediately, freezing what you won't be using within a week or so. Some folks have invested in their own miniature smokers; I simply use my gas grill and a removable smoke pan. If you don't have a smoke pan, try a couple of disposable pie plates for holding the wood chips.

Cran-Cherry Pork Brine

1½ c. pure cranberry juice
1½ c. pure cherry juice
⅓ c. canning or sea salt
⅓ c. packed brown sugar
½ t. mustard seed
½ t. whole cloves
1 t. black peppercorns
¼ t. celery seed
1 bay leaf
3 c. cold water
4 lb. boneless pork picnic shoulder, rolled and tied
2 c. dried cherry wood chips
instant-read thermometer

Make sure you use actual fruit juice in the brine, not "cocktail" or sugar-added juices, which could change the proportions and flavor. Combine all the brining ingredients except the water in a nonreactive cooking pan and bring to a boil, stirring to dissolve the salt and sugar. Remove from the heat, stir in the water, and cool completely. It might be a good idea to make the brine a day in advance, refrigerating it overnight so that it's extremely cold before immersing the pork in it. Poke the pork all over with a skewer or thin sharp knife to aid in the absorption of the brine. Place the pork and brine in a plastic or glass covered container. I like to use a sealable extra-large ziplock bag, which once sealed I place seam-side up in a large bowl. Place the pork in the refrigerator, turning the meat over once a day in the bag, for 5–7 days. Remove from the brine at least 12 hours before smoking it, allowing it to stand on the refrigerator shelf, uncovered, to dry the surface area. To smoke, soak about 2 cups of cherry wood chips in an equivalent amount of water for about ½ hour, until the water is absorbed. Turn on one burner only (preferably a side one) on the grill. (If using a smoker, follow manufacturer's instructions.) Place the soaked chips in the smoke pan or doubled pie plates over the open burner. Once they begin smoking, place the brined pork directly on the rack on the opposite side of the grill. Close the top and adjust the burner so that your grill maintains a constant heat of about 250°F; this is known as a "hot smoke." Smoke the ham, turning it occasionally, until the internal temperature registers 165°F on the instant-read thermometer. This could take up to an hour per pound; if you find near the end of the process it still hasn't heated quite high enough, you may finish cooking it in a 350°F grill or even your oven. Just don't try to hurry the process too much or you may compromise the flavor and texture of your ham. The ham is now ready to be eaten as is. It may be stored in the refrigerator and eaten cold, or reheated and glazed. Because the flavor of this home-cured ham is somewhat mild, I would recommend baking the ham rather than boiling it. Set your oven at 350°F and bake for 20 minutes per pound, adding a little water or other liquid to the roasting pan to help keep the ham moist.

Since cherry-smoked ham doesn't use nitrates or nitrites, the color more nearly resembles fresh pork, but the flavor is that of mild sweet ham.

Vermont Maple Bacon

Bacon is surprisingly easy to make at home. Although you can buy commercial rubs containing sodium nitrate (saltpeter), I prefer not to use it if I can avoid it, especially in something as easy to freeze as bacon.

4 lb. pork belly
½ c. canning salt
¼ c. maple syrup

A 4 lb. chunk of pork belly is easy to manage and will fit nicely into an oversize ziplock plastic bag. As an alternative, use a nonreactive metal, glass, or plastic container with a tight cover that will fit into your refrigerator. Rub the pork belly (rind on) all over with the maple syrup. Then rub the salt evenly all over the surface. Seal it in the plastic bag or other container and refrigerate, turning once a day for 7 days. The salt will draw meat juices from the pork, so it will become wetter as the week goes on. On the seventh day, rinse the pork well, pat as dry as you can, and place on a nonreactive rack (if in doubt, cover it with a double thickness of cheesecloth) and put the whole thing on a cookie or baking sheet. Put back in the refrigerator for another day to thoroughly dry the surface of the meat and form a kind of a soft crust called the pellicle. This is necessary for proper smoke absorption during the smoking process, although as your bacon is technically already "cured," it could be frozen as is. However, it simply won't taste like the "real thing" without this final extra step. After it has drained for 24 hours, the bacon is ready for the slow cooking or smoking process. This may be accomplished by slow baking the pork in a 200°F oven for about 2 hours, until the meat registers 150°F on an instant-read thermometer, cooled, sliced, and frozen. Although it seems an easy procedure, I feel this produces an inferior product. If you don't have access to a smokehouse, your backyard grill may be utilized for smoking small amounts of meat at a time. This is how I cure my bacon and hams. You will need dry wood chips from either fruit or nut-bearing trees or sweet wood such as maple. Check around for premade packets of wood chips; some are all set to be utilized for a single-smoking procedure. The one I use for bacon is also known as a cool smoke, because the temperature is not hot enough to thoroughly cook the meat. *Therefore, whether you use the oven or smoking methods outlined here, the bacon must always be cooked before eating.* As with the previous ham recipe, soak the chips first in a small amount of water. Place them over the lit burner, and once they have begun smoking, place the bacon directly on the rack on the unheated side of the grill. Although your goal is to maintain a temperature of about 200°F, your grill may not go quite this low; 250°F is fine. Smoke the bacon until it registers 150°F on an instant-read thermometer; start checking after about and hour and a half, depending on the size of your meat. Once it has been reached, remove the bacon and chill it well before slicing to use fresh within a week or individually wrapping to freeze for future use.

Maple-and-salt–cured bacon is allowed to stand in the open air of the refrigerator for a day, forming a dry surface called a pellicle, prior to smoking and slicing.

many cuts of pork were preserved in this manner, modern refrigeration and freezing methods have rendered most forms of salt pork obsolete. It's still nice to have your own supply to utilize in recipes such as baked beans and chowders. For a real trip down memory lane you could even try that old standby, salt pork and milk gravy. I've only prepared that dish once, for a very old lady in the nursing home I was employed by back in the early 1970s. I dredged thin slices of the pork in flour, fried them until crisp, and allowed them to hang out on a plate while making gravy. I then made a roux of sorts with the fat left in the pan and a little flour. Milk was added to ensure the proper gravy consistency, while salt and pepper finished out this royal dish. Traditional accompaniment would be boiled potatoes, as I recall. Nostalgia occasionally leaves a little something to be desired . . .

Pork belly, cut into 1 lb. or smaller chunks
3 T. canning salt per pound of pork belly

Rub the salt evenly over the entire surface of the pork. For larger amounts, the salted pork could be placed in a crock, although a pound or two is easier to prepare right in the refrigerator. I utilize a gallon-size plastic twist tie or zip bag that I place, seam-side up, in a bowl. Turn the pork in the bag once a day for about a week. The salt will by now have drawn some of the juices out from the fat pork; this is the brine I remember in the salt pork crock from days gone by. Because I cannot vouch for the safety of keeping a salt pork barrel in this day and age, I would now recommend either using your pork within a week or so or double wrapping it and freezing for future use. Slicing the pork prior to freezing (separate the slices until they have frozen) will make things much easier when you wish to use some at a later date.

Lard

If you do happen to have butchered a pig or two, the easiest way to use up all that extra fat is by rendering it into lard. However, you must not mind the smell of heated pig fat or the rather unique taste lard imparts in order for this exercise in thriftiness to be successful. An added bonus to rendering your own lard is creation of a more pure product than what is available commercially. The most common use of lard is for piecrust production, although I've also seen numerous Mexican and Latin American recipes that call for its use. If you choose to try this ambitious venture, place chopped pieces of pork belly in a large, heavy pan or skillet and maintain them over very low heat for several hours, or until the liquid fat has "rendered" out of the solid. Watch closely; as we all know, hot fat is very flammable! Drain carefully into a heat proof container; once cooled to room temperature, cover and refrigerate to use within a few weeks. What you'll have left in the pan are bits of crispy pork fat, which some folk sprinkle with salt and nibble upon.

Salt Pork

Salt pork, which also utilizes pork belly, is one of the easiest and also most ancient means of preserving meat. It only requires two ingredients—salt and pork—and a nonreactive container for the curing process. Although in times gone by

Roast Pork

Nothing tastes better on a chilly fall night than a juicy, crispy loin of roast pork. Add baked or mashed potatoes, maple-glazed acorn squash, and homemade applesauce and you have a feast fit for royalty. If you're purchasing your pork, read the label carefully and avoid those that have been injected or soaked with watery brining solutions. Investing in a more expensive cut is well worth it when roasting pork; a loin cut will give the desired result. When the kids were little, I sometimes tried to economize by using a blade end roast; the results, while palatable, were disappointing. Too much tough meat and bone made this roast a dull boy indeed—hardly worth the money "saved." Better to braise your blade end roasts and chops for all concerned.

3–4 lb. bone-in pork roast
4–6 medium onions
Salt
Pepper
2 T. butter
Dried sage, optional

Place the pork in a roasting pan of commensurate size, surrounded by the peeled onions. Season all generously with salt and black pepper, sprinkling a little dried sage on the pork if you wish. Put a pat of butter on top of each onion. Add about a cup of water to the roasting pan, enough to cover the bottom and help steam the onions without drowning them. Place the uncovered roast in a preheated 400°F oven for about 10 minutes. Lower the heat to 325°F and cook for about 30 minutes per pound, basting the meat and onions occasionally. When the pork is done, the fat should appear brown and crispy on the outside and the internal temperature should register 165–170°F on a meat thermometer. Remove the roast and onions to a platter and allow it to rest for about 10 minutes. Deglaze the pan with about 2 cups of water or vegetable cooking liquid, heating everything together and scraping down the sides and bottom to incorporate all the savory bits of browned meat. If the roasting pan isn't burner-proof, transfer everything to a medium saucepan before heating. Combine 2 T. flour with ½ c. of cold water and whisk into the boiling pan juices. Adjust to taste with salt and pepper and serve with the pork. This serves 6–8 with leftovers.

Baked Stuffed Pork Chops

Use center-cut pork chops for this recipe and save the less-tender sirloin chops for braising. I offer two stuffing (or topping) options with this recipe, one sweet and fruity, the other more savory. You may use one or both; sometimes it's fun to mix and match. I give an "amount per" recipe for each, so you can bake as many or few chops as you wish. These are quite tasty with baked sweet potatoes.

Per Serving

1 thick or 2 thin center-cut pork chops
Salt
Pepper
Olive oil

Fruited Bread Stuffing

1 thick slice of stale bread
2 T. diced apple, skin on
1 T. diced onion
1 T. diced celery
1 T. raisins *and/or* dried cranberries
1 t. brown sugar
1–2 T. apple *or* orange juice
¼ t. poultry seasoning
¼ t. cinnamon
2 t. butter

Savory Corn Stuffing

1 thick slice of stale bread
2 T. whole kernel corn
1 T. diced onion,
1 T. diced celery
1 T. diced red or green bell pepper
¼ t. cumin
Pinch of salt
Pinch of pepper
Pinch of paprika
1 t. minced fresh cilantro or ¼ t. dried
1 t. butter
1 t. olive oil
1–2 T. milk *or* water

For the fruited stuffing, melt the butter in a small, heavy skillet. Add the onions, celery, and apple and sauté until just tender. Stir in everything else except the bread and juice, cooking just a minute longer. Tear the bread into small

The ingredients for fruited bread stuffing and savory corn stuffing are shown prior to mixing. Fruited bread-stuffed pork chops are baked to golden perfection before enjoying with fresh broccoli and baked sweet potatoes with sugar-'n'-spice butter.

pieces and stir in last. Add the juice as needed just to form a moist but not soggy mixture. For the savory stuffing, melt the butter with the oil in a heavy skillet. Add the onion, celery, and peppers and sauté until they are just tender. Add the corn and all the seasonings and cook a minute longer. Tear the bread into small pieces and stir in. Add the milk or water until the right degree of moisture is reached. If using thick-cut chops, cut a deep slit in each almost to the bone, season with salt and pepper, and place in an oiled baking dish. Boneless chops are even easier; slit them from the fat side almost through horizontally and spread apart to "butterfly" them. Fill each chop firmly with the stuffing mixture, folding over the top if using butterfly-style chops. If using thin-cut chops, pile the stuffing on one chop and place the other on top, pressing lightly. Brush the tops with a little olive oil. Bake in a 375°F oven for about 45–50 minutes, until the chops are nicely browned and the meat and filling are cooked through.

Pork Ribs with Sauerkraut

Braising works well with any of the tougher cuts of pork. This is also a good way to prepare blade-end pork chops. Homemade, canned, or commercially packed refrigerated sauerkraut will do, although each will give you a slightly different flavor.

2 lb. pork spareribs
4 c. (1 lb.) sauerkraut
1 c. beer *or* apple cider *or* apple juice
1 lg. onion, sliced
2 T. butter *or* oil *or* bacon fat
1 tart apple, cored and diced
1 t. caraway seed, optional

Split the ribs into individual or serving-size pieces. Brown the onions and ribs in the fat in a large pan or Dutch oven. Add the sauerkraut, apple and caraway seeds (if using), and the beer or cider. Bring to a boil, reduce the heat, and simmer, covered, for 45 minutes to 1 hour, until the meat is tender. Serve with mashed, creamed, or boiled potatoes or buttered noodles. I think green beans or cooked carrots go very well with this dish also. This amount serves 4.

Beer Bread

If you've broken out the beer for braising the pork ribs anyway, perhaps you'd like to use a little more to make a loaf of beer bread. Start it baking just before you start the ribs to allow for adequate baking time and just a few minutes to cool. Although it is a quick bread and as such requires no yeast or special raising time, the beer flavors the bread, giving it a yeasty taste. If you'd like to bake the bread in less time, divide the batter evenly between two smaller pans, or halve the ingredients and bake it in one.

3 c. all-purpose flour
2 T. sugar
¼ c. butter, melted
1 t. salt
3 t. baking powder
12 oz. (1½ c.) beer

Combine all ingredients in a medium bowl, stirring until just well mixed. Pour into a buttered 9" × 3" bread pan. Bake in a preheated 375°F oven for approximately 1 hour, until golden brown and crusty when tapped. Although a bit feisty to cut when it's fresh from the oven, beer bread is at its finest when enjoyed warm.

Dinner Rolls

On a festive occasion, rolls can make the meal. Thanksgiving surely fits the bill for this, but there's no need to limit such things to holidays only. Homemade rolls with a bit of butter and jam make a tasty breakfast treat. And what's not to like about warm rolls as an accompaniment to just about any meal, from fancy roasts to baked beans? These little bits of golden goodness are easy to make, so why not treat yourself to the real deal? This recipe makes 1 dozen and is very easy to double, triple, or quadruple.

3 T. honey or sugar
3 T. butter
1 t. salt
1 T. active dry yeast
⅓ c. warm water
⅓ c. milk
Approximately 2 c. bread flour

You may wish to heat the milk and water together first or use all hot water from the tap and dry milk powder (scant 2 T. per ⅓ c. water). Stir together in a medium bowl or saucepan with the butter, salt, and honey/sugar until the butter melts and mixture is lukewarm. Sprinkle the yeast over the surface and stir into the mixture until mostly dissolved. Allow to sit and bubble for about 5 minutes. Stir in bread flour to form a soft dough; start with 1 cup and add the rest gradually. When you've added enough, the dough will still be soft but will barely have lost its stickiness. Allow the dough to sit in the bowl, covered with a warm damp cloth, until doubled in bulk, between 30–60 minutes. Using as little flour as necessary, punch down and knead the dough until it is smooth and elastic. Divide into 12 equal balls, rolling smooth between your hands, and place in a buttered 9" round pan. For a double batch, use a 9" × 13" cake pan. Allow to rise in a warm, undisturbed place (if you have a pilot light in the oven, this is a good spot) until doubled again. Bake on a middle to upper shelf in a 375°F oven until golden brown and rolls near the center sound hollow when tapped, 25–30 minutes. Brush the tops with butter while still hot and turn out on a wire cooling rack. These are lovely served warm. If you need to save them, wrap the cooled rolls in well sealed foil and use within a couple of days.

Tourtiére

Our friends to the north in Quebec are the true connoisseurs of *tourtiére*, a meat pie originally made from game or birds, but now from ground pork. Almost a pork meat loaf encased in pastry crust, it will satisfy the heartiest appetites. Some recipes use no potatoes; others may add a few bread crumbs for stability. This version cooks the potatoes along with the pork and onions, beating everything to a semismooth consistency before placing in a double pastry shell. Use of ketchup also varies widely, some considering it integral, others a waste of a perfectly good pork pie. Perhaps you even have a little extra *poutine* gravy squirreled away in your freezer? That would most likely be my choice of topping. If you choose to embellish with ketchup, why not make yourself a batch of homemade to go with? It's not hard and adds dimensions of flavor you'll not get with commercially produced.

1 lb. ground pork
1 c. chopped onion: 1 lg.
2 c. diced potatoes
1 t. salt
¼ t. mace
¼ t. ground allspice
½ t. dried sage
⅛ t. cloves
⅛ t. white pepper
1½ c. water
1 double unbaked piecrust

Slowly cook the pork and onions in a large cast-iron skillet until the pork loses its color and the onions are semitender. Add in everything else except the piecrust and bring to a boil. Cover, reduce the heat, and cook gently for about ½ hour, until the potatoes are nice and soft and the liquid mostly but not completely absorbed. Allow it to cool for a few minutes before either mashing with a large spoon or better yet beating with a heavy-duty mixer paddle to a fine texture. Roll the well-chilled piecrust dough to loosely fit a 9" pie pan. Pour the warm filling into the pan, rolling and fitting the top crust over all. Seal and crimp the edges, poking a few holes in the top for the steam to escape. Brush with milk if you wish. Bake the *tourtiére* in a preheated 375°F oven for 45 minutes, until the crust is golden brown and crispy. Serve warm or cold to 6.

Bacon Birds

Here's another thrifty meal that tastes delicious. If you love stuffing, you'll love bacon birds. You can make these slightly more nourishing by adding a thin scallop of uncooked turkey or chicken to the base of your creation, although you'll then lose the crispy texture of the stuffing oven fried in bacon fat. To keep calories somewhat under control, the stuffing itself is prepared in a different manner than what you'd normally stuff a chicken or turkey with.

Per Person (2 Bacon Birds)

2–4 slices uncooked bacon
2 thick slices bread, toasted
1 t. dried onion flakes
½ t. poultry seasoning
¼ c. milk, more or less

Tear the bread into pieces and combine with the onion and poultry seasoning. Add enough milk to moisten the mixture well without making it too runny. Depending on how rich you wish your birds to be, either lay one strip of bacon sideways on a baking sheet or crisscross two per bird. Mound your filling evenly onto the bacon and bring the strips up over the top to wrap securely. If you wish, poke a toothpick through each, although I don't find this step necessary. Bake in a 350–375°F oven for about 45–50 minutes, until the bacon is crisp and browned. Remove from the baking pan immediately so the birds don't absorb any extra bacon grease. These are tasty served with baked potatoes, which can cook right alongside them in the oven. Perhaps you'd like to throw in some acorn squash to bake as well or broccoli with cheese sauce. This serves as many as you wish.

Baked Beans

Since the salt pork crock no longer exists at my house, I've long since substituted bacon. Feel free to use whichever you prefer. This recipe is a cross between a New England–style maple-baked bean and a Swedish brown bean recipe integrating ginger and vinegar for tang. These beans store well in the fridge and sometimes taste even better heated up. I like to serve them with deviled eggs, steamed broccoli, and homemade rolls.

1 lb. dried beans: great northern, yellow eye, *or* soldier beans
1 lg. onion, coarsely chopped
6 slices bacon *or* salt pork, cut into 1" pieces
¾–1 c. packed brown sugar
½ c. maple syrup
2 T. cider vinegar
1 t. dry mustard
½ t. ginger

Place the beans in a Dutch oven or burner proof roasting pan. Cover with water and bring to a full boil. Remove from the heat and let stand, covered, for at least 1 hour. Alternatively, soak the beans in cold water overnight at room temperature. If you're using a smaller bean, such as a soldier, you may be able to get away with just bringing them to a boil and progressing to the next step. Add the bacon and onion and bring to a boil. Reduce heat to a gentle bubble and cook for about an hour, longer if the beans didn't soak first. Combine the remaining ingredients and add to the beans. Transfer to a bean pot or baking dish if necessary and bake, covered, at 350°F, for about 1½ to 2 more hours, stirring occasionally. Add water if needed to just cover. The liquid should thicken of its own accord to a nice consistency. Remove the cover for the last 15 minutes or so to brown the top. If you happen to have a woodstove that's constantly burning, these can be slow baked or even slow cooked on the top of the stove for the better part of a day. If you'd prefer a vegetarian version, omit the meat and add ¼ c. of butter, or not, as you wish.

Lemon-Ginger Poached Pears

November is also pear season here in New England; they're readily available and inexpensive to boot. Poaching them in lemon ginger syrup adds a little zing and depth of flavor to these autumn fruits. They are quite tasty with the poaching syrup poured over them, and possibly a gingersnap or two to accompany them. Use firm, slightly under-ripe pears for best results. Be sure to select pears which are suited to cooking; some softer varieties are good for eating fresh but will fall to pieces if cooked. It wouldn't hurt to poach a couple extra pears, just in case some come out less well than others. Extras can be eaten just the way they are, integrated into a fruit soup, or even added to a salad of winter greens, toasted nuts, and Roquefort cheese. Try making vinaigrette with the poaching juice to pour over—yum!

Poaching Liquid

¾ c. water
1 c. sugar
1 T. grated lemon zest
¼ c. lemon juice
2 T. diced crystallized ginger
or a 1" piece grated fresh ginger root
4 firm pears, such as Anjou or Bartlett

Bring all the poaching liquid ingredients to a boil in a medium stainless steel or glass saucepan. Add the peeled, cored pears. Reduce heat to a simmer and poach the pears for about 5–10 minutes, until just tender. Remove from heat and allow the pears to cool in the syrup; they'll continue to absorb some of the lemon ginger flavor. Serve warm or chilled. See tips below for using up any extras poaching syrup.

Lemon-ginger poached pears make a nice light dessert. For something a bit fancier, turn them into pears royale.

Pears Royale

This is my absolute favorite pear recipe. It's reasonably easy to prepare, yet sophisticated enough for a special dessert. If you wish whole pears for a fancy presentation, remove the skin from each with a vegetable peeler. Carefully remove the core of the pear with a small sharp knife and/or spoon, being careful not to puncture the surface of the fruit and cut a thin slice from the bottom so the pear will stand upright. Leave the stem and the stem end intact. If your pears are a little too ripe to attempt this, or if you just don't feel like being so fussy, simply slice them in half (peeled or not as you wish), scoop out the center, and simmer. The halved pears are actually able to hold more of the creamy filling and look quite sophisticated with a bit of the chocolate sauce drizzled over all.

1 recipe lemon-ginger pears and poaching liquid
4 oz. cream cheese
¼ c. confectioner's sugar
2 T. reduced poaching liquid (see below)
¼ c. heavy cream
1 T. diced crystallized ginger
2 T. semisweet chocolate mini chips
2 T. diced walnuts
¼ c. heavy cream
¼ c. reduced poaching liquid
1 c. semisweet chocolate chips

Poach the pears as directed in the previous recipe. Allow them to cool in the poaching liquid to room temperature or make a day ahead and chill them overnight. Pour 1 cup of the pear poaching liquid into a small saucepan. Reduce it over medium-high heat to ½ cup and allow it to cool to room temperature. Beat the cream cheese with the 2 T. reduced poaching liquid until smooth. Beat in the confectioner's sugar and ¼ c. cream until the mixture is light and fluffy. Fold in the chocolate mini chips, diced walnuts, and diced crystallized ginger. Combine ¼ c. heavy cream and ¼ c. reduced poaching liquid in a small pan. Cook over medium high until the mixture just comes to a boil. Remove from heat and stir in 1 c. semisweet chocolate chips until chips are melted and the sauce is smooth and glossy. For presentation, place 1 or 2 pear halves in a dessert dish. Spoon or pipe some of the filling into each. If using whole pears, pipe the filling into and around the bottom of each. Drizzle decoratively with the chocolate sauce, passing more to go with as desired. This serves between 4 and 8, depending on pear size and appetites involved. Try mixing any extra poaching syrup with hot tea for a soothing hot drink, or with sparkling water or iced tea for a refreshing cold one. Extra chocolate sauce is rich enough to refrigerate and then form into small rounds. Roll in unsweetened cocoa powder for a new take on truffles.

Pumpkin Cheesecake

If you'd like a change from pumpkin pie this Thanksgiving, why not try pumpkin cheesecake? It's easy to make with either canned pumpkin or your own frozen pureed. Ginger snaps add a nice zip to the crumb crust. Finish it off by swirling with a ginger cream topping. Because it's best made a day in advance to allow for adequate cooling time, it also eliminates one more item from your to-do list on a busy Thanksgiving day.

3 8-oz. pkg. cream cheese, softened
1 c. packed brown sugar
1 c. pumpkin puree
1 T. cornstarch
1 t. cinnamon
½ t. ginger
¼ t. grated nutmeg
¼ t. ground cloves
3 eggs
¼ c. sour cream

Ginger Crumb Crust

1 c. finely crushed gingersnap crumbs
¼ c. sugar
¼ c. butter, melted

Ginger Cream

1 c. heavy cream
¼ c. packed brown sugar
1 t. vanilla
½ c. sour cream
2–4 T. diced crystallized ginger

Combine all the crust ingredients, stirring well to combine. Press the mixture into a buttered 9" springform pan. Beat the cream cheese and brown sugar until light and fluffy. Beat in the pumpkin, cornstarch, and spices. Fold in the pumpkin and sour cream. Pour into the ginger crumb-lined springform pan. Bake at 325°F for about 50–60 minutes, until the top is firm to touch. Run a knife around the edge of the springform pan and allow the cheesecake to cool in the oven for about ½ hour. Remove and complete cooling completely. This can be done a day in advance, if you wish. Refrigerate, covered, until serving time. When ready to serve, remove the springform edge and place the base on serving plate. Whip the cream, vanilla, and brown sugar to soft peaks. Fold in the sour cream. Swirl on top of the cheesecake. Sprinkle with the crystallized ginger. Decorate with candy pumpkins, if desired. Serves 16.

Fresh Orange Cake with Vanilla Nut Frosting

When I was growing up, my dad and his two brothers would get together with their families for Thanksgiving dinner. There would be the traditional turkey, possibly a roast of pork and of course all the side dishes and pies. However, my favorite dessert of the day was the fresh orange layer cake my mother would bake, filled and topped with a creamy white vanilla and walnut frosting.

¾ c. unsalted butter
1¾ c. sugar
1 T. grated orange rind
2½ c. cake flour
2 t. baking powder
½ t. baking soda
1 t. salt
½ c. orange juice
½ c. milk
3 eggs

Beat the sugar and butter until light and fluffy. Add all other ingredients except the eggs and beat until smooth and creamy. Add the eggs and beat until creamy again. Pour into greased and floured pans, either 2 9" round or 1 9" × 13". Bake at 350°F for 30–40 minutes, until the top springs back when lightly pressed with your finger. Cool 10 minutes in the pans before turning out on racks to finish cooling entirely. (If using a rectangular pan, you may prefer to leave the cake in the pan.) Fill and frost with creamy vanilla

nut frosting; garnish with fresh orange slices, if desired. This serves 16.

Creamy Vanilla Walnut Frosting

1 c. milk
⅓ c. flour
1 c. butter
1 c. granulated sugar
1 c. confectioner's sugar
1 t. vanilla
1 c. finely chopped walnuts

Cook the combined milk and flour over low heat until it is very thick. Remove from heat, cover with waxed paper, and cool to room temperature. Beat the softened butter and granulated sugar at high speed until light and fluffy. Beat in the flour and milk mixture and vanilla; the frosting should lighten and become quite thick. Fold in the confectioner's sugar and nuts. Use to fill and frost the fresh orange cake. Decorate with walnut halves and/or fresh orange slices, if desired. Cover and refrigerate leftovers.

Solstice and Other Such Things . . .

DECEMBER DAYS ARE short and sweet, the nights long and dark yet at times quite beautiful. Despite snow, cold, and sunlight lasting for far less of the twenty-four hours than most would prefer, there's a sense of anticipation to December that's felt at no other time. Perhaps it's the solid convergence of holidays lighting the darkest month of the year. Small towns glisten with bowers of white and multicolored lights. Further in the country, the white glow of candlelit windows reflect softly on crystalline icicles hanging from snow frosted rooflines. The occasional solitary evergreen, draped with even more lights, stands guarding the side lawn. December is a month of celebration, whether secular or religious, ancient or newly found. It's also a time to reflect upon the year that has passed—things we've accomplished, perhaps things we need to spend a little more time on in the future. Still, the New Year hasn't arrived yet, so let's enjoy December and the festivities that accompany it; January will come soon enough.

Lights sparkle in December dusk at this country house.

December

Poinsettia Dip

This dip is as easy as it is delicious. Although I prefer it as is, feel free to add some of the optional items listed in the recipe. To make your poinsettia topping, cut pieces of red and green bell peppers into the shape of poinsettia leaves and "flowers," which are really just leaves of a different color. If you happen to have a yellow or orange sweet pepper hanging around wanting to be used, dice a bit for the center of the flower; otherwise, green should do just fine. Serve this with crackers, little slices of baguette bread, corn chips, and/or your favorite dipping vegetables. Cover leftovers tightly to use within a week.

12 oz. cream cheese, regular or reduced fat
½ t. Tabasco sauce
1 large red bell pepper

Optional Add-ins

Diced green, yellow, or orange bell peppers
A bit of chopped cilantro

Roast the red pepper on a metal rack over the open flame of a burner, or under a hot broiler, for about 5 minutes, turning it occasionally for even charring. Once roasted, wrap the warm pepper in a bit of foil for a few minutes. This will cause condensation of moisture and enable you to slip the skin off easier. You may substitute a canned roasted red pepper if you prefer, draining it well before using. In either instance, chop the skinned and seeded pepper coarsely and blend or process it until mostly smooth. If you're using a food processor, simply add your softened cream cheese and Tabasco sauce and process until smooth. I haven't had such good luck with

this when using a blender, so I would recommend removing the pepper to a mixing bowl and beating in the cream cheese and Tabasco until smooth. Stir in any desired extra ingredients and transfer to a small serving bowl. Add decorative touches as desired. Chill the dip, covered, until ready to serve.

Hot Artichoke Dip

Hot artichoke dip may be assembled in advance and refrigerated, covered, until shortly before serving time. It's a nice way to warm up holiday festivities. Refrigerate any leftovers, covered, to reheat in the microwave another day.

1 lb. cream cheese, softened
4 oz. can of chopped jalapeños
14–16 oz. can of artichoke hearts
¼ c. grated parmesan cheese

Drain the artichokes and the jalapeños, reserving a bit of the artichoke juice. Combine all ingredients in oven proof bowl or casserole dish, beating until smooth; add a little of the reserved artichoke juice if necessary. You won't need much of it or the dip may turn out a bit runny. Sprinkle with a little extra grated cheese, if you wish. Bake at 350°F until hot and bubbly, around 30 minutes. Serve at once with crusty bread, bread sticks, crackers, or tortilla chips. Cover and refrigerate any leftovers.

Multigrain Crackers

One of the nice things about making your own crackers is that you can cut them in any shape you desire. For December fun, use your Christmas cookie cutters, make stars on the Fourth of July, or bunnies and chicks for springtime celebrations. Or you may just wish to leave them in circles or squares. However you cut them, these crackers are tasty any time of the year. The onion powder is an optional flavor enhancer if you'd like a little accent of allium; I think they taste fine either way.

½ c. all-purpose flour
½ c. whole-wheat flour
¼ c. rye flour
2 T. cornstarch
2 T. cornmeal
½ c. rolled oats
½ t. baking soda
½ t. baking powder
1 t. salt
1 T. packed brown sugar
1 T. sesame seeds
1 stick (½ c.) cold unsalted butter
½ t. onion powder, optional
¼ c. cold water

Whirl the rolled oats in a blender or food processor until they resemble coarse meal. Combine the white, wheat, and rye flours with the oats, cornstarch, salt, brown sugar, leavenings, onion powder, and sesame seeds. Cut the cold butter into tiny squares and integrate into the dry mixture, either by hand or using a blender or food processor. The mixture should be crumbly, with only tiny flecks of butter showing. Add the cold water to the flour/butter mixture, stirring lightly but thoroughly until everything just clumps together. Gather the cracker dough into a loose ball and wrap in foil, wax paper, or plastic wrap. Refrigerate for at least one hour, or up to 3 days. You may also freeze the tightly wrapped dough for up to a month. Roll half at a time lightly out on a floured board to about ⅛" thickness. Cut with lightly floured cookie cutters, or score into squares, triangles, or whatever with a thin sharp knife. Transfer carefully to ungreased cookie sheets, prick the tops a few times with a fork, and bake in the upper third of a 400°F oven for 10–12 minutes, until the crackers are light golden brown. After a minute or so, gently loosen the crackers with a thin spatula, but don't try to move them until they've completely cooled; they are quite fragile when hot. This recipe will yield approximately 3 dozen crackers, depending on shape and size.

Herbed Cheese Shortbread Crackers

Shortbread doesn't have to be sweet. These easy-to-make shortbread crackers are a perfect example of savory shortbread, just right for enjoying with other appetizers, or all by themselves. Try them as an accompaniment to a bowl of hot soup for a tasty winter treat. The herbs in this recipe are all dried; substituting fresh may alter the shortbreads' flavor and texture.

1 c. flour
½ c. shredded sharp cheddar cheese
½ c. butter
1 t. parsley flakes
1 t. snipped chives
½ t. salt
½ t. paprika
½ t. rosemary
¼ t. thyme
¼ t. dry mustard
¼ t. cracked black pepper

Stir together the flour and seasonings to blend well. Mix in the shredded cheese. Using an electric mixer beat in the softened butter until the mixture is almost ready to hold together and the butter is completely integrated. Form into a 6" cylinder and refrigerate, wrapped in waxed paper or foil, for at least ½ hour to firm everything up. Cut as close to ⅛" slices as you can; mine vary somewhat. Place on an ungreased cookie sheet and bake in the upper third of a 400°F oven for 8–10 minutes, until the crackers are lightly browned around the edges. This is a bit of a balancing act; you don't want your crackers to burn due to the high butter content, but you also need to bake them enough to thoroughly melt in the butter and cheese or they'll crumble to bits before your very eyes. After a minute or two out of the oven, gently loosen them with a thin spatula, but allow the shortbreads to continue to cool on the baking sheet until they've reached room temperature. Carefully remove them to an area where they won't be jostled around; store tightly covered. This makes about 2½–3 dozen crackers.

Christmas-Morn Chocolate French Toast

My mother made an excellent chocolate bread pudding, which was one of my favorite desserts all the years I was growing up. This assembled-ahead French toast boasts the decadence of chocolate custard base, yet is not overly rich. Serve it topped with fresh fruit, honey chocolate sauce, and vanilla yogurt if you're feeling healthy, or whipped cream for an extra bit of indulgence.

4 slices thick-cut rustic-style bread
2 T. soft butter
1 c. milk
2 T. dark cocoa powder
¼ c. sugar
2 eggs
¼ t. Fiori di Sicilia
or 1 t. each vanilla and grated orange zest
2 T. sugar
2 T. finely chopped almonds
Strawberries, hulled and washed
Bananas, peeled
Kiwi fruit, peeled
Honey chocolate sauce
Vanilla yogurt *or* whipped cream

Butter one side only of the bread, using about ½ the butter. Smear the rest of the butter generously

Christmas-morn chocolate French toast tastes even better with fresh fruit, chocolate honey sauce, and vanilla yogurt or fresh-whipped cream.

© Liz O'Brien

374

in a 9" round cake pan; arrange the bread slices, buttered-side up, in the pan. Beat together the cocoa powder, sugar, flavoring, and eggs until smooth. Carefully stir in the milk and pour the mixture evenly over the bread slices in the pan. Cover the pan and refrigerate at least 2 hours, preferably overnight, until the bread has absorbed all the liquid. Uncover the pan and sprinkle the bread slices evenly with the combined 2 T. of sugar and almonds. Bake in a preheated 375°F oven for ½ hour, until everything puffs up and the tops are nice and crusty. Carefully remove the French toast slices from the pan with a spatula, distributing between 4 serving plates. Top with sliced fruits and drizzle with the honey chocolate sauce. Add a dollop of vanilla yogurt or whipped cream, if you dare! This treats 4 to a resplendent Christmas breakfast.

Honey Chocolate Sauce

Honey adds a nice note to this chocolate sauce, blending well with the flavors of the fruit and French toast. Adding a second type of sugar to any sweet sauce recipe also helps prevent formation of sugar crystals, which can turn the creamiest concoction into a training school for rock candy wannabes in short order. For ease in the morning, this may also be prepared a day (or two) in advance; store tightly covered at room temperature.

2 T. honey
2 T. butter
¼ c. dark cocoa powder
¼ c. sugar
½ c. water *or* coffee

Melt together the honey and butter in a small, heavy saucepan. Stir in the cocoa powder and sugar. Lastly, add in the water or coffee and bring the mixture to a full rolling boil. Boil for 1½ minutes, remove from heat, and cool completely before serving. The sauce will initially appear thin, but will thicken slightly upon standing. This makes about 1 cup of sauce.

Frukt Soppa (Fruit Soup)

This was traditional Christmas fare when I was growing up. I guess it's a perfect example of multi-generational ethnic cooking. Do modern-day Swedes enjoy this stew of dried fruits as much as my grandmother did a hundred years ago? It's hard to say, although I'll hazard the guess that it's fully as popular as is fruit cake here in the United States. Even a little dried fruit goes a long way, so this recipe may well last you for a while. December was the one time of year my mother made fruit soup, and she savored every bit of it, no matter how long it took to finally disappear. She added a splash of vinegar for tartness, although I prefer lemon juice. She also flavored and colored it with raspberry syrup, which she referred to as "hallon sås," although this more accurately translates as raspberry sauce. I simply use frozen red raspberries and a few blueberries as well, thereby eliminating any possible transcultural grammatical gaffs.

1 c. dried apples
1 c. dried prunes
1 c. dried apricots
½ c. raisins
½ c. dried cranberries
4 c. water or more as needed
½ c. sugar
4 sticks of cinnamon, about 3" each
2 c. red raspberries
1 c. blueberries
1 T. lemon juice
1 T. quick-cooking tapioca

Place the apples and apricots in a large, heavy saucepan with enough water to cover them. Add the cinnamon sticks, bring to a boil, and simmer for about ½ hour. Add in the prunes, raisins, dried cranberries, tapioca, and additional water if needed to adequately cover all the fruits. Simmer for about 15 minutes longer. Prunes are much softer and more palatable than in days gone by, so they won't need very long at all to stew. Meanwhile, puree and strain the raspberries for a smoother product, although you may just add them whole if you prefer. Add the raspberry puree, blueberries, and sugar to the mixture and simmer an additional 15 minutes. Your fruit soup is now ready to be enjoyed warm or chilled; just don't eat the cinnamon sticks! It's especially tasty topped with cream and accompanied by cardamom bread or Christmas cookies.

Christmas Star Jellied Salad

I love this salad for a Christmas Eve or Day dinner. It's delicious with either ham or turkey. Although I mold it in one large or six individual star shapes, you can use a ring mold or even little custard cups for individual jells. Try to find some star fruit (carambola) for garnish, especially if you don't have a star-shaped mold.

2 pkg. unflavored gelatin powder
2½ c. orange juice
¼ c. lemon juice
¾ c. sugar
¼ t. salt
¾ c. cold water
Assorted fresh fruits for garnish
Mint leaves for garnish, optional

Soften the gelatin in the cold water for about 5 minutes. Transfer to a small pan and heat, stirring gently, until the gelatin is totally dissolved. Combine the orange juice, lemon juice, salt, and sugar in a large bowl and add the gelatin mixture,

Christmas star jellied salad derives its bright flavors and natural golden color from lemon and orange juices.

stirring well until the sugar in entirely dissolved and the gelatin fully integrated. Pour into a quart mold or 6 individual molds that have been set on a cookie sheet for stability. For easier unmolding, you may wish to spray the insides of the molds with nonstick cooking spray or to oil them lightly before filling. Refrigerate until set, at least two hours or overnight. When ready to serve, dip each mold briefly in hot water, running a thin spatula around the edges if necessary to loosen, place your serving plate on top of the mold and flip the entire thing over. The jellied salad should unmold directly onto the plate. Top or garnish with assorted fresh Christmas fruits, such as sliced kiwis, strawberries, pomegranate seeds, and of course, star fruit slices! It will serve 6.

Citrus Poinsettia Salad

When I was growing up, my mother used to buy cans of citrus sections. Oranges and grape-fruit swimming in sugar syrup were combined to make a simple fruit salad. She'd dress them up with French dressing and serve them as a side dish for supper. Here's a little novel something to serve up for Christmas cheer, based on those long-ago salads but updated with fresh citrus sections. It has the added benefit of being fairly light and healthy, helping to off set all those other little indulgences we so enjoy sampling during the holiday season.

2 pink or red grapefruits
2 large oranges, blood oranges if you can find them
1 pomegranate
Leaf lettuce *or* fresh spinach

Cream Dressing

2 T. reserved juices (add a little pomegranate for nice color)
1 T. sugar
¼ c. mayonnaise
2 T. cream

Oil Dressing

3 T. reserved juices

¼ t. salt
Dash fresh-ground black pepper
1 T. honey
¼ c. olive oil

Peel the whole grapefruits and/or oranges. Carefully remove the individual sections of fruit from the surrounding membranes, saving juice that drips out in a bowl or other receptacle. Peel and gently remove the seeds from the pome-granate, again holding it over a bowl to catch any juice that drips out during the process. Place the spinach or lettuce leaves on a serving platter. Carefully arrange the citrus sections to resemble poinsettia blooms (which as we know are really only brilliantly colored leaves). Sprinkle the pome-granate seeds into the center of each poinsettia. Prepare dressing of choice by whisking all the ingredients together until the mixture is smooth and creamy. Serve the dressing on the side to pour over your citrus poinsettias. This serves 6 people as a salad course or as an accompaniment to a holiday buffet.

Spiced Fruit Sauce

My brother and sister-in-law, Marshall and Veronica Wheelock, frequently serve a sweet and piquant raisin sauce with ham. This version carries the concept just a bit further, including the brightness of peaches, pineapple, and maraschino cherries for color and taste.

1 small can sliced pineapple in juice
15 oz. can of diced peaches
¼ c. raisins
6 T. halved maraschino cherries
1 T. vinegar
½ t. ground cloves
½ c. packed brown sugar
1 T. cornstarch
¼ t. salt
Water if necessary

Drain the pineapple and peaches, measuring the combined juices and adding water if needed to equal 2 cups. Dice the pineapple into tidbit-seized pieces. Once upon a time, I could find pineapple tidbits in the store, but no more, and the chunks that have replaced them are too coarse for this sauce. Combine the juice, pineapple, 1 c. of drained and diced peaches (if there are extra, save to use another day), and cornstarch in a medium-sized saucepan, stirring until the cornstarch is smoothly absorbed. Add the rest of the ingredients and bring just to a full boil. Remove from the heat and allow it to cool to room temperature before serving. It may also be made a day in advance and chilled in the fridge overnight. This makes a generous amount of sauce, which is all right because you also have a generous amount of ham with which to enjoy it.

Spiced fruit sauce is the perfect accompaniment to Christmas ham.

Christmas Ham

Christmas Eve just wouldn't be complete without glazed ham. My Aunt Edith and Uncle Russell Hertzberg hosted a family get-together each December 24. The trip to their home on Williams Street, and later to their little house surrounded by pine trees in the hills of Marlboro, was an annual event until I was in my midthirties with children of my own. Baked glazed ham was the traditional star of Aunt Edith's Christmas Eve smorgasbord. Studded with cloves and replete with sweet yellow pineapple slices and bright red maraschino cherries, it made a splendid centerpiece. No matter what on the menu might change, we could always count on glazed ham, limpa (Swedish sweet rye bread), and fruit soup with Christmas cookies. If you are able to find a spiral cut ham, it will make carving all the easier. Whether purchased or home-cured, your ham will be sweet and delicious with a spicy brown sugar glaze. An added bonus is the ease of preparation; you can bake this a bit ahead of time and then set it aside to look splendid while finishing up preparation of the rest of the meal. Be sure to refrigerate leftovers promptly, though. Even if cured, ham is still a meat and as such is highly perishable.

1 precooked bone in ham (7–8 lb.)
1 c. packed brown sugar
2 T. prepared mustard
¾ t. ground cloves
Whole cloves for studding, if desired
1 can pineapple rings in juice
Maraschino cherries
Spiced fruit sauce, if desired
Cornstarch for thickening gravy, if desired

Score the ham into 1" diamonds, inserting a whole clove into each, if desired. Combine the brown sugar, powdered cloves, mustard, and 2–3 T. pineapple juice and set aside. Bake the ham in a preheated 350°F oven for approximately 20 minutes per pound to heat through thoroughly. An hour into the baking process, spread about ¾ of the glaze over the surface, coating it evenly. Adding a cup or two of water to the base of the pan will help prevent burning and provide a nice base for gravy, should you desire. Bake for another hour. Remove long enough to fasten the pineapple rings and cherries evenly over the surface with toothpicks; traditionally, one cherry will fit in the center of each pineapple ring. Gently coat with the remaining glaze and return to the oven for another half hour or so, basting occasionally, to complete the glazing process. Carefully remove to a serving platter and allow the ham the hang out for a few minutes for best results when carving. Stir 1 T. of cornstarch into a cup of cold water and whisk into the pan juices, adjusting amounts of liquid dependent on whether the mixture cooked down a bit in the oven.

Christmas ham, potatoes au gratin, and jellied Christmas star salads share the Christmas Eve table.

Karelian Ragout

The Independent Republic of Karelia, located between Finland and Russia, has a long and intertwined history with both Sweden and Finland. There has been plenty of time over the centuries for the cultures of Scandinavia and of Russia to have intermingled in this little corner of the world. The flavors tasted in Karelian ragout are typical northern European—simple and hearty with just a bit of spice. Stewing meat works fine, although more tender cuts may be used if you wish. Replace some of the beef and pork with a bit of lamb if you feel so inclined; it's also frequently featured in northern European cuisine.

1 lb. beef, cut into 1" pieces
1 lb. pork, cut into 1" pieces
2 T. oil
1 lg. onion, peeled and chopped
2 t. salt
½ t. pepper
1 t. ground allspice
2 T. flour
Approximately 3 c. water

Brown the pieces of meat in a little hot oil in a large, heavy pan or skillet with a cover. Add the onion and continue to brown. Add the salt, pepper, and allspice, plus water to cover. Bring to a boil, reduce the heat slightly, and cook gently for about an hour. Combine 2 T. flour with a little cold water and stir into the cooked meat mixture to thicken. Serve over mashed potatoes or hot-buttered noodles with lingonberry or cranberry sauce on the side. This serves 6–8.

Beef Rib Roast

Perhaps you'd prefer to live it up with a beef rib roast instead of ham for your holiday table; Christmas is a special time! My paternal grandfather came from old New England stock—with probable origins in Northern England and Wales, back in "the day." Beef rib roast is another one of those special occasion dishes we might have once a year if we've been very, very good. Add roasted potatoes and Yorkshire pudding for a taste of jolly old England.

4–5 lb. rib roast
Coarse cracked black pepper
Coarse sea salt
Dry mustard powder, optional
Olive oil

Preheat the oven to 475°F. Place the beef, rib-side down, in a heavy metal baking dish. Don't use glass, which might crack due to the high oven temperatures you'll be using to roast the beef. Lightly rub any nonfatty surfaces of the meat with olive oil. Sprinkle generously with salt and pepper. The salt will draw moisture out of the fat and make it even crispier, although you might want to be more sparing with it over areas where the meat is showing through. Pat on just a bit of dry mustard powder, if you wish; remember it has a pronounced flavor. Roast for 15 minutes and then reduce the oven to 350°F. Continue to roast the beef for 15–20 minutes per pound for a medium rare roast. If you prefer your beef better done, roast for about 25 minutes per pound. These times allow for some cooking to continue taking place once the beef has been removed from the oven. If you don't like really rare beef, you may wish to adjust the time up a little. Just remember, it's easier to remedy an undercooked roast than an overcooked one. Again, an instant-read meat thermometer is an excellent investment, which will take a lot of the guesswork out of it. Once it is cooked to your liking, remove the beef to a warm serving platter and allow it to rest for about 15–30 minutes before serving. This allows the juices to be drawn back into the beef before it is carved. Meanwhile, you have time to set out all your side dishes and bake the Yorkshire pudding. This amount of beef should serve 8–10.

Yorkshire Pudding

Yorkshire pudding is concocted of eggs, milk, and flour and is a traditional accompaniment to roast beef. Although similar in make up to a popover, it's generally baked in one pan rather than individual muffin cups. Using beef fat in place of butter gives the pudding its special flavor.

¾ c. flour
½ t. salt
½ t. dry mustard
2 eggs
1 c. milk
¼ c. cold water
2–3 T. hot beef fat

Optional for an Herbed Pudding (Uses Dried Herbs)

¼ t. cracked pepper
¼ t. tarragon
½ t. rosemary
1 t. parsley flakes
1 t. chives

Once the beef is done roasting, remove it from the pan to rest. Drain off 2–3 T. of the hot fat, placing it in an 8" × 12" or 9" × 9" baking pan. Increase the oven temperature to 425°F. Put the pan in the oven and allow it to heat for about 5 minutes, while you prepare the pudding batter. Combine the dry ingredients with the milk and eggs in a blender container or small deep bowl. Either blend or whisk them smooth. Lastly, add in the water and the herbs, if using, again mixing smooth. Pour the batter into the sizzling hot fat and bake on an upper oven rack for about 30 minutes, or until it is puffed and browned. Cut the Yorkshire pudding in squares and serve it hot from the pan.

*When properly baked,
Yorkshire pudding rises
to the occasion—a fitting
accompaniment to beef
rib roast.*

Roasted Potatoes

These are especially good with roast beef. My preferred potato for roasting in this manner is a red-skinned variety. The thin skin adds texture and color appeal and the flesh is a nice, mealy consistency. Scrub your skins well, leaving potatoes whole if small or cutting into halves or quarters. Mixing and matching is fine, as long as you're consistent about size so that they all cook in approximately the same amount of time.

1 lb. prepared red-skinned potatoes
2 T. olive oil
2 T. butter
¼ t. cracked black pepper
½ t. crumbled rosemary

Melt the butter in a 9" × 9" baking pan. Stir in the olive oil, pepper, and rosemary. Add the potatoes, stirring to coat them all evenly. Place in a 375°F oven for approximately 45 minutes, stirring and turning them once or twice. You will notice this recipe does not contain salt; I prefer to add it at the table, as the potatoes will crisp better without it.

Potatoes Au Gratin

There are probably as many ways to prepare potatoes au gratin as there are types of potatoes and cheese with which to prepare it. In the variation here, we're emphasizing Continental flavors such as thyme and garlic, along with the mellowness of Swiss-type cheese. Simmering the raw potato slices a few minutes in the infused milk draws out their natural starches to provide creaminess without added flour. Utilizing a mandolin, food grater, or food processor will enable you to produce the extremely thin slices you'll need for this recipe. Layering cheese and potatoes with the cheese on top will result in a nice-browned crust to top things off.

Peeled russet potatoes, sliced paper-thin, to equal 4 c.
   ¼ c. butter
   2 c. milk
   1 clove garlic, peeled and halved
   ¼ t. dried thyme
   ¼ t. nutmeg
   ⅛ t. white pepper
   2 c. shredded Jarlsburg *or* Swiss cheese

Melt the butter in a large saucepan over medium heat. Add the milk, garlic, salt, nutmeg, thyme, and white pepper and heat to just under boiling. Add the thinly sliced potatoes, stir to blend, and heat to just boiling. Reduce heat and allow the potatoes to simmer for about 5 minutes. They should turn the milk into a nice creamy consistency but still be a bit crisp. Butter a 6-cup casserole and spread half the potatoes evenly over the bottom. Sprinkle with half the shredded cheese and repeat layers. Place in a preheated 350°F oven for approximately 45 minutes, until the potatoes are fork tender and the top browns nicely. Allow to cool about 5–10 minutes before serving. This will serve 8.

Rich with cheese and butter, potatoes au gratin will enhance a variety of winter meals.

Green Beans Amandine

Green beans make a festive accompaniment to your holiday meals when gussied up with butter-toasted almonds. Hints of lemon, onion, and tarragon enhance the flavor. This dish is at its best when served promptly so that the beans retain their bright green color and the almonds their crunch.

3 c. (12 oz.) fresh-trimmed or frozen green beans
2 T. butter
¼ c. sliced almonds
2 t. lemon juice
¼ t. tarragon
¼ t. onion powder
½ t. salt

Cook or steam the beans until they are just tender, about 10 minutes, or prepare according to directions if using frozen. In a medium saucepan, melt the butter until it is foamy. Add the almonds and cook for a minute or two over medium heat to lightly brown them. Stir in the salt, onion powder, lemon juice, and tarragon just to blend and add the green beans. Mix well to cover the beans evenly and serve to 4–6.

Broccoli with Cheese Sauce

Broccoli with cheese sauce is great for a festive holiday meal where you'd like a spot of color. It's a hearty vegetable dish and can easily be a main course for those wishing vegetarian fare. If you have folks who think they don't like broccoli, try turning it into broccoli with cheese sauce. This recipe may also be made quite respectably with frozen broccoli, so feel free to defrost some of your summer's bounty and enjoy!

1 lg. head broccoli, trimmed and cut in small pieces: approximately 4 c.
¼ c. butter
¼ c. flour
2 c. milk
¼ t. grated nutmeg
¼ t. Tabasco sauce
½ t. each salt and pepper
½ t. dry mustard
2 c. shredded sharp cheddar cheese
¼ c. butter
¾ sleeve saltine crackers
Paprika for topping

Cook the broccoli in boiling water until just tender but still bright green, about 5 minutes. If using frozen, cook just to heat through. Drain well while preparing the cheese sauce and topping. Melt ¼ cup of the butter in a small saucepan; stir in the crushed saltines. Remove from the heat and set aside. In a medium saucepan, melt the remaining butter over medium heat. Stir in the flour and seasonings and cook for a minute, stirring. Add the milk all at once, whisking until smooth. Increase the heat and bring to a boil, stirring to prevent sticking. Add the shredded cheese, stirring until it's just melted. Immediately remove from the heat. Place the hot broccoli in a buttered 2 qt. casserole dish. Pour the cheese sauce evenly over the top and sprinkle generously with the buttered saltine crumbs. Sprinkle with a little paprika and bake in a 350–375°F oven until bubbly and browned, about ½ hour. I've included a couple of baking temperatures in case you're baking something a bit more temperature-sensitive than broccoli and cheese sauce; it will obligingly go along with whichever one your other dish prefers. This serves around 8.

Rotmos

This is another one of those oblique dishes from my childhood that I thought everyone knew about until I started attending school. It turned out there were precious few rotmos fans at the Academy School in West Brattleboro. Rotmos is simply a combination of potatoes and rutabaga that have been cooked and mashed together with a little seasoning. Some recipes call for the addition of beef broth to give it some more strost, although I find milk and butter do just fine all by themselves.

2 c. diced, peeled rutabagas
2 c. peeled, chopped potatoes
1 t. salt and additional for seasoning
½ c. milk
¼ c. butter
Pepper, to taste

Place the rutabagas, potatoes, teaspoon of salt, and water just to cover in a medium saucepan. Cover and bring to a boil. Reduce heat and boil gently, covered, until the vegetables are tender. Drain well and add the butter and milk. Mash until smooth, adding more milk if necessary, and seasoning to taste with salt and pepper. *Rotmos* is especially good with ham, pork, or rabbit.

Cardamom Bread

For years our little church, Trinity Lutheran, held a Christmas fair and bake sale the second week in December, with cardamom bread in an annual starring role. When I was growing up, we bought whole cardamom pods, which we pulled apart in order to release the seeds from their tissue-like dividers. We then banged the waxed paper–encased seeds into a state of semisubmission with a rolling pin. I'm now able to buy the seeds minus the pods at our local food co-op, storing them in my refrigerator and grinding with a mortar and pestle when I'm ready to bake. Although powdered cardamom is also available, it doesn't have the fragrance and flavor of fresh. Some folks like to top their cardamom bread with cinnamon sugar, but I am not one of those people. Either a dusting of pearl sugar or a post-baking blanket of butter almond icing provides what I consider to be a more fitting complement to the cardamom's exotic sweetness. This recipe will yield 4 large braids or 2 dozen coiled and twisted pastries.

1 c. butter
1 c. sugar
1 T. ground cardamom
1 t. salt
2 c. milk
2 T. active dry yeast
2 eggs, at room temperature, beaten slightly
7–7½ c. bread flour, plus more for dusting

Butter Almond Icing

¼ c. milk
¼ c. butter
½ t. pure almond flavoring
4 c. sifted confectioner's sugar

Heat together the milk, sugar, butter, and cardamom until the butter melts. Remove this from the heat and allow it to cool until lukewarm, 120–130°F. You can determine this by dribbling a drop on the inside of your wrist; it should feel comfortably warm but not hot. Stir in the eggs and then sprinkle the yeast over the top, stirring it in as well. Yeast is a finicky little creature; it requires some warmth to raise your dough properly, but must not be overheated or it will die and be of no use at all. Stir in 2 cups of the flour, which will produce a yeasty batter called a "sponge." Allow the sponge to "work" for 5–10 minutes, which it will do by producing bubbles and beginning to expand. Stir in 4 more cups of flour, which should produce a stiff batter. Knead in additional flour to produce dough, which is no longer sticky but which is fairly soft and elastic. Use a light touch; too much flour produces a heavy, dry loaf of bread. I like to use an extra-large mixing bowl

Coiled and braided cardamom bread wreathes, whether plain or with added fruits and nuts, make festive holiday fare.

for the entire procedure, which makes the next step all the easier. Your bread dough now needs to rest and rise for about an hour. I simply place the bowl, covered with a warm, damp dish towel, into my oven, adding a bowl of hot water to raise the humidity and temperature if need be. Once the dough has doubled in size, you get to punch it down, which means doing exactly what it says, with your fist—a great tension release. Depending on your shapes of choice, either section it off into 4 or 24 even portions. For braids, divide each half into 3 equal portions, rolling them into long, thin strips of dough. Braid together the three strips neatly, tucking under the ends once they've been placed crosswise on one end of a greased 10" × 15" baking sheet. Repeat with the second quarter of the dough, braiding and arranging it on the other end of the sheet. Continue this with the other two sections of dough and a second-greased baking sheet. Alternately, coil the braids and fit them into greased 9" round baking tins. If desired, brush the braids with milk or cream and sprinkle generously with pearl sugar. Put them back in the oven to rise again, about ¾ hour this time. Bake on the upper racks of a 375°F oven for 30–40 minutes, until the loaves are light golden and sound hollow when tapped. Carefully remove to cooling racks. If you prefer buns, begin with 24 small pieces of dough. Divide each individual piece into two equal sections. Roll each between your hands into a long, thin strip about 8–10" long. Twist the two halves together and coil into a circle on a greased baking sheet. I would use 3 baking sheets for this number of pastries, two to a row, staggering them slightly so that they don't touch as they expand and bake. If you wish, brush the tops with milk or cream and sprinkle generously with pearl sugar. These will probably only take ½ hour to rise sufficiently. Bake them on the upper racks of a 375°F oven for around 15 minutes, until they're lightly browned and sound hollow when tapped. Carefully remove to racks to cool. If you're icing the braids or buns, frost with butter almond icing and sprinkle with toasted, slivered almonds while still warm. Heat the butter and milk in a medium saucepan until the butter melts. Stir in the almond flavoring and the confectioner's sugar. The icing will have a fairly runny consistency when warm, but quickly hardens when cool, so work quickly to frost your cardamom braids and pastries. Gently reheating the mixture will again soften it, but don't overdo the heating or it may solidify.

Fruited Cardamom Bread

Who needs fruitcake when you can produce a delicious fruited cardamom ring? The amounts of fruit and nuts given here are enough for a half batch of the above recipe, producing two 9" rings or one very large one.

½ c. diced candied red cherries
½ c. snipped dried apricots
½ c. diced candied pineapple
2 T. candied orange rind
2 T. candied lemon rind
¼ c. chopped almonds
¼ c. chopped pistachios
2T. flour

Toss all the fruits and nuts together with the flour to coat evenly. Knead into one-half recipe of the cardamom dough. Although you may braid this if you wish, I prefer to make two large coils. Simply divide each half in two and form each portion into a long thin strip. Coil them together as you would for buns, placing each into a buttered 9" round baking tin. Allow to double in bulk, about ¾ hour rising time, and bake in a preheated 375°F oven for about 40 minutes, until evenly browned and hollow sounding when tapped. Allow to cool about 5 minutes in the pans and turn out on wire racks to finish cooling. Spread with almond butter icing and decorate as desired with cherries, pineapple, apricots, nuts, and/or colored sugar.

Limpa

Limpa is Swedish sweet rye bread flavored with orange rind and anise seed. It's not sweet enough to consider as dessert bread, but makes an excellent accompaniment to a ham dinner or as breakfast bread, by itself or with complementary foods. My mother ate it for Christmas morning breakfast along with her Swedish fruit soup. The amounts given will produce one round, fluffy loaf. If I have more folks around to eat it, I bake 2 at a time; again, this is an easy recipe to double.

1 c. water
1 t. grated orange rind
¼ c. packed brown sugar
2 T. butter
½ t. anise seeds
½ t. salt
1 T. active dry yeast
1¼ c. rye flour
1¾ c. bread flour (approximate)

Heat the water to just under boiling. Stir in the orange rind, anise, salt, brown sugar, and butter. Remove from the heat and allow it to cool to lukewarm (about 120–130°F). Sprinkle the yeast over the top and stir until incorporated. Allow the yeast to work for about 5 minutes and stir in the rye flour. Next stir in about a cup of the bread flour. Add more bread flour a little at a time, kneading in only what is needed to form an elastic dough. Allow the dough to rise in a damp, warm place for about ½ hour. Punch it down and shape into a round, flat patty of dough about 2" thick and 6–8" in diameter. Place in a greased 9" round cake pan and allow it to rise again for another ½ hour. Bake at 350°F on a middle or upper rack until the surface is nicely browned and the loaf sounds hollow when tapped with a knuckle. Quickly rub the end of a stick of butter over the hot top to give a nice shiny glaze. Remove from pan and cool on a wire rack. Once it is thoroughly cooled, bag airtight.

Around our house, it wouldn't be Christmas without limpa.

Rice Pudding

Early December twilights are fine times to have a dish of rice pudding cooking gently in the oven or on back of the woodstove. In my memories, the scents of sweet milk and nutmeg wafting from the oven juxtapose with glimpses of a cool December sun setting by three-thirty in the afternoon. However, many of us no longer have time for lengthy interactions with an oven or stove. Do not despair; you can still have your rice pudding and eat it too! I'm offering a couple of variations, each comforting and delicious in its own way. For sweet dishes such as this, jasmine rice would be my choice. And if you've never invested in a small grater and a few whole nutmegs, now would be a great time to give them a try; the improvement in flavor is amazing.

Classic Rice Pudding

This one takes a while to bake and is the more "old-timey," similar to the rice puddings of my childhood. My mom would pop it on the oven about the time the school bus dropped me off in front of our house. It would sit in the oven baking all the time I was out and about caring for the goats and, during high school, my horse. Of course, by the time I was in high school, I was the one popping the rice pudding in the oven too! It's comfort food, for sure.

4 c. whole milk
½ c. sugar
½ c. uncooked white rice
2 T. butter
¾ t. grated nutmeg
½ c. raisins

You should plan on about 2 hours to complete the cooking of this pudding. Combine 2 cups of the milk, the sugar, rice, and butter in a buttered casserole dish that can hold 6 cups. Place in a 325°F oven, stirring the mixture approximately every 20 minutes. As the milk is absorbed, you should add the remaining 2 cups, about ½ cup at a time. When adding the last of the milk (approximately ½ hour before completion), stir in the raisins and sprinkle the nutmeg over the top. Serve warm or chilled.

Quick and Easy Rice Pudding

Although quick and easy, this is still not an "instant" recipe. However, in the great scheme of things, 45 minutes really isn't all that long a time. The three quarters of an hour the pudding is cooking can easily be spent preparing the rest of your meal, or even ordering some takeout, if you prefer!

2 c. precooked rice
2 c. milk
1/3 c. cream
1/3 c. sugar
½ t. nutmeg
½ t. cinnamon
¼–½ c. raisins *and/or* dried cranberries

This is a handy way to use up leftover cooked rice, or simply cook up a batch for this recipe. Combine the rice, milk, sugar, and nutmeg or cinnamon in a buttered 1 quart casserole or ovenproof bowl. Place in a 350°F oven for approximately 45 minutes, stirring one or twice, until the milk is mostly absorbed. Alternatively, cook in a heavy saucepan stove top over low heat about ½ hour, again stirring a couple of times. Remove from the oven or heat and stir in the cream and dried fruits. Serve warm or chilled.

Crimson Christmas Pudding

There's nothing better than having a freezer full of delicious ripe berries, picked and quick frozen at the peak of their ripeness the summer before. And there's no better way to utilize them than in this smooth ruby red fruit dessert. Serve it topped with whipped cream or by itself, as you prefer. And don't feel that you should only prepare this for Christmas! It's wonderful any time of the year. I prefer a ratio of two to three parts raspberries to any one or two other red fruits, such as currants, strawberries, cranberries, lingonberries, and/or tart cherries. I suppose blueberries or blackberries could be thrown in as well, although then it wouldn't be quite so crimson, would it?

3 c. red raspberries, fresh or frozen (no added sugar)
1 c. red currants or other desired red fruit, again fresh or frozen
1 c. water
1 c. sugar
¼ c. cornstarch
2 T. Chambord or other berry/cherry liquor, if desired

Combine berries and water in a large saucepan. Heat until the fruit is thawed, or until the fresh berries start to lose their juices. Don't allow the mixture to heat too much, as you'll now be pouring it into the blender and blending until smooth. Pour the resulting liquid through a fine mesh wire sieve back into the pan, working the remaining pulp to get as much through as possible while straining out most of the seeds. Stir together the sugar and cornstarch until smooth and add to the pureed berries, whisking to remove any possible lumps. Bring to a boil over medium-high heat, stirring to prevent sticking. Once it has come to a full boil, remove from the heat and stir in the Chambord or other liquor if you chose to use it. Allow the pudding to cool somewhat before pouring into your desired serving dish. Allow to cool thoroughly before serving. This is also tasty when accompanied by crisp butter cookies or gingersnaps. This amount will serve about 6–8 generously as a dessert. It's good for breakfast too.

Baked Apples

As is the case with most fruits and vegetables, some kinds of apples are better suited to baking than others. It's important to pick those apples for the following recipes. Try varieties such as Rome beauty, northern spy, or yellow delicious (but not red delicious, which are specifically grown to eat fresh and are not suitable for cooking). In either case, begin by cutting a thin horizontal slice from the top and then coring the apple about ¾ of the way down. If you don't leave a little base of apple in the center, your fillings will leak out the bottom, leaving you with an empty apple and a sticky mess in the baking dish.

Almond Baked Apples (with Swedish Vanilla Custard Cream and Red Raspberry Sauce)

Once upon a time, I used to pulverize together almonds and sugar to make this recipe. I've since found the almond paste to work every bit as well, and take much less time and effort to boot. It can be found in the baking section of most large supermarkets.

4 large firm baking apples
7 oz. tube of almond paste
2 T. butter
1 t. grated lemon rind
1 egg white
¼ c. sliced almonds
Swedish vanilla custard cream
Red raspberry sauce

Crumble the almond paste into a small deep mixing bowl. Beat in the lemon rind and butter until the mixture is smooth. Lastly, beat in the egg white. Divide the filling evenly between the prepared apples, smoothing a bit over the top cut surface. Sprinkle evenly with the almonds. Place them in a baking pan and add about an inch of water to the bottom. Bake at 375°F for 30–35 minutes, until the apples are just tender. Remove from the oven and allow them to cool slightly before serving.

Almond baked apples, shown here adorned with Swedish vanilla custard cream and red raspberry sauce, are as delicious as they are beautiful.

393

Swedish Vanilla Custard Cream

This rich custard cream is delicious poured over a variety of fruits. Try it over bread pudding or fruit-flavored gelatin, as well.

¾ c. milk
¾ c. cream
⅓ c. sugar
2 egg yolks
1 t. vanilla

Place the milk and cream in a medium, heavy saucepan and heat them to just under boiling. Meanwhile, beat the egg yolks and sugar together. Add a little of the hot liquid to this mixture and then return everything to the pan, whisking constantly. Stir and cook over medium heat to just under boiling; the custard will have thickened slightly but not have curdled. Immediately remove from the heat and stir in the vanilla. Chill quickly by placing the pan into a large bowl of cold water. Once it has cooled to room temperature, pour into a small bowl and refrigerate until you're ready to use it.

Red Raspberry Sauce

2 c. red raspberries, fresh or frozen
½ c. water
1 t. cornstarch
¼ c. sugar
1 T. raspberry liquor, optional

Combine the raspberries and water in a small saucepan and heat them to just under boiling, crushing them with the back of a spoon to help release their juices. Pour into a blender and puree until smooth. Pour the raspberry juice back into the pan through a wire mesh strainer to remove most of the seeds. Stir in the combined sugar and cornstarch. Bring the mixture to a full boil. Remove from the heat and stir in the liquor, such as framboise or Chambord, if you wish. Cool the sauce to room temperature and then chill it until serving time.

To assemble the baked apples, place one into each of four dessert dishes. Carefully pour the custard cream around each. Drizzle with the raspberry sauce. For a decorative presentation, carefully drip teaspoonfuls of the raspberry sauce in small circles onto the custard ringing the apple. Draw a thin, sharp knife around in a single circle, cutting each raspberry sauce circle in half to form a wreath of hearts or leaves.

Pepparkakor (Crispy Ginger Cookies)

These thin crispy Swedish spice cookies are very similar to what you may have seen sold in decorative Carl Larsson tins around

Christmas Cookie Tree

Have you ever tried decorating a Christmas cookie tree? It's especially fun if kids are involved and a great way to showcase your cookie finery. We have a little Norfolk Island pine growing in a corner of our dining room. Actually, it's not so little anymore, so come Christmastime, it makes a dandy Christmas cookie tree. Although we drape a string of mini colored lights on the tree, their use is optional. Either of the rolled cookie recipes below work well for this purpose; poke a hanging hole with a straw or skewer in each cut cookie before baking. The *pepparkakor* cookies roll out into fine little gingerbread folk, just right for hanging out on branches. Spritz cookie wreathes or S-shapes also work well. Rosettes are beautiful but fragile, especially if little fingers are involved in the process, so use extra care. I use colored cotton yarn for hanging the cookies, as ribbons might not be colorfast; that way you'll be able to hang your cookies, and eat them too.

Christmastime—except, of course, the home-made ones taste better! Rather than using butter-based icing frosting for decorating purposes, I prefer a royal-type icing coated with a sprinkling of sparkling sugar. This helps maintain the cookies' characteristic crunch—not to mention, they already contain more than enough butter to satisfy the richest taste buds.

1 c. butter
¾ c. packed brown sugar
¾ c. granulated sugar
⅔ c. water
4 c. flour
1 T. cinnamon
1 T. ginger
1 t. cardamom
1½ t. cloves
1½ t. baking soda

Royal Icing

2 t. dried egg white*
2 c. confectioner's sugar

2–4 T. water
¼ t. almond or vanilla extract

Bring the water and sugars to a boil; remove from heat and stir in the butter until it has melted. Add the dry ingredients to the sugar mixture, stirring well with a wooden spoon. The dough will be soft; chill it, covered, until firm. Roll thin (⅛") on a lightly floured board. Bake on the upper racks at 350°F for 5–10 minutes, until lightly browned (they will burn easily). For the icing, combine the sugar and egg white in a small bowl. Drizzle in the water and flavoring, beating to desired consistency. Add more or less water, as needed to either pipe or spread the icing. Decorate as desired. This recipe makes a bunch, dependent on the size and shapes of the cookies. They keep very well, especially if not iced in advance.

* Although some royal icing recipes call for raw egg white, I don't recommend this due to the risk of salmonella. Powdered egg whites are generally available in the baking section of many supermarkets.

Hjortronbröd (Swedish Sugar Cookies)

This recipe was passed down from Grand-mother to Mother. I never thought too much about the name until I attempted to translate it. "Hjortron" in Swedish refers to cloudberries, a golden berry that grows only in the far north, while "bröd" is more a term for "bread" than a "cookie." Perhaps Hjortronbröd cookies are a preferred accompaniment to cloudberries? Ah, well. These light, not-too-sweet sugar cookies are brushed with egg white and sprinkled with plain or colored sugar before baking. Add a few diced nuts to the topping if you like. They're perfect to include on your Christmas cookie tree should you decide to have one; simply use a straw or skewer to poke a hole in each before baking. After they've cooled, add extra touches of colored icing, or forego the sugar sprinkles and frost them with a simple butter cream. And don't even worry about trying to pronounce "Hjortronbröd;" "Swedish sugar cookies" works just fine.

1 c. butter
1 c. sugar
2 eggs, one separated
3 T. cream
3 c. flour
3 t. baking powder
1 t. almond extract

Cream the butter and sugar until creamy. Beat in the cream, 1 egg and 1 egg yolk, and the almond extract until the mixture is light and fluffy. Stir in the combined flour and baking powder; a wooden spoon would probably work best for this. Chill the dough, covered, for easier handling. Roll thin, cut as desired, and place on ungreased baking sheets. Brush with the remaining egg white which has been slightly beaten with about 1 T. of water. Sprinkle the cookies with desired sugar and chopped nuts. Bake about 10 minutes at 375°F. This recipe makes quite a few cookies, depending on the shapes. They will store well for a couple of weeks, baked, or cut and freeze the unbaked cookies, covered, for up to a month.

Spritz

Spritz cookies are in a category by themselves—a quintessential butter cookie scented with almond. Originally spritz were shaped through a special cookie press called a spritz gun, which unfurls long, narrow ribbons of dough to be shaped into the traditional S-shape or into rings. You can make spritz using a more generic cookie press, but somehow the effect is never quite the same. If you don't possess a spritz gun or a standard cookie press, don't despair! This dough is easily malleable by hand, and some of the variations below lend themselves quite well to this method of shaping.

2 c. soft butter
1½ c. sugar
2 t. almond extract
2 eggs
1 t. baking powder
4 c. flour

Cream the butter, gradually adding the sugar and almond extract. Beat in the eggs until the mixture is light and fluffy. Beat in the flour and baking powder until everything is well combined. This makes a large amount of dough that can then be utilized to churn out lots of classic spritz for bake sales or gifts. It can also be easily divided and used for more than one variation. It's easy to just estimate when you divide the dough, although if you wish to be more exacting it will amount to 1 ⅓ c. dough each if separated into four portions, or 2⅔ c. dough each if halved. The recipes below are gauged for quarter batches of dough.

Spritz cookies are traditionally formed using a cookie press but also may be rolled into balls or formed into a pinwheel to be sliced. They taste equally delicious regardless of shape.

Classic Spritz

Press the dough out into desired shapes, sprinkling with colored sugar and/or sprinkles, if you wish. Bake in the upper third of a 375°F oven for 8–10 minutes, until they are barely brown around the edges. Carefully transfer them to cooling racks. I frequently form and bake plain circles of dough that I transform into "wreathes" by decorating the cooled cookies with a dried cranberry and a sliced almond tinted green, each affixed with a dab of icing.

Pinwheel or Ribbon Cookies

2 T. diced candied cherries
2 T. diced pistachios
2 T. diced almonds
Red and green food coloring

Divide the quartered portion of dough into thirds. To one portion, knead in the diced candied cherries and a few drops of red food coloring. To the second portion, knead in the diced pistachios and a few drops green food coloring. To the third portion, add the diced almonds.* Chill a bit for easier handling, if you wish. Carefully spread one color of dough into a thin panel on a piece of waxed paper; make it a little thicker for ribbon cookies, or thinner for pinwheels. Add a second and then third layer on top of the first, centering them for ribbons, which will be cut in a block, or slightly off center (to the same side each time) for pinwheels, which are rolled up into a cylinder. Carefully square off edges for ribbon cookies, leaving the rolling sides thinner for the pinwheels, roll up if desired, and wrap in waxed paper, plastic wrap or foil. Refrigerate until firm, at least an hour, although you may store the dough for up to a week. Cut into ¼" slices, place on ungreased cookies sheets, and bake in the upper third of a 375°F oven for about 8–10 minutes, until the cookies are barely brown around the edges. Cool for just a minute or two before carefully removing to wire racks to complete the process.

*For variety, try substituting chocolate spritz dough for this portion of the cookie, or add 1 T. of cocoa powder.

Chocolate Spritz

2 T. unsweetened cocoa powder
2 T. sugar
½ t. grated orange zest

Knead the unsweetened cocoa powder, sugar, and orange zest into the quarter portion of dough. Press out into wreathes or S-shapes on ungreased cookies sheets and bake in the upper third of a 375°F oven for about 8 minutes. I like to sprinkle them with green sugar and/or diced pistachios before baking. Chocolate spritz are a bit trickier to test for doneness both because their color camouflages the browning process and the cocoa content combining with the butter and sugar makes these cookies even more prone to burning than most. Just make sure they're done enough, or they may fall apart when you're trying to remove them from the pan.

Sugar Plum Spritz

Green sugar
Candied cherries, halved

Roll portions of dough into balls about ¾" in diameter. Roll each ball in green sugar to coat and place about 2" apart on ungreased baking sheets. Make an indent in each with your thumb or finger and insert ½ of a candied cherry, rounded-side up. Bake at 375°F for about 10 minutes, until the cookies are just lightly browned around the edges.

Rosettes

Of all the Christmas goodies I make, rosettes are far and away the most popular. I don't know how many I've fried over the years, but I'm sure the number is well into the thousands by now. They are not a difficult cookie to make, but are somewhat time consuming. They also require a special piece of equipment called a rosette iron, which is frequently available in kitchen specialty shops, larger department stores, and also by mail order and online. I use 2 at a time, rotating continuously in a deep fat fryer. Although I prefer a cast-iron skillet for most frying, the deep fryer is my conduit of choice for transforming this thin crepe-like batter into crispy little delicacies shaped like snowflakes or roses—hence, the name. In addition to the ingredients listed, I always use corn oil for frying, and confectioner's sugar for sifting over the tops.

1 c. milk
1 t. vanilla
2 eggs, beaten
2 T. corn oil
2 T. sugar
1 c. flour
1 t. salt

Heat your deep fryer, with the rosette iron(s) submerged in the oil to 400°F. Combine in a small, deep bowl the milk, vanilla, corn oil, eggs, and sugar, whisking until smooth. Add the flour and salt, again whisking smooth. Now the fun begins. Working quickly, lift one iron at a time from the hot oil, tapping to remove any extra, and dip it levelly into the batter until it's just even with the top. Don't allow the batter to go up over the top, or you won't be able get it off into the oil. Immediately submerge the iron back into the hot oil. The rosette should slip off in just a few seconds, or you can help it slide with a fork. Allow it to fry a minute or two, until the bottom (which becomes the top once the cookie is fried) appears golden brown. Flip the rosette with the fork and continue frying a minute or so longer. Remove with the fork to a cookie sheet or rack lined with a double thickness of paper towels to cool and drain, open-side down. Sprinkle each cookie with a little powdered confectioner's sugar. Store the rosettes airtight to retain their crispness. You will want to occasionally let the irons stay in the oil a minute or two to retain the proper degree of heat. If the iron is too hot, too cold, or too oily, the batter won't adhere properly. You should also stir the batter so that oil doesn't pool on the top, another deterrent to proper adhesion. This recipe is very easy to halve or double; the amount given produces 5½ to 6 dozen rosettes.

Rosettes are universally loved and equally delicious for Hanukkah, Christmas, and solstice celebrations.

Hazelnut Bûche de Noel

What would Christmas be without a yule log? Here's an edible one made with ground hazelnuts and a little bit of cornstarch—no flour involved. The filling is a rich white chocolate cream, and once rolled into its characteristic shape, the log is frosted with mocha buttercream.

4 eggs, separated
1 c. sugar, divided
¼ t. cream of tartar
¼ t. salt
¼ c. corn starch
½ c. chopped hazelnuts, finely ground
2 T. Frangelico (hazelnut liquor)
or 1 t. vanilla

Filling

4 oz. white chocolate
1¼ c. heavy cream

Mocha Buttercream

2 T. extra-strength hazelnut-flavored coffee
½ c. unsalted butter
1 T. dark cocoa powder
1½ c. confectioner's sugar

Beat the egg whites in a medium mixing bowl with the cream of tartar and salt until they are frothy. Gradually beat in ½ c. of the sugar, until the mixture forms stiff and glossy peaks. Set the egg whites aside and beat the egg yolks (no need to rinse beater) along with the remaining ½ c. of sugar, the cornstarch and the Frangelico or vanilla until they are thick and lemon-colored. Gently fold together the whites and yolks along with the ground hazelnuts. Line a buttered jelly roll pan or 10" × 15" baking sheet with waxed paper; lightly butter and flour that as well. Pour the batter onto the sheet, gently smoothing it evenly. Bake at 350°F for about 15 minutes, until it is golden brown and springs back lightly to touch. Invert the hot cake onto a clean dish towel that has been sprinkled with confectioner's sugar, carefully peel away the waxed paper, and immediately roll up the cake using the shorter side. Leave it to cool entirely, seam-side down. While it is cooling, heat the heavy cream to just under boiling. Break up the white chocolate and add it to the hot cream, stirring until it has all melted. Place the cream mixture in the refrigerator to chill. For the frosting, beat the butter until it is light and fluffy, gradually adding the other ingredients to mix completely. When the cake and filling have cooled, whip the cream to a good filling consistency. Unroll the cake and spread it with the cream mixture to within a half inch of the sides. Carefully roll it back up and place, seam-side down, on your serving plate. Trim the ends if necessary. Spread with the mocha frosting, using the tines of a fork to make wavy barklike designs in the "log." Refrigerate until serving time. This is quite rich, so portion sizes may vary. In general, it should serve 8; be sure to refrigerate leftovers.

Hazelnut bûche de Noel is heavenly Christmas fare.

Yuletide Trifle

Last for the month of December, and the year, is this recipe for yuletide trifle. Whether you enjoy it for Christmas Eve or New Year's Eve, its creamy, fruity sweetness will brighten your holiday table.

Sponge Roll

4 eggs separated
1¼ c. sugar
2 T. orange juice
2 T. water
½ t. grated orange zest
1 t. baking powder
½ t. salt
1 c. cake flour

Custard Cream

2 T. cornstarch
1¾ c. milk
¾ c. cream
1 t. vanilla
½ c. sugar
4 egg yolks
2 T. kirsch *or* Chambord

For Assembly

1 c. heavy cream
¼ c. sugar
1 t. vanilla
½ c. best-quality strawberry jam (I prefer freezer jam)
2 pints strawberries—washed, half hulled, and sliced
2–3 kiwi fruit, peeled and sliced
1–2 star fruit (carambola), peeled and sliced

Prepare the custard cream by combining the cornstarch and sugar in a medium, heavy saucepan. Whisk in the milk, cream, sugar, and egg yolks. Cook over medium heat, whisking constantly, until the mixture bubbles and thickens. Remove from the heat and stir in the vanilla and kirsch or Chambord. Pour into a bowl, cover with waxed paper, and chill for at least two hours. It's fine to make the custard a day in advance, if you prefer. For the cake roll, in a large mixing bowl, beat the egg whites until foamy. Gradually add ¾ c. of the sugar, beating until the mixture is stiff and glossy; set aside. Using the same beater, beat the yolks in a separate bowl, gradually adding the remaining ½ c. sugar along with the juice, water, and zest, until the mixture is pale and thick. Sift or whisk together the flour, baking powder and salt.

Working quickly, fold the egg yolk mixture and the dry ingredients into the egg whites, using a gentle under and over motion and mixing as little as possible to integrate everything. Pour into a jelly roll or 15" × 10" baking pan that has been buttered and then lined with buttered, floured waxed paper. Smooth the batter out to the edges and bake at 350°F until light golden brown and springy to touch, about 15 minutes. Immediately turn out of the pan onto a clean, confectioner's sugar sprinkled dish towel. Carefully remove the waxed paper and roll the cake roll and towel up starting at the long end. Place it seam-side down to cool completely.

When you're ready to assemble, unroll the cake roll and spread the jam almost to the edge. Roll up again and cut into 1" slices; you should

have about 15 slices. Fit them into the bottom of your serving dish. Top with the sliced strawberries and some kiwi fruit. Pour on the custard sauce and pipe or swirl the whipped cream decoratively over the top. Arrange the remaining whole strawberries, kiwi slices, and carambola "stars" decoratively over the top. Serve at once or chill until serving time; refrigerate leftovers. This should easily serve 8–10.

Constructing a trifle is a work of art; pastry cream, sponge jelly roll, and a palette of colorful fresh fruits are the tools of your trade.

Old-Fashioned Household Hints

THESE TIPS ARE compiled from a number of wonderful old books, mostly published in the early 1900s. Some of these are included mainly for entertainment value, but many are just as useful now as they were when first recorded.

Cooking

Dip your knife in boiling water and you can cut the thinnest slice from a fresh loaf.

Pour boiling water over pecans and allow them to stand for a few minutes. Then crack them carefully and the shells can be removed without breaking the meats.

Adding a pinch of soda to the water in which navy beans are soaking will be found to improve them.

Tough meat may be made tender if placed in vinegar a few minutes.

To beat the whites of eggs quickly add a pinch of salt.

A small quantity of green sage placed in the pantry will keep out red ants.

Cold fruits require cold jars; hot fruits, hot jars.

Superior Herb Bitters—Take wild cherry bark, two pounds; juniper berries, one pound; Virginia snake root, half a pound; ginsing, two pounds; orange peel, one pound; cloves, quarter pound; sassafras, half pound. Grind all the ingredients fine. To make the tonic, add ten gallons pure rye whiskey.

To Take Frost out of Fruit and Vegetables—When a thaw approaches put the frozen articles into cold water, allowing them to remain in it until by their plump, fair appearance the frost seems to be out.

If a little flour is sprinkled over meat that is to be minced it will not adhere too closely to the chopping knife.

Remedy for Milk Turning Sour—Add to each quart of milk fifteen grains of bi-carbonate of soda.

Clean dried currants by rubbing them between your hands, in warm water first, then in cold, and repeat this many times, always renewing the water; then lay them on a clean flannel cloth and rub dry; the stems will adhere to the flannel.

Raisins should be cleaned dry by rubbing between two cloths.

You may use the liquor left from pickled peaches, pears, or cherries, for seasoning red cabbage, beans, etc.

The liquor left from brandied peaches may be utilized in mincemeat. In baking mince pies add an apple chopped up fine, the juice of an orange and a very little sugar, just before baking. You will find this quite an improvement.

When broiling steak heat the gridiron before putting it on the meat, and the steak will not stick.

How to Preserve Dill for Your Winter Pickles— Put fresh green dill in wide-mouthed jars and pour vinegar over it. You may use both the dill and vinegar on your pickles.

It is a good plan to make parsley butter in the summer for winter's use. Melt the butter, boil until clarified, then throw in as much chopped parsley as you desire. It is very convenient to use in winter, when greens are scarce, for gravies, etc. You may do the same with goose or any other kind of fat.

In breaking eggs for baking or frying, break each one separately over a cup, it is the safest way; if the egg is bad no harm is done. If you were to run the risk of breaking your eggs all in one bowl you might spoil a whole dozen or more, for it takes but a few drops of a bad egg to do this.

A successful cook should always have a good set of domestic scales.

Milk will keep sweet longer in a shallow pan than in a pitcher.

A mixture of equal parts of lime water and olive oil applied at once is a remedy for burns.

If you once use a small brush for cleaning vegetables you will never do without one.

A coarse grater rubbed over burnt bread or cake is far better than using a knife.

To prevent roasted meat that is to be served cold from drying out and losing its flavor, wrap it in cheesecloth while it is still hot.

Before putting sweet potatoes in the oven, grease the skins and then they can be peeled without any waste of the potato.

Molasses used in cooking should be previously boiled and skimmed. This removes the raw taste.

Only grate off the yellow part of a lemon, as the white pith is of no use for flavoring and is very indigestible.

Drop almonds into hot water to blanch them and then remove the skins. Drop them next into cold water to keep their color.

Before attempting to chop parsley, wash it and squeeze it very dry in a clean cloth.

To remove the odor of onions from hands, crush parsley in them.

Soak rice in cold water for an hour before using

Grape nuts will take the place of other nuts in fudge or other candies very successfully. The result is delicious and inexpensive.

Pour cold water over hard boiled eggs as soon as taken from the kettle, and they will not be discolored.

If you would always remember to measure solids and fluids in exactly the same way success would be far more certain. No cake recipe is followed when you heap the cups or have them level full of sugar and flour and the milk half an inch below the top.

To stone raisins easily, pour boiling water over them and drain it off. This loosens them and they come out with ease.

All cake needs a moderate oven.

Keep the box of baking powder covered.

Never let the cake dough stand any length of time before baking.

To Prevent Lumps in Gravy: Gravy, soups, and thickenings of any sort will not be lumpy if the salt is mixed with the flour before wetting. Stir with a fork instead of a spoon. Better yet, use a small egg beater and the sauce will be perfectly smooth within two minutes.

Never stir sugar and butter together in a tin basin or with an iron spoon, a wooden spoon is better than any other kind.

Be sure the oven is right before the cake is put in and then do not open the door until it has been baking at least ten minutes.

Vanilla Essence or Extract

This is an expensive article when of fine quality, and you may prepare it yourself either with brandy or alcohol. With brandy, the flavor is superior. Cut into very small shreds three vanilla beans, put them in a bottle with a pint of brandy and cork the bottle tightly. Shake it occasionally and it will be ready for use after three months. You may shorten the process to three weeks by using alcohol at 95 per cent. Chop three vanilla beans and pound them in a mortar. Cover them with a little powdered sugar and put them in a pint bottle, adding a tablespoonful of water. Let it stand twelve hours, then pour over it a half pint of alcohol or spirits of wine. Cork tightly, shake it every day, and it will be ready for use in three weeks.

To Dry Corn: Dried corn is sweeter and more satisfactory for winter use than is canned corn. To dry corn pick it while it is young, cut from the cob and dry by spreading over an old platter or old plate and setting in a hot oven or the hot sun to dry. Place the dried corn in a heavy sack and hang

it in a warm, dry place. If after a fortnight it shows no signs of moisture, it is sufficiently dried to keep well. If there are signs of mildew or moisture, take it out and redry it. Do not soak the corn when using it in the winter. Cook it like fresh corn is cooked.

To Improve Olives: when a bottle of olives is opened, pour off the brine and add one table-spoonful of olive oil. Replace the cork and shake the bottle well. Then let it stand about half an hour before using the olives. The disagreeable briny taste will disappear, and the olives will have the rich flavor of the ripe fruit.

Cooked Radishes: When you have too many radishes maturing at the same time, instead of eating a few raw and throwing the others away, try cooking them. Fried, they taste like mushrooms; boiled and mashed, like turnips.

To Make an Ice-Cracking Bag: The only thing needed is a stout piece of white canvas made into an ice-cracking bag. A bag will prevent ice chips from flying around the room when you chip and hammer away at an ice block. Crack off one good-sized piece, put it securely in the bag, give it two or three crushing blows with the hammer, turn it into the colander, and run the water through it.

To Keep the Lid on a Boiling Pot: If you will drop a teaspoonful of butter into the water in which you are boiling dry beans or other starchy vegetables, you will not be annoyed by having the lid of the pot jump off, as it will otherwise do. The butter acts as oil on the troubled water, and keeps it calm and manageable.

Keeping Fruit Fresh for Winter: Grapes, pears, and a number of fall fruits can be kept for winter use very nicely by packing them in sawdust. Of course, wipe them off carefully with dry, soft cloths, taking only the fruit that has just turned and not any that is dead ripe. The sawdust should completely cover every particle of the fruit so that the air is entirely shut out.

Preserved Eggs: Eggs will keep indefinitely if greased with vaseline, the day they are laid, wrapped in tissue paper, placed in a box, small end down, and kept in a cool place. Eggs put away in September, and treated in this way, were just as fresh for Christmas baking as the day they were put away.

To Preserve Green Currants.—Currants may be kept fresh for a year or more, if they are gathered when green, separated from the stems, put into dry, clean junk bottles, and corked very carefully, so as to exclude the air. They should be kept in a cool place in the cellars.

Cream.—The quantity of cream on milk may be greatly increased by the following process: have two pans ready in boiling hot water, and when the new milk is brought in, put it into one of these hot pans and cover it with the other. The quality as well as the thickness of the cream is improved.

Tainted Butter.—Some good cooks say that bad butter may be purified in the following manner: melt and skim it, then put into it a piece of *well-toasted* bread; in a few minutes the butter will lose its offensive taste and smell; the bread will absorb it all. Slices of potato fried in rancid lard will in a great measure absorb the unpleasant taste.

Tomatoes Pie.—Tomatoes make excellent pies. Skins taken off with scalding water, stewed twenty minutes or more, salted, prepared the same as rich squash pies, only an egg or two more.

Pine Apples will keep much better if the green crown at top be twisted off. The vegetation of the crown takes the goodness from the fruit, in the same way that sprouts injure vegetables. The crown can be stuck on for ornament, if necessary.

Eggs in Winter.—The reason hens do not usually lay eggs in the winter is that the gravel is covered up with snow, and therefore they are not furnished with lime to form the shells. If the bones left of meat, poultry, etc., are pounded and mixed with their food, or given to them alone, they will eat them very eagerly, and will lay eggs the same as summer. Hens fed on oats are much more likely to lay well than those fed on corn.

Rice Jelly.—Boil a quarter of a pound of rice flour with half a pound of loaf sugar, in a quart of water, till the whole becomes one glutinous mass, then strain off the jelly and let it stand to cool. This food is very nourishing and beneficial to invalids.

Apple Marmalade.—Scald apples till they will pulp from the core; take an equal weight of sugar in large lumps, and boil it in just water enough to dip the lumps well, until it can be skimmed, and is a thick syrup; mix this with the apple pulp, and simmer it on a quick fire for fifteen minutes. Keep it in pots covered with paper dipped in brandy.

Quince Marmalade.—To two pounds of quince put three quarters of a pound of nice sugar, and a pint of spring water. Boil them till they are tender; then take them up and bruise them; again put them in the liquor, and let them boil three quarters of an hour, then put it into jars, covered as mentioned above. Those who like things very sweet put an equal quantity of quince and sugar; but I think the flavor less delicious.

Raspberry Jam.—Take an equal quantity of fruit and sugar. Put the raspberries into a pan, boil and stir them constantly till juicy and well broken; add as much sugar, boil and skim it till it is reduced to a fine jam. Put it away in the same manner as other preserves.

To Preserve Peaches.—Scald peaches in boiling water, but do not let them boil; take them out and put them in cold water, then dry them in a sieve, and put them in long, wide-mouthed bottles. To a half dozen peaches put a quarter of a pound of clarified sugar; pour it over the peaches, fill up the bottles with brandy, and stop them close.

Cheese is to be chosen by its moist, smooth coat; if old cheese be rough-coated, ragged, or dry at top, beware of worms. If it be over-full of holes, moist and spongy, it is subject to maggots. If soft or perished places appear, try how deep they go, for the worst part may be hidden.

Eggs.—To prove whether they are good or bad, hold the large end of the egg to your tongue; it feels warm, it is new; but if cold, it is bad. In proportion to the heat or cold, is the goodness of the egg. Another way to know is to put the egg in a pan of cold water; the fresher the egg, the sooner it will fall to the bottom; if rotten, it will swim. If you keep your eggs in ashes, salt or bran, put the small end downwards; if you turn them endways once a week, they will keep some months.

Veal.—If the vein in the shoulder look blue or bright red, it is newly killed; but if black, green, or yellow, it is stale. The leg is known to be new by the stiffness of the joint. The head of a calf or a lamb is known by the eyes; if sunk or wrinkled, it is stale; if plump and lively, it is fresh.

Mutton.—If it be young, the flesh will pinch tender; if old, it will wrinkle and remain so. If young, the fat will easily part from the lean; if old, it will stick by strings and skins. Strong, rancid mutton feels spongy, and does not rise again easily, when dented. The flesh of ewe mutton is paler, of a closer grain, and parts more easily.

Beef.—Good beef has an open grain, and a tender, oily smoothness; a pleasant carnation color, and clear white suet, betoken good meat; yellow suet is not so good.

Pork.—If young, the lean will break in pinching, and if you nip the skin with your nails, it will make a dent; the fat will be soft and pulpy, like lard. If the lean be tough, and the fat flabby and spongy, feeling rough, it is old, especially if the rind be stubborn, and you cannot rip it with your nails. Little kernels, like nail-shot, in the fat, are a sign that it is measly, and dangerous to be eaten.

Make Your Own Baking Powder, Saving More than One-Half.—Cream tartar, three ounces, or ten cents' worth; baking soda, one and one-half ounces; corn starch, two ounces. Sift for five minutes or more and put in dry place in can or jar.

A Syrup Suggestion: Do not make syrup of anything but cold water. Stir occasionally, adding sugar to make a thick syrup. Made in this way it will never become hard or granulated as in the case with syrup that has been boiled.

When roasting whole potatoes in an oven, roast thoroughly. Burst them open as you take them out of the oven to prevent them from getting soggy.

To sweeten cream or milk that is just turning take a pinch of soda, wet it a little and stir it in the cream or milk.

To prevent cheese becoming mouldy wrap it in a cloth which has been dipped in vinegar and wrung dry as possible—keep in a cool place.

To improve frosting: A little cream of tartar will improve boiled icing; it will not grain so readily and will be more creamy.

❦

To prevent rice, beans or macaroni from boiling over, put a piece of butter the size of a hickory nut in when cooking.

❦

To prevent milk from sticking when being boiled, rinse out the sauce pan with hot water.

❦

Griddle Greaser: Wrap muslin around the tines of a fork and tie with a cord; dip in grease.

❦

A few kernels of popcorn in the salt cellers will prevent the salt from caking.

❦

Use glass fruit jars to keep raisins moist.

❦

How to Make Good Coffee.—There is hardly anything more interesting to the family than a good cup of coffee. A high grade coffee properly roasted, blended and ground not too fine, will if properly used and made right, make a cup of coffee fit for a king.

❦

Use twelve ounces of coffee to the gallon of boiling hot water. If it has to be extra strong, use sixteen ounces to the gallon. When the water reaches the boiling point, add a little to open the pores of the coffee mixing thoroughly then add the remainder, pouring in slowly until all the good there is in the coffee comes out. To make the coffee clear add a half teaspoonful salt. If followed it will make a cup of coffee fit for any one. Be sure and serve it in hot cups and use hot milk.

❦

Boiled Rabbits.—Sometimes the rabbits that are stewed have a strong flavor. This may be avoided by boiling in plenty of water for fifteen minutes; then drain, cover with fresh boiling water, and stew for an hour and a half. Before boiling the rabbits should lie in cold water one hour.

❦

How to Clarify Fat.—Cut the pieces of fat to be rendered in small pieces. Place in a pan with water to cover. Boil for two hours and drain. When cold you will have a solid lump of white grease, which can be used for cakes or pastry, and is much better than butter or lard.

❦

Sweet Breads a la Rothschild.—Blanch off sweet breads until parboiled in hot water, by adding a sliced onion, some cloves, three or four slices of lemon. When partly done, drain and cool. Then put some butter on your chafing dish and take your sweet breads sliced and put them in the butter. Let it simmer for thirty minutes. Add your pepper and salt and a few sliced truffles and mushrooms to it. When done, make a Bernaise sauce which consists of the yolk of three or four eggs, a little vinegar, a shallot or two, and thicken to suit your taste.

❦

How to Keep Celery.—Celery can be kept a week or ten days by first rolling it in brown paper, then in a towel and keeping it in a dark and cool place. Before you put on the table, put it in a pan of cold running water. This will make it crisp and cold.

❦

For Steaming Potatoes.—Put a cloth over them before putting the lid on. They will take less time to cook and be much more mealy than when done in the ordinary way.

Flowers That Are Good Food.

The food value of flowers is a matter just beginning to interest the scientific world. A botanist says that violets contain considerable nourishment. They formed the basis of a refreshing drink, and in other forms figured conspicuously in the feasts of the ancient Persians. The modern confectioner crystallizes them in sugar.

❦

The old Turkish confections made of rose leaves are declared delicious by those who have eaten them. A number of cooks have discovered that a handful of rose petals imparts a flavor of unparalleled delicacy to desserts of many kinds.

❦

For those who do not care for sweets, the gaily-colored nasturtium offers delights to the palate. It may be used as a filling for sandwiches mixed judiciously with other materials in salad. Its delicious pungency appeals to the epicure, while physicians say it aids digestion.

A favorite Italian dish consists of squash blossoms. When properly prepared this food is both appetizing and nourishing. The yellow blossoms of the common field pumpkin may be cooked in the same way, and to some tastes are even more pleasing.

A ripe tomato will clean the hands after paring fruit. If very much stained use a lemon; digging your fingers into it will also clean your fingernails.

Sliced onions in a sick-room absorb all the germs and prevent contagion. It is a good plan to hang an onion in the nursery.

Vegetables

Parsnips should be kept down cellar, covered up in sand, entirely excluded from the air. They are good only in the spring.

Cabbages put into a hole in the ground will keep well during the winter, and be hard, fresh, and sweet, in the spring. Many farmers keep potatoes in the same way.

Onions should be kept very dry, and never carried into the cellar except in severe weather, when there is danger of their freezing. By no means let them be in the cellar after March; they will sprout and spoil. Potatoes should likewise be carefully looked to in the spring, and the sprouts broken off. The cellar is the best place for them, because they are injured by wilting; but sprout them carefully, if you want to keep them. They never sprout but three times; therefore, after you have sprouted them three times, they will trouble you no more.

Squashes should never be kept down cellar when it is possible to prevent it. Dampness injures them. If intense cold makes it necessary to put them there, bring them up as soon as possible, and keep them in some dry, warm place.

Potatoes boiled and mashed while hot, are good to use in making short cakes and puddings; they save flour, and less shortening is necessary.

Tomatoes should be skinned by pouring boiling water over them. After they are skinned, they should be stewed half an hour, in tin, with a little salt, a small bit of butter, and a spoonful of water, to keep them from burning. This is a delicious vegetable. It is easily cultivated, and yields a most abundant crop. Some people pluck them green and pickle them.

The best sort of catsup is made from tomatoes. The vegetables should be squeezed up in the hand, salt put to them, and set by for twenty-for hours. After being passed through a sieve, cloves, allspice, pepper, mace, garlic, and whole mustard-seed should be added. It should be boiled down one third, and bottled after it is cool. No liquid is necessary, as the tomatoes are very juicy. A good deal of salt and spice is necessary to keep the catsup well. It is delicious with roast meat; and a cupful adds much to the richness of soup and chowder. The garlic should be taken out before it is bottled.

It is a good plan to boil onions in milk and water; it diminished the strong taste of that vegetable. It is an excellent way of serving up onions, to chop them after they are boiled, and put them in a stewpan, with a little milk, butter salt, and pepper, and let them stew about fifteen minutes. This gives them a fine flavor, and they can be served up very hot.

Herbs

All herbs should be carefully kept from the air. Herb tea, to do any good, should be made very strong.

❧❧

Herbs should be gathered while in blossom. If left till they have gone to seed, the strength goes into the seed. Those who have a little patch of ground will do well to raise the most important herbs; and those who have not, will do well to get them in quantities from some friend in the country; for apothecaries make very great profit upon them.

❧❧

Sage is very useful both as a medicine, for the head-ache—when made into tea—and for all kinds of stuffing, when dried and rubbed into powder. It should be kept tight from the air.

❧❧

Summer-savory is excellent to season soup, broth, and sausages. As a medicine, it relieves the cholic. Pennyroyal and tansy are good for the same medicinal purpose.

❧❧

Green wormwood bruised is excellent for a fresh wound of any kind. In winter, when wormwood is dry, it is necessary to soften it in warm vinegar, or spirit, before it is bruised, and applied to the wound.

❧❧

Hyssop tea is good for sudden colds, and disorders on the lungs. It is necessary to be very careful about exposure after taking it; it is peculiarly opening to the pores.

❧❧

Tea made of colt's-foot and flax-seed, sweetened with honey, is a cure for inveterate coughs. Consumptions have been prevented by it. It should be drank when going to bed; though it does good to drink it at any time. Hoarhound is useful in consumptive complaints.

❧❧

Motherwort tea is very quieting to the nerves. Students, and people troubled with wakefulness, find it useful.

❧❧

Thoroughwort is excellent for dyspepsy, and every disorder occasioned by indigestion. If the stomach be foul, it operates like a gentle emetic.

❧❧

Sweet-balm tea is cooling when one is in a feverish state.

❧❧

Catnip, particularly the blossoms, made into tea, is good to prevent a threatened fever. It produces a fine perspiration. It should be taken in bed, and the patient kept warm.

❧❧

Housekeepers should always dry leaves of the burdock and horseradish. Burdocks warmed in vinegar, with the hard, stalky parts cut out, are very soothing, applied to the feet; they produce

a sweet and gentle perspiration. Horseradish is more powerful. It is excellent in cases of the ague, placed on the part affected. Warmed in vinegar, and clapped.

❧❧

Succory is a very valuable herb. The tea, sweetened with molasses, is good for the piles. It is a gentle and healthy physic, a preventive of dyspepsy, humors, inflammation, and all the evils resulting from a restricted state of the system.

❧❧

Elder-blow tea has a similar effect. It is cool and soothing, and peculiarly efficacious either for babes or grown people, when the digestive powers are out of order.

❧❧

Lungwort, maiden-hair, hyssop, elecampane and hoarhound steeped together, is an almost certain cure for a cough. A wine-glass full to be taken when going to bed.

❧❧

Few people know how to keep the flavor of sweet-marjoram; the best of all herbs for broth and stuffing. It should be gathered in bud or blossom, and dried in a tin-kitchen at a moderate distance from the fire; when dry, it should be immediately rubbed, sifted, and corked up in a bottle carefully.

❧❧

English-mallows steeped in milk is good for the dystentery.

Hints for the Home

To Prevent Rust in Deep Pans of Any Sort: Put a few drops of olive or cottonseed oil in them after they have been used and brush this along the seams with a small brush, so that every part of the surface is washed with the oil.

To Clean Discolored Breadboard or Cutting board: Always wash the breadboard with cold water and soap if you wish to keep it a good color. A little silver sand added to the soap will greatly improve the appearance of the board if it is discolored.

Solution for Cleaning Silver and Brass: To one quart of rain-water add two ounces ammonia and three ounces precipitated chalk. Bottle and keep well corked and shake well before using. Wash silver in hot, soapy water and rinse in clean, hot water.

To Make Soap: One can of lye, four gallons of water, four pounds of fat. Put two gallons of water, lye and grease on to boil; when the grease is dissolved add rest of water to boil.

To Destroy Bedbugs and Other Pests: Bedbugs, ants and other pests may be gotten rid of by taking a cake of white soap or a piece of tallow, and with a knife scrape as much as needed, then add an ounce of powdered corrosive sublimate, making a smooth paste. After washing the bedstead with cold salt water, wipe dry and apply the paste to every crevice. This will not evaporate or soak into the wood, as liquids do, but will prove a ready and deadly feast for all partakers. For ants, spread a strip of muslin an inch wide with the paste and tack it around the legs, or under the cupboards, or lay them on the lower shelf under the papers. Put this on after fall housecleaning, and it stays there until spring, when it is all scraped off, the shelves are washed and the paste is renewed.

To Soften Hard Water: For each gallon of water, use two tablespoonfuls of a solution made by dissolving one pound soda in one quart boiling water. This should be bottled and kept on hand. 2. For one gallon water use one-quarter tablespoon caustic soda (lye), dissolved in one cup water. 3. For one gallon water use one tablespoon borax dissolved in one cup water.

To Prevent Flies and Rats: Some experiments with flowers as preventatives of flies and rats and the plan works excellently. Plant old-fashioned mignonette in a window-box outside the kitchen window. The fragrance of this flower, which is so pleasant to us, is extremely disagreeable to flies. As soon as the flowers began to bloom in our boxes, the flies about the rooms disappeared. To rid a place of rats, plant blue-flowered cat-mint around the house, barn, and granary, and when it has grown up all of the rats will have left. Besides being a humble beautifier of the place, the little flower is a real blessing.

Warts—Frequently wash them with a strong decoction of oak bark, or wet lunar caustic, and rub it on the wart a few times.

Growth of Hair Increased and Baldness Prevented—Take four ounces of castor oil, eight ounces good Jamaica rum, thirty drops oil of lavender, or ten drops oil of rose, anoint occasionally the head, shaking well the bottle previously.

Cologne—Take one gallon cologne spirits, proof, add of the oil of lemon, orange, and bergamot, each a spoonful; add also extract of vanilla, forty drops; shake until the oils are cut, then add a pint and a half of soft water.

To Make the Hair Grow Rich, Soft, Glossy, Etc—Take a half pint of alcohol, and castor oil quarter of a gill; mix, and flavor with bergamot, or whatever else may be agreeable. Apply it with the hand.

To Remove Freckles—An ounce of alum, and an ounce of lemon-juice, in a pint of rose-water.

Best Shaving Soap Ever Invented—Take four and a half pounds white bar soap, one quart rain, water, one gill beef's gall, and one gill spirits turpentine; cut the soap thin and boil five minutes; stir while boiling, and color with half ounce vermillion: scent with oil of rose or almonds. Fifty cents worth of materials will make six dollars worth of soap.

To Preserve Fish in a Living State—Fish may be preserved in a living state for fourteen days or longer without water, by stopping their mouths with a crumb of bread steeped in brandy, pouring a little brandy into them, and then placing them in straw in a moderately cool situation.

That an agreeable disinfectant-ground coffee on a shovel of hot coals-will purify the air of a room almost instantly.

A basin of cold water placed in a hot oven will soon lower the temperature.

Rusty flatirons should be rubbed over with beeswax and lard, or beeswax and salt.

Brooms dipped in boiling suds once a week will wear much longer.

To take out iron rust, squeeze lemon juice on spots, cover with salt and place in hot sun or iron with hot flatiron.

For burns make a thick paste of saleratus in water; cover the burn with the mixture, making the application half an inch thick.

To clean mica in stoves wash in vinegar.

Chicken drippings are excellent for greasing tins.

Discolored enameled saucepans are easily made bright and clean by the use of powdered pumice stone.

Keep flowers fresh by putting a pinch of soda in water.

To Clean Leather With Household Items: Leather chairs and leather bindings can be brightened by being rubbed with a cloth which has been dipped in white of an egg. Mix cold starch with soapy water instead of clear, cold water, and the result will be more satisfactory.

Dish cloths should be scalded and washed daily.

What Salt Will Do

A damp cloth dipped in salt will remove egg stains from silver, or tea stains from china dishes.

Salt under bread and cake in oven will prevent scorching on bottom.

Salt is excellent for removing dirt from wash bowls.

Stains

To remove grease stains rub well with alcohol before wetting.

To remove iron rust-wet with a paste of lemon juice, salt, starch and soap and expose to the sunlight.

Fresh ink stains may be removed by repeated soakings in milk.

❧❧

To remove milk and cream stains—Wash in cold water, then in soap and water.

❧❧

To remove tea stains—Sprinkle with borax and soak in cold water. . Soak spot in glycerine, then wash.

❧❧

To remove stains from coffee, fruit and indigo— Stretch surface over bowl or tub and pour boiling water through it from a height to strike the stain with force.

❧❧

To remove stains from scorched fabric— Scorched goods may be restored if the threads are not injured. Wet and expose to sun, repeat several times.

❧❧

To remove mildew stains—First, wet stain with lemon juice and expose to sun; second, wet with paste made of one teaspoonful starch, juice of one lemon, soft soap and salt, and expose to sun; third, wet with paste of powdered chalk and expose to sun.

❧❧

To remove ink stains—Lemon and soda take out some kinds of ink stains. Put the garment on which there is a stain in the sun. Sprinkle the spots with soda and then slowly pour on a few drops of lemon juice. Keep adding soda and lemon juice until the spots disappear.

❧❧

To remove grass stains—Grass stains covered with molasses and left in this condition until wash day are never seen again.

❧❧

To remove a butter grease stain—Cover the grease spot thickly with talcum powder, leaving it overnight.

❧❧

To help un-clog the burners in a gas stove— If irons and pots and pans get all blackened and gas burners cannot be removed to clean; open up all the little holes with a large pin, then hold the nozzle of a vacuum cleaner over the holes and draw out the dirt.

❧❧

To un-stick a glass stopper: Pour a little oil around the top. Let it stand for ten or fifteen minutes, and then try knocking the stopper gently with the back of a knife, giving it an upward motion. Continue this knocking all the way around the stopper. This is the best chance of loosening without any risk of breaking. But if the stoppers of

oil and vinegar cruets are changed every few days, the trouble will be prevented.

❧❧

How to open a jar of fruit or vegetables that has stuck—Place the jar in a deep saucepan half full of cold water, bring it to a boil and allow to boil a few minutes. The jar will then open easily.

Setting Table and Serving Meals

Lay the table cloth with the crease exactly down the middle of the table. Arrange plates, right side up, at equal distances around the table, one inch from edge of table. Place knives at right of plates, sharp edge toward plates, with handle ends one inch from edge of table. Put forks at left of plates, tines up, one inch from table edge. Place spoons at right of knives. Place napkin, neatly folded, at left of forks. Place tumblers at tip of knives, butter plates at tip of forks.

❧❧

Arrange neatly inside of the place settings the steadies (the usual dinner accompaniments), the salt and pepper, vinegar and any oils needed, sugar and cream, milk and water.

❧❧

Place coffee pot and tea pot at right of hostess with cups and saucers before her.

❧❧

Be sure that everything is on the table before beginning to serve meals.

If possible have some little decoration for the center of the table, either a bunch of flowers in season or a little green plant.

All hot food should be served in hot dishes. All dishes should be offered at the left of the guest, if the guest is to help themselves. Dishes placed for the guest must be placed from the right side.

Remove dishes from the right of the guest. Never reach across the guest to place or remove any dish.

If a dessert is served, remove everything from the previous courses before serving the dessert.

After the meal have a time for rest and pleasant intercourse. Cleanliness, good taste, well cooked food and pleasant manners will greatly aid digestion.

General Rules for Table Setting and Dining Etiquette

The room must be in order, clean, free from dust, and well aired. Temperature about 68° F.

The end of the table farthest from the living room door is the head of the table, the opposite end is the foot of the table. The hosts sits at the head of the table and the hostess at the foot.

Upon entering the dining-room all should stand behind their chairs and remain standing until hostess sits.

Do not unfold napkin or begin to eat until hostess does so.

Do not lean arms or elbows on the table. Do not twist feet around the legs of the chair.

Host and hostess should see that guests are kept supplied with food. When offering a second portion never ask a guest if he will "have more" or another piece." It is more polite to say : "Will you have some tea?" or "May I serve you to potato?" or "Let me help you to this piece of meat."

For the Sick

Editor's note: Always consult a doctor, do your own research, and use common sense when considering a remedy of any sort, particularly if you are already taking medication. Even natural remedies can cause adverse reactions in certain individuals. Neither the publisher nor the author take any responsibility for the use or misuse of information, tips, or instructions provided in this book.

It may not be necessary to advise, that a choice be made of the things most likely to agree with the patient, that a change be provided, that some one at least be always ready, that not too much of these be made at once, which are not likely to keep, as invalids require variety, and let them succeed each other in a different form and flavor.

A Great Restorative

Bake two calve's feet in three pints of water, and new milk, in a jar closely covered, three hours and a half ; when cold, remove the fat.

Give a large teacup the first and last thing. Whatever flavor is approved, give it by baking it in lemon-peel, cinnamon or mace, add sugar.

Another

Simmer six sheep's trotters, two blades of mace, a little cinnamon, lemon-peel, a few hartshorn shavings, and a little isinglass, in two quarts of water to one ; when cold, take off the fat, and give near half a pint twice a day, warming with it a little new milk.

Another

Boil one ounce of isinglass shavings, forty Jamaica peppers, and a bit of broken crust of bread, in a quart of water to a pint, and strain it.

This makes a pleasant jelly to keep in the house, of which a large spoonful may be taken in wine and water, milk, tea, soup, or anyway.

Another and More Pleasant Draught

Boil a quarter of an ounce of isinglass shavings, with a pint of new milk, to half, add a bit of sugar, and for a change a bitter almond. Give this at night, not too warm.

A Very Nourishing Veal Broth

Put the knuckle of a leg or shoulder of veal, with very little meat to it, an old fowl, and four shankbones of mutton extremely well soaked and brushed, three blades of mace, ten pepper-corns, an onion, and a large bit of bread, and three quarts of water, into a stewpot that covers close, and simmer in the slowest manner after it has boiled up, and been skimmed, or bake it, strain and take off the fat. Salt as wanted.

A Clear Broth That Will Keep Long

Put the mouse round of beef, a knuckle-bone of veal, and a few shanks of mutton into a deep pan, and cover close with a dish or a close crust, bake till the loaf is done enough for eating with only as much water as will cover ; when cold cover it close, in a cool place. When to be used, give what flavor may be approved.

Beef Tea

Cut a pound of fleshy beef in thin slices, simmer with a quart of water twenty minutes after it has once boiled, and been skimmed. Season, if approved, but it has generally only salt.

Broth of Beef, Mutton and Veal

Put two pounds of lean beef, two pounds of scrag of mutton, sweet herbs, and ten pepper-corns , into a nice tin saucepan, with five quarts of water, simmer to three quarts, and clear the fat when cold.

NOTE. The soup and broth made of different meats are more supporting, as well as better flavored.

Two Ways of Preparing a Chicken. Chicken Panada

Boil it until about three parts ready, in a quart of water, take off the skin, cut the white meat off when cold, and put into a marble mortar, pound it to a paste with a little of the water it was boiled in, season with a little salt, a grate of nutmeg, and the least bit of lemon-peel. Boil gently for a few minutes to the consistency you like; it should be such as you can drink, though tolerably thick.

This contains great nourishment in a small compass.

Chicken Broth

Put the body and the legs of the fowl that the panada was made of, taking the skin and rump off, into the water it was boiled in, with one blade of mace, one slice of onion, and ten white pepper-corns. Simmer till the broth be of a pleasant flavor. If not water enough, add a little more. Beat a quarter of an ounce of sweet almonds, fine, with a teaspoonful of water, boil it in the broth, strain, and when cold remove the fat.

Shank Jelly

Soak twelve shanks of mutton four hours, then brush and scour them very clean. Lay them in a saucepan with three blades of mace, one onion, twenty Jamaica, and thirty or forty black peppers, a bunch of sweet herbs, and a crush of bread

made very brown by toasting. Pour three quarts of water to them, and set them to a hot hearth close covered, let them simmer as gently as possible for five hours, then strain it off, and put it in a cold place.

A Quick Made Broth

Take a bone or two of a loin or neck of mutton, take off the fat and skin, set it on the fire in a small tin saucepan that has a cover, with three quarters of a pint of water, the meat being first beaten, and cut in thin bits, put a bit of thyme and parsley, and if approved, a slice of onion. Let it boil very quick, skim it nicely, take off the cover, if likely to be too weak, else cover it.

Calf's Feet Broth

Boil two feet in three quarts of water to half, strain and set it by. When to be used, take off the fat, put a large teacupful of the jelly into a saucepan, with a half glass of sweet wine, a little sugar and nutmeg, and heat it up till it be ready to boil, then take a little out of it, and beat by degrees to the yolk of an egg, and adding a bit of butter, the size of a nutmeg, stir it all together, but do not let it boil. Grate a bit of fresh lemon-peel into it.

Another

Boil two calf's feet, two ounces of veal, and two of beef, the bottom of a penny loaf, two or three blades of mace, half a nutmeg sliced, and a little salt in three quarts of water, or three pints, strain, and take of the fat.

Panada, Made in Five Minutes

Set a little water on the fire with a glass of white wine, some sugar, and a scrape of nutmeg and lemon-peel, mean while grate some crumbs of bread. The minute the mixture boils up, keeping it still on the fire, put the crumbs in, and let it boil as fast as it can. When of a proper thickness just to drink, take it off.

Another

As above, but instead of a glass of wine, put in a tablespoonful of rum, and a bit of butter, sugar as above.

A Good Eye Wash.

A good eye wash, and one that is safe and harmless, dilute one teaspoon of coarse salt, not the pulverized, in one quart of rainwater. Wash the eyes several times a day, and just before retiring.

A Good Remedy for Colds.

Put ten drops of spirits of camphor in a pint of hot water, drink as warm as possible and keep out of the draft for three hours.

Good Home Remedies

An excellent remedy for stomach or bowel trouble is made by mixing well together two or three teaspoonfuls of wheat flour with warm or cold boiled water, adding a little salt, and repeat the dose until the stomach is strong enough to bear other food. There should be a glassful of the water taken in two doses half an hour apart.

Relief from Burns.

Raw potato, grated, will give almost instant relief. Another remedy is butter, then baking soda.

Remedy for Cough.

One gill sweet oil, one gill honey, one gill St. Croix rum. Tablespoonful three or four times a day. Shake well.

A raisin stuffed with red pepper and laid against the gum will sometimes stop a toothache.

Tips for the Garden

Sound Logic—No food; no cattle--no cattle, no dung--no dung, no grain, is a maxim that ought to be firmly fixed in every farmer's mind.

To Prevent Grass Growing in a Paved Yard—Pour boiling water over the stones whenever the grass shows itself.

Dig Deep for Gold—The following anecdote contains some profitable advice:--"An old farmer, on his death-bed, told his sons, who were not very industrious lads, that he had deeply buried his money in a particular field, which was the most barren land on his farm. In consequence of this information, soon after the old man's death, the sons began to dig (and they dug deeply too) all over the field--and this they did again and again; for it was long before they quite despaired of finding the money. At length, however, they gave up the search, and the land was planted with corn; when, from the deep digging, pulverization, and clearing which it had received in the search for the money, it produced a crop which was indeed a treasure." It might result to the profit of some of our farmers' sons, should they imagine their fathers had deeply buried a bag of dollars in some barren field, and be led to dig in search of the treasure--and though they might not find the expected wealth, their exertions would be amply rewarded, as is illustrated in the anecdote.

Premature Fruit—All immature apples, plums, or other fruit, that fall from the trees ought to be eaten by hogs, or be carefully gathered up and burnt to destroy the eggs or worms therein contained, which will otherwise produce insects to commit depredations next year on your fruit trees.

The Benefit of Toads—Never destroy them; keep them in your garden to destroy insects. They will do more to preserve a garden from such destruction than the labor of man.

To Protect Young Trees from Hares—Young trees in orchards or plantations, where hares can get into, should have prickly bushes tied round their stems, that the hares may be prevented from gnawing the bark off.

How to Prune Flowering Shrubs—Flowering shrubs may be pruned when their leaves fall off. Cut off all irregular and superfluous branches, and head down those that require it, forming them into handsome bushes, not permitting them to interfere with, nor overgrow other shrubs, nor injure lower growing plants near them. Put stakes to any of them that want support, and let the stakes be so covered with the shrug, that the stake may appear as little as possible.

To Expand Tulips and Other Flowers—Tulips, and many other flowers when cut early on a dull, cold morning, are seldom very well expanded. If they are afterwards placed in a warm room, and their stems put to stand in warm water, it will cause them to expand their flowers as well as they would have done on the bed on the brightest day in spring. This is not only applicable to tulips, but to many other flowers as well.

To Free Plants from Leaf-Lice—Mix one ounce of flowers of sulphur with one bushel of sawdust; scatter this over the plants infected with the insects, and they will soon be freed, though a second application may possibly be necessary.

Killing Weeds—Spading the garden in the fall, though beneficial in other respects, will not kill weeds. The seeds of the weeds are not to be frozen out. The only way to get rid of weed seeds in the soil is to allow them to germinate, and then kill the young plants. If taken at the right time this may be done in the garden with the rake. Do not hope to destroy the vitality of weed seeds either by freezing or by burying; as soon as the influences are favorable they will grow as sure as fate.

Substitutions

Spices

Allspice	Cinnamon, cassia, dash of nutmeg, mace; or cloves
Aniseed	Fennel seed or a few drops anise extract
Cardamom	Ginger
Chili Powder	Dash bottled hot pepper sauce plus a combination of oregano and cumin
Cinnamon	Nutmeg or allspice (use only ¼ of the amount)
Cloves	Allspice, cinnamon, or nutmeg
Cumin	Chili powder
Ginger	Allspice, cinnamon, mace, or nutmeg
Mace	Allspice, cinnamon, ginger, or nutmeg
Nutmeg	Cinnamon; ginger; or mace
Saffron	Dash turmeric (for color)

Leavens

Baking Powder (1 tsp)	• 5/8 tsp cream of tartar plus ¼ tsp baking soda • 2 parts cream of tartar plus 1 part baking soda plus 1 part cornstarch • Add ¼ tsp baking soda to dry ingredients and ½ C. buttermilk or yogurt or sour milk to wet ingredients. Decrease another liquid in the recipe by ½ C. • 1 tsp baker's ammonia
Baking Soda	Potassium BiCarbonate
Baker's Ammonia (1 tsp)	• 1 tsp baking powder • 1 tsp baking powder plus 1 tsp baking soda

Herbs

Basil	Oregano Thyme Tarragon Equal parts parsley and celery leaves Cilantro Mint
Bay Leaf	Indian bay leaves Boldo leaves Juniper berries
Chervil	Parsley plus tarragon Fennel leaves plus parsley Parsley plus dill Tarragon Chives Dill Weed
Chives	Green onion tops
Cilantro	Italian parsley (add some mint or lemon juice or a dash of ground coriander, if you want) Equal parts parsley and mint Parsley plus dash of lemon juice Dill Basil Parsley plus ground coriander
Curly Parsley	Italian parsley Chervil Celery tops Cilantro
Dill Weed	Tarragon Fennel leaves
Mint	Fresh parsley plus pinch of dried mint Basil

Oregano	Marjoram (2 parts of oregano or 2 parts of marjoram) Thyme Basil Summer savory
Parsley	Chervil Celery tops Cilantro
Rosemary	Sage Savory Thyme
Sage	Poultry seasoning Rosemary Thyme
Summer Savory	Thyme Thyme plus dash of sage or mint
Sweet Basil	Pesto Oregano Thyme Tarragon Summer savory Equal parts parsley and celery leaves Cilantro Mint
Tarragon	Dill Basil Marjoram Fennel seed
Thyme	Omit from recipe Italian seasoning Poultry seasoning Herbes de Provence Savory Oregano
Winter Savory	Summer savory Thyme Thyme plus dash of sage or mint

Extracts

Almond Extract	Vanilla extract Almond liqueur (use 4-8 times as much)
Brandy Extract	Brandy (1 Tbsp brandy extract=5 Tbsp brandy) Vanilla extract Rum extract
Cherry Flavoring	Juice from a jar of maraschino cherries plus vanilla extract
Cinnamon Extract	Cinnamon oil (1/8 tsp oil per tsp of extract)
Cinnamon Oil	Cinnamon extract (2 units of extract per unit of oil)
Lemon Extract	Lemon zest (1 tsp extract = 2 tsp zest) Oil of lemon (1/8 tsp of oil per tsp of extract) Orange extract Vanilla extract Lemon-flavored liqueur (1 or 2 Tbsp liqueur per tsp extract)
Almond Oil	Almond extract (4 units of extract to 1 unit of oil)
Oil of Lemon	Lemon extract (4 units of extract to 1 unit of oil)
Oil of Orange	Orange extract (4 units of extract to 1 unit of oil)
Orange Extract	Orange juice plus minced orange zest (reduce another liquid in recipe) Rum extract Vanilla extract Orange liqueur (1 tsp orange extract is 1 Tbsp orange liqueur)
Peppermint Extract	Peppermint oil (1/8 tsp of oil per 1 unit of extract) Crème de menthe Peppermint schnapps (1 or 2 Tbsp schnapps for each tsp extract) Vanilla extract (use more)

Peppermint Oil	Wintergreen oil Peppermint extract (4 units of extract to 1 unit of oil)
Rose Essence	Rose syrup Rose water (1 part rose essence is 4-8 parts rose water) Saffron
Rose Syrup	Rose essence Rose water
Rose Water	Orange flower water Rose syrup (few drops_ Rose essence (few drops) Almond extract (use less) Vanilla extract (use less)

Rum Extract	Rum (1 tsp rum extract = 3 Tbsp rum) Orange extract (use less)
Vanilla Extract	Vanilla powder (half as much) Vanilla-flavored liqueur Rum (1 tsp extract = 1 Tbsp rum) Almond extract (use less) Peppermint extract (use 1/8 as much)
Vanilla Powder	Vanilla extract (twice as much as powder)

Weights and Measures

Abbreviations.

t. stands for teaspoon.

T. stands for tablespoon.

c. stands for cup.

pt. stands for pint.

qt. stands for quart.

m. stands for minute.

hr. stands for hour.

Approximate Measure of One Pound.

2 c. milk

2 c. butter

2 c. chopped meat

2 2-3 c. powdered sugar .

3 1-2 c. confectioners sugar

4 c. patent flour

4 c. whole wheat flour

4 1-2 c. Graham flour

2 5-6 c. granulated sugar

2 2-3 c. oatmeal

6 c. rolled oats

4 1-3 c. rye meal

1 7-8 c. rice

2 1-3 c. dry beans

4 1-3 c. coffee

8 large eggs

9 medium eggs

10 small eggs

Proportions Thickening Agents.

1 T flour will thicken 1 c of liquid for soup.

2 T flour will thicken 1 c of drippings or liquid for gravies.

5 T of browned flour will thicken 1 c of liquid for gravy.

Thickening power of corn-starch is twice that of flour.

4 T of corn-starch will stiffen 1 pt. of liquid for pudding.

2 good sized eggs to 1 pt. of milk for custard.

1 egg to 1 c milk for soft custard or baked cup custard.

3 eggs to 1 pt. milk for large mold custard.

1 T gellatin to 1 pt. liquid for jelly cooled on ice.

Weights and Measures.

3 t.=l T.

16 T.=l c.

2 c.=l pt.

2 pt.=l qt.

4 qt.=l gal.

1 c.=½ lb. or 8 ounces.

One quart wheat equals one pound and two ounces.

Four large tablespoonfuls equals one-half gill.

Eight large tablespoons equals one gill.

Sixteen large tablespoons equal one-half pint.

A common-sized wine glass holds half a gill.

A common-sized tumbler holds half a pint.

Four ordinary teacups liquid equals one quart.

Two and one-half teaspoons make one tablespoon.

Four tablespoons makes one wine glass.

Two wine glasses makes one gill.

Two gills makes one teacup.

Two teacups makes one pint.

Four teaspoons salt makes one ounce.

One and one-half tablespoons sugar makes one ounce.

Two tablespoons flour makes one ounce.

Two cups or one pint of sugar makes one pound.

One scant quart wheat flour makes one pound.

Ten ordinary size eggs makes one pound.

Piece of butter size of egg makes one and one-half ounces.

Two cups butter makes one pound.

Four teaspoonfuls equal one tablespoon, liquid.

Four tablespoonfuls equal one wine glass.

Two wine glassfuls equal one gill or half cup.

The Farmer's Cookbook

Two gills equal one coffee cup or sixteen tablespoons.

Two coffee cups equals one pint.

Two pints equal one quart.

Four quarts equal one gallon.

Two tablespoons equal one ounce, liquid.

One tablespoon of salt equals one ounce.

Sixteen ounces equal one pound, or one pint, liquid.

Four coffee cups sifted flour equals one pound.

One quart unsifted flour equals on pound.

Eight or ten ordinary-sized eggs equal one pound.

One pint sugar equals on pound (white granulated).

Two coffee-cups powdered sugar equal one pound.

One coffee-cup cold butter, pressed down, equals one-half pound.

One tablespoon soft butter, well rounded, one ounce.

An ordinary tumberful equals one coffee-cup or one-half pint.

Twenty-five drops thin liquid will fill a teaspoon.

One pint chopped meat, packed, equals one pound.

One pound of brown sugar, or one pound of white sugar, powdered or loaf, equals one quart.

One pound soft butter equals one quart.

One quart Indian meal equals one pound and two ounces.

A tablespoonful is measured level.

A cupful is all the cup will hold leveled with a knife.

One teaspoonful of soda to one pint of sourt milk.

One teaspoonful of soda to one cup of molasses.

Three heaping teaspoonfuls of baking powder to one quart of flour.

Half a cupful of yeast, or quarter of compressed cake, to one pint of liquid.

One teaspoonful of salt to two quarts of flour.

One teaspoonful of salt to one quart of soup.

One scant cupful of liquid to two full cupfuls of flour for muffins.

One cup of water to each pound of meatbone for soup stocks.

One saltspoonful of white pepper to each quart of soup stock.

One teaspoonful of extract to one quart of custard.

One tablespoonful of extract to one quart of cream or custard, for freezing.

One teaspoonful of extract to one plain loaf cake.

A pinch of salt or spice is a saltspoonful.

A few grains is less than a saltspoonful.

Harvest Guide

THIS USEFUL LIST of harvesting tips is from The Illustrated Encyclopedia of Country Living, *by Abigail R. Gehring.*

The vegetable or fruit's stage of maturity and the time of day at which it is harvested are essential for good-tasting and nutritious produce. Overripe vegetables and fruits will be stringy and coarse. When possible, harvest your vegetables during the cool part of the morning. If you are going to can and preserve your vegetables and fruits, do so as soon as possible. Or, if this process must be delayed, make sure to cool the vegetables in ice water or crushed ice and store them in the refrigerator. Here are some brief guidelines for harvesting various types of common garden produce:

Asparagus—Harvest the spears when they are at least 6 to 8 inches tall by snapping or cutting them at ground level. A few spears may be harvested the second year after crowns are set out. A full harvest season will last four to six weeks during the third growing season.

Beans, snap—Harvest before the seeds develop in the pod. Beans are ready to pick if they snap easily when bent in half.

Beans, lima—Harvest when the pods first start to bulge with the enlarged seeds. Pods must still be green, not yellowish.

Broccoli—Harvest the dark green, compact cluster, or head, while the buds are shut tight, before any yellow flowers appear. Smaller side shoots will develop later, providing a continuous harvest.

Brussels sprouts—Harvest the lower sprouts (small heads) when they are about 1 to 1 1/2 inches in diameter by twisting them off. Removing the lower leaves along the stem will help to hasten the plant's maturity.

Cabbage—Harvest when the heads feel hard and solid.

Cantaloupe—Harvest when the stem slips easily from the fruit with a gentle tug. Another indicator of ripeness is when the netting on the skin becomes rounded and the flesh between the netting turns from a green to a tan color.

Carrots—Harvest when the roots are 3/4 to 1 inch in diameter. The largest roots generally have darker tops.

Cauliflower—When preparing to harvest, exclude sunlight when the curds (heads) are 1 to 2 inches in diameter by loosely tying the outer leaves together above the curd with a string or rubber band. This process is known as blanching. Harvest the curds when they are 4 to 6 inches in diameter but still compact, white, and smooth. The head should be ready 10 to 15 days after tying the leaves.

Collards—Harvest older, lower leaves when they reach a length of 8 to 12 inches. New leaves will grow as long as the central growing point remains, providing a continuous harvest. Whole plants may be harvested and cooked if desired.

Corn, sweet—The silks begin to turn brown and dry out as the ears mature. Check a few ears for maturity by opening the top of the ear and pressing a few kernels with your thumbnail. If the exuded liquid is milky rather than clear, the ear is ready for harvesting. Cooking a few ears is also a good way to test for maturity.

Cucumbers—Harvest when the fruits are 6 to 8 inches in length. Harvest when the color is deep green and before yellow color appears. Pick four to five times per week to encourage continuous production. Leaving mature cucumbers on the vine will stop the production of the entire plant.

Eggplant—Harvest when the fruits are 4 to 5 inches in diameter and their color is a glossy, purplish black. The fruit is getting too ripe when the color starts to dull or become bronzed. Because the stem is woody, cut—do not pull—the fruit from the plant. A short stem should remain on each fruit.

Kale—Harvest by twisting off the outer, older leaves when they reach a length of 8 to 10 inches and are medium green in color. Heavy, dark green leaves are overripe and are likely to be tough and bitter. New leaves will grow, providing a continuous harvest.

Lettuce—Harvest the older, outer leaves from leaf lettuce as soon as they are 4 to 6 inches long. Harvest heading types when the heads are moderately firm and before seed stalks form.

Mustard—Harvest the leaves and leaf stems when they are 6 to 8 inches long; new leaves will provide a continuous harvest until they become too strong in flavor and tough in texture due to temperature extremes.

Okra—Harvest young, tender pods when they are 2 to 3 inches long. Pick the okra at least every other day during the peak growing season. Over-ripe pods become woody and are too tough to eat.

Onions—Harvest when the tops fall over and begin to turn yellow. Dig up the onions and allow them to dry out in the open sun for a few days to toughen the skin. Then remove the dried soil by brushing the onions lightly. Cut the stem, leaving 2 to 3 inches attached, and store in a net-type bag in a cool, dry place.

Peas—Harvest regular peas when the pods are well rounded; edible-pod varieties should be harvested when the seeds are fully developed but still fresh and bright green. Pods are getting too old when they lose their brightness and turn light or yellowish green.

Peppers—Harvest sweet peppers with a sharp knife when the fruits are firm, crisp, and full size. Green peppers will turn red if left on the plant.

Allow hot peppers to attain their bright red color and full flavor while attached to the vine; then cut them and hang them to dry.

Potatoes (Irish)—Harvest the tubers when the plants begin to dry and die down. Store the tubers in a cool, high-humidity location with good ventilation, such as the basement or crawl space of your house. Avoid exposing the tubers to light, as greening, which denotes the presence of dangerous alkaloids, will occur even with small amounts of light.

Pumpkins—Harvest pumpkins and winter squash before the first frost. After the vines dry up, the fruit color darkens and the skin surface resists puncture from your thumbnail. Avoid bruising or scratching the fruit while handling it. Leave a 3- to 4-inch portion of the stem attached to the fruit and store it in a cool, dry location with good ventilation.

Radishes—Harvest when the roots are 1/2 to 1 1/2 inches in diameter. The shoulders of radish roots often appear through the soil surface when they are mature. If left in the ground too long, the radishes will become tough and woody.

Rutabagas—Harvest when the roots are about 3 inches in diameter. The roots may be stored in the ground and used as needed, if properly mulched.

❧❧

Spinach—Harvest by cutting all the leaves off at the base of the plant when they are 4 to 6 inches long. New leaves will grow, providing additional harvests.

❧❧

Squash, summer—Harvest when the fruit is soft, tender, and 6 to 8 inches long. The skin color often changes to a dark, glossy green or yellow, depending on the variety. Pick every two to three days to encourage continued production.

❧❧

Sweet potatoes—Harvest the roots when they are large enough for use before the first frost. Avoid bruising or scratching the potatoes during handling. Ideal storage conditions are at a temperature of 55 degrees Fahrenheit and a relative humidity of 85 percent. The basement or crawl space of a house may suffice.

❧❧

Swiss chard—Harvest by breaking off the developed outer leaves 1 inch above the soil. New leaves will grow, providing a continuous harvest.

❧❧

Tomatoes—Harvest the fruits at the most appealing stage of ripeness, when they are bright red. The flavor is best at room temperature, but ripe fruit may be held in the refrigerator at 45 to 50 degrees Fahrenheit for 7 to 10 days.

❧❧

Turnips—Harvest the roots when they are 2 to 3 inches in diameter but before heavy fall frosts occur. The tops may be used as salad greens when the leaves are 3 to 5 inches long.

❧❧

Watermelons—Harvest when the watermelon produces a dull thud rather than a sharp, metallic sound when thumped—this means the fruit is ripe. Other ripeness indicators are a deep yellow rather than a white color where the melon touches the ground, brown tendrils on the stem near the fruit, and a rough, slightly ridged feel to the skin surface.

Recipe Index (by month)

General Index

A

apple
    brown Betty, 292
    crunch, 292
apples, almond baked, 393
applesauce, 272
asparagus, roasted, 143

B

bacon birds, 359
bacon, Vermont maple (smoked), 354
baked beans, 360
beef
    old-fashioned pot roast, 11
    paprikash, 10
    rib roast, 380
    tenderloin, roast, 9
breads
    anadama, 311
    bagels, 37
    baking powder biscuits, 134
    banana bread, 175
    beer bread, 358
    buttermilk biscuits, 310
    cardamom, 386–387
    cheese biscuits, 51
    cinnamon raisin, 7
    classic scones, 176
    corn bread, 74
    cranberry, 310
    cranberry-orange, 74
    dinner rolls, 358
    farmhouse white, 6
    fruited cardamom, 388
    herbed biscuits, 24

Irish soda, traditional, 76
    limpa, 388–389
    naan, 134
    pumpkin, 307
    rustic, 238
    soft pretzels, 38
    sopapillas with strawberry apple dipping
        sauce, 188
    spotted dog, 78
    squash gems, 308–309
    Vermont cheddar onion, 311
bread stuffing, 150
brine, corned beef, 86
broccoli with cheese sauce, 385
brownies, sun butter swirl, 296
brussels sprouts
    roasted, 315
    with blue cheese dressing, 16
bûche de Noel, hazelnut, 401
buns, Easter egg, 112
butternut squash, Napoleon of, 15

C

cabbage, braised red, 315, 348
cakes
    angel food, 126–127
    blueberry, with lemon nutmeg sauce, 264–
        266
    bride's, 192–193
    chocolate layer, with fudge frosting, 30
    coffee, cream cheese, 4
    daffodil, 128
    fresh orange, with vanilla nut frosting, 366–
        367
    fresh peach, 260
    honeybee custard, 204
    maraschino party, 60
    Marie's chocolate zucchini,
    orange chiffon, 266–267
    pudding, 62
    strawberry shortcake, fresh, 186

Sunday sponge, 192
    sweet chocolate, 60
carrots, orange anise glazed, 16
casserole
    scalloped salmon and potatoes, 43
    seafood artichoke, 83
cereal
    breakfast delight, 4
    Scandinavian sunrise, 36
cheese
    Boursin, spread (herbed), 168
    cottage, 172
    cream, 174
    curds, 181
    farmer or pot, 166–167
    garden veggie cottage, 172
    ginseng valley cheddar, 182
    mozzarella, 178
    paneer, 170
    queso blanco, 170–171
    ricotta, 178–179
cheesecake
    pumpkin, 365
    raspberry-chocolate chip, 227
cheese strata, 186
chicken
    barbecued, 218
    broccoli with pasta, and, 155
    cashew-coconut, 154
    cordon bleu, 155
    country-fried, 148
    crispy-baked, 156
    easy oven, supper, 154
    fingers with cranberry-orange dip, 158
    grilled, with peach maple glaze, 247
    provincial, 154
    roast, 152
chili
    garden, 320–321
    with meat, 320
chutney, peach or mango, 257
cobbler, cherry, 56

My Favorite Recipes